Translating the Sugilanon

Translating the Sugilanon: Re-framing the Sign

Corazon D. Villareal

University of the Philippines Press
Diliman, Quezon City
1994

ISBN 971-542-037-0

COVER DESIGN BY JUNE POTICAR DALISAY

Distributed outside the Philippines
by the University of Hawaii Press

Printed in the Philippines by Saint Pancratius Print Inc.

Contents

Part 1

Introduction 3

Chapter I 12
Pre-texts for Translating Hiligaynon Fiction

Chapter II 25
The Semiotics of Translation

Chapter III 36
The *Corrido*: Translation as Sub-version

Chapter IV 54
The Sugilanon in Transit from Hiligaynon to English

Chapter V 96
Translating the Sugilanon into Filipino: Re-viewing the Past

Conclusion 123

Epilogue 130

Part 2

Si Anabella 135

Bunyag-Takas 155

Ang Gaba sang Katubwan 178

Ang Hustisya sa Dagat 212

Sa Lawod sang Pangabuhi 237

Matapok ang Tambis 256

Ang Pagbalik 277

Si Montor 295

Pagpanumbalik 302

Tig-alani 321

Appendix

Selected Bibliography of Materials Relating to Translations in Hiligaynon 347

A Selected Bibliography of Sugilanon 366

References 373

Interviews 387

Index 389

Acknowledgements

This book would not have been completed without

a FELLOWSHIP from the University of the Philippines through the faculty development program of its Department of English and Comparative Literature chaired by Consolacion R. Alaras; and a GRANT from the Philippines-United States faculty development plan

the GUIDANCE of Vivencio Jose and Ernesto Constantino; Luisa Camagay, Nieves Epistola, Bienvenido Lumbera, and Rosario Lucero (my Hiligaynon scholar-confidante); and especially, Prospero Covar

the ADVICE on translation from Lydia Arcellana, Julie Cordero, and Atty. Taleon

the FRIENDSHIP of Isabel, Lydia, Jo, Dayan, and Mailin plus all the fun times at Canopy, Sweet Haven, and 1037; and of course, Lily Rose, Tita, and Jorshie (their absence was their presence)

the EDITORIAL ASSISTANCE of Cristina P. Hidalgo and Anthony Serrano; Nelia Gahol and the editorial staff of U.P. Press, but especially its director, Sylvia M. Ventura

the KINSHIP of my co-Hiligaynons, Quirino Baterna and Jose Golez, through whom permission to publish some sugilanon from the *Hiligaynon* magazine was granted by Liwayway Publications, Inc.; Sol Magahum Dideles for permission to publish her father Angel Magahum's "Si Montor"; and Ofelia Jalandoni for permission to publish her aunt Magdalena Jalandoni's "Si Anabella"

the SUPPORT of Manang, John, Mickey, Manong, Inday, Nonoy, Tata, Magdalen, Violet, Monina, above all, my Mother, who have kept me whole.

Part 1

You do not stand in one place to watch and masquerade.

—Igbo saying

Introduction

The word "Hiligaynon," which now refers to the language and literature of the Ilonggos of West Visayas, is said to be the result of a mistranslation.[1] In the early 16th century, some men living upstream in the Panay River would float bamboo poles downriver and sell these to people for building houses. Once, when some Spaniards came across these men transacting business at the river mouth, they asked some bystanders for the name of the group. Thinking that they were being asked for the occupation of these river navigators, the informants answered *manog-ilig sang kawayan*, meaning "bamboo-floaters." From the contraction *iligaynon*, the Spaniards coined the name *Hiligueynes*, (in keeping with Spanish phonology), and from that time on, in all Spanish historical records, the term became the name of the people in this West Visayas area.

It is difficult to verify the authenticity of this account. The point, though, is that it is not always the correct translation which survives, but the translation that comes within the frame of the prevailing order. In fact, one historian characterizes the history of the Filipino people during the Spanish colonial period (1565–1898) as the "history of the inarticulate."[2] Historians were unable to gather information on the activities and motivations of the Filipinos except through the Spanish government's decrees and circulars (i.e., troops being dispatched here and there to quell uprisings) and Jesuit historical accounts. The latter was valuable in view of the missionaries' purge-and-burn policy towards indigenous documents; these accounts were framed, however, by the clerical line. It was not true, of course, that the Filipinos were wholly inarticulate. The *Noli* and the *Fili* broke into print in the late 19th century (although in Spanish, and therefore limited at first in their circulation among the mestizo elite).

The pattern continued during the American colonial period: one of the first books on the Philippines (1899) was written by an American zoologist who said that in this country he met people ranging from the "highest government officials to the wildest savages."[3] The first translation into English of the *Noli Me Tangere* was done by an American, and many books on Philippine history and culture, the only ones available until the '50s, were written by foreigners. Even Gregorio Zaide, the Filipino author whose Philippine history book is, unfortunately, still widely used in Philippine schools, is concerned more with the colonizers' contributions to Philippine culture and with the chronology of activities of the Filipino nationalist struggle as led by a mestizo elite.

But a nationalist re-awakening in the late '60s led to the rewriting of our story by Filipinos from various disciplines and from different spectrums of nationalist ideology: Renato Constantino, Jose Ma. Sison, O.D. Corpuz, Milagros Guerrero, Oscar Alfonso, Francisco Nemenzo, Bienvenido Lumbera, Prospero Covar, Vivencio Jose, Zeus Salazar, etc. One very influential work is Ileto's *Pasyon and the Revolution: Popular Movements in the Philippines, 1840-1910.*[4] Here, he traces the origins of the masses' participation in Philippine history to the rebellion by a rural-based religious confraternity founded by a Filipino in 1841 and subsequently suppressed. This involvement culminated in the Philippine Revolution against Spain in 1896, but with the coming of a new colonizer in 1899, victory eluded the masses. Ileto, however, sees the continuation of their religious-political ideals in post-1902 mystical and millenial movements. The book is significant because it thrusts the Filipino masses at the center stage of history. To quote Ileto:

> Instead of using preconceived or reified categories of nationalism and revolution as the matrix through which events are viewed, I have tried to bring to light the masses' own categories of meaning that shaped their perception of events and their participation in them.

It is difficult sometimes to distinguish between, on the one hand, what and how the masses actually thought and on the other, what and how Ileto perceives these "categories of meaning" to be. Today, however, the myth of objectivity has been exploded. Instead, the constructed and artificial nature of cultural accounts has been highlighted and ethnography is seen as invention, not representation.[5] Colonial accounts of the experiences of colonized peoples are now seen as the colonizers' convenient subterfuge to mask their own ends. In the process of finding his voice and asserting his presence, can not the Filipino invent his own story too?

I begin the study in this manner to indicate that the translation process is inevitably enmeshed with questions of power. Like other aspects of its Filipino's socio-cultural life, it has existed within the sign frame of the colonizer.

The word "frame" has various meanings. It could refer to an "established order, plan, scheme, system, especially of government."[6] As a verb, it could mean "to enclose in" through "borders." It is basically in these two senses that I used and will be using the word in reference to the sign hegemony of the colonizers, it having a structure with sharply defined borders. One concern of this study, then, is to "un-frame" the sign, to show how translation was utilized in the Spanish period and, later, to enclose a people within a prevailing order.

But to "frame" also means to "contrive (a plot, etc.); to devise, invent, fabricate (a rule, story, theory, etc.); to put together, fashion, compose." It may also mean to "form and construct in the mind; to conceive, imagine." These are engaging meanings, allowing for more creative, dynamic possibilities for translation. Translation may have, in fact, been used to subvert the Spanish order, if we look at the way the *pasyon* was interpreted by its *ladino* translators[7] and the way *corrido* writers had translated and transformed the Spanish corrido. The discovery that one so oppressed can yield power, too, can be both cathartic and exhilarating. It is a prerequisite for liberation.

Yet, what can one really do with broken frames and pieces? Imagine. Construct. Invent. Re-frame a sign system through translation. The use of "re" is significant. The original sense of "re" in Latin is "back" or "backwards" and in the large number of words formed by its use, it has acquired various shades of meaning: 1. the idea of force as in *reluctari* or to struggle against, *repugnare* or to fight against, *recusare* or to refuse; 2. the idea of back to the original place or position as in *recondere* or to put back (usually implying back to one's hands or possession) and, among others still; 3. the idea of "again" or "anew" as in *recreare* or to create again, *reficere* or to make new again, *reformare* or to form again. These are meanings that enter into the "re-framing" of the sign through translation. Indeed, the translator cannot begin with the process without struggling against certain accepted linguistic and cultural norms. And, for it to be truly liberating, she must delve back, rediscover the roots (not necessarily indigenous) of her culture today, and explore how these can be woven into the translation process to help form a new language, and a new sense of Self for the nation. To un-frame then, in order to re-frame: this is the task of the translator.

But why the focus on translation? The Philippine Constitution of 1986 has mandated that Filipino, being the national language, should be the medium of instruction for all courses at all levels (except the foreign language courses). At the turn of the century, however, English became the medium of instruction in the Philippine educational system, and this continued to be the set-up until the post-colonial days of the '80s. Textbooks and instructional materials are written mostly in English, save for the primary grades where the vernacular has been the medium of instruction since the late '40s, and the tertiary level where most social science courses have been taught in Filipino in the past decade. Since teachers are trained to use English as a medium of instruction, the language shift requires a massive translation program in all spheres of knowledge. In the literary field, for example, works from English and other foreign languages need to be translated into Filipino; works in other Philippine languages likewise need to be translated into Filipino.

Full implementation of this provision has been met with protest, particularly from the Visayan regions. But in the University of the Philippines, a five-year program towards fully using Filipino as the medium of instruction was launched in 1989. That year, the Sentro ng Wikang Filipino was set up to initiate and coordinate all relevant language projects such as the compilation of dictionaries, glossaries, and translations. The University's College of Arts and Letters has spearheaded this move towards Filipinization through various innovative activities.

The Constitution further states that the development of the various regional languages shall be encouraged and that Filipino, which is now based largely on Tagalog, shall be enriched and expanded with these languages. English, however, shall be the primary foreign language. Thus, works translated from English are one main avenue through which most Filipinos shall be in contact with foreign cultures. Likewise, English would be the international language through which Filipinos could communicate with the world. With translation's vital role in the production and the dissemination of meaning, translators must be semiotically aware of the politics of knowledge—sensitive to how this could lead to the marginalization of some groups and deeply committed to letting the Filipino image emerge.

Not much, however, has been written on translation in the Philippines. For years the only books available were those of Santiago (1976) and Alejandro (1980).[8] Both were written for pedagogical purposes and certainly did not touch on the issues this dissertation raises. Only four dissertations on the topic have been written so far in the University of the Philippines.[9] In May 1990, a paper on translation was read in a linguistics seminar at the University of the Philippines but few symposiums have been organized on the topic, except under the aegis of the Summer Institute of Linguistics whose main concern is Bible translation. Although papers on translation were presented at a PEN Conference in Manila in 1977, it was only in August 1989 that the first nationwide conference on translation in the Philippines was held. At this one-day conference organized by the Presidential Committee on Culture and the Arts, papers were read by translators working in both Philippine and foreign languages—Kintanar, Tinio, Lumbera, Ordoñez, Schriever, Realubit, among others, and by Robert de Beaugrande (then a guest lecturer at the University of the Philippines). A very interesting paper and one that provided some impetus for this study was that of Resil Mojares which dealt with the politics of translation in Cebuano literature. There seems to have been no follow-up to this conference, although another nationwide conference on translation was held at the University of the Philippines in August, 1991.

Hiligaynon (Hiligaina, Panayana, Ilonggo) is considered one of the eight major languages of the country which, according to

Ernesto Constantino, has 105 languages, possibly even more. It is the lingua franca in the West Visayas, which consists of Iloilo, Capiz, Antique, Aklan, Romblon, and Negros Occidental and in some portions of Davao and Cotabato in Mindanao. Its literature is neglected, compared to Tagalog literature, whose writers have traditionally benefited from their proximity to Manila where both material and cultural resources have been centralized since the 16th century. Moreover, the most prestigious literature during the last decades in the Philippines has been its writing in English, up until recently when even some of the most outstanding writers in English have shifted to writing in Filipino.

My decision to write about translation using as corpus the *sugilanon* (short prose), not the novel, is a practical one. Readers are likely to have time only to read translations of short works; the translated sugilanon is then the best way to introduce Hiligaynon literature to them. Besides, except for Marcella's collection of the sugilanon and Lucero's translation of this, the genre has been relatively unnoticed.[10] On the other hand, a number of studies have been made on the novel, especially those of the major novelists—Jalandoni, Muzones, and Norada. I read about 200 stories published in the *Hiligaynon* over an eight-year period from 1966–1973, and chose eight stories to translate from Hiligaynon into English and Filipino. The stories were selected for narrating various aspects of Hiligaynon life; they are the writers' unconscious record of a society whose milieu is largely rural, its rhythm pastoral, and its concerns sometimes pre-technological. The selection of these stories and the decision to translate them are really a way of declaring my oneness with some Hiligaynon scholars who are quite explicit in their view of the responsibility of the writer/translator. In the introduction to *Sugilanon*, Lucero writes: "Layunin ng antolohiya ng maikling kuwentong Hiligaynon ang kilalanin at ilantad ang temang pagtutol laban sa panlipunang kaayusan."[11] ("This anthology of Hiligaynon short prose aims to convey the theme of protest against the existing social structure.") In another book, Hosillos says:[12]

> Ang kadamuan sang maayo nga sugilanon amo yadtong nahanungod sa kaimolon, pangtinguha, pag-antos, gutom, ang antad sang imol kag ang manggaranon, ang wala patugsiling sa isigkatao, paglaom, mga sugilanon nga may pagpahilabot ukon *social involvement*. Mga sugilanon nga

> makatuytoy, makatandog sang balatyagon. Mga tema nga mapuslanon kag mainuswagon tuhoy sa pagpangabuhi sa idalom sang pungsodnon nga demokrasya.
>
> (Most worthwile stories deal with poverty, strivings, sufferings, hunger, the gap between the rich and the poor, the lack of concern for one's fellowmen, aspirations. Stories dealing with social involvement. Stories which can guide, touch the heart. Relevant themes leading towards a life under a democracy.)

In a country with a long colonial history and a still dominant neo-colonial presence, it is not just insensitive but callous to ignore the central issue of the class struggle. In fact, a number of sugilanon in this study deal headlong with these themes, such as "Ang Gaba sang Katubwan," "Bunyag-Takas," and "Sa Lawod sang Pangabuhi," even "Si Anabella"; and tangentially, "Ang Hustisya sa Dagat" and "Tig-alani." But I also include stories dealing with experiences which cannot be reduced to the aftermath of colonial encounters. Should the translator, for instance, ignore a boy's initiation into the twists and turns of love, a young man's pained discovery of his own mother's deceit, or an old couple's anxieties over age and separation? Marxism itself is not an absolute truth; its insistence on universalism derives from the fact that capitalism and its structures have become universalized and, on this premise, Marxism chooses to edit out voices and experiences not falling within the binary struggle between classes.[13] Besides, neo-Marxists now affirm that expressions of protest may be found within the absences or the margins.[14] The stories are the Hiligaynon writers' perceptions of their society; unenlightened or not, these perceptions, their own truth, must be acknowledged before new directions are charted. The truth must be un-framed to be able to re-frame.

In this book, these twin processes are reflected in my choice of one of the vernacular literatures as corpus for translation, my decision to make inroads into English and into Tagalog through translation, and my attempt to locate the translation of the sugilanon in a historico-semiotic context.

The choice of the period is symbolic. These were tumultuous years, as most awakenings are, a time for the most fervid of nationalisms; but whatever form it took, the nationalist resurgence led to a rediscovery of our culture and a reviewing of our history.

In literary history, it marked a decline of Philippine literature in English and the resurgence of interest in and a re-evaluation of Philippine vernacular literature. This had been backgrounded with the introduction of American and English literature and its literary canons.(My effort here is thus a participation in, and a celebration of, the re-emergence of our vernacular literature). Moreover, these years are the midpoint in the development of the sugilanon; it is, therefore, a vantage ground for looking back to its beginnings and for looking toward its future. This is why aside from these eight, I shall also translate two stories by the pioneer sugilanon writers, Magdalena Jalandoni and Anghel Magahum.

The book consists of two parts. Part 1 discusses the politico-semiotics of literary translation in Hiligaynon literature from the 18th century up to the present, especially in connection with the sugilanon. It also discusses the possibilities of a liberative orientation towards translating Hiligaynon fiction. But in the cycle of theory and practice, it is important for theory to guide the translation process even as it validates theory itself. Part 2 thus includes my translations of ten stories from Hiligaynon into English and also translations of the same stories from Hiligaynon into Filipino. I refer to these stories in my discussions on translation in Part 1. The Appendix has a selected bibliography of translations into and from Hiligaynon, and a selected bibliography of the sugilanon published in the *Hiligaynon* from 1937-1938 and 1966–1973.

NOTES

1. Santiago Alv. Mulato, *Ani*, III, 2 (Manila: Cultural Center of the Philippines, June, 1989), 3.
2. William Henry Scott, "History of the Inarticulate," *Cracks in the Parchment Curtain and Other Essays on Philippine History* (Quezon City: New Day Publishers, 1982), pp. 18–27.
3. Dean C. Worcester, *The Philippine Islands* (New York: The Macmillan Co., 1899).
4. Reynaldo C. Ileto, *Pasyon and Revolution: Popular Movements in the Philippines, 1840–1910* (Ithaca, New York: Cornell University Press, 1979).

5. James Clifford and George E. Marcus, eds. *Writing Culture: The Poetics and Politics of Anthropology* (Berkeley: University of California Press, 1986), p. 2.

6. J.A. Simpson and E.S.C. Weiner, eds. *The Oxford English Dictionary*, VI (Oxford: Clarendon Press, 1989), pp. 140–42.

7. Vicente L. Rafael, *Contracting Colonialism* (Quezon City: Ateneo de Manila University Press, 1988).

8. Alfonso O. Santiago, *Sining ng Pagsasaling Wika* (Manila: Rex Bookstore, 1976) and Rufino Alejandro, *Ang Sining ng Pagsasalin* (Manila: Rex Bookstore, 1980).

9. Lilia Antonio, "Pagsasakatutubo sa Pagsasalin: Ang Nilalaman at Pamaraan ng Pagsasalin ng Nobela sa Panahon ng Kolonyalismong Amerikano (1912–1940)," Unpublished Doctoral Dissertation, University of the Philippines, 1987.

   Mariano Javier, "Joseph Montano's Travels in the Philippines and in the Malay Archipelago (1879–1881): A Translation and Critical Evaluation," Unpublished Doctoral Dissertation, University of the Philippines, 1990.

   Nilo Ocampo, "Pagsasalin sa Filipino ng *Rizal: Philippine Nationalist and Martyr*," Unpublished Doctoral Dissertation, University of the Philippines, 1994.

   Josefa Schriever, "The Cultural Dimension of Translation: An Analysis of the Relay Translation of Selected French Texts into Tagalog and P/Filipino from English," Unpublished Doctoral Dissertation, University of the Philippines, 1994.

10. Juanito C. Marcella, *Bahandi-i* (Manila: Lyceum Press, Inc., 1970); Rosario Cruz Lucero, *Sugilanon* (Manila: De La Salle University Press, 1991).

11. Lucero, xv.

12. Lucila V. Hosillos, "Introduksyon," in Marcella, *Bahandi-i*, xi.

13. Ronald Aronson in "The Post-Modern Condition: The End of Politics?" in Sarah Harasym, ed. *The Post-Colonial Critic* (Routledge: New York and London, 1990), p. 22.

14. For instance, Herbert Marcuse, in *Counter-revolution and Revolt* (Boston: Beacon Press, 1976) writes that "very rarely is proletarian class consciousness explicitly revealed in the work."

I cannot understand what indigenous theory there might be that can ignore the reality of 19th century history. As for syntheses: syntheses have more problems than answers to offer. To construct indigenous theories one must ignore the last few centuries of historical involvement. I would rather use what history has written for me.

—Gayatri Spivak

CHAPTER I

Pre-texts for Translating Hiligaynon Fiction

My roots are Hiligaynon. I was born in Capiz, have relatives in Capiz, Iloilo, Aklan, and Antique, and although I have lived in Manila since I was seven years old, I never really forgot the language of my birth. It was mainly the language of my home and the one I speak when relatives congregate (which is quite often).

It was about three years ago, while reviewing for my comprehensive examination for my Ph.D in Philippine Studies, that I worked on translating into English, "Si Anabella," a short prose work by Magdalena Jalandoni, a Hiligaynon writer. The story was part of her *Hinugpong nga mga Sugilanon 1936-1938* (Anthology of Short Prose). This was to be the first of the stories I would translate for my dissertation. A good choice, I thought, since along with Anghel Magahum, Jalandoni was the pioneer in the Hiligaynon narrative form called the *sugilanon*. Moreover, she received the Republic Cultural Heritage Award for Literature in 1969, the highest honor the Philippine government could give for cultural achievement.

"Anabella" is a nostalgic trip to the '30s. The beau serenades his love with a violin on a moonlit and starry night, they dance in the spacious sala of his palatial home to the strains of a full orchestra, they are the envy of everyone on the dancefloor. But he is rich and his mother takes him away from his lover. Anabella, however, waits patiently for his return and eventually they are reunited. The pace is slow, almost dragging (although this is not surprising if we consider that in Hiligaynon, the term sugilanon suggests a leisurely conversation, usually in a drawing room or some bench under a tree; the Ilonggos are also known to be *cariñoso*, or gentle and warm in both their speech and ways). In a way, "Anabella" confirms what critics have listed as the weaknesses of vernacular literature in the Philippines: "a cloying romanticism," "a lack of concern for technique," and thus a looseness in form (episodic plots), "didacticism," and "sentimentalism."[1] Added to these is stylized or conventional characterization. When the story is translated into English, these features are heightened—the effect is downright mushy, contrivedly didactic and offensive to the taste of any one who has read Poe, Anderson, Hemingway, Lardner, and Faulkner. These were the big names in the American short story during Jalandoni's time, their works devoured by most educated Filipinos then.

Was this all that a literary awardee could produce?[2] Should I not have eschewed the translation of "Anabella" for stories with socially realistic themes and a dynamic, but restrained style? Or, even if it were to be included in my collection of translations, should I not have tempered its romanticism and sentimentalism? After all, current translation theory has debunked the concept of complete equivalence in translation for a reader-oriented theory. And yet, despite the newer breed of writers like Muzones, Yap, and Norada, who wrote in a different vein, this type of story continued to appear in the *Hiligaynon* on to the '70s and, when *Hiligaynon* ceased publication, in the *Yuhum*. It is obvious then that the sugilanon writer, unlike his counterpart in the Filipino short story in English, looks back to different roots.

The Hiligaynon narrative tradition dates back to the oral literature of the pre-Spanish times, to epics, myths, legends, tales, short narrative poems, some of which survive in their acculturated forms among unChristianized ethnic groups. If we search, however, for sources with some form or structure written or institutionalized in some way (like the short story which is an inscribed genre), its beginnings can be traced to 19th century works: the *composo*, the *corrido*, the *Almanake* and the *pananglet.*[3]

The composo is a narrative poem consisting of five to ten quatrains or longer and intended to be sung. In the 19th century, the *manogcomposo* (singer-composer of the composo) was the chief source of news in the town. The composo was basically of two types: a message from government authorities, or an account of an incident in the manogcomposo's town or adjacent ones. The latter could deal with stories like a couple's undying love, a love triangle, or the activities of a certain *tiniente* (chief of the Spanish civil guards) believed to be a notorious *aswang* (a type of bad spirit that flies without a torso).

The corrido (which is believed to be the precursor of the composo) is a narrative poem set to music and chanted; it is written in octosyllabic verses arranged in quatrains. Sometimes the corrido was concerned with melodramatic situations in realistic settings, but often it had fantastic plots involving foreign characters. Corridos were not written or published until the late 19th century, and when they did get published, they were hard to secure since they did not enjoy ecclesiastical imprimatur. In short, these were non-mainstream. I shall deal with the corridos in a separate chapter.

What did get published with ease were the *Almanake* and the pananglet. The former was a yearly publication of the La Panayana Press in Iloilo, and it consisted of some 50–100 pages in a book 5-1/2 inches long and 7 inches wide. It included a calendar, advertisements, articles on medicine and agriculture, facts on Iloilo towns and parishes, and interestingly, translations and adaptations from Spanish and other European sources. For instance, published in its 1893 issue was *Daigon sa Noche Buena* (Carols on Christmas Eve). In its 1896 issue was *Ang Doctor Nga Nakahibalo Sang Tanan* (The Doctor Who Knew Everything). In the Ayers collection of the Newberry Library (Edward Ayers was a collector of materials on Indian Studies, but when he heard in 1898 that the Philippines was going to be annexed to the U.S., he instructed his agents to get whatever documents on the Philippines he could get hold of) I found a version of the *Daigon* published earlier in Manila in a 3x2-inch pamphlet. Apparently, some narratives compiled in the *Almanake* had already floated in small, individual pamphlets.

The *Daigon* was partly a direct translation, partly an adaptation of Spanish Christmas carols. A narrative in quatrains, this would be sung by carolers as they went from house to house trying to reenact Joseph and Mary's search for an inn (there was then a custom of lighting fires along the road for the carolers; hence, the name *daigon* which comes from the word *daig*, meaning "to light"). It is worth noting some features of the text in the edition. The title appearing on the cover page is in Spanish: *Noche Buena*. Inscribed in the title page is the approval of the Board of Censors in the words, *con las licencias necesarias*. The key words in Christian doctrine remain untranslated from Spanish or Latin; some of these are *Mesias, Divino Verbo, Dios*, and *Gloria in Excelsis Deo*. Spelling and orthography are Spanish-based, i.e. *cong* for *kung*, *tauo* for *tawo*. The first two lines in the starting quatrain are in Spanish:

Por siempre sea bendito
el Señor Sacramentado
cabay pang hatagan camo
sing cagab-ihon nga maayo.

(May you forever be blessed
pious Master of this home,
may you have
a good evening.)

The closing carol is *Villancicos de Noche Buena*, a tribute to the Holy Family wholly in Spanish. Interspersed within the whole text are pictures of European religious art. In short, although written largely in Hiligaynon, the work is framed within a Castilian sign system.

The most popular religious works were the 31-day devotion to the Blessed Virgin or *Flores Por Maria*, and the various novenas. Both of these included texts of prayers and songs, as well as those of the pananglet ("for example" in Hiligaynon), also called *ejemplo* ("for example") in Spanish. In the *Flores*, the pananglet was a short account of the conversion of a sinner due to the assistance of Mary; in the novena, it was usually an anecdote of a miraculous incident in a saint's life. The pananglet would begin with *Guinasuguid nga*... (It is told that...), or *May isa ca olitao*... (There was a young man...). It would end with an exhortation:

Gani pamalandungun ta... (So let us reflect on...). Says Mojares: "All narrative literature published before Paterno and Rizal partakes of the exemplum. A standard feature in pulpit oratory and religious writings, it appears in lives of saints, manuals of conduct, books of meditation, sermons and like works."[4]

An example of the pananglet is found in a novena for the souls in purgatory. Translated from a Spanish source by Bishop Mariano Perfecto, the novena was published in Manila by the Imprenta de Amigos del Pais, Calle de Anda in 1882. Its complete title is *Calantahon nga tacus mapamalandongan sang mga casaquit sa purgatorio cag novena sa mga calag nga may matahum nga mga ejemplo sa tagsa ca adlao; decenario sa mga casaquit ni Jesus cag versos ni San Gregorio Papa nga may maramu nga indulgencias*. Translated, this is: "Hymns meditating on the sufferings of the souls in purgatory and novena for these souls with appropriate anecdotes/examples for each day; meditations on Christ's sufferings and verses by St. Pope Gregory with a lot of indulgences."

The work is composed of a hymn of seven stanza quatrains and a novena which consists of a listing of good deeds, an act of contrition, an *oracion* (invocation) and a *pangamuyo* (supplication). The novena proper begins with two prayers in Latin: one, to be prayed if the soul being prayed for is that of a male, the other, for that of a female. The ejemplo for the first day then follows, and next, the oracion. The same sequence is done for each day of the novena. The ejemplo for the first day deals with a miraculous incident in the life of Judas Machabees, said to be a leader of God's Chosen People in the Old Testament. Judas had slain Gorgias, the enemy commander, but in the battle, Judas' army had also suffered many losses in lives. Seeing this large casualty, Judas raised 1,500 pesos to be offered at the temple for the souls of their dead. Meanwhile, Gorgias was succeeded by Nicanor, a ruthless general who had a huge army and a lot of elephants and horses. On the eve of the battle between the armies of Judas and Nicanor, while Judas was thinking of a way to offset the advantage of the enemy, he fell asleep. Then appeared to him the souls of the prophet Jeremiah and the Chief Priest Onias, who told him: "Take this precious sword which is only one of those which God will send your army: through this you will prevail over the enemy of Israel." True enough, Judas' small army won over Nicanor's 3,500 men.

An oracion of two paragraphs comes next and the following is a part of it:

> *Nagahapa aco sa imo mga tiil, nagasimba aco sa imo, matam-is gayud nga Jesus; cag tungud sang mga casaquitan nga ginbati sang imo nga masulub-on nga Iloy, nagapangamuyo ako sa imo nga luason mo na ang mga calag sa Purgatorio, didto sadto nga mga casaquitan, labi na ang calag ni N (ngalan sang namatay)....*
>
> (I lie prostrate before your feet, I come to worship you, oh sweet Jesus; and through the sufferings borne by your sorrowful Mother, I implore you to free the souls of purgatory from their sufferings most especially the soul of N (name of the deceased....)

I cite this ejemplo and its oracion in some detail because there is a correspondence between the image of the suffering Anabella and the image of the sorrowful mother found in a lot of prayers and religious literature. The fact is that many other female characters in Hiligaynon fiction are cast in the same mold (what a Filipino theatre director has termed as the Mater Dolorosa image); this results from the use of melodramatic situations and adjectives which limit rather than characterize. Also, we get to understand what critics have complained about as the "looseness in form" or episodic character of vernacular stories (Magahum's adventure stories, for instance); this can be traced partly to these anecdotal accounts in the novenas, all of which are independent narratives, united, however, by a common rhetorical/religious purpose.

However, a further look at the ejemplos (as well as other religious literature most of which are in translation) suggests a purpose beyond the religious. Take for example, the ejemplo for the third day in the novena just discussed. It shows the reader the consequences of committing venial sins by citing personalities who have long suffered in purgatory as a result of these small "sins": a nine-year old girl who had chatted inside a Church; Catalina of a noble Roman family and a good friend of Santa Monica (San Agustin's mother) who was, however, vain; a priest who did not bow his head while reciting the *Gloria Patri*; and Fr.

Damiano's sister who listened to lewd songs (*cancion nga malao-ay*). The ejemplo for the fourth day narrates the story of a painter who appeared to a member of the Carmelite Order while she was praying. He told her that when he faced the Supreme Judge, some souls cast into hell and some others cast into purgatory took him to task for an indecent painting which he had done for a certain gentleman. Luckily, some saints whose paintings he had also done testified that he did indecent paintings when he was a young bachelor but had since shifted to religious paintings. It would seem then, from the above examples, that the ejemplo did not just impart good morals but also encroached upon the Filipino's individuality and freedom.

These ejemplos were but a portion of a larger colonial discourse, mainly in translation, that appeared geared towards the Filipino's complete submission to the established order. There were, for example, the *vidas*. The vidas or lives of the saints were narratives like the ejemplo but longer, and not part of a larger work like a novena or a sermon. (It is of interest to note here that some of Jalandoni's earliest writings were vidas). One such biography was *Vida ni Santa Zita, Criada o Hinuptan* (Life of St. Zita the Servant). This was written in Spanish by Fr. Francisco Butiña, S.J.; translated into Hiligaynon by Mariano Perfecto; and then published by the Imprenta de Santa Cruz in Manila in 1888. Meant to lift the spirits of the poor, especially the hired servants, this vida is built around one of Christ's lines in the Sermon of the Mount: "Blessed are the poor in spirit for theirs is the kingdom of heaven." It tells of St. Zita's patience, good cheer, industry, and virtuousness despite too much work and problems like the harshness of her masters and intrigues from her co-servants. This advice would have been commendable except that it may have encouraged downright slavishness; there is no instance at all where the servant is made to stand up for her rights (or, did she have any?). Aside from anecdotes on St. Zita's life, there is a listing of servants of various types who had become saints. One cannot help thinking this is merely a semiotic device to strengthen the Spanish hegemony. (In the same way that priestly classes in more ancient societies had sought to keep their power through various means, i.e., the Egyptian priestly class and the Brahmins through a monopoly of script culture, or the Pharisees by invocation of a plethora of Old Testament laws.)

Even the dictionaries and grammar books bore the semiotic imprint of the clerico-political order. For instance, *Arte del Idioma Bisaya-Hiligaino*, written by Fr. Mariano Cuartero and published in 1890, bears the ecclesiastical imprimatur and some religious pictures. Hiligaynon grammar is explained with Spanish grammatical categories as the basis. In the *Gramatica Hispania-Visaya*, a Spanish-Hiligaynon/Kiniray-a dictionary (1841) by Fr. Alonso de Mentrida, Church approval is indicated in the title page with the line *con superior permiso*, and religious references are made in various parts of the book.

One book, very popular because it determined one's acceptance in a society where the Church as an institution was supreme, was the *Cahologan Sang Confesion General* (Significance of the General Confession) translated from Spanish into Hiligaynon and published by D. Pedro Perez, Maestro de Primera Ensenanza, in 1884. Everyone who wanted to make a good Reconciliation had to go through this book.[5] More than 200 pages long, thicker than most books published in the period, the manual details in very specific terms every word, every movement, every twist of thought considered to be sins against each commandment, thus severely circumscribing behavior.

For example, the section on the fourth commandment, "Thou shalt honor thy father and thy mother," reenforces an authority-centered society in which hierarchies are not to be broken. The husband is asked, for instance, whether he has seen to it that his wife has followed God's wishes or if he has taken good care of his children and treated his servants well. Aside from these, he is asked if he has allowed his wife to talk for a long while with another man, or if he has allowed her to be away from their home for some extended time. The woman, on the other hand, is asked if she has respected her husband at all times, or if she has followed his commands and decisions especially with regard to their children and their servants. Furthermore, she is made to recall if she ever was lacking in respect for government authorities, judges, priests and other people needing to be respected. But very interesting too is the section on the sixth commandment. This details the speech, gestures, and thoughts considered indecent (in the process of which the section almost becomes a piece of lewd literature in itself). Added to these are prescriptions on what types of art and literature are acceptable.

We shall quote these lines below because they are relevant to our discussion of translation and the Hiligaynon narrative:

1. *Con nagcanta icao o nagbuhat o con naghuad icao sang mga calantahon nga malao-ay, con guin todloan mo sina ang iban o con guin pahuad mo sila: cag nian basi may natago icao nga calantahon nga malao-ay.*
(If you sang, composed, or copied indecent songs, if you taught these songs to others or allowed them to copy these; or, if you are keeping copies of these songs.)

2. *Con nagsuguid ikaw sang mga sugilanon nga malao-ay.*
(If you have recounted indecent stories.)

3. *Con nagsulat icao o nagbasa sang mga canta o mga libro nga malao-ay, pananglet ang mga corrido, ang mga novela, con ang mga comedia; con man ara sa imo ini nga mga tolon-an; o con nasayuran con sin-o ang may-ara.*
(If you have written or read indecent songs and books, for example, corridos, novels, and comedias; also, if any of these materials are in your keeping, or if you are aware of anyone who has these in his possession.)

4. *Con nagsaut icao; subong man con nagtan-ao icao sang mga saut con sang mga comedia con may liban pa nga calingauan nga quinalibutan cag macagda sa pagcacasala.*
(If you danced; also, if you watched people dancing in the comedia, or in some other worldly or sinful show or entertainment.)

5. *Con nagpinta icao sing may bayhon nga malao-ay, cag con guinbutang mo ina sa dayag dira sa imo balay; subong man con nacasayod icao nga ang iban may ila sina.*
(If you have sketched indecent figures and if you have displayed these in your home; likewise, if you know of anyone who has this type of paintings).

The above are a few examples of Spanish colonial discourse, but a further study of this reveals certain patterns. This literature was of a type: religious works mostly in translation—novenas for saints, religious hymns/carols, books of conduct, guides for confession and prayer books, bibles, spiritual exercises, etc. The other important books were the tools for translation—

diccionarios, vocabularios, and *dialogos, cursos de lengua*, and *artes*. Translation was largely unidirectional, that is, from Spanish into Hiligaynon, using Spanish as linguistic and cultural reference. Translation was also strictly monitored by a central authority; each published work bears the imprimatur of the bishop, or of the Board of Censors (which was made permanent in 1856). A good number of works, although in Hiligaynon translation, were published in Manila by printing presses owned by the friars. It was not until the late 19th century, with the establishment of Libreria Panayana (first, a bookstore and then later also a printing press), by Mariano Perfecto who was an immigrant from Bicol, that secular publishing was introduced. Translations then adhered to the formal equivalence model in which the target text had to be the same as the source text since religious dogma could not be compromised.[6] The model, however, elaborates a code of submission and abdication of intellectual discrimination.

The translated works reveal not just the design to impose Spanish hegemonic imprint but also the attempt to control the reader's whole being by a deadening of the creative spirit, paradoxically in the guise of purifying the spirit by ridding it of all carnal or worldly desires. Thus depriving the artist of some of the most elemental themes of life, like for instance, what Goethe observed among the revelers in a Roman carnival:

> [...]the course of these follies [draws our attention] to the most important stages of human life as when a vulgar Pulcinella indecently reminds us of the pleasures of love to which we owe our existence, when a Baubo profanes the mysteries of birth in public places, when so many lighted candles at night remind us of the ultimate ceremony.

Thus, too, trying to deprive the Filipino of what Goethe refers to in the same account as "...that freedom and equality [which] can only be enjoyed in the intoxication of madness."[7]

I have traced in a preliminary way the possible sources of the sugilanon in the narratives of the 19th century and the body of religious works of which they were a part. This was by way of showing that this (as perhaps all vernacular literature) should be taken on its own terms, that in determining the canons by which it is to be judged, critics and translators must be cognizant of the narrative within the narrative. But I have also endeavored to suggest that this linguistic enterprise is inevitably enmeshed in issues of power. What texts are translated? In what directions are these translations—from what language to what language? For whom and to what ends? What omissions, additions, elisions, appropriations are done in the process? What is the Grand Frame used?

Evidence shows that the Filipinos did not yield wholesale to these colonial impositions. In a book earlier cited, *Contracting Colonialism: Tagalog Translation During the Early Years of Spanish Rule*, Vicente Rafael explains in detail how the *ladinos*, the priests' native assistants in translating religious literature from Spanish into the vernaculars, subverted its centralizing claims.[8] In an earlier book on Tagalog poetry under Spanish colonial rule, Bienvenido Lumbera illustrates how the ladinos demonstrated their originality especially in their insightful rather than conventional depiction of the characters of the *Pasyon*.[9]

Secular works, some a mixture of the sacred and the profane, floated both clandestinely and freely in the second half of the 19th century. These were the propaganda works written in Spanish by the *ilustrados* (the *mestizo* elite), the revolutionary writings in Tagalog and the other vernaculars in the twilight years of the colonial era, like the corridos, the *zarzuelas*, the *moro-moros*, and the comedias. Secular forces unleashed themselves especially in the first two decades of American rule through original (not translated) works in Spanish and the vernaculars. It appeared that the translation cord had been broken.

But as the 20th century wore on, certain developments brought translation to the fore: the policy of using English as a medium of instruction, the institutionalization of Tagalog as the national language, the rise of mass media and media monopolies, the continued concentration of resources in Manila, and the formation of the radical left. As new forces emerge and power configurations shift, it is valuable for translators to consider the questions earlier raised especially in the selection of works to be translated and the making of decisions on how to translate.

It is not, however, enough to be aware of the power relationships involved in translating. We must look for means to resist power. Thus, the more important questions should perhaps be: How can translation be used to subvert power? How can it be used by the Filipino to image his Self and articulate his Being and Presence?

NOTES

1. See Leonard Casper, "Introduction: Writing in the Vernacular," *Salimbibig*, edited by Joseph Galdon (Quezon City: Council for Living Traditions, 1980) pp. 4–6; also, Lourdes de Castro, "Hiligaynon Literature," in Roger Bresnahan, ed. *Literature and Society: Cross-Cultural Perspectives* (Makati, 1976).

2. Magdalena Jalandoni is a towering figure in Philippine vernacular literature. She wrote 122 short stories, 26 novels, seven novelettes, five corridos, eight narrative poems (100–1000 stanzas), 231 short lyrics compiled in four volumes, seven long plays, 24 short plays, and dialogues in verse compiled in two volumes, seven volumes of essays including translations from Spanish into Hiligaynon, and two autobiographies. This list was compiled by Sr. Socorro Evangelista, S.Sp.S. in "Magdalena Jalandoni, Hiligaynon Novelist," Unpublished Dissertation, Ateneo de Manila University, 1977.

3. This was suggested by Sr. Socorro Evangelista in the dissertation cited above.

4. Resil Mojares, *Origins and Rise of the Filipino Novel: A Generic Study of the Novel until 1940* (Quezon City: University of the Philippines Press, 1983).

5. This emphasis on Confession may have influenced the use of the framework of the confessional which was popular in Hiligaynon and other vernacular narratives up to the 1930s. See Mojares, *Origins*, p. 253.

6. In Jay Siskin, "A Medieval Semiotics of Translation," *Semiotica*, LX, 1–2, pp. 103–28, the same formal equivalence model is noted with regard to the Hebrew experience. Only one form in the matrix code corresponds to the target code. The emphasis results from the belief that Hebrew form and their referents are contingent and sanctified since Hebrew was the language of creation and of revealed truth.

7. Johann Wolfgang von Goethe, *Italienische Reise*. 2 vols. (Frankfurt am Main: Insel Verlag, 1976), pp. 676-77. Cited in Clifford and Marcus, 1986.

8. Vicente L. Rafael, *Contracting Colonialism.*

9. Bienvenido Lumbera, *Tagalog Poetry 1570–1898: Tradition and Influences in its Development* (Quezon City: Ateneo de Manila University Press, 1986).

So that everything is a sign that can be used to tell a lie (since everything that serves to tell a lie can be used in the right circumstances, to tell the truth).

—Umberto Eco

CHAPTER II

The Semiotics of Translation

A growing body of works suggests directions for translation in a post-colonial setting. One pioneering and engaging study is Tzvetan Todorov's *The Conquest of America: The Question of the Other.*[1] Dealing with the theme "the discovery the self makes of the other," (by "self" he refers to European culture and by "other" to Indian culture), he documents the ways by which Columbus' and Cortes' interpretations of Indian culture were colored by the form of their faith and the belief in the superiority of their own culture. For instance, having learned the word *cacique*, Columbus was interested more in what Spanish word it corresponded to than in what it signified in the Indian scheme of things; having settled in Indian land, he was more preoccupied with proper names (which only serve as indices of nature) than with words which serve for human comunication with the indigenous people. Todorov concludes that the system of signs which prevailed were those of the dominant ideology of the Spanish *conquistadores*. Hence, it is important, he says, to examine the weapons of conquest since conquests do not belong only to the past.

In another article, Jorge Klor de Alva, an anthropologist from Princeton, shows how Spanish missionaries transposed oral classical Nahuatl in Mexico into written form, using European grammatical and lexicographic canons.[2] Although their explicit goal was the proselytization of the natives, the claims of religious discourse were actually used in support of Spanish claims to sovereignty; thus, Nahuatl and the subsequent linguistic uniformity among its speakers dislodged the authority of the native priests in favor of the missionaries; delegitimized, and in some cases, erased regional dialects; and stunted the creative process of indigenous writing.

In a study on the Swahilis, Fabian makes us privy to translation encounters in Africa.[3] Here, he points out that the impositions of control (and acts of resistance) occur mainly through the linguistic moves in the process of translation. A politics of language is encoded in the selection of texts, vocabulary, and styles. Cheyfitz shows that the triad of translation, communication, and transmission of power was the driving force of Anglo-American imperialism in the conquest of the American Indians in the New World.[4]

These works suggest that apart from the initial battle the outcome of which was determined by military superiority, the real battle was really that between two signifying systems. The power of the written word was pitted against the power of orality. The colonizers sanctified the written word by linking it with religious literature and with a superior culture, and constructed all channels of communication based on these, thus marginalizing and in some cases obliterating the native's language and culture. In effect, they succeeded in translating experience for and on behalf of the colonized.

The contemporary translator therefore cannot be oblivious of the realities encoded in his texts. Todorov acknowledges, for instance, that by comparing Columbus and Cortes, and then Cortes and Montezuma, he has become aware that the production as well as reception of the forms of communication—"even if they are universal and eternal aren't accessible to the writer's free choice, but are correlated to the ideologies in force and can therefore become the sign."

It is then simplistic shortsightedness to view translation as a neutral linguistic process in the way Catford defines it: "an operation on languages, a process of substituting a text in one language for a text in another."[5] Or to "postulate certain target-source relationships usually on pragmatic and/or semantic grounds."[6] It seems, in fact, that the nature of the translation process militates against such perfect equation, that although translation has a central core of linguistic activity, it belongs most properly to semiotics, the doctrine which studies sign systems or structures, sign processes and sign functions.[7]

Viewing translation within a semiotic framework could unmask false claims to objectivity by imperious translators and may open possibilities for releasing suppressed meanings or even create new ones. Why this is so stems from the nature of translation as a semiotic process itself. Jakobson was probably the first to write of translation in semiotic terms. He claimed that all communication consists of translation; meaning is attached to the linguistic sign and consists of the translation of that sign "into some further, alternative sign especially a sign in which it is more developed."[8] Subsequent translation theorists have considered translation as semiosis. For instance, to Gorlee, translation[9]

> takes as its point of departure (simple or complex) a verbal sign—word, sentence, text—as referring to its object(s). Tracing back the particular way in which a sign is encoded—its ground—is followed by the creation in the mind, of the interpretant, the meaning of which is equivalent to, or a more developed version of the meaning of the first sign. This interpretant also becomes a sign which is the starting point of a second triadic relation.

To Frawley, translation is "an act of sign production: the new code derived from the matrix code and the virtual target code is a semiotic unit, capable of interpretation as that and not solely as a secondary sign or derivative semiotic unit."[10] Hatim views translation as "the process which transforms one semiotic entity into another under certain equivalence conditions to do with semiotic codes, pragmatic action and general communication requirements."[11]

Implicit in these concepts of translation is the presence of a translator as producer of meaning or sign-giver—someone investing the sign with meaning and developing a "secondary," "developed," "alternative," or "derivative," sign. This feature is inherent to the sign. As Peirce writes: "A sign or representamen is *something which stands to somebody for something in some respect or capacity*[12] [Italics supplied]. To Buhler, what makes possible this "standing for" is the ability of the sign-user to take up a particular "set" or *Einstellung* vis-a-vis the physical reality of the sign, regarded as a material entity with sense; in effect, to "besoul" it.[13] If a translator invests the sign with meaning, it follows that the concept of the sign standing for an object apart from it, in the manner of a one-to-one correspondence is illusory. The idea then of translation as an objective event is untenable. In a study, for example, of Leon Ma. Guerrero's translations of Rizal's *Noli* and *Fili*, Benedict Anderson meticulously documents how Guerrero intervenes in Rizal's works by adding to, subtracting from, and modifying the original probably to suit "the demands of the state" which serves as his "strategic compass." [14]

Implied, likewise, in the above concepts is that of translation as an on-going process that cannot be terminated. This derives from the nature of the sign and a semiosic view of culture. Says Peirce:[15]

> The meaning of a representation can be nothing but a representation; the interpretant is nothing but another representation to which the torch of truth is handed along; and as representation, it has its interpretant again. Lo, another infinite series.

What defines language is not the words themselves but the relation of signification and once the mind recognizes this, man's *umwelt* or universe, is opened up to infinity, according to Sebeok.[16] Eco looks at culture as a continuous generation of new interpretants by a society of interpreters..."culture continuously translates signs into signs and definitions, into other definitions, words into icons, icons into ostensive signs."[17] To Volosinov, "what's important for the speaker about a linguistic form isn't that it's a stable and self-equivalent signal but that it's an always changeable and adaptable sign."[18]

This vision of an unlimited semiosis and of man as semiotically defined can be a point of departure for resisting a sign hegemony. For if the object is illusory and the interpreter and the interpretant are the determining features of the sign, then no unitary meaning can be imposed permanently. And if the translator is a sign-giver, can he not then intervene at some point in the semiotic web, (to use Sebeok's term), break its patterns or construct a counter sign-system even if this involves some clandestine moves? If knowledge and order are not some "putative inner world of autonomous consciousness and sense but a field of expressions," can he not, being himself a Sign and a Sign-giver, draw an alternate field? The translator can reconstitute and restructure his semiosic environment to create an *umwelt* specific to the Filipino, yet linked to the universal network of signs. This is an exciting prospect partaking of the abductive quality of the sign.

That these counter-semiotic potentials of translation can be realized has been documented. In an article entitled " 'Failing to Marvel': Atahualpa's Encounter with the Word" (1991), Patricia Seed contrasts four interpretations of the encounter between King Atahualpa and his court on the one hand, and Fray Vallaverde and Spanish soldiers on the other, in Cajamarca Plaza (in Peru) on November 16, 1532.[19] The core event seems to be Vallaverde's presentation of the Bible (Summa?) to Atahualpa who throws it, flagrantly. Fray Jerez interprets Atahaulpa's act of flinging the book as barbarous; a failure to marvel among those whom Jerez's countryman, Sepulveda referred to as "little men in whom you will scarcely find traces of humanity, who not only lack culture but do not even know how to write." Garcilaso, a mestizo, reduces the misunderstanding between the Spaniards and the Indians to a problem of translation, the message distorted because of the stupidity of the Indian interpreter and the lack of Quechua equivalents for Spanish religious concepts. Eventually then, he demeans Quechua language and culture.

The other two accounts put the meeting within an indigenous frame. Tito Cusi approaches the encounter from a position of cultural equality; his uncle had flung the book because earlier, Vallaverde had poured into the ground the *chicha* which Atahualpa had offered to him in a golden cup. But it is Poma's account that is the most telling from the point of view of the awakened colonized. Upon receiving the book, Atahualpa was said to have exclaimed: "What? How is it that it does not tell me? It does not even talk to me, that book!" Then, majestically seated in his throne, the Inca king flung the book in his hands.

Another interesting study is Regina Harrison's *Signs, Songs, and Memory in the Andes: Translating Quechua Language and Culture* (1989).[20] Harrison translates Quechua songs, poems and other folk literature into English with her fellow Americans as target audience. In this she demonstrates a remarkable sensitivity to Quechua culture—their thought patterns, their categories, as well as their centuries of contact with Spanish culture. These, in order to see the "cultural continuities and semantic dislocations within the texts she translated." Other than translations, her book also cites studies on Quechua culture. An example of these is Santacruz Pachacuti Yamqui's *Relacion de las antiguedades deste reyno del Peru*, an account which intersects somewhat with the events in the Seed article, but interesting in the original way by which Yamqui is able to weave in Andean orality within Spanish cultural codes. His description of Inca and Spanish personages stresses the iconicity of the signs of their office rather than indices to designate names:[21]

> [...]the aforesaid Pachucutiyngayupangui sits with his Topayngayupangui, and Amaro Ttopaynga, all three sitting on their royal seats, made of gold, all three are dressed up in their royal woven headbands and their royal fringe, and the old [king] held his scepter and royal standard, made of gold, he and Topayngayupangui with his scepter of gold, and the other one without a scepter, only a royal war club, made of gold.

Also, each person is described in reference to a higher being in Yamqui's hierarchical scheme: Pizzaro is the human sign of Charles V, while Vallaverde in his miter and cape, that of St. Peter. This disposition for details of royal insignia, spectacle and social stratification is believed to derive from Yamqui's exposure to the *tocapu*, an Inca geometrical system adorning the clothes of nobles.

But another excellent study (cited by both Seed and Harrison) in this genre of conquest narratives, and one that establishes the solidarity of the Filipino with peoples of similar historical experience is Vicente Rafael's *Contracting Colonialism: Translation and Christian Conversion in Tagalog Society under Early Spanish Rule*. It shows how language was used as an instrument of the Spanish empire in the Philippines, specifically, as a tool to mold the Tagalog's thought and language according to the formulas, ritual phrases, and inflections of 16th century Castilian culture. It is particularly fascinating in the way it documents the ladino's strategies to deflect and refract the meaning imposed by the dominant ideology in a variety of texts: the *pasyon*, prayers for the dead, prayers for confession, and other religious literature.[22]

Most translation theorists have identified cultural considerations as indispensable for any translation theory (Nida and Taber, 1969; Steiner, 1975; Hornby, 1989; Newmark, 1988; Hatim, 1990, etc.) but few have focused on the interrelationship of culture and translation in a post-colonial setting. What is needed by Filipino translators as well as their fellows in the Third World is an inventive poetics of translation that takes into account the historical and cultural antecedents of the nation.

However, in negotiating between a linguistic text in a source semiotic system to another linguistic text in a target semiotic system, the Hiligaynon translator is confronted with certain issues. If the equivalence of the source text and the target text is denied, what are the boundaries of translation? If the objects of translation are not to be taken as isolated units in a vacuum but rather in a continuum, what should be the point of departure for the translator of Hiligaynon fiction? How can this emancipatory perspective influence the lexical, syntactic, and stylistic choices of the translator?

We would have to return to Peirce's classic definition of a sign: "A sign or representamen is something which stands to somebody *in some respect or capacity*" [italics supplied]. Signs then are generated according to a certain "ground" or from a given context, that is, "in some respect or capacity." Thus, although versions of translation are potentially unlimited, the semiotic process being unlimited, these versions can only occur within a given universe of discourse or, to borrow from Buhler, a common perceptual or "spatial" field.

What is the nature of this ground and who sets it? Tentatively, it would be solely the author of the source text and the translator. But did not Rimbaud say *Je suis un autre*? Others are also I's. And Bakhtin: "Every use of the I presupposes a you...the word is half someone else's?" The occasion of a text's creation and/or translation by an individual subject is merely one of its generative or potentially meaningful contexts. The ground of the text consists then of the system of conventions underlying its genre. And, since it is not just the author but the conventions themselves which may be locked in certain hegemonic frames, the translator is engaged continually in a subversive enterprise.

But first the Filipino translator must zero in on these conventions. These would, first of all, consist of his colonial experience, the pre-texts to Hiligaynon fiction. These would also be linguistic—the specific qualities of Hiligaynon vis-a-vis the target languages and the cultural codes embedded in it. It is interesting to note, for instance, the terms for translation in Hiligaynon. The simplest term is formed by prefixing the affix *gin* to the name of a language, as for instance, the word *ginbinisaya* meaning "made into Bisaya" (Hiligaynon is one of the Visayan languages); another term is *luad* which means to "copy" or "imitate." These terms assume perfect equivalence in translation. But other terms connote invention and discovery. There is *hubad* (echoing the Tagalog term *hubad* which means "naked") meaning "to open, solve, untie, or bind." Still another word is *lubad* which likewise means "to untie, to open, to disentangle."

Also used is *ginbiao*. *Biao* refers to a "spring" or to "any pool of clear, pure water." Then the word *ginpahamtang*. *Hamtang* means "firm" or "stable" as in *Hamtang na ang ila balay* or "Their house is sturdy now." A translated text then should rest on some solid foundation.

In enacting the double movement of resistance and envisioning, the Hiligaynon translator must be conscious of the obscured or suppressed meanings within the signs in his language, lay these bare as in the sense of *hubad/lubad*; perhaps give birth to new words, new meanings, or new structures as suggested by *biao*; in short, be semiotically aware of the potentials of his own language in relation to the target language.

Other than the historical and the linguistic, the translator also needs to look into the literary conventions that entered into the shaping of the genre, for in determining what to keep and what to invent, in attempting to find the mean between the impulse to facsimile and the impulse to create in the tension of which the craft of translation lies, it would help to understand the genealogy of the sugilanon. And since certain features of language "knit together with specific points of view, specific approaches, forms of thinking, nuances, and characteristics of the given genre,"[23] the linguistic choices of the author and the translator may be governed in part by generic considerations.

In thus directing the semiotic movement of the sugilanon towards its liberatory goal, the translator will have to acknowledge its singularity as a genre and discover the literary antecedents within its intertextual space. Genre membership is a key point in the process of transfer between two semiotic systems.[24] But in the ceaseless continuum in which one finds the "trace" of a sign in what went before and in what will follow, where does the translator, she who would be Sign-Giver, begin?

NOTES

1. Tzvetan Todorov, *The Question of America: The Question of the Other*, trans. Richard Howard (New York: Harper and Row Publishers, 1982).
2. Jorge Klor de Alva, "Language, Politics, and Translation: Colonial Discourse and Classic Nahuatl in New Spain, ed. Roseanna Warren, *The Art of Translation: Voices from the Field* (Boston: Northwestern University Press, 1989), pp. 143–62.
3. Johannes Fabian, *Language and Colonial Power: The Appropriation of Swahili in the Former Belgian Congo 1880-1938* (New York: Cambridge University Press, 1986).
4. Eric Cheyfitz, *The Poetics of Imperialism: Translation and Colonization from The Tempest to Tarzan* (New York: Oxford University Press, 1991), pp. 104-41.
5. J.C. Catford, *A Linguistic Theory of Translation* (London: Oxford University Press, 1965), p. 27.
6. Gideon Toury, "Translation: A Cultural-Semiotic Perspective" in *Encyclopedic Dictionary of Semiotics*, ed., Thomas A. Sebeok, (Berlin: Morton de Gruyter, 1986), pp. 1111–24.
7. Susan Bassett McGuire, *Translation Studies* (London and New York: Routledge, 1988), p. 13.
8. Roman Jakobson, "On Linguistic Aspects of Translation," in *On Translation*, ed. R.A. Brower (Cambridge: Harvard University Press, 1959), pp. 232–39.
9. Dinda Gorlee, "Wittgenstein, Translation, and Semiotics," *Target* (International Journal of Translation Studies) I:1, 1989, p. 83.

10. William Frawley, "Prolegomenon to a Theory of Translation," in *Translation: Literary, Linguistic, and Philosophical Perspectives*, ed. William Frawley (Newark: University of Delaware Press, 1984), pp. 159–75.

11. Basil Hatim and Ian Mason, *Discourse and the Translator*, (London and New York: Longman, 1990), p. 105.

12. Charles S. Peirce, "Logic as Semiotic: The Theory of Signs" in *Semiotics*, ed. Robert Innis (Bloomington: Indiana University Press, 1985), p. 5.

13. Karl Buhler, "The Key Principle: The Sign Character of Language," pp. 70–86.

14. Benedict Anderson, "Rereading Rizal," *The Manila Chronicle*, Sept. 26–Oct. 2, 1992, p. 11; "Noli Bowdlerized," *The Manila Chronicle*, Oct. 3–9, 1992, p. 10.

15. Charles Peirce, cited in Umberto Eco, "Drift and Unlimited Semiosis," Distinguished Lecturer Series, Indiana University, 1990, p. 4.

16. Thomas A. Sebeok, "Semiotics in the United States," *American Signatures* (Norman: University of Oklahoma Press, 1991), introduction.

17. Umberto Eco, *A Theory of Semiotics* (Bloomington: Indiana University Press, 1979), p. 71.

18. V.N. Volosinov, "Toward a Marxist Philosophy of Language," in *Semiotics*, ed. Robert Innis (Bloomington: Indiana University Press, 1985), pp. 47–65.

19. Patricia Seed, " 'Failing to Marvel,': Atahualpa's Encounter with the Word," *Latin American Review* XXVI, 1, 1991, p. 7.

20. Regina Harrison, *Signs, Songs, and Memory in the Andes, Translating Quechua Language and Culture* (Austin: University of Texas Press, 1989).

21. *Ibid.*, pp. 58–60.

22. The ladinos were the native assistants to the Spanish missionaries in the writing and translation of Spanish texts into the vernaculars. They were often the most educated among the Filipinos and many of them turned out to be poets who produced some of the most original works by Filipinos during the Spanish period. See

Bienvenido Lumbera's *Tagalog Poetry* (1986) which was cited earlier.

23. Michael Bakhtin, "Epic and Novel" in *The Dialogic Imagination: Four Essays*, ed. Michael Holquist (London: University of Texas Press, 1981), p. 289. Four Essays, trans. Caryl Emerson and Michael Holquist.

24. Hatim and Mason, p. 70.

Each poet must slay his poetic father; he must displace his precursors by a revisionary misreading which creates the historical space for his own poetry to take place.

—Harold Bloom

CHAPTER III

The *Corrido*: Translation as Sub-version

The *sugilanon* has been implicitly considered as the short story and thus, subject to the standards of the Western short story. Says, for instance, Juanito Marcella, former editor of the *Hiligaynon*: "ang karamihan sa mga maikling katha sa Hiligaynon ay hindi pa nakahabol sa mga maikling kathang nailathala ng pananakop ng mga Amerikano" ("most short stories in Hiligaynon have not yet come up to the standards of those written during the American period").[1] The same attitude seems to hold true for the Cebuano sugilanon. In 1937, the editors of *Bisaya* awarded Marcel M. Navarra's *Ug Gianod Ako* (I Was Carried Away) the top prize in a contest; they cited its being comparable to Edgar Allan Poe's "The Pit and the Pendulum" and Hawthorne's "The Ambitious Guest." In 1968, 30 years after the publication of Magdalena Jalandoni's *Tampad sa Kasanag*, Mr. Marcella was to hail as the model for the sugilanon Julius Flores' *Ang Gaba sa Katubwan* mentioning as criteria the qualities we normally associate with Western short stories: a well-defined plot, well-motivated characters, a singleness of impression, and an economical style. (Today, of course, we know that it is not easy to straitjacket even the Western short story itself. See, for instance, Lohafer and Clarey's *Short Story Theory at the Crossroads*, 1989).[2]

Lucila Hosillos, for example, speaks of the short story genre in the Philippines, but seems to do so only in reference to the works of Filipino writers in English:[3]

> Indeed, when one reads the Filipino short story in English such as the works of Manuel Arguilla, Nick Joaquin, Edith L. Tiempo, N.V.M. Gonzalez, Francisco Arcellana, Gregorio Brillantes, to name a few, one gets the impression that the genre is endemic in the Philippines and did have a long development. The truth is that... Like the novel, it has no ancestor in the Philippine literary tradition.

Nothing is mentioned of the sugilanon and its origins.

The Corrido and the Sugilanon

But the preponderance of sugilanon not meeting these standards suggests that it develops from a tradition different from that of the short story and that the sugilanon writer looks up to different models.

A good point of departure in locating the sugilanon in its semiotic continuum would be the corrido. There are various reasons for surmising this. Magdalena Jalandoni, who was the second Hiligaynon writer to come up with an anthology of sugilanon (the first was Anghel Magahum in 1935), actually began her career as a corrido writer. She wrote her first corrido, *Padre Juan kag Beata Maria* (Father Juan and Blessed Mary) in 1904 when she was ten, and her second one, *Don Juan Gonzaga* when she was twelve. She then wrote other corridos: *Lucibar*, *Pontivillar*, *Principe Recarredo*, and *General Monfredo*.[4] One of the most popular tales of Marta Jalandoni, the other Jalandoni of Hiligaynon fiction and noted for her gothic tales, was *Kasingkasing sa Botelya* (Lover in a Bottle) which Mojares called the "half-way form" since it had European characters and setting like the corrido but was written in prose like the novel. As late as 1951, Conrado Norada, called the most popular Hiligaynon novelist today, wrote *Bokay nga Owak* (The White Raven), a corrido in novel form.

It is worth noting that Iñigo Ed. Regalado, an incisive and original critic of vernacular literature, traces the origin of the vernacular novels to the *awit* and the corrido.[5] These, he says are merely a continuation of the latter and that there is no radical difference between them other than that the novels are in prose while the awit and the corrido are in verse. The same observation is made by Resil Mojares and Damiana Eugenio, who note that most vernacular novelists began as corrido writers.[6] This was, of course, a measure of the popularity of the corridos. In fact, the influence of the *pasyon* in Hiligaynon culture has been noted to be much less than that of the corrido, unlike the case among the Tagalogs to whom the pasyon was very popular. Among the major linguistic groups in Luzon and the Visayas it was the Hiligaynons who came up last with a vernacular version of the pasyon. This was with the publication of Mariano Perfecto's translation of the *Pasyong Pilapil* entitled *Kinabuhi cag Pasion ni Jesucristo nga Aton Guinoo* in 1885, in contrast to the Iloko version which appeared in 1621 and the Tagalog version in 1704.[7] The genealogical link, therefore, between the corrido and vernacular prose is very real. (Until recently when the word *sugilambong* was introduced for the novel, the term sugilanon referred to both the short story and the novel). In short, a study of the corrido would be useful to the translator in mapping out the sugilanon's intertextual sphere.

More intriguingly, as mentioned in the first chapter, reading the corrido was declared immoral by ecclesiastical authorities. Was its content an occasion for sin? Or was it perhaps an occasion for native resistance to their control? In looking for a liberative context for translating the sugilanon, the corrido may then be a good starting point.

The Corrido as Translated Text

Moreover, the corrido was largely a literature in translation. Most Tagalog corridos were translations from Spanish and other European sources, and most corridos in the vernacular literatures are believed to be translations from Tagalog. In Hiligaynon, where they were the earliest narrative poems, the majority, like the popular *Don Juan Tiñoso*, *Doce Pares de Francia*, *Bernardo Carpio*, and *Haring Villarba* were translations from Tagalog and Spanish. For instance, all of Magdalena Jalandoni's corridos were translations from Tagalog and Spanish, except for *General Monfredo*. Here we take the term "translation" in a broader sense to include Jakobson's three categories.[8] The corrido can thus inform the translator not only of the narrative conventions antecedent to the sugilanon, but also of those peculiar to the Philippine experience.

But what was the corrido? How did it enter the consciousness of the Hiligaynon as well as the other vernacular writers? Why was reading it declared sinful by ecclesiastical authorities?

Kept in the rare manuscript collection of the Lilly Library in Indiana University are transcripts in yellowed leaves of paper, material evidence of two events in Panay: one was said to have occurred in January 1627 when San Nicolas of Tolentino was believed to have appeared to an *indio* (as the Spaniards then called the Filipino) by the name of Luis Alagan de...as he was fishing by a riverbank in *Pueblo del Rio*; the other event happened one day in 1618, when a cross was seen falling from the sky at the estero Mapana in Panay. These two documents are part of an original manuscript collection by Augustinian friars on the Visayas in the 17th to the 18th century.

It was events of this nature that struck the corrido writers' imagination. It dealt with *occurridos* or events that were out of the ordinary, such as visions or apparitions. Along with these were tales of adventure and romance: love found, love unrequited, abductions and seductions, plunder and escape. It was a genre (or perhaps mode of thought?) in which the miraculous, sometimes indistinguishable from the fantastic, mingled with the earthy and secular. Peopled with kings and queens, princes and princesses, and set in exotic places far from the Philippines, it made for a heightened narrative appealing to readers fed only with religious literature such as the *ejemplo* in the novenas and the sermons.

Corridos or metrical romances, are long narratives in verse drawn mainly from European romances of chivalry, folktale, and religious literature.[9] Tagalog writers distinguish between the dodecasyllabic heroic-chivalric awit and the octosyllabic five-line legendary corrido. In Hiligaynon, however, no such distinction is made. The plot is complex, and there is much repetition both of situation and narration, a moderate use of stock phrases or epithets, and a leisurely narrative pace due partly to the padding of lines to complete the proper metrical length. The corrido is highly conventionalized; romance heroines are extremely beautiful and virtuous, heroes are gallant and brave, battles and single combats are described in hyperbolic and stereotyped images, beginnings and endings are formulaic.

It is usual for the corrido to be blamed as one of the sources of the weaknesses of vernacular literature. Lucila Hosillos writes: "The dodecasyllabic heroic-chivalric awit and the octosyllabic five-line legendary corrido adopted from the metrical romance, accustomed Filipinos to sterotyped plot, setting, and fairy-tale ending."[10] Anghel Magahum in his preface to his novel *Benjamin* (published in 1907 and 1918, this is considered the first Hiligaynon novel) says that his work combines the motives of the exemplum and the chronicle, a "mirror" of the "true happenings of life...things we see with our own eyes from day to day." Quirico Abeto, a journalist-critic from Iloilo at that time, hailed the novel for breaking away from literature "far removed from reality." Obviously, the context of Magahum and Abeto was the corrido. Encarnacion Gonzaga, one of the first products of the American educational system and the first to do a master's thesis on Hiligaynon culture (1917), dismissed the corridos as having "no literary beauty whatsoever."[11] But the most summary dismissal comes from Trinidad Pardo de Tavera in an article *The Heritage of Ignorance* (1924) which described the corridos as "all lengthy, exaggerated, puerile, and absurd in the extreme."[12]

The fact, though, was that the corridos were popular. Eugenio asserts that "they captivated the imagination of a people who as yet knew very little of the outside world. These romances provided a temporary release from the harsh realities of existence." Dean Fansler noted that even in the early decades of the 20th century the lives of heroes[13]

> such as Jaime del Prado and Bernardo are sung by the small boy driving the cattle to pasture, by the peasant working in his paddy field or by the itinerant beggar travelling from one town fiesta to the next. Even in social gatherings the apt introduction into the conversation was moralizing or didactic lines from some well-known corrido.

A. E. Manuel writes: "Indeed, everybody found in the metrical romances endless entertainment, drawing from them quotations to prove a point, reciting them, singing them, and even dancing to their musical renditions."[14]

The picture of the corrido drawn by these scholars is by no means that of a "puerile," unimaginative genre; the corrido, it seemed, animated the Filipinos, touched their lives in a fashion that the ejemplo did not. It endured in their society long after the repressive regime—responsible for this supposed retreat into fantasy—had gone. There is much fertile ground there, possibly enough emancipatory energy. Interestingly, this may come from the fact that the corrido was a literature in translation.

It is useful to look back briefly into its beginnings. The corrido did not get published until the late 18th or early 19th century but it was believed to have been written already at the onset of the second half of the 18th century. The basis for this belief is that Jose de la Cruz, one of the few writers who signed the corrido they wrote, lived in 1746-1829. The earliest accounts of its origins come from Barrantes' *El Teatro Tagalo*:[15]

> It is not doubtful that together with the harnesses of war, Legaspi's soldiers brought from Mexico the romances and narratives of our popular literature and a few books of knight errantry which, reaching the indios already altered, were in turn altered by them either because of poor reading in the foreign language or because of incomplete or monstrous recitations, which might be the origin of their *corridos* the name of which signifies no other thing than the printed leaflets circulated from hand to hand, copies sold or sung on the streets by blind men, well, street literature of the crowd, the populace.

Fansler, in his pioneering article on Philippine metrical romances, (1916) does not speak of how or when these found their way into the Philippines; however, he conjectures that they are European-based.[16] He writes in particular of the popularity of the Constance saga of which he found five versions in the Philippines. This he subdivides into Groups I and II. Group I is definitely European but he stops short of pointing to a specific European source for the different versions except for "Adela," which has identical localities, personages, incidents, and motifs as the *Historia del Rey de Hungria*. What is worth noting is his remarks on the stories in Group II:

> Group II seems to represent a development that took place in the Islands themselves and resulted either from an unconscious misunderstanding and subsequent confounding of the Constance and Cinderella stories, or from a studied departure from the fixed traditions for the purpose of emphasizing some particular phase of these essentially didactic motifs.

The corrido translations then were not mainly linguistic but literary, i.e., a transfer in terms of motifs, characters, and story outline. There was very likely a minimal attempt at a word-for-word, line-by-line translation. Both Fansler and Barrantes also speak of a misreading of the corridos; they hint at its appropriation by the poet for his own ends, and its alteration as it was passed on from one reader to another. The corrido is in a sense a vulgarization of the source text, their readers translating these in an off-hand, loose way.

The missionaries, in contrast, pursued their translation work methodically, beginning with the compilation of translation tools like dictionaries and grammar books. The first Hiligaynon-Spanish dictionary, for example, was compiled by the Augustinian friar, Fray Alonso de Mentrida, in 1637 (this was just soon after the first Spanish settlement in Panay). A reprint was done in Manila in 1841 and a second volume added in 1842 by another Augustinian, Fray Julian Martin, in Tigbauan, Iloilo. A Spanish-Visayan dictionary was also found within the Dalrymple loot, possibly compiled in the first half of the 18th century.[17] The oldest grammar book in Spanish and Hiligaynon is Raymundo Lozano y Mejia's *Cursos de la Lengua Panayana*, published in 1876 and reprinted in 1892. Another book, *Arte del Idioma Bisaya-Hiligaino* by Fr. Mariano Cuartero, was published in Jaro, Iloilo in 1890. All these use Spanish as a frame of reference (the final product after all is the translation of Spanish religious texts for the indios). All seem to demonstrate that even linguistic correctness is assured by ecclesiastical authority. Cuartero's *Idioma*, for example, does not treat Hiligaynon as distinct but as a language to be compared to Spanish. Thus, sections are arranged according to Spanish grammatical categories, such as tenses (recent studies show that "aspect" is more applicable to Filipino grammar than tense), case, and parts of speech. Other than the usual publication data, the title page bears the author's name and

Cuartero's ecclesiastical position. In the *Diccionario* by Mentrida, the title page indicates Mentrida's church position and the words *con superior permiso* show ecclesiastical approval. The dictionary ends with the lines *LAUS DEO*.

The overriding concern, then, in translating religious literature was the linguistic fidelity of the Hiligaynon version to the Spanish source text to ensure the passage of Christian doctrine to the readers in unadulterated form. It is significant to note that most of the religious texts I have examined use the term *ginbinisaya*, an indication that the source text and the target text were viewed in neutral terms. This neutrality, of course, was only more apparent than real, in view of the overarching ideological *intentio*. Asad devalorizes this linguistic type of translation claiming that "linguistic patterns are not meanings to be translated; they are rules to be systematically described and analyzed." Quite applicable to the translator-missionaries, considering their disregard for the categories of meaning among their target audience in the name of linguistic-clerico fidelity.

What seems more promising for an inventive poetics of translation is Talal Asad's concept of cultural translation. To Asad, the translator "constructs the discourse as a cultural text in terms of meaning implicit in a range of practices and therefore, the construction of cultural discourse and its translation seem to be facets of a single act."[18] The statement was made in a different context, given as an advice to the foreigner transported to and translating in a setting not native to him. And yet, in a sense, in interpreting and appropriating the corrido to his own purpose, altering it, even distorting and fitting it within his ever- changing semiotic milieu, the corrido poets (one cannot speak of singularity here) were engaged in the dual yet single act of translating. And thus, articulating. From the point of view of the colonizer, any departure from the original in/on whatever point in the semiotic continuum would be a "misreading," or a "poor reading," or a "confounding." From the point of view, of the colonized/receptor, however, any alteration is a "creative misreading"—the continuous construction and reconstruction of signs in his cultural system.[19]

The Corrido as Creative Mis-reading

We must point out that the corrido translators were not as concerned with staking a claim to some authority as their religious counterparts were. Although some of the former made the pretense of using "translated by" in the title page to lend authority or authenticity to the text, most of them used terms in their various vernacular languages synonymous to "localized," "modernized," "corrected," "adapted." In Hiligaynon, one of the terms used was *ginbiao*. (*Biao*, it will be recalled, means "spring.") All these suggest the idea of the translator as an innovative sign-giver, although by no means a dogmatic or an infallible one. The following title illustrates the point: *Vida ni San Alejo, Confesor nga anac ni Don Eufemio cag ni Don Aglais sa imperio sang Roma. Guincuha sa año Christiano, cag guinbiao sa pulong nga Panayanhon ni Mariano Perfecto.*

Moreover, most corridos, even up to the establishment of secular printing presses in the late 19th century, did not bear the publisher's name or the publishing date and usually indicated only the initials of the author or pseudonyms like "Enepe." Unlike in the religious texts, the author's position was not indicated. These features survive in later corridos. For instance, the corrido, *Story of Edmundo, Son of Merced in the Kingdom of France* is unsigned but indicates that it is taken from a *novela* and "composed by one who enjoys writing the Tagalog language, Manila, 1909"; the author of *Hada Parubanu* signs herself mysteriously as *Isa ka Bagonhon* (a native of Bago) and the writer of *Ang lahog nga pulos Milagro sang duha ca Bata nga si Cente cag si Tonio, nga cabataan sang duha ca Babae nga Pulos Francisca* (1928) quite disarmingly refers to herself as *Isa ka Curiosa* (One Who is Curious).

Although partly religious, the corrido was devoid of the legalistic, imperious air which greets the readers as they leaf through the first pages of the novenas and the vidas. Like the novenas, the corrido begins with a religious invocation but this is to ask for enlightenment for his narrative account. This is in contrast to the title page of religious texts which have to bear an *imprimatur*; everything that follows is thus considered doctrinally correct.

The invocation at the start of *Prinsesa Florentina* shows the corrido poets' concern for divine enlightenment:

O Dios nga Ginuong Mahal (O God, dear Lord)
Nga hari nga sa tanan (King of all)
Imo ako nga tabangan (Please help me)
Sining akon igasaysay (With what I will say).

Kag ikaw, Birhen nga himpit (And thou perfect virgin)
Nga emperatriz sa langit (Queen of heavens)
Ining akon igasuguid (This which I shall say)
Ginasalig ko sa imo (I entrust to you).

Usually, this is followed with a stanza in which the poet offers an apology to the reader for the former's lack of wisdom and artistry, followed by a request to overlook the poet's shortcomings. In the foreword to *Florentina*, for example, the author defends corridos from their detractors who ridicule them for their lack of realism. Despite this flaw, he says that the youth owe much to the corridos because from them, knowledge has sprung. This description of the features of the corrido may appear trivial, but as Edward Said has demonstrated, beginnings in narrative accounts are crucial.[20] They lay down the means for legitimizing authority for a particular version of events. For the corrido writer, such authority clearly was not derived from an ecclesiastical imprimatur; hence, the absence of publication data, the preference for initials rather than the fully-spelled name of the author (to delude or elude?), and the absence of clues as to version and source. Instead, there is a direct appeal in the invocation to the Final Authorities (not to a Censorship Board) and a plea for understanding from the audience. The plea at the beginning is reiterated as the corrido closes. For example, *Corrido Sang Mucuhanoclog nga Cabuhi Nga nadangat Sang Pito Ca Mga Infantes de Lara Cag Sang Macalolooy nga Ila Amay sa Reinong España* ends almost on the same vein with which it begins. The following are its last two stanzas:

Acon guinapangayo sa tauo nga macabasa
iya nga dispensahon ang acon nga mga letra
cag ang mga verso nga may culang o may sobra
sanglit ang nagbuhat dili guid poeta.

Busa guinapangayo co
ang patauad nga bug-os
cabay man macasambit ang tanan
nga cristianos
sadtong capahuayon nga wala
pagcatapos
ang gloria sa langit cag ang
LAUS DEUS.

(May I request the reader
to please be patient with my words and the verse that
may be too much or too little
for this comes from someone who is not a poet.

So let me ask
for your pardon,
may all pray,
may all Christians pray
for that peace
eternal
glory in heaven and
GLORY TO GOD.)

There is something clandestine here, a flaunting of accepted sources of authority, an indication that the corrido although derived, shall be its own being, and that although it respects religion it will refuse to conform wholly to its institutional features. It was therefore the alternative literature of its time.

Barrantes' account on the genealogy of the corrido may not altogether be complete; some scholars believe on the bases of its strong religious elements that these were written by missionaries with the assistance of the ladinos. In fact, some corridos were called ejemplos. But the ladinos were not exactly the passive assistants that the missionaries deemed them to be. It appears, in fact, that it was they who kept alive the secular and folk impulses of the Filipino imagination through the corridos and the corrido-based *comedia* and *moro-moro*. Writes Lumbera on the Tagalog ladinos:[21]

> In the 18th century, they [the ladinos] adapted the Spanish romances into Tagalog thus producing the awits and the corridos that were to be the only secular works authorized for publication during the long Spanish era. From the dramatic presentations in Spanish during great religious occasions, they adapted the theatrical techniques and devices of the *loas* in creating secular dramas based on the plots of romances; thus, ideas and sentiments missionaries would edit out found their way again into Tagalog literature because of the ladinos.

Cecilia Nava suggests the same appropriation or secularization with regard to the Hiligaynon corrido. The survival, she says, of one "gross" corrido published in 1908 by the Libreria Panayana entitled *Ang Nagsagad Caon Santol nga Tinubol* (The One Who Ate Too Much Santol and So, Became Constipated) and another hilarious corrido entitled *Vida nga Matahum ni Capinahan cag ni Bulanbulan sa Barrio nga Malapit sa Madiaas*, n.d. (The Beautiful Life of Capinahan and Bulanbulan in a Barrio near Madiaas) shows that the corrido did not just deal with the miraculous and marvelous.[22]

> Revealing dimensions hitherto unexplored of the protean form which includes obscenity, satire and graphic depiction of toilet humor, the above mentioned corridos appear to show that the oppressed Indios' lean reading fare was not necessarily confined to the deadening monotony of devotional literature due to the stringent standards of the *censura*.

It is claimed that the origins of the corrido may not be purely European. Fansler (1921), in his discussion of sources and analogues of Filipino popular tales, suggests that some metrical romances may have been derived from folktales which were in turn partly derived from Asian folktales. He points to Juan's adventures (number 17 in his collection) as the basis for the metrical romance on the *Adarna Bird* which was printed in six languages—Tagalog, Pampango, Hiligaynon, Cebuano, Ilocano and Bicolano. Also, he traces the source of the Tagalog metrical romance on *Edmundo, Son of Merced in the Kingdom of France* to two tales belonging to the *Magic Ring* cycle (Fansler,

1921, p.87). In another study (1937), Fansler writes that he found 54 *maerchen* (serious, droll, animal) to represent oral popular versions of 28 corridos; in short, some corridos were literary versions of much older native material. It may be too sweeping, therefore, to speak of our metrical romances as simply derived from European sources since our popular tales which have had an influence on them have their origins worldwide such as in Arabic, Hindu, and other Asian tales. In fact, Fansler writes that a comparison of the corrido with the Malayan *hikayat* "might reveal hitherto unsuspected relationships."[23]

The origins of the corrido, then, are complex. What is suggested, however, is that it was a literature in translation. Furthermore, its translation was a collective enterprise shaped and reshaped by various participants: soldiers, sailors, priests, ladinos, writers, chanters, singers, anyone who had it in his heart to tell and enjoy a story. With the corrido, we bracket the issue of fidelity to the source text; this was the concern of those anxious to preserve the accurate passage of doctrine—not of the corrido writer. It is significant that with regard to religious texts, we speak of editions, but with the corridos we speak of versions within and between languages and of the tales they have spawned. *Don Juan Tiñoso*, for example, is said to be the bases for various tales nationwide.

To quote Benjamin:[24]

> ...no translation would be possible if in its ultimate essence it strove for likeness to the original. For in its afterlife—which could not be called that if it were not a transformation and renewal of something living—the original undergoes a change.

The corrido was, in other words, the imaginative space the Filipinos had set aside to engage in the earthy, the carnivalistic, the fantastic, the bawdy, the exuberance of life and spirit shunted aside in a medieval order. It was not surprising that the missionaries looked upon it with suspicion and summarily dismissed it as heretical. Toribio Minguella, an Augustinian friar (1878) writes: "...alas for history and theology when they take into account a hero of the past or any saint whatsoever, then the anachronisms and material heresies vie for their attention."[25] Even while the *Comision Permanente de Censura* allowed the publication of the corrido in the 19th century as liberal ideas filtered into the Spanish colony, the Church pursued the audience of the corrido like lost souls in the language it deemed most effective: threat of purgatorial pain or infernal damnation; hence, the strict injunctions within the section on the sixth commandment of the *Confesion General* earlier mentioned.

The corrido's liberative potential was evident not only in the creative sphere but in the political arena as well. It was a medium to protest against the colonizers' injustices. Albanya in *Florante at Laura* (hailed as the best corrido both in poetic power and allegorical force) was recognized as the Philippine society during the Spanish period. San Juan claims that *Florante* is "unquestionably the first anti-feudal poem of epic dimension" reflecting in essence "the struggle of different social classes at that crucial juncture in our history." Writes Hosillos:

> Balagtas [one of the few known authors of the corrido] adopts the generalities of the genre but invents details of scene, plot, and action, character, and psychology specific to his narrative purpose [which] enables the poet to reveal the forces that negate truth, freedom, and justice....[26]

Reyes has the following to say:[27]

> ...examined not as reflection but as refractions and even negations of reality, the awit and the corrido would appear to set up an alternative world different from nineteenth century realities. In these works, what was presented was a simplified ideological pattern more acceptable than the complex of ideological forces that conditioned the people's lives.

It seemed, in fact, that the corrido had a tremendous influence on our principal nationalist figures during the last decades of the Spanish colonial period. When Jose Rizal set out for Spain, it is said that one of the books he lugged along was *Florante at Laura*. But there is a more detailed story than this.[28] In April 1895, about a year before the outbreak of the Philippine Revolution, Andres Bonifacio and his closest advisers in the Katipunan trekked up to the mountains of San Mateo, about 20 miles southeast of Manila. Their aim: to reach the cave of Bernardo Carpio. This trip was widely interpreted as a search for a haven should the revolutionaries have to retreat. But Bonifacio and his men reached the cave on Good Friday and once there, wrote with pieces of charcoal the battlecry "Long Live Philippine Independence!" Each *katipunero* then signed his name on the wall with trembling hands and tears in his eyes.

In the light of this act, the trip could not merely be labeled as "exploratory." Bernardo Carpio is the hero of a Philippine corrido based on *Mocedades de Bernardo del Carpio* by Lope de Vega, or a popular version of it. The *Mocedades* is basically about the adventures of Bernardo Carpio, the bastard son of a courtier and the sister of the king of Spain. He had grown up to be a great general with a keen sense of justice and zeal to defend the Spanish crown and Christianity. But the Philippine version weaves changes into the original story, the most significant of which is the addition of a different closing episode. In Bernardo Carpio's continuing search for idolaters, he comes upon a cave with a churchlike entrance guarded by two lion statues. A lightning bolt hits one of the statues, and Bernardo Carpio chases the lightning into the cave even against the admonition of an angel. The cave closes in on him. However, it was a widespread belief among Filipinos that Bernardo Carpio did not die; he was merely asleep and would one day rise to save the Filipinos from oppression.

This Messianic detail was of utmost significance. "Bernardo Carpio" was one of the most popular corridos in the Philippines. It was translated into five languages: Tagalog, Ilokano, Hiligaynon, Cebuano, and Bikolano. This is not to mention the versions within each language. Two Tagalog versions, for example, have been found: *Historia Famoso ni Bernardo Carpio* (1919) and *Ang Walang Pagkupas na Kasaysayan ni Bernardo Carpio* (1949). In Hiligaynon, there are two known versions: *Vida ni Bernardo Carpio cag ni Doña Jimena* (1911) and *Historia sang dalaganan sa guinharian sa España* (1922). In an informal survey which Fansler conducted among 175 of his students at the University of the Philippines (circa 1921), which group he claims to be representative of all regions of the Philippines, 104 replied they had either read in their dialects or had seen acted in their fiestas the life of Bernardo Carpio; 85 made a similar report on the "Twelve Peers." This is to say nothing of Bernardo Carpio as the subject of legends in various parts of the country. When, furthermore, we consider the somewhat clandestine manner in which the corrido chapbooks or manuscripts circulated from hand to hand (so much so that the *Confesion General* pronounced it sinful for one to have in his possession a corrido manuscript or not to report anybody else who had a copy of it), the corrido assumes a subversive character much like the circulation of mimeographed copies, leaflets, and manuscripts of the underground movement in the Philippines today. The corridos were the subjugated masses' versions of a prior narrative.

Bernardo Carpio was a redemptive figure whose anointment Bonifacio and his men had to seek before the revolution could commence. Through the corrido of Bernardo Carpio, translated from the *Mocedades*, then transfigured and transformed within the Filipino semiotic system, revolution and romance had become conjoined.[29]

NOTES

1. Juanito Marcella, "Ang Panitikang Hiligaynon," in *Mga Piling Akdang Pilipino* ed. Efren Abueg (Manila: Kampi and Pioneer Printing House, 1970), p. 149.

2. Susan Lohafer and Jo Ellyn Clarey, *Short Story Theory at the Crossroads* (Baton Rouge and London: Louisiana State University Press, 1989).

3. Lucila V. Hosillos, "The Transmutation of the Western Short Story," *Originality as Vengeance in Philippine Literature* (Quezon City: New Day Publishers, 1984), p. 92.

4. "Magdalena G. Jalandoni: Writing at 85," *Pamana*, 29, December 1977, pp. 4–5.

5. Iñigo Ed. Regalado, *Ang Pag-unlad ng Nobelang Tagalog* (Manila: Institute of National Language, 1939).

6. Resil Mojares, *Origins and Rise of the Filipino Novel, A Generic Study of the Novel until 1940* (Quezon City: University of the Philippines Press, 1983), pp. 180–83; 250–53.

   Damiana Eugenio, *Awit and Corrido: Philippine Metrical Romances* (Quezon City: University of the Philippines Press, 1987), xxix.

7. Mojares, p. 51.

8. Roman Jakobson, "Linguistic Aspects," pp. 232–39.

9. Eugenio, *Awit and Corrido.* This is the most comprehensive study of Philippine metrical romances, especially with regard to sources and analogues. I owe much of my historical background on the corrido to this book.

10. Hosillos, *Originality as Vengeance*, p. 24.

11. Encarnacion Gonzaga, "Bisayan Literature From Pre-Spanish Times to 1917." Unpublished Master's Thesis, University of the Philippines, 1917, p. 21.

12. Cited in the introduction of Eugenio, *Awit and Corrido*.

13. Dean S. Fansler, "Metrical Romances in the Philippines," *Journal of American Folklore*, XXIX (1916), pp. 204–05.

14. Arsenio E. Manuel, cited in Eugenio, *Awit and Corrido*, xv.

15. Vicente Barrantes y Moreno, *El Teatro Tagalo* (Madrid, 1889), pp. 20–21.

16. Dean S. Fansler, "Metrical Romances," pp. 203–81.

17. This dictionary is one of the documents catalogued in the Asian Studies Research Institute's Occasional Papers No. 2, Catalogue of Philippine Manuscripts in the Lilly Library by C.R. Boxer at the Indiana University. These comprise the major part of an important collection of original manuscripts relating to the Philippines and the Spanish Roman Catholic Mission in East Asia. They were looted from the Augustinian convent of San Pablo during the British Occupation of Manila in 1762–1764 when they were acquired by Alexander Dalrymple (1737–1808).

18. Talal Asad, "The Concept of Cultural Translation in British Social Anthropology," in *Writing Culture, The Poetics and Politics of Anthropology*, ed. James Clifford and George E. Marcus (Berkeley: UCLA Press, 1986), p. 160.

19. Harold Bloom in *The Anxiety of Influence* (New York: Oxford University Press, 1973, p. 70) writes: "Each poet must slay his poetic father; he must displace his precursors by a revisionary misreading which creates the historical space in which his own poetry takes place." All poems are in a sense translations or "creative misreadings" of previous ones.

20. Edward Said, *Beginnings and Methods* (New York: Columbia University Press, 1976).

21. Lumbera, *Tagalog Poetry*, pp. 36–39.

22. Cecilia Locsin Nava, "Pagtan-aw sa Kalibutan: A Study of Ilonggo History and Society in the Novel of Ramon L. Muzones," Unpublished Dissertation, College of Arts and Letters, University of the Philippines, 1990, p. 189.

23. Dean S. Fansler, "Philippine Folk Literature, A Sypnotic Study on an Unpublished Manuscript Collection of Folktales," *Philippine Magazine*, XXXIV (May 1937), pp. 208-09.

24. Walter Benjamin, "The Task of the Translator," *Illuminations* (New York: Harcourt and Brace, 1955), pp. 69–82.

25. Cited in Eugenio, xiii.

26. Hosillos, *Originality as Vengeance*, p. 51.

27. Soledad Reyes, "The Romance Mode in Philippine Literature," *Philippine Studies*, 32 (1984), pp. 163–80.

28. Recounted in Ileto, *Pasyon*, pp. 122–27.

29. It may be interesting to explore the literature on the Mexican corrido. The Philippines and Mexico had close economic, political, and cultural relations with Spain for almost three centuries; studying this genre's Mexican counterpart may reveal unexpected data on the origins of the corrido and its revolutionary potentials. See, for example, Maria Herrera-Sobek's *The Mexican Corrido, A Feminist Analysis* (Bloomington, Indiana: Indiana University Press, 1990).

Let us invent
letter by letter
The word we shall say when it happens
A tender word
that will define us
with perfect seriousness.

—Vicente Rodriguez Nietzche

CHAPTER IV

The Sugilanon in Transit from Hiligaynon to English

Tracing the connection of the *sugilanon* to the *corrido* does not mean the latter is its only source; that certainly would be an oversimplification. But various strands in our narrative tradition—tales, legends, songs, poetry, the *ejemplo*—converge in the corrido and diverge from it. The linkage provides the translator with an understanding of the nature of the sugilanon and allows him to take it on its own terms in the actual translation process. To quote Rifattere: "Every work of art is a dialogue between the present and past works of arts."; Jorge Luis Borges: "Every writer of fiction creates his own set of precursors."; and Barthes: "Every work of art is a mirage of citations." These seem to refer alone to original creative writing, but if we note Octavio Paz's statement that "no text is entirely original because language itself, in its essence, is already a translation," then the line between the writer and the translator is thin, indeed. If we note further that both the source text and the translated texts are interpretants co-equal in an infinite semiosic process, then a writer is a translator and the translator, a writer (as Terry Eagleton claims, for instance).[1] And both engage themselves in intertextual probings/musings.

Moreover, the corrido was the site of an ideological struggle in which secular and local forces via the translators wrested control over the process of sign production from religio-imperialist dominion. Thus, marking the sugilanon's affinities with the corrido clears the ground for an inventive or liberative poetics to guide and energize its translation, a strategy made imperative by new power alignments formed after the Spanish era. The corrido connects the sugilanon to a revolutionary or alternative tradition. Any discussion, then, of Philippine language and literature inevitably touches the political.[2] This is not mere paranoia, especially when we cross the intertextual space between a homegrown vernacular and an international language with an imperialistic track record. There is real danger here. As Talal Asad writes: "...because the languages of Third World societies...are 'weaker' in relation to Western languages (and today, especially to English), they're more likely to submit to forcible transformation in the translation process than the other way around."[3] In fact, this danger has also been observed by Rogelio Sikat with regard to the borrowing of English words by Filipino translators: *"Hindi dapat sumobra ang panghihiram pagka't masisira, kundi man mawawasak, ang batayang wika. Tulad ng agos, tatangayin ito patungo sa Ingles."*[4] (The translator should borrow [English words] moderately, or else, the receiving language [Filipino] will be damaged, if not destroyed.)

Such dominance is due to two factors: the prevailing political-economic order in which Western nations have the greater ability to manipulate the latter, and the fact that Western languages produce and deploy "desired" knowledge more readily than Third World countries. In an article entitled "Literary Colonialism: Books in the Third World," Philip Altbach documents the fact that the products of knowledge are distributed unevenly in the world. Industrialized countries notably the United States, Great Britain, France, and to a certain extent West Germany and the Soviet Union [and now, Japan] dominate the field. These same countries control systems which distribute knowledge; they own the publishing houses which produce the scholarly journals, magazines, films and tv programs the rest of the world consumes. And since English has been the principal conduit for such knowledge, most people in the Third World are predisposed to accept as truths concepts expressed in the language.

In fact, the question of English in the Philippines has always been a political one, the language having been historically associated with elitism.[5] Its use alienated administrators from the people, giving enough room for the abuse of power and enough distinction for its speakers to enjoy unearned privilege. It divided society into classes on the basis of the buying and selling of labor power since those who could speak English well went on to occupy positions of power.[6] Because it has made the Filipino accept both Western and capitalist values to the detriment of his own culture, it has, in the words of one nationalist, become the medium for "the miseducation of the Filipino."[7] English, in short, has been the language of the dominant elite and their alien partners in the country. It continues to be so up to now.

But the domains of Filipino have expanded greatly this past decade, especially in the educational system, the church and the mass media, and to a limited degree, in business and government.[8]

Also, the most vital writing is now being done in Tagalog and the other vernaculars. These developments have actually been acknowledged in the 1987 Philippine Constitution, which is supportive of Filipino as the eventual sole medium of instruction:

> Sec. 7. For purposes of communication and instruction, the official languages of the Philippines are Filipino and until otherwise provided by law, English.
> Sec. 9. The government shall take steps to initiate and sustain the use of Filipino as a medium of official communication and as a language of instruction in the educational system.

So why translate the sugilanon into English? If the domains of English are shrinking, who would read these English translations?

Yet, translations from Hiligaynon and other vernaculars into English have continued to appear long after the first simple attempts of Gonzaga in her master's thesis in 1917 and the student translations in the Bisayan volume of the Beyer Collection (1921)—and even after the demystification of English in recent years. Translation projects have been done largely at the University of the Philippines Visayas Center in Iloilo; at the Cultural Center of the Philippines through publications like *Ani* and *Lahi* (now defunct), and its Regional Literature Series; at the University of the Philippines Press in Quezon City through occasional publications like Eugenio's *Awit and Corrido* and

Damaso, et al., *Philippine Drama: Twelve Plays in Six Philippine Languages*, which was a translation of vernacular plays into English (interestingly, Ernesto Constantino remarks it was a "translation in need of a translation,"); the Toyota Foundation's Translation Series, most of whose grantees come from universities. Apart from these, there are translations of vernacular texts appearing in various theses and dissertations, and books on vernacular literature, the number of which have risen recently.

That these translations go on largely in academic settings is reflective of the academic domain of English. But it also reflects an intention to reach out beyond the margins of one's culture since a significant percentage of books are sent to libraries abroad. Circulation among the masses (for whom comics and the radio [now mainly in Filipino and the vernaculars] are the favorite media), is almost nil. Ironically, however, it is not just from the elite and the middle class that the plea to keep English in schools comes, but from the educated spokesmen of the masses, the teachers.[9] Their main argument: the dominant elite can use their private resources to study English, but not the unaffluent ones who can study the language only within the regular school curriculum. Therefore, the new language policy aggravates even more the dominance of the elite, especially in view of the fact that "upper class, upper middle-class, and upwardly mobile urban Filipinos" have in recent years been cultivating their facility not just in English but in Filipino.[10] Their dominance, linguistic or otherwise, would be even more total. Thus, Emy Pascasio, on the basis of empirical studies on the present role and domains of English in the Philippines, has predicted that "if English is denied to the rural Filipino and the culturally deprived urban Filipino, one important avenue for upward social movement becomes closed to him."[11]

Worth considering, likewise, is the loss of the Filipino's competitive edge in international conferences and educational venues where English is still the dominant medium for communication. If certain countries like Japan, China and Korea are developing or strengthening their programs in English for a stronger international linkage, why then should we drop English? Some English-speaking nationalists have gone as far as using Filipino even in foreign venues, whether or not the audience understands the language; they insist that those interested in our culture should learn the language first. But this insistence is unpragmatic, in view of the fact that the Filipino does not enjoy the global English network. Save for researchers, Filipinophiles, and foreigners at work in the country, we cannot expect any large group to be enthusiastic about our culture if they have to learn our languages first. We note here the case of Ngugi wa Thiong'o of Kenya. Reacting to "literature in colonial schools and universities whose entire way of looking at the world...was Eurocentric," he declared his farewell to writing in English in his book *Decolonizing the Mind*.[12] "From now on," he said, "it is Gikuyu and Kishwahili all the way." His works, however, continue to be available in English translations, some of which he does himself. There are valid arguments, then, for English although these should not by any means sidetrack us from supporting a language policy built on Filipino as a national language developed and enriched through the other vernacular languages. What is needed is a tilt in the balance where English is not to be dropped totally but studied on our own terms.

But can English sever its ties from elitism and cultural imperialism? Eagleton traces how English studies in the universities in England have been used alternately to promote capitalist ideology and to liberate readers from it.[13] In a fascinating study, Ashcroft et al. (1989) discuss how the twin processes of abrogation and appropriation have been utilized in post-colonial literature in English, thus demonstrating the liberative potentials of the language.[14] Of particular interest is the ingenious manner in which the Rastafarians have evolved subversive strategies against English, this being the only way for linguistic emancipation where there is no native language in which to "reject the language (and hence, the vision) of the colonizers."[15]

In the Philippines, English has been both a conduit for colonial values and a dynamic medium in the liberation from colonial consciousness (the same holds true for Filipino and Spanish).[16] Thus, mainstream Philippine literature in English has accommodated works as diverse as the committed poetry of Emmanuel Lacaba and the elitist poetry of Jose Garcia Villa. The Department of English in the University of the Philippines has produced graduates who have co-opted themselves in a repressive system, but also true liberals and even revolutionaries like Jose Ma. Sison and Carolina Malay. It appears then that while English paves the way for reading and writing that are open to "forms of regulation, exploitation, and denigration," it contains within itself "potential modes for resistance and affirmation."[17]

Unleashing these potentials, however, would depend on a number of factors. First, on the translator's consciousness of the inherent qualities of Hiligaynon, the language and culture to be transposed into English. This would help him approach the task of translating from a position of equality, (a condition necessary for any democratic encounter between languages).[18] The time for a dominant language to make totalizing claims is past; the era for the fraternity of languages is here. It would do the translator well to note what Bakhtin wrote in explaining the burst of creativity in such periods as the Renaissance:[19]

> The world becomes polyglot, once and for all and irreversibly. The period of national languages, coexisting but closed and deaf to each other, comes to an end. Languages throw light on each other: one language can, after all, see itself only in the light of another.

The translator must cultivate what Bakhtin called a "Gälilean consciousness" in which many languages are encompassed and enter into dialogue with one another, mutually illuminating each other.

Second, the translator should acknowledge the sugilanon's distinctness as a genre and hold a respect for the vernacular traditions from which it draws. In a discussion of the Filipino short story in English, Andrew Gonzalez laments the writer's failure to integrate native narrative traditions into their stories and to include indigenous discourse conventions and techniques (for example, the repetitive pattern of folktales or a certain seriality in design). Writing about Nick Joaquin, considered widely as one of the outstanding Filipino prose writers in English, Gonzalez acknowledges that the writer depicts the Filipino way of life, but notes that Joaquin's mode of narration is entirely Western.[20] In fact, this inadequacy of Philippine literature from/in English in reflecting our semiotic milleu should be one justification for translating the sugilanon into English. English is our window to the world but how much of Philippine culture is depicted in Philippine literature in English? Our vernacular and ethnic literatures would be lost to the world forever. Already, Rosario Lucero laments the neglect of vernacular literature:[21]

> Were it not for its marginalized status, vernacular literature would be capable of being more fully expressive of the Filipino identity. Metro Manila literature is beset with themes of angst, cosmopolitanism, bourgeois ambivalence, alienation, and other such metaphysical concerns; in its themes and forms, it is necessarily limited for it is derived from the monolithic, capitalistic structure of the city.

In fact, except for efforts from academe (as mentioned above), it would have been presumptuous to translate our vernacular literature into English: after all, what is there to showcase? Hiligaynon-related translation has been handled largely by the editors of a Manila-based monopoly that has controlled Philippine media and Philippine vernacular literature since the '20s. What stories to publish and what stories to translate from the vernacular literatures have therefore been determined mainly by commercial motives. Translations have been of two kinds. Stories written in Tagalog and published in *Liwayway* have been translated into the various vernaculars and subsequently published in the company's vernacular magazines like *Hiligaynon*, *Bisaya* (Cebuano), and *Bannawag* (Ilocano). Foreign literature, mostly romances, like *The Three Musketeers*, etc. have been translated into the vernaculars. Much of the translation has been directed inwards from a centralized authority originating in Manila; Hiligaynon and other vernacular literatures have not had a chance to be known outside of their respective regions. In short, not much has changed in the status of vernacular literature and the direction of translation since the Spanish period.

Critics, in fact, tend to focus on translation of foreign works and their influence on Philippine culture. Says Lumbera:[22]

> The growth of any national literature is always abetted by its contacts with foreign literatures and translations are the records of these contacts. The literary merits of the translation are not half as important as the information they provide on the entry of certain literary types and themes into Tagalog literature.

Writes Hosillos:[23]

> The translator's purpose, aside from deriving pleasure in the whole creative process of translating literature from one language to another, may be to make available to his own culture and society certain values, attitudes, ideas, even temperaments and sensibilities in the work he has chosen which he may not find in the literature of the culture and language he is translating in.

Third, it would be profitable for the translator to consider and experiment with a Filipino variety of literary English. Although English was introduced to the Filipinos by the Americans via American and English works in the educational system and in the mass media, the form in which it developed is distinctly Filipino as some studies prove. The first such study is Jean Edades'.[24] However, she puts these Filipinisms side by side with their American English expressions, implying the former to be substandard. More scientific studies are those of Llamzon (1969, 1983), who used the term "standard Filipino English," implying stratification among its users; that of Alberca and Gonzalez (1978), which focuses on the phonology, lexicon, and syntax of Filipino English in the mass media; those of Dar (1973) and Ponio (1974) which are cited in the Gonzalez and Alberca study; and Aranas (1990). No one has made a formal study of the literary English of Filipinos except Gonzalez, who observes the use of a new English code by Filipinos. For instance, characters in Filipino literature in English manifest speech patterns almost directly translated from the local languages, or use code-switching. Young Filipino writers in English whom I interviewed recently told me that they have received feedback from fellow American writers in various workshops on the differentness of their English.

The concept of a Filipino variety of English is crucial for an inventive poetics of translation. For if we continue to measure Filipino literary English against the canons of American and English semiotic systems (which many still do, even in the English Department of the University of the Philippines), then English translations of vernacular literature on which expectedly the first language idioms, patterns, and other conventions shall be carried over, may be declared inferior immediately. In fact, known Third World writers have been more than emphatic in their insistence upon their own kind of English. Raja Rao, for instance, in his preface to *Kanthapura* (1943) declares:[25]

> We cannot write like the English. We should not. We can write only as Indians. Our method of expression therefore has to be a dialect which will some day prove to be as distinctive and colorful as the Irish and the American. Time alone will justify it.

Chinua Achebe writes:[26]

> Can he [an African] ever learn to use it [English] like a native speaker? I should say, I hope not. It is neither necessary nor desirable for him to do so. The price a world language must be prepared to pay is submission to many different kinds of use....The African should aim at fashioning out an English which is at once universal and able to carry his peculiar experience....It will have to be a new English, still in full communion with its ancestral home, but altered to suit its new African surrounding.

Rao, Ngugi, Achebe have been joined more recently, by a younger generation of transcultural writers including Ben Okri, Timothy Mo, Salman Rushdie, Kazuo Ishiguro, Vikram Seth, and Michael Ondaatje who continue to re-invent English literature and English.[27]

To reject the reality of Filipino English is to continue capitulating to an imperial educational system which has installed in the Philippines and in other parts of the world a "standard version of the metropolitan language as the norm, and marginalizes all variants as impurities." It is to allow the English language to perpetuate its own conceptions of "truth," "order" and "reality." As Vikram Seth says: "The English language has been taken over, or taken to heart, or taken to tongue, by people whose original language historically it was not."[28]

One other question pertains to the target audience for these texts translated into English. Would readers not be more interested in literature originally written in English or translations approximating English in the United States and England? According to Toury, "a translation occupying no position in the target literary system will not be regarded as a literary translation, simply because it fails to be a literary text according to the target's conception and norms."[29] In which case, what is the use of translations in Filipino English?

Crystal and Kachru estimate, however, that roughly every third person in the world uses some variety of English as a non-native speaker, English being one of the few languages in the world used by a majority of people who speak it as a second, third, or nth language.[30] Moreover, it has been acknowledged even by native English users (Steiner, 1975) that the linguistic centre of English has shifted—and not only demographically.[31] "It does look," he says, "as if the principal energies of the English language...its genius for acquisition, for innovation, for metaphoric response, had also moved away from England." Using various terms such as "world Englishes," or "englishes," a group of scholars from all over the world have made it their principal concern to study these varieties of English. Most notable among these are Kachru (1982, 1986),[32] Bokamba (1982), Smith (1987), Strevens (1982), Quirk and Widdowson (1985), Quirk (1990), McCrum (1986). Their studies dwell partly on the literatures of these English varieties, coining terms like "contact literatures" (Kachru 1982, 1986), English literatures (Thumboo, 1991), Commonwealth literatures, and post-colonial literature in English (Ashcroft, et al., 1989).[33] The audience for English, in other words, is no longer monolithic; its use and usage have been decentered.

Operational problems in the process of translating mainly revolve around the movement/the proper relation of source text to target text. An oft-repeated dictum is that "a translation that is faithful is not beautiful while that which is beautiful is not faithful." The conflict between source and text cannot be resolved simply by rejecting a formal translation in favor of a dynamic translation which, according to Nida, aims at producing in the receptor an effect equivalent to that the source text made on the original audience.[34] The matter of equivalence or fidelity needs to be re-viewed in the light of semiotic theory.

In the Peircean sense, a sign is not only something which stands for something else; in order for it to be a sign, it must function as a sign, i.e., be interpreted, at least potentially. Eco, in *Semiotics and the Philosophy of Language* distinguishes between dictionary-like definitions "which establish bidimensional semantic relations whereas the encyclopedic universe possesses a labyrinthine quality creating multi-dimensional pragmatic relations which stimulate choice and interpretation."[35] In the *Blue Book*, Wittgenstein writes: ..."the sense is not the same as the sentence," but one interpretation among others, "a shadowy being capable of lying."[36] The locus of the problem thus shifts from the matter of equivalence to the matter of interpretation.

Even-Zohar, an Israeli theorist on translation, writes on the problem of translatability:[37]

> It is of no great value to "discover" that it's always of a lower problem that a translated utterance be identical with its original. A more adequate question seems rather to be under what circumstances, and in what particular way, a target utterance, text b, relates to a source utterance, text a.

The term equivalence, therefore, is an extremely fluid concept, the process of translation being determined both by the interpreter and the circumstance (hence, the impracticality, for instance, of attempts at backward translation to test the accuracy of a translation, since no translation can ever be equivalent to the source text or another translation version).

The circumstance, the constant which looms large in the translation of Hiligaynon fiction and thus one that cannot be ignored is a translation milieu marked by unequal relations of power. If the corrido writer adhered to this criterion of fidelity, then he would have worked at an iconic translation or complete resemblance with the original, thus allowing himself and his readers/listeners to be absorbed in a unitary semiotic system. His choice was the opposite, of course, and we are all witness to the liberation of the corrido and its lovers by the translator/writer.

However, translating Hiligaynon into English presents quite a different problem from the corrido. The receptor language here is the dominant language and the source language, the "weaker" language. It becomes the task of the translator to adhere to the source as much as he can to elide absorption of the vernacular language and literature into an imperial culture. Equivalence is thus relative to the conditions of translation production.

In resolving problems of translating the sugilanon into English in favor of the source and target texts, we shall juxtapose semiotic units between Hiligaynon and English and allow these to interanimate and interilluminate each other. This method provides the opportunity to explore "difference on equal terms" and to define our self as distinct from the other. As a text coming into being in the intersection of two languages and cultures, the translation contains forms (and content, form being content) from English and also those functionally peculiar to Hiligaynon. As such, English is reconstituted into english. I shall use the term "english" to indicate the "various ways in which the language has been employed by different linguistic communities in the post-colonial world."[38] It is the language I am translating to, as well as that used by authors outside of the imperial centers of Great Britain and the United States. I shall draw examples from the sugilanon I have translated into English and into Filipino. These are: "Si Annabella" (A), "Ang Gaba sang Katubwan" (GK), "Ang Hustisya sa Dagat" (HD), "Matapok ang Tambis" (MT), "Pagpanumbalik" (P), "Sa Lawod sang Pangabuhi" (SLSP), "Ang Pagbalik" (AP), "Tig-alani" (TA), and "Si Montor" (SM), and "Bunyag-Takas" (BT).

The discussion will begin with the word, move on to syntax, and then to the rhetorical aspects of discourse. These do not reflect the sequence of my translation method since the translation process is rarely linear; like writing, it involves re-writing. The translation process begins with a careful reading and proceeds with re-readings of the original and the evolving translated text both in parts or in wholes. The reader is central to translation for it is he/she who connects the text, the interpretant (the translated text in all its stages and versions), and the intertext to effect the semiotic transfer from sign to sign. Such interconnections are a major concern of a translator using my particular framework. Based on my experience, these occur in one or more of retroactive readings. Frequently, there is the push and pull between the subjective and the objective, between the spontaneous and the deliberate, through which tension a translator inevitably goes.

Culture and the Word

Let us consider the following sentence from one sugilanon and its literal English translation:

1. *Nagahigda siya sa banig sa tupad ni Agueda*. (GK)
1a. Was lying he on the sleeping mat beside Agueda.
1b. He was lying on the sleeping mat beside Agueda.

The word "sleeping mat," although readily understandable, is too general a term for *banig*. A banig is a mat woven from buri palm leaves, sometimes dyed in various colors. It is cool to sleep on, and so it is preferred to a mattress in a country where temperature ranges from 85-105 degrees fahrenheit all year round. The connotation of banig is different from that of other mats used in the United States or Africa. It is a culture-specific term and can thus be retained.

Here is a sentence from another sugilanon (TA):

2. *Magpanghinaw ka na didto sa pantaw kag magsalo....*
2a. Will wash hands (habitual task) you already there in the *pantaw* [italics supplied] and join me...
2b. Go wash your hands now in the kitchen balcony.

"Kitchen balcony" is almost equivalent to *pantaw* but the phrase does not quite convey its exact meaning, which is a roofless, railless terrace at the back of houses in rural areas. It is used for stocking water and washing dishes, and leads to a backyard where cooking is done on hot coal during special occasions. There are other culture-specific terms on which certain decisions need to be made such as "*Tiya* Semang," and "*Tiyo* Mente." In Hiligaynon, *Tiya* and *Tiyo* literally mean "aunt" and "uncle," respectively, but these are also attached to the names of middle-aged people older than the speaker, as a sign of respect, whether or not these are his relatives. Another culture-specific term is *kumpare* in the sentence:

3. *Naguntat siya sang pagbaligya sang botelya sang kuhaon siya sang kumpare ni Tatay niya nga kabulig sa talyer sini.* (HD)
3a. Stopped he the peddling of the bottle when taken in by the *kumpare* of father his as assistant in the machine shop of this (man).
3b. He stopped peddling these when his father's friend took him in as an assistant in his machine shop.

It is inadequate to substitute just "friend" for *kumpare* or "Mrs." or "Mr." for *Tiya* and *Tiyo* because of the peculiar social network implied by the Hiligaynon terms.

Certainly, a translator cannot expect perfect equivalents for culture-specific terms in view of the different semiotics of cultures. The matter of loss of meaning in translation is conceded even by those who would not interpret the Sapir-Whorf hypothesis literally. I have opted, however, to keep the above Hiligaynon words and quite aggressively retain a significant number of Hiligaynon terms for which no English terms come close in meaning. I have refused to substitute any English words for them although I italicize them in the translations. This is in recognition of the pluricentric audience of English today, a concrete step to shape and appropriate a language whose growth and existence is no longer determined by a monolithic audience. It is a deliberate attempt to formalize the cross-cultural nature of "english" as contrasted to "pure English."

There is the question, though, of whether or not these culture-specific terms are to be left unexplained. It would be instructive here to draw from the works of "english" writers who use translation.[39] The affinity between translators and writers which was remarked about earlier on seems to be especially true with regard to "english" writers. Says Naipul on the predicament of the Indian or Indian-descent writer in English: "It is an odd, suspicious situation: an Indian writer writing in English for an English audience about non-English characters who talk their own sort of English....I cannot help feeling that it might have been more profitable for me to appear in translation."[40]

It appears that the writers seldom leave culture-specific terms undefined. N.V.M Gonzalez, for example, in *A Season of Grace* uses a lot of terms specific to the culture of Mindoro, but their meanings do not escape the reader outside of it. Such transparency is due to the various strategies he employs to explain these terms—from simple juxtaposition of terms like "trousers and camisa de chino" and "catcha cloth" to more extended definitions by context. He uses these devices in such a way that they blend quite naturally with the rest of the text. In the following sentence, the meaning of "batel" is clear: "A batel came up the river where enough wood had been split." And in the following paragraph, the meaning of "yuro" emerges in the conversation:

"Well, Rosa," said the midwife, "you could have sent your Pablo up the river to trade dried fish for yuro."

"Thank God. He's left."

"Surely, people in the interior have started making yuro these days. This visitor of yours would have been surprised to know that there's a starch that comes from the buri palm and that in this way God keeps us quite well provided for. Yuro's something for the stomach really."

In Chinua Achebe's *Things Fall Apart*, Ibo terms are made clear, as in the following sentences (although he italicizes them, unlike Gonzalez's *A Season of Grace,* in which we feel the more assertive presence of Filipino terms):

> His own hut, or *obi*, stood immediately behind the only gate in the red walls.

> He even remembered how he had laughed when Ikemefuna told him that the proper name for a corn cob with only a few scattered grains was *eze-agadi-nwayi*, or the teeth of an old woman.

Sometimes, the meaning is not immediate. *Egweg-wu* is first mentioned in Chapter 1 of the novel, but its meaning is made fully clear only in Chapter 10.

In Ngugi's *A Grain of Wheat*, Kihika's song is not explained although its meaning—and significance—emerges once the over-all semiotics of the novel is grasped. This process of allusion, according to Ashcroft, et al. "installs linguistic distance itself as a subject of the text whose "maintenance in the cross-cultural text is of profound importance to its ethnographic function."[41]

It seems then that the translator is obliged to explain, explicitly or implicitly, the Hiligaynon terms she opts to keep; addition of text to clarify meaning becomes justified in the translation process, as long as it is done unobtrusively.

The translator should also explore the possibilities of loan translations. Successful loan translations have the advantage of transparency as a result of their literal translations of words and collocations from a foreign language. Consider, for example, N.V.M.'s "stove-box," "coconut-shell dipper," or "coconut-shell charcoal"; Rao's "to skin off your back" or Narayan's "If I hear your voice, I'll peel the skin off your back."

The Syntax of "english"*

The translator should, likewise look into the use of Hiligaynon syntactic patterns in the translated text. This would make for a more dramatic metaphoric entry into English in the process of which it undergoes transformation into "english." The works of "english" writers are infused by native-language syntactic patterns. For instance, a favorite device of R.K. Narayan is the verbless sentence fragment which is similar to the discourse patterns in Kannada and Tamil as seen in the following sentences: "Don't touch, not completely dry yet," and "We must be serious about it, no time to joke, no joking matter" (*The Painter of Signs*, New York: Viking, 1976 p. 135, 69). In Gabriel Okara's *The Voice* (London: Andre Deutsch, 1964, p. 13) the subject-object verb order is simulated from Ijaw discourse structures in the following excerpt:

> It was the day's ending and Okolo by a window stood looking at the sun behind the tree tops falling.... Okolo at palm trees looked. They were like women with their hair hanging down, dancing, possessed....

The matter of literalness is seen often as an inadequacy of the translation since it requires certain fixed relationships between codified elements in the two respective systems. Likewise, the work in the process of translation acquires a semiotic dynamism unique to the target language to which the translator is simply hard put not to submit. This becomes palpable to the translator, as he/she sees the translation, hears it, and feels it in the process of its fulfillment in the target language. Non-idiomatic expressions

---

* To be consistent with the headings in this book, this heading should read: "The Syntax of English"; but in view of the explained significance of "english," we are keeping the lower case **e** in this heading.

and patterns usually characteristic of literal translations thus become intrusions or contrivances.

But a literal translation may be evidence of the text's ethnographic or differentiating function, an insertion of the "truth of culture into the text." Referring to Whorf's observation that the Shawnee does not speak of "cleaning (a gun) with the ramrod" as Americans do, but of "directing a hollow moving dry spot by movement of tool," Schultz writes that Whorf was actually demonstrating that idiomatic translation by itself is *insensitive* toward what Bakhtin refers to as "the brute materiality, the typicality [of a culture]...in how the world is seen and felt, ways that are organically part and parcel with the language that expresses them."[42] Even Zohar writes:[43]

> Since translational activity participates when it assumes a central position in the process of creating new primary models, the translator's main concern here is not just to look for ready-made models in his home repertoire [in this case, the target language] into which the source texts would be transferable. Instead, he is prepared in such cases to violate home conventions. Under such conditions the chances that the translation would be close to the original in terms of adequacy (in other words, a reproduction of the dominant textual relations of the original) are greater than otherwise. But from the point of view of the target language the adopted translation norms might for a while be too foreign or revolutionary.

Literalness installs the self within an adopted vehicle, signals not just the refusal to be overwhelmed by such a vehicle but the determination to shape it. The tension between the idiomatic and the non-idiomatic thus animates the internal aesthetics of a work being translated into a dominant language. The translation becomes the venue for enacting the struggle between center and margin. It is inadequate, therefore, to dismiss a translated work simply on the basis of its literalness; rather, we could enlarge the frame so as to include literalness as a positive criterion for judging translations. Note, for instance the following lines from "Pagpanumbalik" (Remembrances):

4. *"Nakapamasyar ka?" ang hambal ni Tiya Biana sang magatubangay sila sa balkon sang balay kag matapos makabisa si Luisa.*

4a. "You've dropped by?" Tiya Biana asked when they stood facing each other in the balcony and *Luisa raised her mother's hand to her forehead.* [italics supplied]

5. *"Inso, husto na anay ina," nabatian niya ang panawag sang asawa.*

5a. "Inso, that's *enough already,*" he heard his wife call.

6. *"Nakasukad na ako." pahibalo ni Tiya Biana.*

6a. "The rice is *ladled out* now," Tiya Biana told him.

The italicized phrase in sentence 4a may be considered unidiomatic in English, but the gesture referred to is specific to Philippine culture, and no English term can convey this as visually as the above formally translated phrase. Keeping the word "already" in sentence 5a sounds awkward but in Hiligaynon as well as in other Filipino vernacular languages it is common to use particles like *anay*, *gid*, *lang*, *gali*, etc. This linguistic practice has to be reflected then in "english." In English, it is customary to use the statement "The table is ready." However, among the Hiligaynon and other Filipinos, the staple food is rice (for some, rice is the only food), and the term *sukad* which means "to ladle out rice" becomes a generic term for any kind of meal prepared on the table.

This matter of idiomatic syntax enters into decisions on how to translate dialogues. Just what type of English uneducated and undereducated characters native to the Philippine countryside should speak is problematic for the translator of the sugilanon. Most are farmers, fishermen, rural housewives, country boys and lasses who speak Hiligaynon unadulterated by Tagalog or English. It would be useful at this point to look into the works of post-colonial writers both in the spirit of solidarity with their experiences and a genuine interest in the strategies they employ.

Some characters use pidgin while the narrative account itself, is kept in "english" or English. The following passage from Adisa's "Duppy Get Her" demonstrates the shift between pidgin and "english":[44]

> The clouds stand back, way off in respect. The sun, heedful of his power, gyrates and snarls. Lilly glances at him just as he flaps his ears, emitting fire from his nostrils; she checks her laughter. So awed is she by the sun's fire she scarcely breathes. After some moments, Lilly mumbles: 'Lawd, de sun mitey tonight, sah. Look im on im way home nuh.' Suddenly, the turning of the child in her belly elicits a laugh that escapes deep from her womb.

V.S. Naipul's *A House for Mr. Biswas* offers another possibility: standard or educated English is substituted for Hindi speech while "english" is conveyed as spoken.[45] These two levels are noted in the following excerpt:

> "Ma said you beat her," Savi said.
>
> Mr. Biswas laughed. "She was only joking," he said in English.
>
> "She upstairs, rubbing down Myna," Savi said, in English as well.

R.K. Narayan, in *The Financial Expert*, uses grammatically correct English to the point of stiffness. It is not just the financial expert who does so, but the supporting characters. The peasant says, for example, that "We should not talk about others unnecessarily" while the policeman declares that Margayya "has come after his son, Balu, about whom a card has emanated from here." Weir[46] comments that Narayan must have had two reasons for using this style: to convey the idea that the characters in this South Indian village of Malgudi speak grammatically in a language not in English, or that Narayan is trying to show the foibles of the characters through stilted speech.

Characters speaking in formal or academic English are not unusual even in Philippine writing in "english." Note, for instance, this heated discussion between the peasant couple Sabel and Doro in *A Season of Grace*:

> It buzzed in the air like a bumblebee. The stick broke when the blow fell.
>
> "One more step toward that baby and I'll—"
>
> "Kill me, kill me now!" Sabel cried, offering her body for him to beat up as he pleased.

"One more word and I'll give you a thrashing you won't forget!"

"But one more word," says he!

"Just one more!" Doro cried, raising his stick again.

"Why not? And, may I ask, why have you brought me here? To be bedmate only? To be your housekeeper only?"

"It's but now you complain."

"Why, if I may ask?"

"Yes, why?"

"So you've somebody to flog." (p. 106)

Apart from mother tongue patterns embedded in this conversation, a certain academic texture is evident. However, these do not seem to detract from the intensity of the characters' emotions or obtrude into the text's semiotic unity.

Various strategies, then, may be used singly or in combination, depending on the situation of the characters.

As for the characters in the sugilanon included in my corpus here, it would definitely be unnatural for them to use American slang or English idiomatic expressions. These are not within the repertoire even of educated Filipinos. One possibility then would be for the characters to code-switch between Hiligaynon and English in the same way that Manilans code-switch between English and Tagalog if they wish to make their English sound informal. But the Hiligaynon in the sugilanon examined in this study does not distinguish between formal/informal or educated/uneducated registers. Moreover, with the exception of English terms included in the sugilanon with an urban setting like "Ang Pagbalik" and stories which appear later in the *Yuhum*, characters do not code-switch or use pidgin.[47] Neither is social stratification indicated by speech. Code-switching may thus be an inappropriate solution to the problem of dialogue. More suitable would be a straightforward "english" in which Hiligaynon patterns and culture-specific terms are embedded. This should not be too formal or academic, however, as to sound unnatural. Take, for example, this excerpt from a translation of the Cebuano sugilanon *Ang Hunsoy Sungsongan Usab* (The Empty Clay Pipe):[48]

> "Whoever said you won't pay me back, Malta? I'm only thinking of Teroy who has been complaining of intense stomach ache ever since he has been losing sleep because of

his standing guard with the soldiers every Tuesday evening. I don't care if my children and I subsist only on bananas, but I want Teroy always to eat well-cooked corngrits so his ailment will not worsen. If only the soldiers had not obliged the volunteers to keep watch with them at night, nothing would have happened to Teroy. According to him, this is the first time he has experienced such intense pain."

This sounds stilted not because of the Cebuano structures overlapping with the target language but because of the translator's academic voice. Otherwise, the Maceda collection is a fine example of translating a regional literature into Filipino and a foreign language.

Other than Hiligaynon syntactic patterns, there are other issues falling within the sphere of the conflict between source and target. One concerns the indexical use of pronouns, adverbs, and adjectives. Take the following sentence:

7. *Ginsunod pa ini sang iya panulok tubtob nga nilamon ini sang kadulom didto sa kipawkipawon nga unhan.*
7a. Was followed even this/it with her looking until swallowed there in the dimness ahead.
7b. She even followed it with her looking until it was swallowed up in the dimness ahead.

Wolfenden writes that *ini* in Hiligaynon generally means "this."[49] But *ini* may sometimes mean "it," "he," or "she."[50] For instance, in the sentence, *Amo ini* (This it) or (This is it), ini means "it." In actual usage, however, the term could refer to persons either male or female. The personal pronoun used for the third person is usually the word *siya*, but the writer's choice of ini is preferable since although it refers to the person Narding, he is an unimportant, even a repulsive figure to Esang at this point. The use of ini, likewise, is part of the interchangeability between indices in Hiligaynon for the animate and the inanimate. For example, we use *patay*, meaning "to kill" in the sentence *Patya ang suga*, meaning "Kill the light"; or, we use *guba* meaning "destroyed" in relation both to an object and a person. There could be two other versions of sentence 7:

7c. She followed him with her eyes until he was swallowed up in the dimness ahead.

7d. She followed the figure with her eyes until *it* was swallowed up in the dimness ahead.

Of the four versions, it is the last one that most closely approximates the impersonal ini in Hiligaynon. Still, the translated text seems awkwardly wordy with the phrase "followed the figure with her eyes." However, it is common in Hiligaynon as well as in other Philippine languages to weave in references to the body in various expressions. These present some problems when translated into English, because the translations may sound wordy or too literal. Here are some more translated sentences (b versions) which keep these body references, thus sounding literal:

8. *Nakita niya nga maluya nga naghalin si Narding.* (TA)
8a. Saw she (ligature) wearily (ligature) left the personal Narding
8b. She *saw* (italics supplied) that Narding looked weary

9. *Kumopo si Agueda sa dughan sang bana.* (GK)
9a. Clung the (personal) Agueda to the chest of husband.
9b. Agueda clung to her husband's *chest* (italics supplied).

10. *Sa pagligad pa sang pila ka adlaw, ang mga kapatagan nga sang wala pa lang madugay nga lagtom kon tanawon, karon nagbalhin na ang duag.* (GK)
10a. With the passing still of few (ligature) days,the plain that of not yet a long time that dark green when looked at, now changed already the color.
10b. After a few days, the ricefields which just shortly before were dark green *when looked at* (italics supplied) have changed colors.

11. ...*kag lumosot gikan sa tilaok ni Agueda ang isa ka malawig kag makatilingil nga tiyabaw.* (GK)
11a. ...and slipped from the throat of Agueda the one (ligature) long and deafening (ligature) scream.
11b. Then burst forth from Agueda's *throat* (italics supplied), a long, piercing scream.

12. *Makita niya ang pagsabuwag sang kasanag sang bulan sa palibot, sa mga kahilamunan nga ginbasa sang talithi.* (TA)

12a. Can see she the strewing of the brightness of the moon on the surroundings, on the grass that was made wet by the showers.
12b. She *saw* (italics supplied) the light cast by the moon all around her, on the grass now moistened by the showers.

13. *Nagadangat sa iya igsilimhot ang alisbong sang nagagulang na nga mga humay upod sa mayami nga dapya sang hangin*. (TA)
13a. Was/is reaching to her sense of smell the odor of the maturing already (ligature) the grain accompany the cold ligature touch of wind.
13b. The odor of the maturing grain seeped into her *nose*, wafted there by the cool *touch* (italics supplied) of the wind.

Various Filipino scholars (Covar, 1988; Agpalo, 1973) have observed the Filipinos' propensity for the anatomy not only in idioms, figures of speech, proverbs and other expressions, but also in the process of conceptualizing. The translator would have to be conscious of this fact but he has to select which body images to keep or delete within the context of the sentence or even the semiotic structure of the story. For instance, it appears that in sentence 7 "watched" would be a better choice than "followed the figure with her eyes"; it is a leaner expression and thus more expressive of the action. A better version, then, is the following:

7d. She watched him walk away until he was swallowed up in the dimness ahead.

In sentence 9 "chest" does sound awkward in English; it is the word "heart" which is customarily used in similar English expressions. But *dughan* or "chest" recurs in various yet similar contexts in other texts I have examined. This frequency is not a matter of statistics but an indication of the fact that using the term dughan is part of the conventions of the Hiligaynons. I have decided thus to use the word "chest" and not "heart" which seems more idiomatic. I have opted though to drop "when looked at" in sentence 10 because it does seem superfluous in the translation. But "she saw" in sentence 8 is essential as a way of showing Esang gloating over her having rejected her suitor. The last two sentences (12 and 13) are taken from the same paragraph describing her surroundings. In sentence 12, which is the opening statement, "she saw" is important because it conveys Esang's awareness of the beauty of the night which contributes to the romantic atmosphere appropriate for the coming *harana*. In sentence 13, the overt reference to the body (nose/sense of smell) need not appear in the translation since the context has already been set by the previous sentence. Thus, the final version is:

13b. The cool wind wafted the fragrance of matured grain.

There seems to be a tentativeness in the indexical functions of adverbs and adjectives where in English these would be more definite. The word *unhan* (ahead) in sentence 7 and *wala pa lang madugay* (just shortly before) in sentence 10 are not specific on the distance in time and place referred to. Hiligaynon is, in fact, replete with these expressions. A particular way of looking at space or, better still, non-space, is manifest in Hiligaynon sentence structures; thus, problems of dangling and misplaced modifiers do not arise. Here are some examples from sugilanon texts with the literal translation following each one:

14. *Nagahigda siya sa banig sa tupad ni Agueda.* (GK)
14a. Was/is lying he in the *banig* at the side of Agueda.
14b. He was lying on the *banig* beside Agueda.

To make the English translation clear, we would have to switch the positions of the prepositional phrases:

14b. He was lying beside Agueda on the *banig*.

Another instance where the same problem arises in a literal translation of the sentence into English is the following:[51]

15. *Pagkatapos, ginlansang niya ang iya panulok sa bangkay nagahulatholat sa igahambal sang tenyente.* (GK)
15a. Then, was nailed by him the his looking/eyes at the corpse was waiting a bit at what will probably be said by the lieutenant.
15b. Then he nailed his eyes on the dead man, waiting for the lieutenant to speak.

In this case, I have decided to keep this literal translation to reflect the structure of the Hiligaynon text; anyway, it is clear to everyone that a dead man does not speak. Here, literalness is not just an acceptable choice; it becomes an assertive act. The problem, however, is more difficult in extended sentences with a string of modifiers as in the next sentence:

> 16. *Kon ngaa nabutang nila ang kaugalingon sa tungatunga sang duha ka banas nga hindi maghilisanto, nagasalasala, ginakurog, wala sing pagalutsan pakadto sa matam-is nga kahilwayan?* (GK)
> 16a. As to why were able they to place themselves in the midst of two (ligature) paths that do not jibe, are being confused, are trembling, there is none will slip from will go to sweet peace?
> 16b. As to why they got themselves in the midst of these paths, clashing, dazed, trembling, with no way to slip into bliss of peace?

Here, the translator needs to consider the context emerging in the translated text as a result of the modifier string. In the above example, the sentence had to be restructured to avoid confusion:

> 16b. How did they get themselves into this dilemma, leaving them dazed, trembling, and unable to slip into the bliss of freedom?

It appears that the nature of sentences, particularly of predicates, in Hiligaynon is different from those of English. What Bloomfield writes about sentence types in Tagalog applies to Hiligaynon as well, (except for the equational type).[52] We shall cite from his work not only because Hiligaynon, Tagalog and other Philippine languages are similar, but also because his point of reference is English, which is relevant to our discussion here.

> In a predication, the more object-like component is called the subject; the other part, the predicate. English has only one type of predication. Tagalog has five types of predication with this common feature: either the subject precedes and a particle [aj] intervenes, or the reverse order is used without the particle...[of the latter there are] four narrative types in which

the predicates are transient words which denote things in four different relations to an action.

In the next chapter on syntax, Bloomfield writes:

> In Tagalog, the parts of speech are full words and particles but here, the full words are subdivided into two classes we may call static and transient. The latter resemble English verbs in forming a special kind of predicate (the narrative type with four subtypes mentioned earlier) and in showing morphologic distinctions of tense and mode, but they differ from English verbs because on the one hand, they are not restricted to the function of predicate and, on the other hand, there exist non-narrative predicates.

Bloomfield's reference to the four narrative types explains the concept of focus and, related to it, the system of affixation in Tagalog and Hiligaynon. That there exist non-narrative predicates tells us that we cannot speak of a strict noun-verb dichotomy and of a verb (transitive)-direct object dichotomy in the construction of Hiligaynon sentences. Sentences without verbs to express action are normal:

17. *Ang iya liog masakit pa gihapon bangod sa pagkuga sang pakaisa.* (HD)
17a. His neck smarting still because of the strangling by his cousin.
17b. His neck was still smarting from being strangled by his cousin.

18. *Karon sirom na.*(GK)
18a. Now twilight.
18b. Twilight had fallen.

Wolfenden has devised a more elaborate classification of clauses in Hiligaynon but he also discusses non-verbal clauses in which non-verbs manifest the predicate slot.[53] Some of these are: the descriptive clause which has a descriptive phrase manifesting the predicate such as sentences 17 and 18 above; the equational clause which has an *ang* class noun phrase manifesting the predicate slot such as *Ang ginbakal niya ang bayo* (What she bought the dress); interrogative clauses like *Sa diin si Benigno?* (GK) the literal translation of which is "Where Benigno?"

Also there is no subject/object dichotomy expressed in the case of third person pronouns nor male/female distinctions in pronoun forms. In all these, *siya* is used for the singular form and *sila* for the plural form.

19. *Mahambal* siya *kuntani, siguro masiyagit, apang maabtik* siya *nga binutong ni Benigno pabalik sa banig*.(GK)
19a. *She* wanted to say something, even scream, but Benigno held her down.

(In this connection, it is interesting to note that the Rastafarians in Jamaica consider "me" and "we" as objects of the sentence and governed by the subject in the way in which the slaves were dominated by the whites. Thus, the Rastas insist on the use of "I" for the personal pronouns in all positions).

The above features are a linguistic articulation of the Hiligaynon identity. An awareness of these can somehow be an assurance that in the intersemiotic negotiation between Hiligaynon and English, the translator shall not be overwhelmed by a language that has enjoyed dominance in the production of meaning, even as he considers the overall context of the target semiotic code.

The Rhetorical Aspect of Fil/english

In Hiligaynon it is not just the outlook towards space that is peculiar but the way time is segmented. For instance, the following paragraph describing Esang's immediate reaction to her first kiss is revealing. Here the sentences in the paragraph are itemized for convenience in our discussion:

20. *Naga dalagan nga nagahibi siya*. (TA)
20a. Was/is running while crying she.
20b. Crying, she ran off.

21. *Subong sang may kahaladlukan sa duong nga ato nga luyag palalagyuhan.*
21a. Like that there is/was something fearsome in place (ligature) that there which like *will have cause to escape from*.

21b. Like there were something terrifying from which she wanted to flee.

22. *Pagsampot sa ila ugsaran, daw wala sa kaugàlingon nga pumongko siya sa halintang sang hagdanan.*
22a. Reaching at their stairs, as if not in herself that sat she on the stair of the staircase.
22b. When she reached their house, she sat on the staircase, dazed.

Since these come from the same paragraph, all its verbs in the English translation should have the same tense. However, this is problematic for the translator since in Hiligaynon, distinctions between tenses are not sharply defined. In fact, it may be better to speak of aspect or mode, instead of tense with regard to Visayan verbs.[54] Aspect, according to Nida, is "a semantic category which specifies the point of view taken by the speaker with respect to an event, e.g., completed or incompleted, beginning, continuing, or ending, real or imaginary, etc."[55] Elmer Wolfenden writes on the matter of aspect in Hiligaynon:[56]

> The aspect of a verb shows whether or not an action has begun. It may appear to be equivalent to the category of tense in European languages but it does not actually relate to points in a spectrum of time. Verbal action can be related to time in Hiligaynon but it is accomplished specifically by the inclusion of time words in the sentence (e.g. yesterday, today, etc.) rather than by verb inflection.

Ruiz takes off from Nida (1964) and defines aspect as "the kind of action indicated by the verb. Aspect may also identify a type of process, a quality, a state." On the usual confusion between aspect and time, he says that the completed aspect is often equated erroneously with the English past tense. But the frame of reference is not the same; the one in tense is time; the one in aspect is kind of action.[57] This matter of aspect versus tense may be the reason why Filipino writing in English is sometimes tense-inconsistent.

How does the translator cope with this time feature? In the above example taken from "Tig-alani" (Harvest Time), it is not clear, for instance, whether *nagadalagan* and *nagahibi* should be translated in the present or past tense since the marker *naga-* is a

Hiligaynon prefix simply indicating the quality of action, that is, durative action. *Palalagyuhan* means "will have cause to escape from" denoting incompleted action. The other verbs like *pumongko* denotes completed action. The translated text in English becomes coherent and smooth if the past tense is used consistently for all verbs, since the story has already occurred. Often, the translator can base his choice on the predominant time quality of the story, which in this case, is the past. There are instances, however, when a shift in tense may be necessary even in the translated text. The paragraph cited above (sentences 20–22) is followed by two paragraphs entirely narrated in the present; there is not a single marker of past action. Describing the barrio during harvest time, this section comes midpoint in the story and is set off from the two halves by extra spacing. These are semiotic devices used to suggest the cycle of harvest time in the farm, an event that transcends the temporality of Esang's and Narding's experience.

Sometimes, the setting is set off from the rest of the story through the present mode. In "Ang Gaba sang Katubwan" (The Curse of the Sugarcane Fields), the scene of Agueda waiting for her husband who was arrested by the military is separated from the rest of the narrative through the present mode. The shift suggests intensity, emotion that cannot be mediated by time. This change will have to be reflected in the English translation to reflect this. Moreover, the shift would still be consistent with the stylistic convention of the sugilanon, notwithstanding its possibly being misconstrued as inconsistency in tense. (It may be of interest to note here that in the novel *A Season of Grace*, p. 99, a similar shift in tense occurs possibly to suggest Sabel's continuing fear of her husband and insecurity about their life).

Related to this tension between aspect and tense, is the matter of sequencing narrative action in the sugilanon. This could result in some awkwardness in the English translation. In English, the following discourse units may be considered as fragmentary or not coordinated logically:

23. *"Yatis nga awa ina, a!" Kag liniso ni Lucio ang iya baroto kag linagas ang isda nga malip-ot sang ikog.*(HD)
23a. "Damn (ligature) *awa* this, a!" And turned the personal Lucio the his banca and chased the fish with short the tail.

23b. "Damn that *awa*!" Lucio swung his boat around to chase the fish with the short tail.

24. *Iya na karon nahangpan ang masubo nga pagsugilanon sang iya mga ginikanan sadtong Domingo sing hapon kag ang ila paghipos kag pagduyo sang mga inadlaw nga masunod.* (BT)
24a. By her already now was understood the sad (ligature) conversation of her the parents that Sunday in the afternoon and their will be silent deliberately and their will be gloomy in the days that followed.
24b. Now she understood her parents' dispirited conversation that Sunday afternoon and their silence and their melancholy in the days that followed.

Both 23a and 24a are practically literal translations. I decided to revise the former because the repetition of "and" is aesthetically jarring, notwithstanding its acceptability in an "english" mode. Thus the sentence:

23b. "Damn that *awa*!" Lucio swung his boat around to chase the fish with the short tail.

But I retained 24b. The repetition of "and" conveys a sense of deliberateness; the puzzle is now being put together piece by piece as a result of some realization by the character.

In other instances, the translator assumes an even more active role—omitting, adding, rearranging details to enable the paragraph to make sense or appear logical in the target system. Compare, for instance, the two translations of the same paragraph from one sugilanon (AP):

25. *Apang sa pagkamatuod, indi lang kay ini ang tunay nga maga kabangdanan. May iban pa. Nagaut-ot ini sa iya painuino, sa iya pagkatao. Nahatagan gid lang siya sang diutay kag makadali nga katawhayan sa sulod sang sinehan, bangod siguro sa kalaka sang mga tao dire kag subong man kay sa liwan na ini nga lugar. Pagkatapos sang duha ka adlaw kag duha kagab-i nga pagbiyahe, nakaabot siya sa sini nga siyudad nga liwan ang mga talan-awon, liwan ang mga kalye, liwan ang pulong nga iya nabatian.*
25a. But in truth, not only were these the real reasons. There was/were others. Gnawed these at his thoughts, at his being.

Was given only he a brief respite and peace inside the moviehouse, because perhaps few the moviegoers here and too in a different this ligature place. After two days and two nights of traveling, was able to reach this city in which different the scenery, different the streets, different the language that he heard.
25b. But these were not the only reasons why he could not sleep; there were others. And these gnawed into his thoughts, into his whole being. He was given a brief respite inside the moviehouse, perhaps because the moviegoers were few, and the place was new. After two days and two nights of traveling, he had reached this city where the scenery, the streets and the language were different.

It seems then that rhetorical organization (semiotically defined, this would be the arrangement of signs to suit the sign structure or matrix of a discourse unit) may be affected by a people's peculiar way of viewing time and space which is embedded in their language. Kaplan's point that paragraph patterns vary cross-culturally may have some bases. In the Philippines, a number of studies have been made on the discourse structures of specific languages largely through the Summer Institute of Linguistics (Longacre, 1968 and Grimes, 1975, among others). These are, however, outside of the eight major languages of the country and deal chiefly with orature.

Related to the problem of rhetorical organization is redundancy since this affects the movement of the sequence of signs. If translated literally, many sentences in Hiligaynon would appear wordy. Note, for instance, the following sentences and their translations:

26. *Ginpasikto siya sang isa sang mga suod nga tinao ni Komander Marcos, si Pitong Barbasan, natungod sa kamatuoran sang nagalagaw nga balita nga magakampanya si Simeon Arriola sa maabot nga Sabado sa Bay-ongan.* (GK)
26a. Pitong Barbasan, one of Commander Marcos' most trusted aides, checked out with him *the truth of the rumor circulating* that Simeon Arriola was planning to campaign in Bayongan *this coming Saturday* (italics supplied).

The Hiligaynon text, however, does not strike the reader as wordy.

Sometimes, redundancy even contributes to a certain effect. In "Tig-alani," the redundancy in the opening lines is appropriate for a description of the farm just before harvest time since this is an interlude in which activities in the farm are almost at a standstill.[58] The details convey the sense of waiting for the harvest. On another level, they also suggest narrator Esang's anticipation of approaching womanhood since the farm is described through her point of view as she sits by the window.

> 27. *Magulugal-om sang hapon sina. May diutay nga tulotalithi nga nagtupa pag-abot sang kasisidmon. Wala man lang dugay. Naghuyophuyop ang hangin. Amat-amat nga naghawan ang nawong sang langit kag pumakita ang masanag nga bulan kag ang madamo nga bituon.*
>
> 27a. It was a little cloudy that afternoon. At twilight, it drizzled lightly. But just for a short while. A gentle breeze blew now and then. Slowly, the sky cleared, and then shone forth the bright moon and the many stars.

Note that the translation keeps "But just for a short while" and "the many stars" when these should be deleted by someone who uses Western criteria in judging stories, such as a lean or economical style. Notice, likewise, the string of Hiligaynon words like *magulogalom*, *tulotalithi*, *naghuyophuyop*, and *amat-amat* in which the root word is repeated. In Hiligaynon as well as in other Philippine languages, the root word is repeated to express diminutiveness or a small degree or amount of something. This string of words describes a mild and pleasant weather appropriate for a village waiting for good times to come and, of course, for the slow rhythm of rural life. In fact, repetition of signs may be considered a marker of the bucolic genre since this slackens narrative movement and thus is in itself an iconic representation of the slow rhythm of rural life and its cyclic patterns. Repetitiveness is therefore functional both to the language and the sign matrix of the story.

In "Paypanumbalik," the various forms of redundancy create a narrative pace suitable for the speech and lifestyle of a retired couple. In "Si Anabella," redundancy merges with a floridness of style characteristic of the corrido and the early sugilanon. The following are some lines uttered by Anabella's lover:

> 28. *Bella, ang halintang nga kawayan sang inyo hagdanan nga akon ginsakaan, ginatan-aw ko sing subong sang siniad sang mga malahalon nga marfil nga napanidsiran sing mga bulawan kag pilak kag natampokan sing malahalon nga bato. Ining lagawan nga akon ginadayunan amo ang Olimpo nga napun-an sang kasanag kag sang himaya sa diin nagaluntad ang isa ka libo nga kaanyag nga akon ginasimba kag pagasimbahon ko tubtub sa akon kamatayon.*
> 28a. Bella, the steps (ligature) bamboo of your staircase that were climbed by me, being looked at by me (ligature) like sliced the precious ivory that was inserted with (ligature) the gold and silver and was studded with precious stones. This sala which by me staying in that the Olympus that was filled with light and bliss where coming from the one thousand the beauty that I am worshipping and will be worshipping until my death.
> 28b. Bella, the bamboo stairs of this house are to me like pieces of ivory rimmed with gold and silver and studded with precious stones. This sala is Mt. Olympus filled with brightness and bliss for herein dwell a thousand graces which I worship now and will go on to worship until I die.

Even in the relatively compact "Bunyag-Takas," which was written by someone educated in the U.S. and very much exposed to its literary canons of unity and compactness in the short story, "redundant" lines appear, as in the following example:

> 29. *Sugod sadto, nasat-uman na niya ang pagbag-o sang iya tingog, ang paglain sang iya panulok, ang pagbalhin sang iya paghulag.*
> 29a. Since then, was able to notice by her the changing of her voice, the changing of her appearance, and the change of her moving.
> 29b. Since then, she noticed an alteration in her voice, a differentness in her appearance, a change in the way she moved.

Perhaps, then, semiotic redundancy is framed not just within the semiotic construct of the individual sugilanon, but within that of the tradition of its language and genre. A repetitive style and the multiplication of plots are evident in the epics and other folk literature surviving among the non-Christian ethnic groups. Significantly, these have also been noted in the corrido, an essentially oral genre, to which we traced the lineage of the sugilanon, and even in Tagalog and other vernacular novels written in the first half of the century. Long-drawn, melodramatic scenes are an essential ingredient in Philippine movies, even in those directed by its most talented directors. Watch, for example, the award-winning *Pacita M* (1992) or even the famed Lino Brocka films. With regard to the novels, repetitiveness may have been a result of its serialization in commercialized magazines. The redundant, in short, is very much alive in our semiotic consciousness.

It is a consciousness influenced by what may be a lingering orality in our vernacular cultures which have not quite completed the transit from orality to literacy. Careful selectivity of details producing the tightly pyramidical plot which is considered the mark of a good short story has been observed as a result of print culture.[59] The author acquires a different feeling of expression and organization unlike that of the oral performer whose creativity was both enhanced and limited by a live audience; now he can write his story in solitude and with deliberation. In the West, the movement towards a carefully structured narrative reached its peak in the detective story, beginning with Poe's *The Adventures of the Rue Morgue* in 1841, and continues all the way to the twentieth century with writers like Anderson and Hemingway. It was picked up by Filipino short story writers in English who were largely Manila-based and taught by American or American-educated litterateurs.

But the sugilanon does not follow the same history. We pointed out its precursors in the narratives found in the novenas and other religious texts. These were printed but the manner in which the Filipinos responded to them was largely oral and dramatic (note the ways we have appropriated the *pasyon*, the *cenaculo*, novenas and lives of saints). We also traced its affinities with the secular narrative that was the corrido whose heroes continued to be written about in various romances printed in Philippine vernacular literature well in the '50s and even up to the '70s. The sugilanon, which first got written in the '30s with the stories of Jalandoni and Magahum, is therefore framed within an oral-based literature.

It is crucial, then, for the translator to keep in mind the sugilanon's intertextual field to understand this looseness both in style and plot. The translator cannot, should not rid her translation of this quality, but find ways to integrate it within the aesthetics of each sugilanon while in the process of being translated into English.

The sugilanon, however, is evolving, and so is Hiligaynon. The translator needs to see the development of the genre so he can shift frames where necessary and employ appropriate linguistic and literary strategies. One notes, for instance, a brisk and economical style in some newer stories such as Leothiny Clavel's "Hustisya sa Dagat" (Vengeance in the Sea), Julius Flores' "Ang Gaba sang Katubwan" (The Curse of the Sugarcane Fields) and "Ang Pagbalik" (The Apparition). There have been changes in the portrayal of character, as well. Most sugilanon, especially the earlier ones, tend to depict the characters in a formulaic and stereotyped manner. Linguistically, this type of characterization manifests itself through indexical and iconic signs rather than the symbolic; likewise, in conventional instead of innovative signs. Hence, the problem of clichés.

In Jalandoni's "Si Anabella," for example, the hero is handsome and righteous, the heroine is beautiful and virtuous, and the hero's mother, condescending. These character portrayals in clear, antithetical strokes (good-bad, beautiful-ugly, poor-rich, etc.) are linguistic signs of perceiving and ordering reality in the medieval mode—reminiscent of the corrido and the religious texts which move within the sugilanon's intertextual whirl. Such binary ordering is carried over in the later stories like "Matapok ang Tambis" (The Branch is Still Brittle) and "Tig-alani" (Harvest Time) where the rural lass is both coy and haughty and the beau persistent and resourceful.

Writing, with its drive toward carefully itemized introspection and elaborately worked out analyses of inner states of soul and of their inwardly structured sequential relationships, resulted in the drawing up of round characters.[60] The sugilanon, whose affinities with oral literature is more marked than that of the scripted narrative, inevitably produced flat characters initially. It has also been observed that the age of print has resulted among Protestant circles, the advocacy of private, individual interpretation of the Bible, and among Catholics, frequent private confession of sins, and concomitantly a stress on examination of conscience.[61] The Spaniards appeared to have encouraged such introspection, judging from the plethora of religious texts to which the Filipinos were exposed. Inwardness took the form of sentimentalism and melodrama in the characters rather than a certain roundness or complexity of motivation.

In other stories, though, the antithesis becomes less sharp. For example, in "Ang Hustisya sa Dagat," the strangler is seen as a psychological victim of an oppressive father, while in "Ang Gaba sang Katubwan," the violent husband is caught within forces too large for him to cope with. The sugilanon writer's intertextual sphere is widening and changing in various ways, and along with this, his manner of perceiving and ordering reality. Now, for example, shades of character and psychological insight are taking the place of absolute contrarieties. In sum, the translator must be semiotically aware of such shifts and have these reflected in the translated texts.

The Translator and Fil/english

The discovery of specific characteristics of the sugilanon runs parallel to the discovery of problems in translating it from the Hiligaynon semiotic system into English. Translation, then, becomes an occasion to understand the linguistic and cultural conventions embedded in the sugilanon. The translated text is what Bakhtin refers to as "an artistically organized system for bringing out different languages in contact with one another, the carving out of a living image of another language."[62] In translating from Hiligaynon into English, the Filipino translator draws herself and the reader into the process of coming to know her own language (and culture), Hiligaynon, as "it's perceived in someone else's system, an ideological translation of another's language, and an overcoming of its otherness—an otherness that's only contingent, external, and illusory."[63] The translator comes to realize that in the creation of another entity in the semiotic movement, she does need to consider the target semiotic system—but within the grounds of the source text. She/he must, in short, have both the linguistic and cultural competence to perceive these grounds.[64] In the context of a post-colonial theory of translation, these would refer to cultural forces in which the historical-political is central; the translator must, to use Gayatri Spivak's term, be guided by what history has written for her.[65] Inevitably thus, the post-colonial translator writes not in English (although earlier I used this term provisionally), but in Fil/english.[66]

In accepting the sugilanon's formative traditions and recognizing its identity (in mutability), the translator becomes both the mediator and creator of an inventive poetics of translation.

By an inventive poetics of translation we mean the translator's resistance to the colonial network of power through variations in the translation act. It is the breaking of the hegemonic frame and the triumphal re-framing of his culture. The corrido writer recreates the European metrical romance; the ladino devises countersignals; the translator today abrogates and appropriates English.

But what is really important is the mode of thinking that goes within these forms of resistance. For power is not only ubiquitous but protean. Its most insidious form—and its most liberating—may be just within us. What we need, then, is a mind, individual, creative, open-ended, and aware that power is semiotically realized. No one then need construct a frame for our culture and history. We translate our various selves to find our SELF—gingerly, but ably.

NOTES

1. Terry Eagleton, "Translation and Transformation," *Stand* XIX 30 (1977), pp. 72–73.

2. Vivencio Jose, "Identity and Liberation in Philippine Literature," *Kultura*, vol. 2, no. 2 (1987), pp. 3–11.

3. Asad, "Concept of Cultural Translation," p. 157.

4. Rogelio R. Sikat, "Kasaysayan Bilang Panitikan: Pagsasalin at Ebalwasyon ng *The Forest* ni William Pomeroy." Unpublished Master's Thesis, University of the Philippines, May 1990.

5. This, notwithstanding the observation that the politics of language among writers has eased considerably the choice of language; writers are now dictated more by practical rather than by ideological considerations, according to Isagani Cruz in "The Future of Philippine English," *The Role of English and its Maintenance in the Philippines*, ed. Andrew B. Gonzalez (Manila: Solidaridad Foundation, Inc., 1988), p. 125.

6. Pascual Capiz, "Politics and the English Language," *Diliman Review*, VIII, 1–3 (January-September 1960), pp. 307–09. Also, in Nieves Epistola, "English in the Twenty-First Century Philippines," Paper read at the annual convention of the Linguistic Society of the Philippines. Manila: Philippine Normal College (May, 1986).

7. Renato Constantino, *The Miseducation of the Filipino* (Quezon City: Alemar-Phoenix, 1966).

8. Andrew Gonzalez and Lourdes Bautista, *Language Surveys in the Philippines 1966–1984* (Manila: De La Salle University Press, 1986).

9. The proceedings of the PESCLA Convention, Department of English Studies and Comparative Literature, University of the Philippines, October, 1989.

10. Lourdes Bautista, "Domains of English in the 21st Century," in *The Role of English and its Maintenance in the Philippines*, p. 75.

11. Emy Pascasio, "The Present Role and Domains of English in the Philippines," in *The Role of English and its Maintenance in the Philippines*, p. 114.

12. Ngugi wa Thiong'o, *Decolonizing the Mind: The Politics of Language in African Literature* (New Hampshire: Heinemann, 1986).

13. Terry Eagleton, "The Rise of English," *Literary Theory* (Oxford: Basil Blackwell, 1983).

14. Bill Ashcroft, Gareth Griffiths and Helen Tiffin, *The Empire Writes Back: Theory and Practice in Post-colonial Literatures* (London and New York: Routledge, 1989). Another interesting article is Oluwole Adejare "Translation: A Distinctive Feature of African Literature in English," *Language and Style* (1987). This is the only study dealing with translation and the appropriation of English have come across with.

15. Other than Ashcroft, et al., the Rastafarians' language is also discussed in Robert McCrum, et al. *The Story of English* (New York: Viking Press, 1986).

16. Nieves B. Epistola, "English in the Twenty-First Century Philippines," Paper read at the Annual Convention of the Linguistic Society of the Philippines. Manila: Philippine Normal College, (May 3, 1986).

17. Jane Batsleer, *Rewriting English* (London: Methuen, Inc., 1985), p. 5.

18. Ngugi wa Thiong'o discusses the precondition with regard to the meeting between African and Western languages in "English: Language of the World?," *The Yale Journal of Criticism* IV, 1 (1990).

19. M.M. Bakhtin, 1940, "Epic and Novel" in *The Dialogic Imagination*, ed. M. Holquist (Austin: University of Texas Press, 1981), p. 12.

20. Andrew Gonzalez, "Poetic Imperialism or Linguistic Creativity?" Dr. Braj Kachru shared this material with me during my visit at the University of Illinois at Urbana-Champaign in May 1991.

21. Rosario Cruz Lucero, "Vernacular Literature: Philippine Literature's 'Other'," *Kultura*, vol. 2, no. 4 (1989), p. 13.

22. Bienvenido Lumbera, "The Literary Relations of Tagalog Literature," in *Brown Heritage*, ed. Antonio Manuud (Quezon City: Ateneo de Manila University Press, 1967), p. 310.

23. Lucila V. Hosillos, "Notes on Translation," *The Literary Apprentice*, vol. XLIX, no. 1 (1976–1977), pp. 130–31.

24. Jean Edades and J.H. Hernandez, *English for Filipinos* (Quezon City: Hernandez and Edades, 1953).

25. Raja Rao, *Kanthapura* (London: Oxford University Press, 1943), viii.

26. Chinua Achebe, "English and the African Writer," *Transition* 18, 27–30.

27. These writers are featured in Pico Iyer, "The Empire Writes Back," *Time*, vol. 141, no. 6, February 8, 1993.

28. Cited in Pico Iyer, p. 48.

29. Gideon Toury, "Translation" in *Encyclopedic Dictionary of Semiotics*, ed. Thomas A. Sebeok, p. 1120.

30. Braj B. Kachru, "The Second Diaspora of English," in *English in its Social Contexts: Essays in Historical Sociolinguistics*, eds. William Machan and Charles T. Scott (New York: Oxford University Press, 1990). What I read was the manuscript handed to me by Dr. Kachru himself.

    David Crystal, "How Many Millions? The Statistics of English Today," *English Today* 1 (1985), 7–9.

31. George Steiner, *Why English?* (1975, pp. 4–5), cited in Braj Kachru, "The Sacred Cows of English," *English Today* 16 (October 1988), pp. 3–8.

32. Braj Kachru is probably the most prolific researcher on English as an international language. I had the occasion to meet him in May 1991 at the University of Illinois in Urbana-Champaign, where he heads the Division of English as an International Language.

33. Braj Kachru, *The Alchemy of English: The Spread, Functions and Models of Non-native Englishes* (Urbana, Illinois: University of Illinois Press, 1986 and 1990).

    Edwin Thumboo, "The Pragmatics of Meaning: Language as Identity in New English Literature," *Pragmatics and Language Learning*, Monograph Series vol. 2 DEIL, University of Illinois at Urbana-Champaign, 1991.

34. Eugene Nida and Charles Taber, *The Theory and Practice of Translation* (Leiden, Netherlands: E.J. Brill, 1974), p. 159.

35. Umberto Eco, *Semiotics and the Philosophy of Language* (Bloomington: Indiana University Press, 1984), p. 46.

36. Cited in Dinda Gorlee, "Wittgenstein, Translation and Semiotics," *Target* (The International Journal of Translation Studies, 1:1, 1989), pp. 69–94.

37. Even-Zohar, "The Position of Translated Literature Within the Literary Poly-System," *Poetics Today* 11:1, Spring 1990.

38. Ashcroft, et al., p. 8.

39. This study uses the term "english" to refer to literatures written outside of the U.S. and Great Britain. But other terms have been used: "new English" (Weir, 1982) and "non-native English" (Kachru, 1982). The word "english," though, most dramatically reflects the multi-cultural appropriations of English.

40. Cited in Ann Lowry Weir, "Style Range in New English Literatures," in *The Other Tongue*, ed. Braj Kachru (New York: Pergamon Press, Inc., 1982), p. 310.

41. Ashcroft, et al., p. 57.

42. Emily A. Schultz, *Dialogue at the Margins* (Wisconsin: University of Wisconsin at Madison Press, 1990).

43. Evan-Zohar, p. 50.

44. Opal Palmer Adisa, "Duppy Get Her," in *Caribbean New Wave*, ed. Stewart Brown (New Hampshire: Heinemann, 1990), p. 2.

45. V.S. Naipul, *A House for Mr. Biswas* (Harmondsworth: Penguin, 1969), p. 194.

46. Weir, pp. 311–12.

47. See, for instance, Sebastian A. Tacal's "Nagre-entry si Takoy sa Abu-Dhabi," *Yuhum,* June 29, 1987.

48. Teresita G. Maceda, trans. *Mga Piling Kuwentong Sebuwano, Marcel M. Navarra* (Quezon City: University of the Philippines Press, 1986), p. 248.

49. Wolfenden, pp. 174–75.

50. Rev. J. Kauffmann, *Visayan-English Dictionary* (Iloilo: La Editorial, n.d.), p. 340.

51. When the accent falls on different syllables in the reduplicated word, the root meaning is diminished in some way. Thus *nagahulatholat* means "waiting a bit." Please see Wolfenden, p. 87. The dubitative mode is signified by the affix *iga-*. It suggests uncertainty as to whether the action will be performed. No real aspect is correlated with this mode since if the action took place, there is no more uncertainty to it. From Wolfenden, p. 134. Therefore *igahambal* suggests uncertainty as to what will be performed.

52. Leonard Bloomfield, *Language* (New York: Holt, Rinehart and Winston, 1933), Chapter 11.

53. Wolfenden, pp. 220–29.

54. Leonardo Mercado, "Visayan Grammar," *Philippine Studies*, vol. 20 (1972), p. 213.

55. Nida and Taber, p. 197.

56. Wolfenden, p. 116.

57. Macario Ruiz, "A Study of the Behavior of Hiligaynon Verb Roots with Particular Reference to the Actor and Goal Focus Affixes," A Report Submitted to the National Science Development Board (Iloilo City: University Research Center, Central Philippines University, 1968), pp. 13–14.

58. The problem of redundancy is dealt with by Susan Suleiman in "Redundancy and the Readable Text," *Poetics Today* 1 (April 1980), 119-42.

59. Walter J. Ong, *Orality and Literacy* (London: Routledge, 1982), pp. 147–51.

60. Ong, pp. 151–55.

61. The connection between religion and characterization was observed earlier by Ian Watt in *The Rise of the Novel: Studies in Defoe, Richardson, and Fielding* (Berkeley: University of California Press). Rpt. 1957.

62. Bakhtin in Holquist, 1981, p. 361.

63. *Ibid.*, p. 365.

64. Isagani R. Cruz, "The Future of Philippine Literature in English," p. 131. Cruz cites these prerequisites for a reader to understand Philippine literature in English. These are also applicable to a translator who is, first of all, a reader.

65. Spivak in Harasym, ed. *The Post-Colonial Critic*, p. 69.

66. Prof. Sylvia Ventura suggested this term to denote "Filipino English."

Book, leave me to walk in shoes full of dust and none of mythology: go back to your shelf; I, down the street shall go.

—Pablo Neruda
—trans. by Corazon Villareal

CHAPTER V

Translating the Sugilanon into Filipino: Re-viewing the Past

I have not lived in the Visayas for a long time although I was born there. In 1957, when I was just a child, our family boarded an interisland vessel for Manila. The ship docked in Manila, I remember nothing except the row of "police cars" parked in the pier, and my father saying that our table glass had broken in transport. It was only in 1982 when, upon invitation of the Cultural Research Association of the Philippines, I returned as a member of a panel to speak on various aspects of Philippine culture to selected teachers in Iloilo. I returned again in February 1992 to interview Hiligaynon writers, scholars, and teachers in connection with this study on translation.

But really, the interview was not my only purpose. I had read a lot on Hiligaynon culture in various libraries in Manila and the United States and have come across works by the Hiligaynon literati. I am familiar with the works of the most well-known Hiligaynon writers: Magdalena Jalandoni, Ramon Muzones, Conrado Norada, Serapion Torre, Anghel Magahum, Delfin Gumban and others. In the process of selecting the sugilanon to be translated into Filipino and Fil/english, I have read some of the most prolific sugilanon writers: Jan Marcella, Quirino Baterna, Ernesto Javellana, Ismaelita Floro-Luza, Antonio Joquiñó Sr.,

Julius Flores, Luisa Defante Gibraltar, Romeo Roullo, Elizabeth Batiduan. I became familiar with the works of the few scholars who have pioneered in Hiligaynon studies: Lucila Hosillos, Doreen Fernandez, and Rosario Lucero, who are based in Manila, Leoncio Deriada and Santiago Alv. Mulato in Iloilo, and Cecilia Nava in Negros. Although exposed largely to Filipino and English in Manila, I managed to keep a Hiligaynon vocabulary and let it grow by reading Hiligaynon works picked up here and there through the years. Recently, through my translation work in Hiligaynon, I came in close contact with native Hiligaynon speakers and have consulted the few dictionaries available on Hiligaynon of which the most comprehensive is Kauffman's (published just before the turn of the 19th century). Sometimes, in fact, I surprise some friends who have been long-time residents of Iloilo and Capiz, with my knowledge of Hiligaynon.

But I had to come back to Iloilo. I felt some absence in this learnedness. I wanted to step foot once again in Panay, the land of my birth—breathe its air, feel its trees, kneel in its churches. The place is different, I have been told: you find footprints of the dwarf on the soil, you must defer to some invisible beings living in the trees, you draw in the living breath of the wind, and you see mestizo fairies stalking out of St. Clemens Church before the Consecration in the Mass. I wanted to experience that which Bakhtin had termed as the "brute materiality" of a culture, something that I feel is indispensable to a translator. The Hiligaynon's laughter and gesture; his lusts and desires; his every step and plodding; his breaking wind, his getting stung—the Hiligaynon's breath and soul. One has to look around, listen, savor the living signs of Hiligaynon culture. Such a visit was not enough for me to feel its wholeness. But for a lover who must move on, does not another rendezvous with one's love hold promise of a continuing affair?

Translation: Languages Coming Together

A oneness, perhaps, to which we can compare the process of translating a literature in the vernacular into the national language? To quote the editor of *Kurditan* (1988), a collection of short stories in Ilocano translated into Filipino:[1]

> It may be said that this book comes from the fervent wish for a marriage of Ilocano literature with our national literature. Based on the notes and commentary in this anthology, one observes that almost half of the stories were translated by the authors themselves. We think this is a pleasant discovery since it shows that Ilocano fictionists, after all, can write in the national language.

The publication of regional literature translated into Filipino like the *Kurditan*, *Sugilanon* (1991) and *Marcel Navarra: Mga Piling Kuwentong Sebuwano* (1986) is cause for celebration. This is a concrete way of realizing the following provision in the Constitution of 1987:

> The national language of the Philippines is Filipino. As it evolves, it shall be further developed and enriched on the basis of existing Philippine and other languages. (Article XIV, Sec. 6).

The language policy of the University of the Philippines (1990) supports this provision:

> Along with this [developing the national language], we should also develop and energize our *local and regional cultures and languages* because it is from this spring that we can enrich and strengthen Philippine civilization. (1.3)

The policy also recognizes the importance of translation.

> A vigorous translation program should be encouraged and supported. (2.2.8)

The idea behind these propositions is not really new. Way back in 1974, the SALIPI or the Samahan para sa mga Literatura ng Pilipinas (Association for National Literature) published *Literatura ng Pilipinas*. In its editorial, Ernesto Constantino and Rogelio Sikat explained that "a national literature is not composed of or should not be composed only of the literature in one language of one ethnic group."[2] They stressed that the journal was using Filipino, which to them is the language of our national literature, and not Tagalog or English. In the formation of our national literature, translation is valuable because it is through this that the various ethnic literatures could be translated into Filipino, or the national language. In short, our national literature can be formed only with the union of our different languages and literatures in a medium known and accepted by many as the national language.

The process seems simple enough. Yet why did it take so long for these ideas to be incorporated in the Constitution and the language policy of the premier state university in the country? What is the prospect of implementing a serious and wide-ranging program of translation in the country?

Politics in Translating

Answering this question entails looking into the system of translating regional literature in the Philippines. One institution which had for years been very influential in deciding what should be published and in what language it should be published was the Roces Publications, which started publishing in the 1920s. It pioneered publication in the vernacular magazines and Tagalog comics and held virtual monopoly of these for decades until the sale of the rights to *Liwayway* and other magazines to Hans Menzi of Bulletin Publications in the 1980s. The Roces-owned company published the *Liwayway* (Tagalog), *Bannawag* (Ilocano), *Hiligaynon* (Hiligaynon), *Bisaya*, (Cebuano), and *Bikolnon* (Bicol).

The publisher's policy was to translate the novels, short stories, and articles written by Tagalog writers in its lead magazine *Liwayway* into the languages of its sister magazines. This was to the great advantage of the company. First, because it did not have to hire a separate group of writers for the other magazine. The publisher spent for only one set of writers—those based in Manila whose original script they paid for. It did not pay the writers for the rights to have their works translated into the other vernaculars. For instance, according to Mario Cabling, when the company used his stories in the *Liwayway* for translation in the other magazines, the only fee he received was for the original story in Tagalog.[3] He said he did not care; he did not understand the translations anyway. (Besides, was it not a privilege to be published by a monopoly with a nationwide circulation? And if at all he protested, would he have been able to look for another publisher?) Secondly, the company did not even have to hire translators, for the task of translating was assigned to the regular editorial staff of each magazine. The practice continued up to the 1970s, when Liwayway Publications called for the suspension of translations from Tagalog since by then, Tagalog was widely understood all over the Philippines.[4] Thus, it was possible to circulate the *Liwayway* nationwide.

It can be gleaned, for example, from the first issues of *Hiligaynon* in the mid-'30s (which fortunately are still preserved in the company's library) that the fiction and essays in its pages were translation of works by Tagalog writers like Gregorio C. Coching, Fausto J. Galauran, Lazaro Francisco, Gervasio B. Santiago, Rosalia Aguinaldo, Tony Velasquez, Susana de Guzman and others. (Kindly look at the selected bibliography of sugilanon in the appendix.) The principal translators from Tagalog into Hiligaynon were Abe S. Gonzales, who was the editor of *Hiligaynon* before WWII, and the members of the editorial staff: Jose J. Guevara, Ulises M. Vadlit, Prax S. Villaluz, and the soon-to-be novelist, Ramon Muzones. Muzones was the most productive translator until the publication of his sugilanon "Hara" (Queen) on June 28, 1938 and his highly successful first novel *Tibud nga Bulawan* (The Golden Jar) on October 11, 1938. After that novel, he devoted himself to writing fiction. Along with Magdalena Jalandoni and the younger novelist Conrado Norada, Muzones dominated the pages of *Hiligaynon* for over forty years until it ceased publication in 1973 because of poor circulation. But other translators followed, and the mass translation of the works of Tagalog writers like Nemesio Caravana, Efren Abueg, Clodualdo del Mundo, Pablo S. Gomez, and Mars Ravelo continued.[5] This was the responsibility of the editorial staff of *Hiligaynon*. The only difference was that the translators' names no longer appeared in the bylines. Translation as a profession was eclipsed, and the emergence of would-be Hiligaynon writers was stunted, for other than these translations, what were frequently published were the works of the three writers mentioned. After all, they already commanded a readership; the magazine was a sure hit at the newsstands.

Very noticeable, too, was the fact that although these three writers were famous in the Panay region and were talented writers, their works were not translated into Tagalog in the *Liwayway* and into the other vernacular languages in its sister magazines. In short, Hiligaynon culture (as well as other vernacular cultures) was unable to contribute to the formation of Filipino as a national language which is provided for in the Constitution of 1986 and the Language Policy of the University of the Philippines in 1990. Neither could Hiligaynon take part in the formation of a national literature in the process. In this, it was the monopoly of commercial magazines which played a major role since they had a wide circulation and the greatest number of publication outlets for writers.[6] Thus, according to Rodolfo Salandanan, current editor of *Liwayway*, in the '60s when television and other forms of entertainment were not yet popular, the circulation of *Liwayway* reached 200,000, and that of *Bannawag* about 148,000. The only anthology I know of works translated from Hiligaynon into Tagalog is an academic work, not commercial: the book *Mga Ginto sa Iloilo* (Golden Treasures from Iloilo), compiled and translated by Felicisima Torres Campos, a native of Bulacan, south of Manila, who is married to a native of Iloilo.

But it was not just the magazines that dictated the direction of translation and what works had to be translated. For from the very beginning, the National Capital Region, particularly the Manila area, was the seat of government and of culture as well. (In Chapter I, for instance, I mentioned that during the Spanish period, most religious publications and their translations were published in Manila.) The Linangan ng mga Wika sa Pilipinas (formerly the National Language Institute in 1936, then renamed the Institute of National Language in 1938), has encouraged and produced projects geared to propagating the idea that our national language is Pilipino which is actually Tagalog-based.[7] For instance, the *Diksyunaryo ng Wikang Filipino* (Dictionary of the Filipino Language) which it published in 1989 with the Instructional Materials Corporation of the Department of Education, Culture and Sports and National Bookstore, Inc., is a monolingual dictionary in Tagalog, not Filipino, for while it includes words derived from English, it does not include words from other regions. The tradition it comes from is apparent in the words of Ponciano Pineda in the preface: "This year, on the occasion of the 200th or bicentennial anniversary of Francisco (Balagtas) Baltazar, we have completed the publication of the *Diksyunaryo ng Wikang Filipino* in special memory of the Poet of Our Race." Thus, the Institute's role in the growth and development of the national language has been limited in a sense.

Neither has the Department of Education been very helpful in developing a national language based on the various regional languages. Being part of the Department of Education, the Institute's language perspective has been implemented in schools nationwide by national supervisors in Pilipino whose idea of the language was Tagalog. At present, the current process of selecting and producing textbooks has not really facilitated the propagation of Filipino. The Executive Committee in charge of formulating the policies for this process is the Instructional Materials Council, which is composed of the Secretary of Education, Culture, and Sports, the Head of the Bureau of Education for Elementary Education, the Head of the Bureau of Education for Secondary Education, and two other members chosen by the Secretary of Education. If there is need to produce new textbooks, the Council makes this need known through a call for manuscripts. A panel of evaluators chosen by the members of the Council examines these manuscripts. It would be interesting to find out the composition of this panel, especially its stand regarding the national language, but let us put this aside for now and turn our attention to its criteria for selecting books for public schools. These are the following: the minimum learning competency skills expected of its grade or level, completeness of material, and for the courses in English and Filipino in the secondary level, adherence to the canon formulated by the SLATE Project of the Language Study Center of the Philippine Normal Unversity in 1988. Nothing is mentioned of the nature of our national language and the role of the regional languages in its development. This is of no concern to textbook writers because the kind of Filipino used now is "liberal" and open to foreign words.[8]

But if we study the SLATE Report, the domination of Tagalog writers is clear. Except for Marcel Navarra of Cebu, Reynaldo Duque and Pedro Bukaneg of Ilocos, the works included in the canon are those of the Tagalog writers such as Liwayway Arceo, Genoveva Matute, Edgardo Reyes, Rogelio Sikat, Domingo Landicho, Teo Antonio, Ponciano Pineda, Alejandro Abadilla, Lope K. Santos, Amado Hernandez, Patricia Cruz, Rolando Tinio, Bienvenido Lumbera, Faustino Aguilar, Andres Cristobal Cruz, Virgilio Almario, and others. Except for Bienvenido Lumbera who has expressed his agreement to a Filipino based on all our languages, no one has shown a clear commitment to this idea provided for in our Constitution.

It is not surprising that such a canon was arrived at. The SLATE panel in Filipino (as well as in English) was composed of delegates from the National Capital Region; not a single one came from outside of it. Also noticeable is that this conference was a project of the Language Study Center of the Philippine Normal University headed by Alfonso Santiago, a well-known Tagalista. If we recall, Mr. Santiago published *Sining ng Pagsasaling-Wika* (1976) that dealt only with *external translation*, or translation vis-a-vis foreign languages and not with *internal translation*, or translation between and among languages within the country.[9] It is this second type of translation which we need in order to develop a language based on all regional languages. We must also note that the Philippine Normal University is the site of the Pambansang Samahan sa Linggwistikang Filipino, Inc. which is known for its view that Filipino is mainly Tagalog although open to foreign influences.[10] If we consider the fact that the one in charge of the selection and production of elementary textbooks is the Language Study Center of the Philippine Normal University, not the Instructional Materials Corporation, the force of Tagalog-based Filipino is clear, and the constitutional provision of Filipino is a mere legal fact. Thus, in the words of Rogelio Sikat: "Filipino is Tagalog. But this Tagalog is liberal...Call it Tagalog or Filipino, the National Language is here." His basis: the survey of the Philippine News Agency that in 1989, 92 percent of Filipinos could speak and understand Tagalog, as compared to the 25.4 percent in 1935.

It is hard to disregard this observation. But it is also hard to discount the various protests against Filipino which is Tagalog-based. The vehement objections in Cebu are well-known. It may be true that these come mainly from the politicians, but they are the ones in a position to enact legislation affecting the direction and growth of languages. For example, the Provincial Council of Cebu has appropriated one million pesos for the translation of Tagalog works into Cebuano.[11] Recently, in Iloilo, the Provincial Council passed a resolution to the effect that Hiligaynon shall be used in its sessions and not English or *Tag*Filipino. In August 1989, the Ilonggo Language and

Literature Foundation, Inc., an association of writers and scholars in Iloilo, issued a manifesto objecting to Executive Order No. 335 and suggesting that then-President Aquino take certain measures like the following:[12]

> ...to repeal or suspend the implementation of Executive Order No. 335 until such time as there is a program for the emergence and growth of the national language through democratic means which give the indigenous languages of the Philippines equal opportunity and to contribute to the national language as constituent languages.
>
> ...to work for budgetary allotments for the development and propagation of the constituent languages through research for the retrieval, publication and propagation of their grammar, orthography and dictionary with the exclusion of Tagalog, as this language has already been given top priority for the past 54 years.

In Cagayan de Oro City, in particular at the Xavier University, results of a survey made among its teachers and students show that they prefer English to Filipino.[13] These developments are contrary to the intention of the Constitution to develop a national language based on all Philippine languages, but it is clear that these reactions stem from the common perception that Filipino is Tagalog. In short, because of political factors not within the control of the other regions, they had to learn Tagalog. This does not mean that they accept the language, though. Neither does this mean that it is already their first language. In fact, to quote Pacifico Aprieto:[14]

> There seems to be no escaping the fact that Filipino and English are both second languages for most teachers and pupils throughout the country. Language difficulty forces well-meaning teachers to circumvent the bilingual requirement, sometimes resorting to the local language or vernacular to impart instructions, a practice that has been found to be effective in the teaching and learning situation in the countryside.

This problem of language will surface again and again and will continue to gnaw at the unity of the nation, especially its cultural unity.

Tagalog or Filipino?

For instance, if there is no such national language as Filipino, a national literature cannot be formed. This was the problem that confronted the Division of Literature of the Department of Media, Visual Arts, and Literature of the Cultural Center of the Philippines, now headed by Herminio Beltran. Since 1989, the Center has given writing grants to writers in English, Filipino, and four other major languages: Hiligaynon, Cebuano, Ilocano, and Bicolnon, in acknowledgement of the value of our regional literatures. But in one of the meetings of the coordinators in the region, Leoncio Deriada, Coordinator for Hiligaynon, asked why Tagalog was not one of the language categories of the writing grants. If, indeed, Filipino is not Tagalog, it was just proper that the categories for Filipino and Tagalog be separate.

But is there really a difference between Filipino and Tagalog? And if they are at all different, what are their differences? Because the regional coordinators of the Center could not resolve the issue, Beltran called a symposium on the matter in February 1991. Those who attended were writers and teachers of language and literature from the University of the Philippines (U.P.), Polytechnic University of the Philippines (P.U.P.), Ateneo University, De La Salle University, and others, as well as representatives of the Sentro ng Wikang Filipino (Center for Filipino) of U.P. The discussion was heated. For instance, Bayani Abadilla and Cesar Torres of P.U.P. insisted that as far as the use of Filipino was concerned, nobody could beat Tagalog. This did not escape the attention of Florentino Hornedo, who has Ivatan and Ilokano blood: if they, non-Tagalogs, have struggled to study Tagalog, why don't the Tagalogs find time to study the other regional languages? The group also queried the representatives of the Sentro ng Wika as to their research on the difference between Tagalog and Filipino, but at that time the latter did not yet have a report on the issue. The meeting adjourned without the problem being resolved. Even so, the regional coordinators for literature of the Cultural

Center of the Philippines decided that beginning in 1992, there would be a writing grant for Tagalog which would be a separate category from Filipino. This was perhaps upon the insistence of the regional coordinators on the right of their languages and literatures to participate in the formation of our national language and culture. After all, what harm would such an experiment do?

But how difficult it is to capture this concept of Filipino as defined in the Philippine Constitution. What appears is that this is not yet a reality. Despite the hindrances discussed previously, is there still hope that Filipino will evolve? What is the role of translation in achieving this goal? How can the translator give reality to Filipino? Looking closely at the works recently written by writers with regional roots, the translator would notice their attempts at creating Filipino. The concept does not seem too abstract, after all. In fact, the formation of Filipino has begun.

When I researched in the Liwayway Publications library, I found out that Reynaldo Duque, who is an Ilocano writer, was the newly-appointed Assistant Editor of *Liwayway*. I was curious; I wanted to know how it happened that he had penetrated a bastion of Tagalog writers. But since I was meeting him only for the first time, I could not bring myself to ask him the question. When I inquired regarding his process of translating (he is both writer and translator), he mentioned something which caught my attention. This was the observation of his fellow writers, Jun Cruz Reyes and Rosario Lucero, regarding the works he translated from Ilocano to Filipino: "How come, Rey, your work is written in Tagalog, but when you read it, you get the feeling it's Ilocano?"[15] A casual observation, yet one I think which held the clue to what must be Filipino. I badgered him: "How do you do that, Rey—you write in Tagalog yet sound Ilocano?" It was hard to answer this, he said; he didn't think about this at all. Just that when you read the work, it does not stammer; it is smooth. I know that writers avoid questions on how they write; they are like intrusions into the process of creation. But when I coaxed him into answering me (gently though), he did reply. He said the grammar and syntax of Tagalog must be studied. Attention should also be given to creating an Ilocano setting and character. For example, one should not use "*Anak ng kulog!*" ("Son of thunder!") because this is a Tagalog expression; instead, one should use "*Anak ng kidlat!*" ("Son of lightning!") because the phrase corresponds to the Ilocano expression "*Anak ti sal-it*!" Also to be included are Ilocano words with no equivalents in Tagalog, like "*sardam*" (early evening) or "*bit-ang*" (a kind of fence peculiar to the Ilocos area). Other than these, the style in the original must be retained; thus, one should not cut the long sentences in Ilocano.

We can probably understand the interweaving of these elements when we read the stories that Duque translated from Ilocano to Filipino. One is "Ang Gamugamo sa Lampara ni Julio Madarang" ("The Moth in the Lamp of Julio Madarang"), a story he wrote in Ilocano and subsequently translated into Filipino for publication in *Liwayway* on December 29, 1986 and January 5, 1987. A second translation version of this story won the First Prize in the Cultural Center's Short Story Contest in 1987. The text I use here, though, is the third version; this was published in the *Kurditan*. Another story Mr. Duque translated for the *Kurditan* is "Pista" ("Fiesta") written by Pacifico Espanto and published in the *Bannawag* on March 3, 1958.

The translated versions use Ilocano words having no equivalents in Tagalog like *dinengdeng* (a vegetable dish with fried or broiled fish and fermented shrimps); *ading* (younger sister, and also a general term for any female younger than the speaker, connoting respect or fondness); and *Tata* (an old man; also suggesting respect). But sometimes, Ilocano words are used even if these have equivalents in Tagalog, such as *Manong* (Kuya), and *balasang* (maiden). A famous song in Ilocano is reproduced in the Filipino translation but its translation into Filipino is placed in a footnote in "Pista." These details contribute to integrating Ilocano elements into the translated story. It is hard to say how the translator has interwoven Ilocano structures into Tagalog because of my limited knowledge of Ilocano, but can one say that the following sentence taken from "Julio Madarang" sounds Tagalog?

> *May itinatarak na balaraw ng lumbay ang pangungulila sa dibdib ng karimlan...at mula sa sugat na nilikha ng itinarak ng pangungulila na balaraw ng lumbay sa dibdib ng karimlan ay umagos nang buong laya ang dugong hihilamos sa mukha ng bagong silang na umaga.*

(There's a dagger of sadness that loneliness thrusts into the heart of darkness...and out of the wounds from this dagger that loneliness stabbed into the heart of darkness flowed freely and profusely the blood that was to cleanse the face of the new day.)

It should also be mentioned that Duque used the word *buhat* which, in the context of his translation means "work." This is neither Ilocano nor Tagalog, but Hiligaynon. He borrowed from Hiligaynon! A surprising but welcome move and certainly a good model for the formation of Filipino.

In the case of Hiligaynon, it is worthwhile for the translator to note how Rosario Cruz Lucero's works contribute to the formation of Filipino. Let us look, in particular, at "Demonyo" (Demon) and "Komedya" (Comedy). "Demonyo" won the first prize in the Short Story Contest of the Cultural Center of the Philippines in 1988, and "Komedya" was one of the three stories which won in the Cultural Center Contest in 1990. These are original works in Filipino, not translations like Duque's "Julio Madarang," but if we focus our attention on the dialogues in Lucero's stories, we notice that Lucero took pains to translate into the receptor language (Filipino) the natural way Hiligaynons from Negros speak. Let us look at the following excerpt from "Komedya":[16]

> *Nagulantang si Barangay Kapitan Elizardo Lerga nang marinig niya ang bati ni Manang Didit sa labas. "Oy! Sardo, maistorbo ka lang pero daw ginatanghali 'ka ata ng gising."*
>
> *Bumangon si Tiyo Sardo at dumungaw sa bintana habang pinapahid ang tulog sa mga mata.*
>
> *"Baka nakalimutan ni'yong ngayong umaga natin ipupulong ang ating kababaryo para simulan ang pag-eensayo ng moro-moro," patuloy ni Manang Didit. "May mga nagapunta na sa tindahan ni 'Nay Marianing. Aantayin ka na lang namin doon."*

> (The barangay captain, Elizardo Lerga, was awakened when he heard Manang Didit call from outside the house. "Hey, Sardo, I think I'm waking you up, but it's late in the morning."
>
> Sardo rose and looked out of the window, still rubbing off the sleep from his eyes.

"It might have slipped your mind—this morning, we're suppose to rehearse for the moro-moro," Manang Didit continued. "Some have already gone to 'Nay Marianing's store. We'll wait for you there.")

In the English translation, Hiligainized Filipino is not reflected. In the original Filipino version, however, this Filipino variety is seen in the use of Hiligaynon affixes with verbs in Filipino, in the retention of typical Hiligaynon expressions like *daw*, and in phonological modifications like *aantayin* for *hihintayin*.

Here is another dialogue taken from Lucero's story, entitled "Demonyo."[17]

"Huu," sumimangot si Virginia at kinulubot ang ilong, "kasi, masyado siyang malaki at pangit at mabalahibo. At ang nakakapangilubot sa lahat, ang panghi gid ya bala. Amoy natuyong ihi—katulad ba nung banyong pinasukan natin doon sa plasa."

Matitigil ang kuwentuhan kapag biglang bubulyawan si Virginia ni Tiya Ason, ang kanyang nanay at kusinera nina Nena, "Hoy, Inyang! Tigilan mo na nga iyang mga kuwento mo! Pag nalaman ng ina niya, tayong dalawa gid ang madadale niya."

("Yes," Virginia frowned, twisting her nose, "you see, he's so huge and ugly and hairy. And what's so creepy is, he smells so much of urine. Long dried up urine. You know, like what we smelled in the comfort room at the plaza."

The conversation would break off only when Tiya Ason, Virginia's mother and cook of Nena's family, would snap at her, "Hoy, Inyang! Stop that! If her mother gets to know of these, she's sure to get us!")

The story uses two languages: that of the narrator is Tagalog, that of the characters is Tagalog that sounds Ilonggo (which is the name given to informal Hiligaynon). Various strategies were used to achieve this effect, although of course, these would be obvious only in the Tagalog original. For instance, verbs in Tagalog are again formed through the use of Hiligaynon affixes, like *nagapunta* (*maga* in place of *um* or *mag*) and *ginatanghali* (*gina* instead of *in*). There are changes in spelling to suit the Hiligaynon phonology like *huu* for *oo*; *aantayin* para sa *hihintayin*; or *ata* for *yata*. Favorite Ilonggo expressions like *daw*, *gid*, and *daw bala*, are also used. The passages also reflect the way Ilonggos pronounce Tagalog pronouns. For example, *ni'yong* is used in place of *ninyo*. Instead of *Pag nalaman ng ina niya iyan, tayong dalawa gid ang madadale niyan*, (which uses the Tagalog pronouns *iyan* and *niyan*) the line reads as: "*Pag nalaman ng ina niya, tayong dalawa gid ang madadale niya.*"

On the whole, then, the stories were written in a language that is neither Tagalog nor Hiligaynon. Could this be Filipino? If not, the language suggests directions for the formation of the national language Filipino, and our national literature. Thus, the judges in Gawad 1988 (a literary contest sponsored by the Cultural Center of the Philippines) observe:

> ...one of the favorable changes apparent in the entries concerns the shift of the stories' setting from Manila to other regions, whose issues sometimes become the concern of some of the stories. Related to this is the creation of "languages" that arise out of the attempts at adopting regional concerns in a rather popular manner.

Some Translated Sugilanon: An Analysis

It is also worth looking at the stories translated from Hiligaynon. We can count these with our fingers: "Taghoy" (Lamentation). This is Jan Marcella's Tagalog translation of his sugilanon entitled "Panaghoy Sang Ginahandos nga Palpal," (Lamentation of a Stake) which was published in the original Hiligaynon in *Bahandi-i*, a collection of sugilanon in Hiligaynon. Marcella translates this into Pilipino in Abueg's *Ang Manunulat*.[18] Lucero does a translation of the same story in *Sugilanon*, an anthology which translates into Tagalog a number of sugilanon taken from *Bahandi-i*.[19] "Bunyag-Takas" which I translate in Part 2 of this book is also included in the *Sugilanon* and so it would be enlightening to compare the strategies used by two translators of the same story. (Hosillos, by the way translates her own story "Bunyag-Takas" into English under the title "A Refusal of Ritual.")[20]

Lucero's translation seems to be more literal than Marcella's. The difference in titles illustrates this point:

J.M. *Taghoy* (Lamentation)
R.L. *Panaghoy ng Minamasong Tulos* (Lamentation of a Stake Driven into the Ground)

Marcella also deletes lines from the original such that sometimes what is left is a mere summary. This difference in translation strategy is seen in the following English versions:

J.M. "This son of yours who ran in the last election, he must be somewhat well-off, Mang Danoy."
"Well-off? Oh, no. He wouldn't have run in this election, but his friend coaxed him into it."

R.L. "This son of yours who ran in the last election, he must be somewhat well-off, Mang Danoy."
"If you speak of property, Mang Tante, my son doesn't have any. All he's got is daring and wit. He doesn't really want to get into this because he knows how messy it is, especially now when what's needed is a lot of money. But his friends coaxed him into it. Maybe, because my son was number one councilor in the last polls."

We note Lucero's care in bringing out each detail in the original Hiligaynon. (The translator is probably very careful when she/he is translating someone else's work; also we are not privy to the belt-tightening measures of the editors in *Ang Manunulat*, where Marcella's translation appeared). But Lucero's efforts have paid off. In Lucero's version of the title, the metaphor reflecting Mang Danoy's sad experience with an oppressive master surfaces. Also, the reader understands clearly the motivation of Mang Danoy's son in joining the elections through Lucero's more detailed translation.

Marcella's Tagalog translation, however, sounds more Ilonggo. For instance, he keeps some Hiligaynon words and italicizes them even if these have their equivalents in Tagalog, like for instance: *nakatibong* (carrying a burden on one's shoulders); *mataptapan* (covered); and *pinadayawan* (raised, as from the ground). Marcella also uses Hiligaynon words having no equivalents in Tagalog like *bakibaki* (even out) and typical Ilonggo expressions like *man* in the dialogues. He Hiligainizes Tagalog pronouns like *sila* into the Visayan *nila* (which was also observed in Lucero's "Demonyo"):

Original: *Pag-abot nila sa ligwin na kulokatamnan...*
(When they would get deep into the woods...)
J.M.: *Pag darating nila sa liblib na gubat...*
R.L.: *Pag darating sila sa liblib na gubat...*

But there are two aspects which Lucero and Marcella seemed to have neglected. In translating the following passage from the original Hiligaynon, both of them dropped the Hiligaynon word *sumoklip* (seized) and *kalawasan* (body):

Original: *Ang tingog ni Mr. Tante may kahinay kag kapung-awon nga kadalomon sa palamatin-an ni Tyo Danoy.*

Apang indi tingog ni Mr. Tante ang sumoklip sa iya kalawasan. Tingog ni Don Lucas ang ginaaningal sang amo.

J.M.: *Nguni't hindi tinig ni Mr. Tante ang narinig ni Mang Danoy. Tinig ni Don Lucas ang gumitgit sa kanyang pandinig.*

(But it was not Mr. Tante's voice that Mang Danoy heard. It was Don Lucas' voice which rang in his ears.)

R.L.: *Mahina ang tinig ni Mr. Tante at parang naririnig ni Mang Danoy na may matinding kalungkutan ito. Nguni't hindi tinig ni Mr. Tante ang narinig ni Mang Danoy. Tinig ni Don Lucas ang gumitgit sa kanyang pandinig.*

(Mr. Tante's voice was low and Mang Danoy noted some deep sadness in it. But it was not Mr. Tante's voice that Mang Danoy heard. It was Mr. Lucas' voice that rang in his ears.)

The verb *sumoklip* has vigor and so much is lost if this idea is not included. Also, the word *kalawasan* suggests the intensity of Mang Danoy's emotion. I likewise used *kapanglawan* rather than the more popular *kalungkutan* because the former is closer in sound to the original Hiligaynon word, *kapung-awan*. Here is my version:

C.V.: *Mahina ang tinig ni Mr. Tante, at sa pandinig ni 'Tay Danoy, may matinding kapanglawan. Nguni't hindi tinig ni Mr. Tante ang sumakop sa kanya. Tinig ni Don Lucas ang umalingawngaw sa kanyang pandinig, sa buong katawan niya.*

(Mr. Tante's voice was low, and to Mang Danoy, it carried some deep sadness. But it was not Mang Danoy's voice that seized him. It was Don Lucas' voice that rang in his ears, that shook his whole body.)

I shall next explain the strategies I have used in conveying Hiligaynon language and culture in my target language. Like the aforementioned writers and translators, I focus on word or lexicon and then proceed to the level of discourse or syntax. This procedure is only for purposes of analysis and does not actually reflect the translation process, which is recursive rather than linear. In the course of my explanations I shall compare my translations with those of Rosario Lucero in her collection *Sugilanon* (Sug). The stories to be discussed are: Lucila Hosillos' "Bunyag-Takas" (BT), Leothiny Clavel's "Ang Hustisya sa Dagat" (DH), and Ismaelita Floro-Luza's "Sa Lawod sang Pangabuhi" (LP). The intention is not to judge which is the better translation because each translation has its own merits depending on the framework the translator uses. Sometimes, though, the analysis of a translation becomes clearer when it is compared to other versions.

In looking for a word equivalent in the target language, I usually choose that which sounds like the word used in the source text. For instance, for the word *binghal* (snap at) in "Sa Lawod sang Pangabuhi," I could have used various Tagalog words having the same meaning, such as *bulyaw*, *sikmat*, and *singhal*, but I chose *singhal* because aside from being the closest in meaning to *binghal*, it also sounds like *binghal*. I have also coined compound words in the target language which is Tagalog/Filipino.

Hil: *"Ano ka bala?" balik nga binghal ni Lorna.*
("What's the matter with you?" Lorna snapped back.)
Tag: *"Ano ka ba?" balik na singhal ni Lorna.*
C.V.: *"Ano ka ba?" balik-singhal ni Lorna.*

Although some Hiligaynon words have rough equivalents in Tagalog, I retain the Hiligaynon terms if they give a dimension that cannot be found in the receptor language. Take *handurawan* (BT), for instance. Its meaning is close to the word *guniguni* in Tagalog, or to the borrowed word *imahinasyon*. But according to Santiago Alv. Mulato, who is known to writers in Iloilo as the *Bahathari (Prince) of Hiligaynon and Kiniray-a*, *handurawan* comes from *handum* (desire) and *larawan* (picture). Thus, I do not translate *handurawan* into Tagalog. The same holds true for *magdigamo*. This can be matched only with *paghahanda ng pagkain* (preparing the meal). In Hiligaynon, the word for "full moon" is *ugsaran*. The word comes from the root *ugsad*. When the moon makes its first step in its ascent towards the zenith, the horizon on which the full moon rises is considered its first step. Thus, *ugsaran* for full moon.

It is also important to keep the words which deal with Hiligaynon beliefs like the word *gaba* in the sugilanon "Ang Gaba sang Katubwan" (meaning "punishment," which has a connotation similar to the Hindu concept of *karma*). Terms on kinship have also been retained like *Tiyo* (literally "uncle" but also used for Mr.), *Tiya* (literally, "aunt" but also used for Mrs.), *'Noy* or *Toto* (terms of address for a boy or a man younger than the speaker), *Inday* (term of endearment for the females), *Manang* (elder sister) and *Manong* (elder brother). I keep these terms especially when they refer to non-relatives of the speaker, because these show the well-known *cariño* (tenderness, demonstrativeness and caring) of the Ilonggo. To refer to the character entering a house, I use *umakyat* (go up the stairs) rather than *pumasok*, since the former is more appropriate to the house in the barrio where people generally need to go up a bamboo staircase before entering the door.

On the level of discourse, I prefer literal translation. This leads to a more vivid character portrayal and a fuller expression of the characters' experience. Take the following examples:

Hil: *Kag sa nawong ni Lorna, amat-amat niya nga namasnahan ang pagkulap sang gal-om.* (LP)
R.L.: *Napansin niya ang unti-unting pagdidilim ng mukha ni Lorna.*
(He noticed Lorna's face slowly darkening.)

C.V.: (my translation in Part 2 of LP): *At napansin niyang ang mukha ni Lorna ay unti-unti nang nabalot ng dilim.* (He noticed a pall gradually cover Lorna's face.)

Or these lines excerpted from "Bunyag-Takas" (BT):

Hil: *Dungan sang paghumlad sang iya paghangop sang ila kahimtangan nga daw wala katibwasan, nabatyagan niya ang pagbalhin sang iya lawas kag ang iya kahuluy-on kon may masat-oman siya nga may nagatulok sa iya.*
R.L.: *Kasabay ng kanyang hangaring maunawaan niya ang kanilang kalagayan na tila walang kaluwagan, naramdaman niya ang pagbabago ng kanyang katawan, at ngayo'y nahihiya na siya kapag nahahalata niyang may nakatitig sa kanya.*
(Along with her wish to understand their miserable condition to which there seemed no end, she felt some change in her body, and now she would get self-conscious when she caught someone staring at her.)

C.V.: *Sabay sa pagladlad ng bagong pag-unawa na walang kaibsan ang kanilang kalagayan, napansin niya ang pag-iiba ng kanyang katawan at ang kanyang pagkahiya kapag naramdaman niyang may nakatitig sa kanya.*
(Along with unfolding realizations that their misery was unrelieved, she began feeling a transformation in her body and a self-consciousness when she noticed someone looking at her.)

The author of "Bunyag-Takas" often uses noun phrases where verb phrases may be used. Thus, in my translation of the sugilanon into Filipino I usually leave the noun phrases intact. That is why the two translation versions above are different: I use *pag-unawa* (understanding) while Lucero uses *maunawaan* (to understand); I use *pagkahiya* (self-consciousness) while she uses *nahihiya* (to be self-conscious). I translate the phrase *paghumlad sang iya paghangop sang ila kahimtangan nga daw wala katibwasan* into *Sabay sa pagladlad ng bagong pag-unawa na walang kaibsan ang kanilang kalagayan* ("Along with *unfolding realizations* [italics supplied] that their misery was unrelieved"). Lucero translates the phrase into *Kasabay ng kanyang hangaring maunawaan niya ang kanilang kalagayan* ("Along with her wish *to understand* [italics supplied] their miserable condition to which there seemed no end").

In the following line from "Ang Hustisya" (HD), the literal translation conveys a certain dimension.

Hil: *Nagbagrot ang ngipon nga dumalagan siya sa kusina kag sa daku sang kaakig, binali ang liog sang manok.*
R.L.: *Nanggigigil na tumakbo siya sa kusina at sa tindi ng kanyang galit ay binali niya ang leeg ng manok.*
(Trembling, he ran to the kitchen and from so much anger broke the neck of the rooster.)
C.V.: *Nagngangalit ang mga ipin, tumakbo siya sa kusina, at sa laki ng galit, binali ang leeg ng manok.*
(Gritting his teeth, he ran to the kitchen, and enraged, broke the rooster's neck.)

Nagbagrot is not just vivid; it is onomatopoeic as well, since it suggests the sound of someone very angry. A literal translation is therefore needed to let these features emerge.

But sometimes a literal translation sounds roundabout, like version 1 below:

Hil: *Sugod sadto, nasat-uman na niya ang pagbag-o sang iya tingog, ang paglain sang iya panulok, ang pagbalhin sang iya paghulag.* (BT)
Version 1: *Mula noon naramdaman na niya ang pagbabago ng kanyang boses, ang pagpapalit ng kanyang pagtingin sa buhay, ang pag-iiba sa kanyang pagkilos.*
(Since then, she felt a certain newness in her voice, a difference in her appearance, and a change in her behavior.)

Version 2 is smoother and more active:
Version 2: *Magmula noon, napapansin na niya ang pagbabago ng kanyang tinig, ng kanyang pagtingin sa buhay, ng kanyang pagkilos.*
(Since then, she noticed a change in her voice, in her appearance, in the way she moved.)

Dialogue is sometimes unnatural, like the version that follows:

Hil: "*Pinatay kuno si Indo paagi sa pagkuga.*" (HD)
Version 1: "*Pinatay daw si Indo sa pananakal.*"
(They say Indo was killed by strangulation.)

The non-literal translation is smoother, like versions 2 and 3 below:

Version 2: "*Pinatay raw si Indo. Sinakal siya.*"
("They say Indo was killed. He was strangled.")
Version 3: "*Sinakal kuno si Indo. Patay!*"
("They say Indo was killed. Strangled!")

On the whole, however, a literal translation is more suitable than a non-literal one for the framework I am using.

(This discussion assumes, of course, that the basis for the translation is accurate. One gauge of the translator's respect for the source culture is his effort to make sure his copy of the original is correct. Mechanical mistakes may arise from the textual production, a process which begins with the writer, and continues on to the printing and translation. I noticed some textual differences, for example, in my study of the three stories just mentioned.)

In short, there are various ways of relating lexicon, grammar, discourse, and pragmatics in order to let Hiligaynon language and culture emerge in the Tagalog translation.

But this position appears to contradict the experiences of some translators. For instance, Rolando Tinio writes: "A translated work must always sound as if the work were originally written in the language into which it has been translated. Nobody is interested in translation for being a translation."[21] Jose Lacaba also writes:[22]

> In all instances, I strive not to make my target language sound like a translation. Although I try to capture, even if faintly the rhythm of the original, what I more often come up with is a reconstruction, which on the whole uses the rhythm, structure, and idiom of modern Tagalog (Pilipino, or Filipino, or whatever my language should be called).

These views of two of our most talented writer/translators should not be ignored. A work that sounds translated does grate on the ear—it indicates roughness and sloppiness, not smoothness or care. But what if the work sounds Visayan, or Ilocano? In the context of the marginalization of regional languages and culture, this aspect merits our concern. Based on what had been discussed with regard to the works of Lucero, Duque, and Marcella, this regional peculiarity in sound is distinct from "sounding translated." The presence of the source language and culture is felt, but this is woven into the receptor language and culture so that the translation is "smooth and does not stammer." It is in the push and pull of these forces that works in Filipino are created.

But there appears to be some artificiality in this perspective; it becomes a hindrance to the translator's freedom to convey the life of the original translation. Ask any translator/writer what language he would like to translate to or write in—Tagalog, Filipino, or Pilipino—and you will receive no definite answer. For example, in this consultation I mentioned, on the issue of Filipino and Tagalog held at the University of the Philippines in 1991, Herminio Beltran recounted to me that when he asked Efren Abueg what language category he would choose in the literary contests of the Cultural Center of the Philippines, he simply said: "I don't care!" Lilia-Quindoza Santiago answered, on the other hand, "In both!"

In fact, Mr. Beltran said that this question of whether to use Filipino, or Tagalog, or Hiligaynon, etc. may just be a preoccupation of academics. Perhaps so. But if the debates in that conference (participated in by well-known writers) were so heated, is it really true that writers/translators do not care about the problem of language?

It is worthwhile noting that this language issue has been a central concern of regional writers. According to Resil Mojares, this problem is probably more important to the Hiligaynon and the Cebuano than that which divided Tagalog writers between the camps of Salvador P. Lopez and Jose Garcia Villa in the '30s. Mojares writes:[23]

> Rather, like their Cebuano counterparts, Hiligaynon novelists got caught up in the "rearguard action" on the language issue after Tagalog came to be adopted as the national language. Consequently, up to the '70s this remained a major concern of major writers like Muzones.

It can also be recalled that from the '20s up to the '40s, the language issue was the bone of contention between two groups of Hiligaynon writers: the purists who wanted to eliminate all Spanish terms from Hiligaynon, and the non-purists who borrowed freely from Spanish. Among the first group were the members of the Academia Bisaya: the poet Zaragoza Cano, the komedya writer Eriberto Gumban, and the poet-novelist-playwright Serapion Torre.[24] The desire to use pure Hiligaynon and along with this, the expression and development of an experience unique to Hiligaynon culture through this language, motivated Magdalena Jalandoni, Serapion Torre, Ramon Muzones, and others to write.

Thus, the translator strives to make the Hiligaynon language present in the receptor language. But since life is language and language is life, he/she breathes Hiligaynon life and culture into the receptor language. Filipino is the language and life of the Tagalog, Hiligaynon, Ilokano, Isinay, and every ethnic group in the Philippines.[25] In the attempt to realize the dream of writing in Filipino, not in *Tag*Filipino, we can give more importance to the languages and cultures of other regions. Because these were concealed by the dominant culture in Manila and the Tagalog region, they must re-surface and exist on equal terms with each other through the medium of a national language.

To unravel and create—this, then, is the task of the translator. The task sounds formidable. That is why translating is an act of presumptuousness. But if both the medium and the subject are Filipino, is not the translation process an act of courage?

The sugilanon I have translated is the result of my desire to share the language and culture of Hiligaynon with the readers. But I, too, am a recipient of such sharing. For when we left for Manila when I was seven years old, I left behind a rich heritage. Now I come back—not to give seminars—but to listen to its voice. And put together the broken pieces.

NOTES

1. Reynaldo Duque, Jose Bragado and Hermilinda T. Lingbaoan, *Kurditan: Mga Kuwentong Iluko* (Manila: Gumil Manila, 1988), v. (My translation.)

2. Ernesto Constantino, ed., "Editorial," *Literatura ng Pilipinas*, vol. 1, number 1 (Quezon City: Samahan para sa Mga Literatura ng Pilipinas, 1974), ii.

3. Interview with Mario Cabling at the Liwayway Publishing, Inc. Office, Pasong Tamo, Makati, Metro Manila on January 23, 1992. Mario Cabling was features editor of *Liwayway* from 1972–1985 and literary editor from 1985–1987.

4. Interview with G. Rodolfo Salandanan of Liwayway Publishing, Inc. on January 28, 1992. Mr. Salandanan is currently the editor-in-chief of *Liwayway*.

5. Interview with Erniesto Javellana, sugilanon writer and staff member of *Hiligaynon* magazine from 1965—1973, the period from which come most of the translated stories in Part 2 of this book. According to him, Nestor Jamolangue, editor-in-chief of *Hiligaynon*, also translated stories from Tagalog to Hiligaynon.

6. TagFilipino comics have been very influential in the propagation of Filipino. Filipino comics have, ever since, been published in Tagalog even if they were circulated nationwide. This practice was made possible perhaps because the comics are illustrated and thus it is easy to follow the story without fully understanding the lines. Please see Corazon D. Villareal, "Ang Industriya ng Komiks: Noon at Ngayon" ("The Comics Industry: Yesterday and Today") *Kultura*, vol. 3, no. 3 (Manila: Sentrong Pangkultura ng Pilipinas, 1990), pp. 47–55.

7. Andrew B. Gonzalez, *Language and Nationalism* (Quezon City, Metro Manila: Ateneo de Manila University Press, 1980). Gonzalez discusses the Tagalog issue in many parts of the book, especially in Chapters 3 and 4.

8. Interview with Ms. Cristina Gonzalez Pinera, supervising editor for Filipino, Instructional Materials Corporation, Quezon City, January 24, 1992.

9. This term is borrowed from Josefa Baldoz-Schriever, who did a dissertation on translation. Please see p. 11.

10. Kindly see Pambansang Samahan sa Linggwistikang Pilipino, Ink. *Linggwistika at Panitikan* (*Linguistics and Literature*), (Manila: Rex Book Store, 1985).

11. This information comes from Dr. Clara Ravina. When she was president of the Language Education Council of the Philippines (LEDCO), she consulted with teachers from Cebu and other provinces.

12. According to this Executive Order, Filipino (which is now still largely Tagalog) should be used in all official documents of the government.

13. This is according to Dr. John Ballweg, exchange professor of Virginia Tech at Xavier University in Cagayan de Oro.

14. Pacifico Aprieto, "The Philippine Textbook Project: From the Textbook Board Secretariat to the Instructional Materials Corporation," (Quezon City: Instructional Materials Corporation, 1987), p. 25.

15. Reynaldo Duque was National Fellow for Translation of the U.P. Creative Writing Center in 1991. Duque won a number of Cultural Center and Palanca Awards for works written in Ilocano and translated into Filipino.

16. Rosario Cruz Lucero, "Komedya," *Ani*, vol. IV, no. 3 (Manila: Sentrong Pangkultura ng Pilipinas, September, 1990), p. 82.

17. ________________, "Demonyo," *Ani*, vol II, no. 4 (Manila: Sentrong Pangkultura ng Pilipinas, December, 1988), p. 65.

18. Juanito Marcella, trans. "Taghoy" in *Ang Manunulat*, ed. Efren Abueg (Manila, 1970), pp. 24–30.

19. Rosario Cruz-Lucero, *Sugilanon* (Manila: De La Salle University Press), 1991.

20. Lucila Hosillos, "A Refusal of Ritual," *Lahi* 2 (Manila: Cultural Center of the Philippines), January, 1980.

21. Rolando Tinio, "An Approach to Translation." Paper read at the Seminar on Translation Sponsored by the Presidential Committee on the Arts, (Intramuros, Manila: August, 1990).

22. Jose. F. Lacaba, *Sa Daigdig ng Kontradiksyon* (Manila: Anvil Publishing, 1991), xv. (My translation.)

23. Mojares, *Origins*, p. 309.

24. Doreen Fernandez, *The Iloilo Zarzuela*, (Quezon City: Ateneo de Manila University Press, 1978), p. 81. Sr. Socorro Evangelista's dissertation also discusses this language issue among Hiligaynon writers.

25. Please see, for example, Ernesto Constantino, *Isinay Texts and Translations* (Tokyo: Institute for the Study of Languages and Cultures of Asia and Africa, 1982). This is an important step towards giving importance to various etholingusitic groups, both

major and minor. At present, Dr. Constantino is working on a dictionary of about 105 languages in the Philippines. This should be of immense help in the formation of a national language.

'Baw kanami bilog liwan ang bulan dali kita tubiganay, garabay shatbong, lagsanay...

—Milagros Geremia

Conclusion

To unframe and re-frame the sign. This is a theme structured in different forms in recent scholarship on various aspects of Philippine culture—"to unmask ideology and valorize the Utopian," "to deconstruct and reconstruct," "to discover subjugated knowledges, resurrect them or let their authors insurrect." This has been an obsession for some, and the decision to build my essay around this twin ideal signals that I stand principally aligned to this school. For a people whose memory and present reality are haunted by the colonial and feudal encounters and for whom the nationhood remains fugitive, this obsession can be no other but a magnificent one.

But it is also fraught with risks (as all obsessions are) and one must fend these off, distance herself repeatedly from them or be framed by the frame one seeks to unframe. I refer partly to the fact that for these twin tasks we usually turn to Western theory to deconstruct and validate ourselves. To Bakhtin, Barthes. Foucault, Althusser, Jameson, Marcuse, etc., whose preoccupation is to strike at the core of the nature of oppression and liberation. And for this, their theories serve us well. But they start off from a school of philosophy deeply rooted diachronically and synchronically in the West and although a good number of scholars have had the devotion and the acumen to understand them, some have only managed to write muddled discourse. Thus, we need to use them discriminately and apply them gingerly. To put it differently, when Lenin exhorted workingmen of all countries to unite and fight, he probably could not know that there was a world of difference between the autoworker in Detroit and the assembly worker in Manila. When terms like "minority" and "marginalized" appear in recent American scholarship, these refer to Mexican migrants, Afro-Americans, etc., whose "poverty" cannot quite compare with poverty and squalor in the Philippines.

And so, it was at first with some unease that I used the words "sign" and "semiotics," knowing that at least from the point of view of Eco and Sebeok, this project of a general science of signs has continued throughout the whole history of Western thought. That it can be traced to the time of Galen and the Stoics, that the idea of a general theory of all types of signs made its appearance in England in the seventeenth century especially in the writings of John Locke, who defined semiotics as "the business whereof is to consider the nature of signs the mind makes use of for the understanding of things, or conveying its knowledge to others." And that for two centuries semiotics remained in hibernation and that only towards the nineteenth century did it make its dramatic reappearance in the works of Charles S. Peirce and Ferdinand de Saussure from which two schools the science of semiotics today may be traced.

But when in the fall semester of 1990 I braved the cold early mornings to listen to the lectures on semiotics by Thomas Sebeok, Director of the Research Center for Linguistic and Semiotic Studies at Indiana University,[1] I did not do so for the intricate definitions and delineations on semiotics (which he did, though rarely technically) but for the narratives he told about the sign. His analysis, for instance, of the play of signs in "E.T." which he entitled "Enter-Textuality: Echoes from 'E.T.' "; his explanation of the semiotics of circus and how animal trainers use the stick as an indexical sign so as not to intrude into the social space of the tiger or the lion; his biography of Ulysses Grant which he has quite intriguingly entitled *I Think I am a Verb*; or, his views on the Quinlan case (would a blob of tubes be still considered human or merely an iconic representation of the person?). Interesting, although remote from the immediate concerns of a student from the Third World, reading and translating the sugilanon. Still what struck home was that the sign can pulsate; it lives. And because the sign lives, it can be seized from semiotic jargon and be used to approach a topic such as translating the sugilanon.

This sounds rather impressionistic. If we recall, however, Peirce's definition: "A sign is something which stands to somebody for something in some respect and capacity," or of Saussure: "A sign is made up of a signifier (a sound image or graphic equivalent) and a signified (the concept of meaning)" and that "the relation between the signifier and the signified is an arbitrary one," we notice in both definitions the presence of a sign-giver—in Peirce, the interpreter for whom the sign stands for something in some respect or capacity, and in Saussure, the presence of someone or a community responsible for the arbitrary meaning of the sign. Furthermore, what a sign stands for may be absent, may not even exist, or at least not be present anywhere at the time I use the sign; and thus, "the fundamental characteristic of a sign is that I can use it to *lie* (since everything that serves to tell a lie can also be used to tell the truth). Thus, the very nature of the sign partakes of life since it involves/engages man/woman in the dialectic of truth-giving and lying, and privileges them as sign-givers or sign-makers. This is of tremendous appeal to me or, I suppose, to anyone whose history is framed within a sign not of his/her own making and who is determined to imagine or invent his/her own sign-frame.

But in what sense is translating the sugilanon a process of unframing and re-framing the sign? To answer this, we cannot speak any longer of a sign-function established between two elementary units, as between a word and its meaning. We speak of a sign as a system. This was already present in Peirce's "to stand for" but was vigorously underlined by Saussure when he insisted that language is a system, a network of oppositions in which each sign acquires its value on account of the presence or absence of other signs. The notion of system need not be confined to verbal language alone but to various systems of signs in a culture.

What I sought to un-frame was that the process of translating the sugilanon/vernacular literature is largely determined by power relations. What to translate, in what direction translation is made, what omissions, additions, elisions to make, what shape or form the target language must take—the answers to these often lie outside of the individual writer. The translation process occurs within the confines of a particular sign-system dictated upon by a ruling order. In the nineteenth century, for instance, the translation process was closely tied up with the production of discourse which stood ostensibly for religious ideals but which in reality represented a design to cast the Filipinos in total subservience. The frailocracy having been in control of the means of production, specifically the printing presses, readily influenced the type and the direction of translation; in fact, published literature was largely in translation.

In the early twentieth century, when the institutions of the new colonial order were not yet in place, there was a surge in original works both in Spanish and the vernaculars. But in the '20s and onwards, with the establishment of a print monopoly not only in journalism but also in popular comics and magazines, a systematic translation program was revived under terms dictated by the publisher and editors of the Manila-based monopoly. Thus, works translated were almost always in one direction—from Tagalog into Hiligaynon, Ilokano and the other vernaculars. Although Hiligaynon literature produced prose writers who wrote well and voluminously like Magdalena Jalandoni, Ramon Muzones, Conrado Norada and Quirino Baterna, it was not until 1969 that Jalandoni was recognized nationally through the Republic Cultural Heritage Award, Muzones through the Gawad Pambansang Alagad ni Balagtas for Fiction in 1988, Norada through the Gawad Pambansang Alagad ni Balagtas Award for Fiction in 1990, and Baterna through the Gawad Pambansang Alagad for Fiction in 1993. Even so, not a single one of their works appeared in translation in *Liwayway* and they were thus deprived of national stature in real terms. The translator as an intermediary among the regional cultures and between the regional cultures and the declared national language was never acknowledged; he had no rights except to be paid as a regular staff member of the publication. There was probably no effort to raise the quality of translation since no one, certainly not the Tagalog author who quite often could not understand the vernacular, was paid extra for the translation of his work.

This print monopoly was, in fact, only part of a larger discourse which was not only physically and financially based in Manila but was also premised on the assumption that all cultural productions from that hub stood for what was central while the cultural productions in the regions stood for what was peripheral. From the time Commonwealth Act No. 184, or the National Language Law, was enacted and the National Language Institute which it established chose Tagalog as the basis of the national language, the language had enjoyed the status of a national language, even if it had undergone various name changes to assuage regional hurt. It grew, it developed steadily and consistently, because Tagalog writers wrote and had more opportunities for publishing, mainly because they resided in the Manila area, site of the printing presses (as of old), and various publication companies. Manila has been the venue for the Palanca Awards, which sealed a writer's prestige provided he wrote in English first of all, and later, in Tagalog in its various names. It has been the seat of the country's top universities where scholarship and criticism were expectedly focused on the center. Only one thesis, for example, is known to have been written on Hiligaynon literature in the '50s.[2] The Institute of National Language, the Textbook Board of the Department of Education and the Linguistics coterie at the Philippine Normal College formed a formidable flank in propagating through textbooks a national language which was hardly different from Tagalog and a Philippine literature which was mainly Tagalog literature.

But of course we need not dwell on the marginalization that Tagalog itself had undergone with the institution of an educational system using English as a medium of instruction and a curriculum which equated language studies with English, and literature with American and British literature. For a time, especially in the '50s and the '60s, Philippine literature was Philippine literature in English. Although Philippine literature written in Spanish appeared in translation in textbooks in English, not even the best of Hiligaynon literature saw itself translated and printed. In short, through a sign system which privileged Tagalog and English, Hiligaynon and the other vernaculars were marginalized twice over. Thus, a sign system in which the center has stood for what is superior and all-pervasive and the off-center for what is inferior and faint had to be re-framed.

But what does re-framing the sign mean? What is the translator's role in the process? This involves a re-valorization of both the translator and the translation act. Having realized that translation is determined by power relations, the translator must seize the initiative from the wielders of power (the translator can, being himself/herself a Sign-Giver and the Sign being capable of telling both truth and lie). This means a voice in the choice of works to translate and the language to translate from and to. A respect for the work and language he/she uses as source, and the determination even within artistic-political confines to shape the language to which he will translate the work. When these are effected, the Sign which draws distinctions between central and periphery shall have been dismantled for a Sign in which these are dissolved. Hiligaynon is Ivatan is Aeta is Ilokano is Kiniray-eng is Filipino. The epigram-become-poem leaps into the text.

Pabay-i ang Bulan
ni Milagros Geremia

'Baw kanami
Bilog liwan ang bulan
dali kita
tubiganay, garabay
shatbong, lagsanay
pabay-i ang tibi
ipabinit ang bitamaks
ti ano gid
kon d'yan run
ang Miyami Bays
ti ano gid
kon Kung Fu Kids
ang now showing
sa balay ni Mal-am Tasing
(nga may bata nga obersis
amo r'a nga may bitamaks)
mabayad pa timo ka pisos
(mahal bay kuryinti sa Antiki)
ti ano gid
kon paamanan nanda
ka sini nga nagaubauba
nagbilin si nanay
nga indi gid maglantaw ka--
ano?
nagaubauba?!
sa diin?!
ano oras maumpisa?!
pabay-i ang tubiganay
pabay-i si nanay
pabay-i ang bulan
mabilog pa man r'a liwan.

NOTES

1. Thomas A. Sebeok was Director of the Research Center for Linguistic and Semiotic Studies at Indiana University up to 1991. He is considered "America's most active and, for some years, its lone semiotician." Cited by Gregory Colomb, "The Semiotic Study of Literary Works," in *Tracing Literary Theory*, ed. Joseph Natoli (Urbana-Champaign: University of Illinois Press, 1990), p. 311.

2. Yolanda Velasco, "A Critical Study of Magdalena Jalandoni as a Novelist with Special Reference to *Ang Bantay sa Patyo*," Unpublished Master's Thesis, University of the Philippines, 1952.

Epilogue

I ended in lightness and frolic, drawing the readers into a game of translating by saying that since what needs to be translated is not just one physical printed text but various cultural texts towards the formation of a national language and literature, translation is a collective enterprise—an endeavor that need not begin from the customary center.

But it was partly to conceal certain nagging thoughts, as one puts on a veneer sometimes to disguise some fears. Although the Sign has been unframed and the way to its re-framing paved, can mere awareness or even actual steps taken to re-frame the sign, hold? The Sentrong Pangkultura ng Pilipinas has taken concrete measures to decenter Philippine literature through regional grants for writing and writing workshops, and the provision of a publishing venue for regional creativity through the *Ani*. Indeed, these are worthy beginnings. But the *Ani* is more of a literary journal, and its circulation pales in comparison with the comics and popular magazines. Although the writers I met in Iloilo were very pleased at the new attention given them, still, how far can ₱5000-₱10,000 in funds for a writing workshop go? The structures that I have referred to—the publications monopoly and the textbook clique—are still active. This recent spur of activity in regional writing, how much influence can it really wield compared to that of the tv and the movies which are also held at the center by monopolies or near-monopolies?

And over in Iloilo, to my disappointment, *Yuhum*, the only magazine in Hiligaynon today other than the recently revived *Hiligaynon*, serializes stories about sophisticated characters from Manila rather than about characters in the region and their experiences, thus abrogating its role as the promoter of Hiligaynon culture. At Central Philippine University (which ranks 11th in the whole Philippines according to the most recent DECS evaluation), the moderator of publications could only show publications in English and say quite frankly (but lamentably) that he had no plans of encouraging Hiligaynon writing. At the Iloilo National High School, the biggest in the province, and alma mater of Conrada Norada and Lucila Hosillos, there are two student newspapers, one in English and the other in Tagalog. Neither features writing in Hiligaynon.

But Agustin Misola glows when he shows me his UMPIL Award for Poetry in Hiligaynon (1990) and very generously gifts me with his books of poetry and his novels (he owns a printing press after all); Raymundo Italia, *hacendero*-politician turned poet, invites me to a poetry writing workshop for Central Iloilo high school teachers at Duenas, Iloilo; Flaviano Manalo, occasional sugilanon writer and moderator of publications for the University of San Agustin, shows me a copy of the most recent issue of the *Augustinian Mirror* which, except for his sugilanon, is solely in English—he tells me, though, of a newly formed poetry guild in the university and of their forthcoming CCP-sponsored poetry workshop in Hiligaynon; Santiago Alv. Mulato, the anointed Bahathari, frail and in his '70s, looks forward to the publication of his *Maragsod* (from *Maragtas*, meaning history, and *sugod*, meaning beginnings) or, the etymology of words in the Hiligaynon language; Leoncio Deriada chuckles with delight, his tummy shaking, boasting that in a recent competition for writing grants there were more entries in Hiligaynon and Kiniray-a than in TagFilipino, and that the *Hari sang Binalaybay* contest (King of Poetry) first held in 1926 with the battle between Eriberto Gumban and Serapion Torre and last held in 1952 with Santiago Alv. Mulato as King, shall be revived with a donation from the Italia family; it is not only Oebanda or Lucero who writes in Hiligaynon or Kiniray-a but also a security guard, students, a bamboo-craftsman, teachers, a radio technician, lawyers, a palm-reader, businessmen, etc. An editorial staff for the new *Hiligaynon* has now been formed at the Liwayway Publications in Makati (will their vision be different from their forebears?). Quirino Baterna, sugilanon writer-turned-realtor and UMPIL Awardee for Hiligaynon Fiction (1993), has drawn from personal funds to sponsor a sugilanon contest. These are more than just stirrings of new life.

Back here in Manila, a Tagalog scholar researches on literary criticism among the various regional groups; another Tagalog scholar speaks of ethnicity and Filipinicity; a Tagalog poet-essayist-critic supports the idea that in CCP writing contests, the Tagalog category should be made separate from Filipino; a Tagalog anthropologist critiques some linguistic and social science researches that pass off Tagalog-based data as Filipino; some members of an English department schooled in John Donne and Shakespeare break away from the cord to research on the Iloko zarzuela and the Cebuano drama, or to write a play in Bikolano; Herminio Beltran frets on how to apportion his limited budget for regional literature.

When I see these and remember the glow in Misola's eyes and the shaking of Deriada's tummy, then I know.

The Sign shall be re-framed.

Part 2

Si Anabella

Magdalena Jalandoni

Tuman kasanag sang bulan, walay labot nga masanag ang kabalayan kay gab-i ini sang paskua sang pagkatao ni Hesus. Ang mga dalagko nga gawang sang pulupalasyuhon nga puluy-an ni Don Juanso Navarro napangwawa sa sini nga gab-i kag tuman nga linanton sang orkestra ang mabatian sa maubus niya nga panalgan, kay isa ka hubon sang ginabantog nga daigon ang ginpasaka sang mga maalwan nga tagbalay.

Gikan sa duha ka aranya nga katya, nagawas-ag sang daw adlaw nga kasanag ang maasul-asulon nga mga bombilya kag sa tunga sang mahalwag nga lagawan mamanahan sing maayo ang nawong sang kadalaganhan nga nanginkatapu sadtong ginabantog nga daigon. Sa tunga sining dili magkubus sa napulo kag anum ka mga lin-ay nga mga bataon kag maayo-ayo, lumutaw sa ila ang kaanyag ni Anabella, isa ka lin-ay nga may kalibugan sang katsila, may tindug nga makabibihag kag may nawong nga sarang isa ka bulak. Ang iya tingug nga matam-is, malanyug kag makalulomay, bumalani sang mabinatyagon nga kasing-kasing ni Tito Navarro, ang bugtong nga manunubli sang manggaranon nga tag-balay. Kay wala sing kasing-kasing nga dili malumay sa pagtan-aw sang kanaya-naya ni Anabella...Nagasaya sia kag nagabayo sing puti nga nasinamayan sang pula, imol sa malahalon nga mga hias, apang manggaranon sa kaayo-ayo, kaangay sa bituon nga nagabanaag sa maitum nga langit kon kagab-ihon.

Ang inamba sang mga malulu nga bilyansiko, ang sinaut kag ang linanton gumuob sa lagawan nga ginapasundan sing mainit nga pamalakpak. Mation-tion pumakita si Tito nga nagabitbit sang malahalon niya nga biolin kag umingud sa luyo ni Anabella sa pagpangabay sing isa ka ambahanon sa dalaga. Ining makabibihag nga manogdaigon wala magpapilit, umamba sia sing isa ka malulu nga *kundiman* nga binuylogan sang lanton sang malahalon nga biolin ni Tito Navarro. Sang pagkatapus, gumuob ang mainit nga pamalakpak sa sulod sang balay, kag ang wala lamang makaamot sa pagpakita sang iya pagdayawa amo si Donya Julia, ang palabilabihon nga iloy ni Tito.

"Sus, sin-o nga bathara ang ginayauban ni Tito ko? Manogdaigon? Makahuluya. Dili ko igtugot nga mabuyok ang akon anak sa isa ka Anabella nga imol," ang nakumod sang nagapangakig nga iloy sa iya hulot.

Sang paglumbos sang daigon, pinapalong ni Donya Julia ang mga masanag nga mga suga sa ila lagawan, kag sa tingug nga puno sang gahum kag pamasul, dinala niya si Tito sa iya hulot kag sumiling:

"Anak ko, indi ko ikagtugot nga maghigugma ka kay Anabella. Buot ako karon nga mangasawa ka sing isa ka babae nga labaw sa aton sa manggad kag sa pagkatalahaon."

"Nanay, ngaa pagkataas sa imo kon manghuluhambal ikaw? Indi bala matuod ang mga imol kag mga manggaranon kon magkalamatay nagasalamo ang ila mga tul-an didto sa patyo?"

"Anak, labaylabay ang ginapanabat mo kay indi ka maluyag nga sabdongon ang imo handum. Buot ko siling nga indi ka magduaw sa puluy-an ni Anabella, kay kon mahibaloan ta, ti ambot lang dira sa imo."

"Maluoy ka Nanay, ayaw pagtamaya inang dalaga nga imol, apang manggaranon sa kaligdong kag sa kaayo-ayo."

"Apang Tito, ngaa nga nagabuang ka sa babae nga wala gani makakilala kon sin-o ang amay? Indi daw ako buot nga magduaw ka liwan sa iya puluy-an."

Sang madason nga gab-i.... Sa ugsaran sang isa ka balay nga kawayan kag nipa nga nahandongan sang isa ka magapa nga akasya, tumunog ang mamingaw kag malulu nga lanton sang biolin nga naga-tuaw sang pilisanguon sang isa ka kalag nga nawad-an sing kalipay. Mation-tion bumukas ang isa ka gawang kag ang gumawa si Anabella sa pagsiling:

"Tito, indi ko ikagtugot nga magseranata ka sa tun-ogan. Nagamata kami ni Nanay kag saka diri sa ibabaw kay bukas sa imo ang ganhaan namon."

Ang ulitao nanagbalay sa hagdanan kag si Anabella sumugata sa iya nga malipayon ang nawong kag dinala sia sa lagawan sa pagtanyag sing isa ka lingkuran.

"Wala ka makabuylog sa daigon karon nga gab-i?" namangkot si Tito.

"Wala, kay naglagnat ang pamatyag ko sang paghalin ko sa inyo kagab-i....Tito, sa indi na ako magdaigon sa inyo balay."

"Ngaa man? Ginapakakubos mo ang amon kahimtangan kon magsubong ka sina."

"Tito, nahuya ako sa imo mga ginikanan....Indi ako angay sa inyo, kag untatl na ang pagduaw diri sa balay."

"Ngaa nga mag-untat ako? Bella, ang halintang nga kawayan sang inyo hagdanan nga akon ginasakaan, ginatan-aw ko sing subong sang siniad sang mga malahalon nga *marfil* nga napanidsiran sing mga bulawan kag pilak kag natampokan sing malahalon nga mga bato. Ining lagawan nga akon ginadayunan amo ang Olimpo nga napun-an sang kasanag kag sang himaya sa diin nagaluntad ang isa ka libo nga kaanyag nga akon ginasimba kag pagasimbahon ko tubtub sa akon kamatayon...."

"Tito, ayaw ka pagkabuyo sa isa ka damgo nga bunga lamang sang hamuok nga katulogon. Manggaranon kamo kag sa tunga sang manggad yara ang kinaugali nga pagpakakubos sa mga imol nga tagsubong sa akon. Dumduma, nagapangabuhi ako sa tinuluan sang balbas sang akon iloy, kag sa tunga sang iya paghilibion nagatug-an sia nga hatagan niya ako sing dunggahanon nga ngalan, katapusan nga palanublion nga sarang ko maangkon sa iya...."

Si Anabella humibi kag tumabon sang iya agtang ang linabag sang kulong niya nga buhuk nga nangin angay sa binan-i nga sukla nga pumutus sa isa ka mutya nga labing mahal.

"Gugma ko, ayaw ka paghibi," ang nasabat ni Tito nga tumulok sing malulu kay Anabella, "walay sapayan nga imol ikaw, higugmaon ta sing labi sa mga maanyag nga bathara sa kalibutan kay sa imo panulok yara ang kabuhi, sa imo yuhum yara ang himaya, kag sa imo tingug yara ang tulalay sang walay kamatayan nga gugma...."

Lumigad ang pila ka adlaw. Sang isa ka hapon nga nagakadagas ang mga bukad sang akasya sa ila ugsaran, nabaton ni Anabella ang isa ka sulat nga nagasiling:

Bella, indi ako makabatas magtapak sing katapusan sa inyo ugsaran kag ginhimo ko ini nga sulat nga amo na lamang ang paalam nga igabilin ko sa imo. Dili ko mapaiway ang ginabuot sang akon mga ginakanan nga nagatulod sa akon sa pagkadto sa Amerika. Huo, makadto ako didto sa paghimpit sang akon pagtuon sa biolin, kag ayhan magaulot ang malawig nga tinuig sa aton pagkitaay. Ang hitabu magapilit sa pagpahilayuay sa aton nga duha, apang sa gihapon magabuylog sa akon ang pagsalig nga pakamahalon mo ako, subong nga ako dili magligab sa pagtuman sang akon panaad sa imo.

Ang magahigugma sa imo tubtub sa kamatayon,

TITO NAVARRO

Tinabon ni Anabella ang sulat sa iya nga mata kag magnguy-ngoy nga subong sang bata nga diutay kag ang iloy nga bumatyag sing daku nga kaawa sa iya anak, dinapulay ang abaga sini kag magsiling:

"Anak ko, tun-i ang paglimot sa kahagugma nga manggaranon nga dili angay sa imo. Sa luyo sang isa ka imol nga bana nga aton kaangay, magabulahan ka nga subong sang mahimayaon nga pispis nga nagasuyup sang matam-is nga dugo sang mga bulak."

"Nanay, luas kay Tito, ang kabulahanan isa ka damgo nga dili nakon makita."

Ang mga inadlaw naghadagas sa duldogan sang binulan, kag ang binulan sa duldogan sang tinuig, kag ang tinuig tumangò sing ikalima sa pulundan sang panahon.

Kutub sang pagtaliwan ni Tito, lima na ka tuig ang lumigad nga si Anabella kag ang iya iloy nadula sa ila dalan kag tuhay na nga mga tinao ang tag-iya sang ila balay. Ang sinugid-sugid madamo sing sari, kag ang balita nga ginapaalinton sang ila mga kilala amo nga si Anabella nahimo manunubli sang napatay niya nga amay, kag sa karon, tunay na sia nga tag-iya sang isa ka matahum nga puluy-an sa malinong nga bahin sang Manila. Ini nga balita wala maglisding sa makatuoran, kay sa lakat sang lima ka tuig, si Anabella subong sang nagdamgo sing matahum sa iya katulogon kag nagmuklat ang iya mga mata sa pagtan-aw sang makakulunyag nga kamatuuran sadto nga damgo.... Ina na sia ang ginasugid nga bathara sa sidlangan nga tag-iya sadtong puluy-an nga nagatagu sang isa ka libo kag isa ka katingalahan. Sia ang tunay nga manunubli sang dako nga manggad nga binilin sa iya sang manggaranon niya nga amay nga dili liwan kundi ang dako nga pumalatikang nga katsila nga si Don Eduardo Aguilar. Ini nga tao, wala sing liwan nga manunubli kundi ang bugtong niya nga anak nga 'si Anabella nga binilin niya sa iloy sini sang iya pagpasipalad sa pagpangita sing pilak.

Apang, magabaylo ayhan ang bugal sa pagkamapainubusan ni Anabella? Kon sang una ginkaakigan sia sang iloy ni Tito Navarro nga nagapangaluyag sa iya, karon ginhandum na sia nga pangumagaron sini nga babae. Karon, madamo na nga Don kag nga Donya ang nagahandum nga mangumagad sa iya kag karon madamo na nga kasingkasing ang nagapakighalad sang paghigugma sa iya kag ang isa nga nagasalimuang sa pagpangaluyag kay Anabella, amo si Lirio Aguilar, ang bataon nga katsila nga hinablus sang iya amay.

"Lirio, pasayloha ako, kag dili na ako makahigugma sa imo. Ang ulitao nga wala pa diri amo ang handum ko nga pagabanahon," ang masunson nga ginasabat sang dalaga sa iya pakaisa.

"Kag sin-o inang bulahan nga tao nga imo ginahandum? Isugid sa akon...."

"Indi ko masugid sa imo," humibi si Anabella kay ang iya kasing-kasing daw malumos sa kahidlaw kay Tito Navarro.

Lima na ka tuig nga naghilayuanay sila ni Tito kag nagdugang pa gid ang iya kahidlaw sang isa ka gab-i nga lumanton ang biolin sa isa ka hulot sang otel nga kaiping sang ila balay. Ang ginalanton sadto nga biolin amo man ang mga kundiman nga ginapabati sa iya ni Tito. Naghibi sia sa pagpanganibaw sadtong matam-is nga handumanon sang iya kabuhi kon maglanton sa kagabihon ang katingalahan nga biolin nga iya ginapamatian.

Sa sini nga adlaw nagahilapit na ang kaadlawan sang paskua sang Pagkatao. Si Anabella nagahanda sing masadya nga tinipun-tipon sa sulud sang iya puluy-an nga pagahiwaton sa malipayon nga gab-i sang Paskua. Si Lirio amo ang isa sang nagapanikusog nga magmadlaagon sini nga tinipun-tipon ang isa ka pandita sang lanton nga bag-o nag-abut diri halin sa Amerika.

Umabot ang mahimayaon nga gab-i sang pagkatao. Ang engkantohanon nga puluy-an ni Anabella punu sang ginatus nga mga tumalambong, punu sang lanton kag sang kasanag. Sa tunga sadtong lagawan nga nalam-us sang sidlanganon nga mga puni, masaksihan ta ang inalun-alon sang mga sukla, ang dinabadaba sang mga brilyante kag ang inalisbong sang mga pahumot.

Sa tunga sang hinigugma nga bataon nga tumalambong, si Lirio Aguilar tumindug kag magsiling:

"Talahuron nga mga dinapit, hinabu ini nga mamati kita sang lanton sang isa ka pandita sa biolin nga bag-o naghalin sa Amerika kag ginapadungug ko ang pagpakilala sa inyo kay Tito Navarro...."

Ang guban nga pamalakpak tumugob sa lagawan kag pumakita sa tunga sang mga talahuron nga pinandapit ang makabibihag nga dagway sang bansagon nga manoglanton. Nagapanapot sing lubos puti kag nagabitbit sang malahalon nga biolin ang tuo niya nga kamot.

Sa tapus sia makaduku sang iya ulo, winas-ag ni Tito ang katingalahan nga lalantunon nga nagpabati sa tanan sing dili matapus nga pagdayaw. Isa ka mainit nga pamalakpak ang gumuob sa lagawan sang pagkatapus, kag ang wala makabuylog sa pagtukap sang iya kamot amo si Anabella nga dumuko sa iya lingkuran kag maghibi sa tagu lamang. Mation-tion pumalapit si Lirio sa iya luyo nga nagadapit sa manoglanton kag magsiling:

"Bella, ginapadungug ko ang pagpakilala sa imo kay Gg. Tito Navarro, ang sampaton nga manoglanton nga bag-o naton nabatian."

Si Anabella tumulok kay Tito nga puno sang luha ang iya mga mata kag dungan sa pagdahu niya sang kamot sini, sumiling:

"Tito, wala ako makalimot sa imo...."

Isa ka madalum nga hibubun-ot ang ginapautwan ni Anabella kay daw mamudmod ang iya tagipusuon. Si Tito umuyat sa mahumok niya nga kamot kag sumabat:

"Bella, sa gihapon ginahigugma ko ikaw, kag walay tion nga malimot ako sa imo."

Ang mga saksi sadtong masadya nga tinipun-tipon sa balay ni Anabella, sang lumigad ang pila ka adlaw, sumaksi liwan sa maduagon niya nga kasal kay Tito Navarro, ang bugtong niya nga kahagugma nga wala magkalimot sa iya.

Ini nga hitabu natuon sa kaadlawan sa tatlo ka Hari kag sang paghalin sa simbahan sang bag-ong kasal, kumadto sila sa diutay nga *Belen* sa ila puluy-an sa paghalad kay Ninyo Hesus sang balaan nila nga gugma, subong sang pagdulot sang tatlo ka Hari sang malahalon nila nga mga halad.

Halus lang sila makahalin didto, isa ka suluguon ang nagtunghol sa nobya sing isa ka sulat. Ini nga sulat binukasan nila kag amo ini ang natugan.

Gng. Anabella ni Navarro:

Pinalangga ko nga anak:

Sa ubos makaligad ang lima ka tuig kutub sang pagdaigon ninyo sa balay, gintugot sang kapalaran nga mangin-umagad ko ikaw. Ang panahon nagalakat kag sa tagsa niya ka tikang nagapakita sang pagbaylo sang mga butang. Kon sang una gintamay ko ikaw kag gin-kaakigan tungud nga imol ikaw kag kubos kaayo sing kahimtangan kon itupad sa akon anak, karon wala ako sing sarang masiling kundi nga pasaylohan ako, kag pasayloha ang akon pagkapalabilabihon. Karon pa lamang ang akon pagkatalupangud nga ang manubu may pagtaas, kag ang mataas may pagnubu kon iwakli sang kapalaran. Sa sining bulahan nga kaadlawan sang inyo kasal, isa ka haluk ang ginadulot ko sa imo, haluk sang isa ka iloy nga walay paglus-aw tubtub sa kamatayan.

Ang nagapalangga sa inyo,

JULIA

From *Hinugpong nga Sugilanon*
(Collection of *Sugilanon* 1936-1938)

Anabella

Magdalena Jalandoni

The moon shone brightly that Christmas night. *Don* Juan's palatial home was illuminated and its large doors were wide open. Its first floor was filled with the strains of music by a well-known orchestra whom the gracious hosts had earlier welcomed upstairs.

Bluish bulbs from two crystal chandeliers radiated light as bright as day on the spacious living room where young women from a famous group were singing. There must have been no less than sixteen of them and all were pretty, but the one who stood out was the beautiful Anabella, a young Spanish mestiza with a lovely bearing and a flower-like face. Her soprano voice, sweet and gentle, captivated Tito Navarro, the sole heir of the owner of the house. For indeed, no one could resist the charm of Anabella. Dressed in a white *baro* and *saya* with red stripes, she wore no expensive jewelry, but was as beautiful as a star glowing in the night.

The songs, the dance and the orchestra numbers all drew warm applause. Then, with his precious violin in hand, Tito approached Anabella to request her to sing. The alluring lady did not refuse. Accompanied by Tito's violin, she sang a tender *kundiman* which the audience heartily applauded. Only *Doña* Julia, the proud and haughty mother of Tito seemed displeased.

"*Sus*, who is this goddess Tito adores? A singer? How shameful! I shall not allow him to be smitten by someone as poor as Anabella," the mother grumbled in her bedroom.

After the carolers had left, *Doña* Julia ordered the lights turned off. She then called Tito into her room and in a tone full of authority and rebuke, she said:

"My son, you cannot carry on this way with Anabella. You ought to marry a woman with more wealth and name than we have."

"Mother, why must you be so snobbish? At death, do not the bones of the poor and the rich mingle?"

"You're changing the topic because you don't want me to stop you. Really, Tito, you must not see her again. If you persist, then you better watch out."

"But have a heart, mother! Don't be harsh! Anabella is poor but lovely and decent."

"Tito, I don't understand! Why must you go crazy over someone who doesn't even know who her father is? Listen, I don't want you to visit her at her house—never again."

The following night, at the doorstep of a bamboo and nipa house shaded by the drooping branches of an *acacia*, the plaintive tone of a violin drifted out to soothe a soul that seemed to have lost all joy. After some moments, a door opened and Anabella appeared, saying:

"Tito, I can't let you serenade me out there in the chilly night. Mother and I are still awake; come up. You're welcome."

After the young man said his *tagbalay* at the staircase, Anabella went down happily to meet him. Then, she led him to the sala where she offered him a seat.

"You didn't join the carolers tonight?" Tito asked.

"No. After coming from your house last night, I caught a cold...Tito, I will not go carolling at your house again."

"Must you belittle us so?"

"It's just that I cannot face your parents. I'm not worthy of your family; so please, you've got to stop seeing me."

"Why must I, Bella? The bamboo stairs of this house are to me like pieces of ivory rimmed with gold and silver and studded with precious stones. This sala is Mt. Olympus filled with brightness and bliss for here dwell a thousand graces which I worship now and will continue to worship until I die."

"Tito, you must not believe in a dream that comes only from deep sleep. You are rich, and among your kind, it is usual to look down on people like me. Just think, I live only on the solemn pledge of my father that someday he will give me his name. This is the only legacy I may be able to get from him."

Anabella wept, her forehead covered by the curls of her hair which seemed like silk hiding a precious pearl.

"My love, do not cry," Tito consoled Anabella as he looked at her tenderly. "No, it doesn't matter that you are poor. I shall love you more than any beauty in this world for in your eyes is my life, in your smile is my happiness, and in your voice is the song of my undying love."

A few days passed. One afternoon, when the acacia was shedding its leaves, Anabella received a letter which said the following:

> Bella, I cannot bear to bid you goodbye at the doorstep of your house, so I am writing this letter instead to say, 'farewell.' I can no longer go against the wishes of my parents; they're pushing me to fly to America. Yes, I shall go there to take further studies in the violin and the long years will come between us. Circumstances have forced us apart, but I shall keep with me the hope that you will continue to love me even as I vow never to break my promise to you.
>
> From him who will love you till death,
>
> TITO NAVARRO

Anabella covered her eyes with the letter and sobbed like a child. Her mother, feeling pity for her, stroked her shoulders and said:

"My child, you must learn to forget a lover who isn't right for you. If you marry a man of your own status, you shall be as happy as a bird sipping sweet nectar."

"But mother, without Tito, happiness will only be a dream unfulfilled."

The days turned into months, the months into years, until five years finally passed.

After Tito left, Anabella and her mother gave up their house and another family came to live there. There were all kinds of rumors. But what Anabella's friends spread was that she had been made sole heir to her father who had died. Now, she was the owner of a beautiful house in a quiet neighborhood in Manila. This was not far from the truth. In the last five years, it was as if Anabella had dreamt a delightful dream, and upon waking, her eyes beheld the dream come true. She was now known as the bright star in the east—owner of a house of a thousand wonders and heiress to the great wealth of her father. He was none other than the Spanish businessman *Don* Eduardo Aguilar who had left Anabella and her mother many years before to seek his fortune.

But did Anabella change? Did she become proud? Tito's parents who despised her once, now wanted her to be their daughter-in-law, and so did a lot of *Dons* and *Doñas*. Many suitors raved about her. One of them was Lirio Aguilar, the young nephew of her late father.

"Lirio, forgive me, but I cannot give my love to you any more. I've pledged to marry another man," Anabella repeatedly told her cousin.

"And who is this lucky man?"

"I'm sorry but I can't tell you," she replied. And Anabella wept because her heart was filled with longing for Tito.

Tito had been away for five years, but she pined for him even more when she would hear the sound of the violin from a hotel beside her house. The melody was that of the same *kundiman* Tito would play to her during those happy days. And each night she would hear this song, she would recall the sweet memories with her lover.

Christmas was drawing near. Anabella was preparing to host a grand party at her house on Christmas night, and Lirio was one of those arranging for an accomplished violinist to perform at the gathering. He had just arrived from America.

On that joyful Christmas night, Anabella's home was simply enchanting. Hundreds of guests came, music filled the place, and the lights were ablaze. In the huge parlor dazzlingly bedecked, silk rippled, diamonds sparkled, and perfume permeated the air.

In the midst of the young guests, Lirio Aguilar stood up and said:

"Most worthy guests, we are privileged to have here tonight, a violin virtuoso who has just arrived from America. May I introduce to you, Mr. Tito Navarro."

Applause broke out in the living room and among the guests that had now drawn close together, appeared the handsome face of the well-esteemed musician. He was dressed entirely in white and was holding an expensive violin in his right hand.

After taking a bow, Tito played his violin music, enthralling everyone. The guests cheered him with great enthusiasm; the only one who did not congratulate Tito was Anabella who had bowed her head and was weeping silently in her seat. Lirio brought the violinist up to her and said:

"Bella, I have the pleasure to introduce to you, Mr. Tito Navarro, the master violinist."

With tears welling in her eyes, Anabella looked at the young man, and shaking his hand, she said:

"Tito, in my heart, I have never forgotten you."

Anabella sighed deeply for she felt as if her heart would crumble from the pain. Tito reached for her soft hands and replied:

"Bella, I have loved you always and not for a single moment did the thought of you leave me."

Those who were present at the celebration that night were also on hand at the joyous wedding of Anabella to Tito Navarro, her one and only love. This event coincided with the feast of the Three Kings. From the Church, the newly-married couple went straight home to pray at their small *Belen*. There, they offered their enduring love to the *Santo Niño*, in the same way that the Three Kings had gifted Him with their precious presents.

The couple had just finished praying when a servant handed a letter to the bride. They opened the letter which said the following:

Mrs. Anabella Navarro

My dear children:

Five years after you had come caroling at our house, fortune willed for you to become my daughter-in-law. Time passes; at every single step, it brings on changes. I scorned you for being poor and socially inferior to us but now there is nothing more I can do but beg for your forgiveness. Forgive me for my arrogance. Only now have I realized that the lowly can rise and the high and the mighty can fall, if fate so decrees. On this happy day of your wedding, I give you a kiss, one that shall remain unfaded until I die.

Love,

JULIA

Si Anabella

Magdalena Jalandoni

Lubhang maliwanag ang buwan; maliwanag din ang pamamahay dahil gabi ito ng pagsilang ni Hesus. Nakawangwang ang malalaking pintuan ng malapalasyong tahanan ni Don Juanso Navarro at ang tanging naririnig sa unang palapag ay ang himig ng orkestra; nanggaling ito sa isang tanyag na pangkat ng mang-aawit na tinanggap ng magiliw na maybahay.

Mula sa dalawang aranyang kristal, kumalat na tila araw na liwanag ang malaasul na bombilya sa maaliwalas na salas na kung saan kitang-kita ang magagandang binibining bumubuo sa bantog na pangkat. Sa gitna nitong di-hihigit sa labinsiyam na magandang dalagita, lumitaw ang kariktan ni Anabella: isang dalagang may gandang Kastila, may tindig na nakabibighani, at may mukhang tulad ng isang bulaklak. Ang tinig niyang matamis at mataas ay bumihag sa maramdaming puso ni Tito Navarro, ang tanging tagapagmana ng mayamang maybahay. Sadyang walang pusong di-naaakit kung makamalas sa kagandahan ni Anabella. Naka-saya siya at nakablusang puti na pinaguhitan ng pula, walang mamahaling alahas ngunit pinagpala ng kagandahang tulad ng bituing nagniningning sa kadiliman ng gabi.

Ang magigiliw na awit, ang mga sayaw at tugtugin ng orkestra na pumapailalang sa bulwagan ay sinundan ng matinding palakpakan. Ilang sandali pa, lumabas si Tito na bitbit ang isang mamahaling biolin at lumapit kay Anabella para humingi ng isang awit sa dalaga. Hindi na pinilit ang kabigha-bighaning mang-aawit, kumanta siya ng isang makababagbag damdaming kundiman na sinaliwan naman ng mamahaling biolin ni Tito Navarro. Pagkatapos nito, pumailalang sa buong bahay ang matinding palakpakan. Ang tangi lamang hindi nagbigay ng papuri ay si Donya Julia, ang mapangmatang ina ni Tito.

"Sus, sinong diyos-diyosa itong ginasuyo gid sang Tito ko? Isa ka mang-aawit? Makahuluya...! Indi ko ipahihintulut magumon ang aking anak diri kay Anabellang mahirap lamang," ang pagngingitngit ng ina ni Tito sa kwarto.

Pagkaalis ng mga mang-aawit, iniutos ni Donya Juliang patayin ang maliwanag na ilaw sa kanilang bulwagan, dinala niya si Tito sa kanyang silid, at sa tinig na malakas at naninisi, kinausap ito:

"Anak ko, indi ko gid mapahihintulutang umibig ka kay Anabella. Nais ko nga makapag-asawa ka sang babaye nga higit sa aton sa kayamanan at pangalan."

"Nanay, bakit man napakamapagtaas niyo kung gasalita? Indi bala, sa kamatayan napaghahalo ang mga buto sa libingan, dukha man o mayaman?"

"Anak, kung anu-ano ang pinagsasabi mo para lang indi kita mapigil sa nais mo. Basta, indi ko gustong dumalaw ka kay Anabella. Pag nalaman ko, ti ambot sa imo."

"Maawa ka naman, 'Nay. Huwag kang malupit sa dalagang mahirap ngunit mayaman naman sa kagandahan at kabaitan."

"Tito, ba't ka ba nabubuang sa babaeng indi nga nakakikilala sa kanyang tatay? Basta't ayaw kong dumalaw ka uli sa kanyang bahay."

Sa sumunod na gabi...sa may hagdanan ng bahay-kawayan at nipa sa lilim ng malaylay na akasya, tumunog ang malungkot at makabagbag-damdaming himig ng biolin; kaaliw-aliw ito sa pusong namimighati. Ilang sandali pa, bumukas ang pintuan at lumabas si Anabella. Ang sabi niya:

"Tito, indi ko gusto nga mahamugan ka sa paghaharana. Gising pa kami ni Nanay. Umakyat ka, at bukas ang pinto namon sa imo."

Nagmagandang-gabi si Tito. Masayang-masaya na sinalubong siya ni Anabella. Dinala sa salas at pinaupo roon.

"Indi ka nagsama sa mga nagkaroling?" tanong ni Tito.

"Indi. Nilagnat ako pagkagaling sa inyo kagab-i...Tito indi na ako aawit sa inyong tahanan."

"Bakit naman? Minamaliit mo kami kung gawin mo iyan."

"Nahuya ako sa imo nga mga magulang, Tito...indi ako bagay sa iyo; at tigilin mo na ang pagdalaw mo diri."

"Ba't ako titigil? Bella, ang bawat baitang nitong kawayang-hagdanang aking hinahakbangan ay parang piraso ng mamahaling marmol na nasidlan ng mga ginto't pilak at pinagtamnan ng mga mamahaling bato. Ang salang ito ay Olimpong puno ng liwanag at sanlibong biyaya at kagandahang ginasamba ko at sasambahin hanggang kamatayan."

"Tito, indi ka mahalina sa isang panaginip na bunga lamang ng isang mahimbing na pagkatulog. Mayaman kayo, at sa mga mayayaman nariyan ang ugaling mangmata sa mga dukhang tulad ko. Alalahanin mo, nabubuhay lamang ako sa tulo ng pawis ng aking ina, at sa kanyang paghihirap, nangangako siyang bibigyan niya ako sang marangal nga pangalan, katangi-tanging pamana na maangkon ko sa kanya."

Umiyak si Anabella at natakpan ang kanyang noo ng mga ikid ng kanyang kulot na buhok na kasingtulad ng sutlang bumabalot ng mamahaling perlas.

"Mahal ko, indi ka na mag-iyak," sagot ni Tito, habang magiliw na tumingin kay Anabella. "Wala sa akin kung mahirap ka. Palanggaon kita nang higit pa sa maririkit na diyosa sa buong mundo dahil sa iyong mga mata nariyan ang buhay; sa iyong ngiti, nandiyan ang kaligayahan, sa iyong tinig, ang awit ng walang kamatayang pagmamahal...."

Lumipas ang ilang araw. Isang hapong nangaglagas ang mga bukadkad ng akasya sa may hagdanan nila, natanggap ni Anabella ang mga sulat na nagsasabi:

> Bella, indi ko matiis tumapak ng huling hakbang sa iyong hagdanan, kaya't ginawa ko itong sulat nga amo na lamang ang maging paalam ko sa imo. Indi ko matanggihan ang kagustuhan ng aking mga magulang na nagtutulak sa aking pumunta sa Amerika. Huo, pupunta ako roon para makasa ang aking pagtugtog ng biolin at maari sigurong mamamagitan ang maraming taon sa ating pagkikita. Nagpupumilit ang mga pangyayaring paghiwalayin kitang duha, ngunit

nakakapagluwag sa loob ko ang pagtitiwalang pakamahalin mo ko, tulad ko ring hindi kailanman sisira sa aking pangako sa iyo.

Ang gapalangga sa imo hasta kamatayan,

TITO NAVARRO

Tinakpan ni Anabella ng sulat ang kanyang mga mata at ngumuyngoy na parang isang batang maliit. Nakaramdam ng malaking pagkaawa ang ina sa kanyang anak, at nagsabi:

"Anak ko, pag-aralan mong limutin ang kasintahan mo. Mayaman siya, alangan kita sa ila. Sa piling ng isang banang dukha tulad natin, magiging mapalad ka at maligaya kagaya ng masasayang ibon na sumisipsip ng matamis na dagta ng bulaklak."

"Nanay, kung wala si Tito, ang kaligayahan ay parang panaginip na di ko kailanman makikita."

Ang mga araw ay sumapit sa buwan, ang mga buwan ay naging mga taon, at ang mga taon nama'y sumapit sa ikalimang hagpang ng panahon.

Mula nang umalis si Tito, limang taon na ang nakalipas na wala si Anabella at ang kanyang ina sa kanilang kalye; at iba na ang nakatira sa kanilang bahay. Marami ang naging usap-usapan tungkol sa kanila, at kumalat sa kanilang mga kakilala ang balitang naging tagapagmana si Anabella ng yumao niyang ama, at ngayon, ligal na siyang may-ari ng isang marangyang tahanan sa isang tahimik na distrito sa Maynila. Hindi lumihis sa katotohanan ang balita. Pagkalipas ng limang taon, parang nanaginip si Anabella ng isang magandang panaginip at namulat ang kanyang mga mata sa kalugod-lugod na katotohanan ng kanyang panaginip. Isa na siya sa pinakamaganda sa silangan at maybahay ng isang tahanang nagtatago ng isang libo at isang bagay na kamangha-mangha. Siya ang tunay na tagapagmana ng malaking kayamanan ng masalaping Don Eduardo Aguilar, ang tanyag na Kastilang mangangalakal. Walang ibang tagapagmana ito kundi ang bugtong niyang anak na si Anabella na iniwan niya sa ina upang makipagsapalaran at makahanap ng pera.

Ngunit pumalit kaya ang kahambugan sa kababaang-loob ni Anabella? Kung noong una, hinamak siya ng ina ni Tito Navarro na nanliligaw sa kanya, ngayon ninanais na siyang maging manugang nito. Ngayon, marami ng don at doñang naghahangad maging manugang siya at ngayon marami na ring mga puso ang umaalay sa kanya ng kanilang pagmamahal. Isa sa mga nahihibang sa kanya si Lirio Aguilar—isang binatang kastila na pamangkin ng kanyang ama.

"Lirio, ipagpaumanhin mo ako, at indi kita maaring ibigin pa. Isang binatang wala pa rito ang nais kong pakasalan," ang laging sagot ng dalaga sa kanyang pinsan.

"Sin-o itong mapalad na napupusuan mo? Sabihin mo sa akin."

"Indi ko maaaring sabihin sa iyo," umiyak si Anabella dahil ang kanyang puso'y parang malunod sa pananabik kay Tito Navarro.

Limang taon nang nagkahiwalay sila ni Tito at nadagdagan pa ang kanyang pangungulila nang isang gabi, tumugtog ang biolin sa otel na katapat ng kanilang bahay. Ang itinugtog ay tulad rin sa mga kundimang pinaririnig sa kanya noon ni Tito. At umiyak siya sa pag-aalala ng kanyang matamis na kahapon kung tumutugtog tuwing gabi ang kahanga-hangang biolin.

Nalalapit na ang Pasko ng Pagkatao. Naghahanda si Anabella ng masayang pagtitipun-tipong idaraos sa kanyang tahanan sa maligayang gabi ng Pasko. Si Lirio ang isa sa mga nagsikap na mag-anyaya rito ng isang ekspertong biolinista na kararating lang sa Amerika.

Dumating ang masayang gabi ng pagkatao. Sa malaenkantadong tahanan ni Anabella na puno ng sandaang panauhin, pumailanlang ang magandang himig ng biolin.

Sa gitna ng mga kabataang dumalo, tumindig si Lirio Aguilar at nagsabi:

"Kagalang-galang na panauhin, pagkakataon itong makarinig tayo ng musika ng isang ekspertong biolinistang galing lang sa Amerika. Ikinalulugod kong ipakilala sa inyo si Tito Navarro...."

Isang masigabong palakpakan ang sumanib sa bulwagan at lumitaw sa gitna ng mga panauhing nangatag-op, ang nakabibihag na anyo ng bantog na biolinist. Nakagayak siya ng puro puti, at bitbit ang mamahaling biolin ng kanyang kanang kamay.

Pagkasaludo nito, pinakawalan ni Tito ang alindog ng musikang bumighani sa lahat. Isang masigabong palakpakan ang umugong sa bulwagan; ang tangi lamang di-pumalakpak ay si Anabella. Nanatili siyang nakayuko sa kanyang upuan at lihim na umiiyak. Ilang sandali pa lumapit si Lirio sa kanya, yakag ang biolinista at nagsabi:

"Bella, ikinararangal kong ipakilala sa iyo si G. Tito Navarro, ang dalubhasang musikong napakinggan lang natin."

Tumingin si Anabella kay Tito, puno ng luha ang mga mata at sabay sa pag-abot niya ng kanyang kamay ay nagsabi:

"Tito, indi gid kita nalimtan...."

Bumuntong-hininga ng malalim si Anabella dahil pakiramdam niya'y parang mawawasak ang kanyang puso. Hinawakan ni Tito ang malambot niyang kamay, at nagtapat:

"Bella, hanggang ngayon, ginamahal ko ikaw, at indi ako nakalimot sa iyo ni anumang sandali."

Makalipas ang ilang araw, ang mga nagdalo sa masayang pagtitipong iyon, dumalo uli sa maligayang kasal ni Anabella kay Tito Navarro, ang katangi-tangi niyang minamahal na hindi rin nakalimot sa kanya.

Nataon ang pag-iisang dibdib na ito sa kapistahan ng Tatlong Hari. Pagkaalis sa simbahan, sinadya ng mga bagong kasal ang maliit na Belen sa kanilang tahanan upang mag-alay sa Niño Hesus ng kanilang walang-katapusang pag-ibig, tulad ng paghahandog ng Tatlong Hari kay Hesus ng mga malahaling alay. Saglit lang silang nakaalis dito nang isang utusan ang umabot sa kanila ng isang sulat. Binuksan nila ito at binasa:

Gng. Anabella Navarro:

Minamahal kong anak:

Halos limang taon taon na ang nakalipas mula nang mamasko kayo sa aming bahay, ipinahintulot ng kapalaran na maging manugang ko ikaw. Nagalakad ang panahon at sa bawat hakbang nito nagapakita ng pagbabago ang mga bagay. Kung noong una ginghamak kita at gingkagalitan dahil ikaw ay mahirap at alangan sa katayuan ng aking anak, ngayon wala akong maaring sabihin kundi humingi ng pagpaumanhin, at patawad mo sa aking pagmamataas. Ngayon ko naunawaan na ang hamak ay nagiging dakila din, at ang mapagmataas ay nagiging hamak din kung siyang itulot ng kapalaran. Nitong maligayang araw ng inyong kasal, isang halik ang dulot ko sa iyo, halik ng isang ina at walang-pagkupas hanggang sa kamatayan.

Ang nagapalangga sa inyo,

JULIA

Bunyag-Takas

Lucila V. Hosillos

Nabatyagan niya ang pagbalhin sang iya kalawasan. Magasulod na karon sa isa ka bulan nga daw sa indi niya mahangpan ang iya kaugalingon. Karon pa lang niya mabatyagan ini nga balatyagon. Ginhimutaran niya ang iya nawong sa matin-aw nga tubig sang bubonbubon nga iya ginkutkot sa bibi sang suba. Wala sia sing may nakita nga pagliwat sang iya pangbayhon, apang nabatyagan niya nga may naglain sa iya pangguyahon. Nagpadayon sia sang iya pagpanglaba kag gindalidali niya ang pagpangbunlaw sang mga panapton sang iya mga manghod kay nagasingkal na ang init. Kinahanglan nga makapauli na sia kag makadigamo sa pag-abot ni Tatay kag ni Nanay niya halin sa talamnan.

Ginsaylo niya ang iya panulok sa malayo. Sa unhan nagakipawkipaw sa initan ang atop sang ila balay. Ang banas nga nagaubay sa suba pakadto sa dalan mahawan, apang ang nagasipak pakadto sa ila balay masiot. Wala pa magaid ang karabaw nga ginagamit ni Tatay niya sa pag-arado sa puno sang pahu sa kilid sang ila balay. Wala pa sila makatapos sa talamnan.

Malinong ang iya palibot sanglit ang halos tanan sa baryo nagaarado kag nagabungkag sang talanman. Sa tunga sang kalinong naghari sa iya ang mga balatyagon kag painuino nahanungod sang iya kaugalingon nga indi niya mahangpan. Nagaisahanon sia. Ang iya mga ginikanan kag kautoran daw sa nagapalayo nga palayo sa iya. Daw indi niya madab-ot ang ila mga panghunahona kag balatyagon. Daw indi niya mapasayod sa ila ang iya mga ginabatyag kag ginaisip.

Sa sini nga mga tinion, daw malapit pa sa iya ang pag-igot sang kawayanan sa tabok-suba. Daw nakahangop pa sang iya balatyagon ang mga alibangbang nga nagapulopalapit sang buot maghapon sa mga bulak sang lumboy nga iya ginapahandungan. Ang katagsing sang tagwati daw nagapanungkad sing iya balatyagon kag nagapamangkot kon ano ang iya ginapanundom. Kag ang magagmay nga pagbaludbalod sang tubig nga nagadapyadapya sa iya mga tiil sa balas daw nagapakigabyan kag nagapakighambal sa iya balatyagon.

Hinali nga nagtambong sa iya panghandurawan ang dagway sang iya amay. Maniwang apang mapag-on sing panglawason. Maugdang sing pangnawong kag manayanaya sing pangguyahon. Ang panghulag kag panulok daw banawan sang matawhay nga pamatyagon kag maayo nga kabubot-on. Apang ini nga kaayo sang pamatasan kag sang kapiot sang ila pagpangabuhi amo ang ginahalinan sang alawayon ni Tatay kag ni Nanay niya. Tungod sang pagkahumok sang tagipusuon sang iya amay, indi ini makahibalo makigsuay sa tag-iya sang duta nga ila ginaagsahan bisan ginasaklam sini ang ila bahin sang patubas nga humay. Kon makigsuay gid man ang iya amay madali nga dayon naman paubos kag ginakahuya ang pagsabat bisan sa kay Pablo nga engkargado lang ni Don Ramon. Kapin pa gid kon ang iya ginaatubang ang Senyor ukon ang Senyorito nga si Ramoncito. Ang iya amay wala na nagapaathag ukon nagapamalibad. Daw apa kag wala na sing nahibaluan nga inughambal. Nagayuhomyuhom kag nagakulokadlaw na lang. Nagahuo nga nagasulusaludo kag nagatangutango. Tungod kay nahibaluan sang ila mga amo nga maayo sing kabubot-on ang iya amay ginapadak-an sila sang hilikuton nga wala ginabayari, ginadaya sila sa isipay sang humay, kag ginapasobrahan ang ila utang ukon mga balayran.

Ungon ang kahalimbawa sa ini nga mga hitabo sa iya dughan kag painuino. Daku ang pagbasol niya sa iya amay kag kon kaisa nagaapin sia sa kay nanay niya kon ini magpangakig sa iya amay. Apang kon makita niya ang nawong sang iya amay nga wala gid sing landong sang kaakig, aligutgot, ukon dumot, nagalain ang iya kabubot-on sa iya iloy.

Ang pagpamintaha sang ila mga amo nagpukaw sa iya dughan sang mapait nga katahap kag daku nga kahadlok apang indi pa gid maathag sa iya lamharon pa nga panghunahona kon tungod sa ano. Sa ila mga kaingod nga masunson nagapamati sa pag-away sang iya mga ginikanan wala sia nagakahuya kundi nagapangakig, kay iya nasat-uman nga nagakalipay ini sila sing tagu kay may labi pa sa ila kapiot sing pangabuhi. Karon, samtang nagapanglaba sia, nagapalangluya ang iya lawas sa pagpanumdom sang ila kahimtangan.

Sa sulod sang isa ka bulan daw sa hinali nga tinuboan sia sing buot. Daw may nagpukaw sang iya balatyagon kag panghunahona tuhoy sa ila kahimtangan. Sa hinali nga nagbugtaw ang iya kaugalingon sa mga libog kag hapdi sang ila pagpangabuhi. Tungod ayhan ini kay nagahinalaga na sia? Indi sia mahim-os. Wala nagapahimuyong ang iya panghunahona kag balatyagon. Wala pahuway ang iya pagpainuino, bisan naga digamo sia, nagatanom, nagapangani, nagapangahoy, kag kon kaisa bisan ginahambal sia. Nanuhaytohay nga mga bagay kag palanundomon ang nagasabaysabay sa iya panghunahona, handurawan kag dalamguhanon.

Dungan sang paghumlad sang iya paghangop sang ila kahimtangan nga daw wala katibawasan, nabatyagan niya ang pagbalhin sang iya lawas kag ang iya kahuloy-on kon may masat-uman sia nga may nagatulok sa iya. Karon iya nadumdoman ang natabo sa iya sadtong nagligad nga simana sing ila pagdugok sa piyesta sang San Rafael. Ang tagpakilala sang reyna nagbinalaybay sang masunod nga mga dinalan:

Si Inday
Pahu nga nagapanglumbay
Ang dagway
Bulak nga nagakamung-ay.

Ang katam-is sang mga tinaga nga ini iya ginbatyag nga ginapatungod kag ginapatuhoy sa iya. Nabatyagan niya nga daw nagpamukadkad ang iya balatyagon kag ang iya panghunahona, ang iya bilog nga lawas kag ang mga bagay nga natungod sa iya pagkababae. Sa bug-os niya nga pangabuhi, amo pa lang sadto nga hitabo niya mabatyagan ang iya kaugalingon nga pagkatao, nga sia gali nagaginhawa, nagahulag, nagadako, "nagapanglumbay" kag nagapamulak.

Sugod sadto, nasat-uman na niya ang pagbag-o sang iya tingog, ang paglain sang iya panulok, ang pagbalhin sang iya panghulag. Ginlain niya ang panghusay sang iya buhok, ang pagsul-ob sang iya panapton, kag ang iya paglakatlakat. Sugod sadto, iya nabatyagan nga sia may pagkaibog sa mga bagay nga iya makita sa iban, pagkahisa sang maayo sing pangabuhi. Iya nasat-uman ang halos wala katibawasan nga pagpangagsa sang duta. Bisan daw ano nga panikasog sang bug-os nga panimalay kag pagpatial nila sa ulanan kag initan, wala nagadugang ang ila patubas. Tigaylo nga mabuhinan ang ila utang, tapat gani nga nagadugang.

Apang kon nagbaylo ang iya panuloktulok sa mga tao kag mga bagay, nagabalhin man ang panulok sang mga isigkatao sa iya. Namulalongan niya nga kon kaisa maukod nga ginatulok sia sang mga ulitao, kapin pa sadtong adlaw nga Mierkoles nga adlaw sang tiyenda sa banwa kay nakasul-ob sia sing maayo-ayo nga bayu kag nakapanghipid. Apang indi pa niya mahangpan ang mga kahulogan sini nga mga bagay. Nahibaloan niya nga ginasat-om sang kon sin-o man nga nagahimutad sa iya nga ginalikaw niya ang iya panulok sa daku nga pagkahuya kag pagkagumon sang iya balatyagon kag panghunahona.

Karon, sa iya pag-isahanon, daw masinggit sia sa iya mga ginikanan, kaingod, kag sa bilog nga kalibutan nga kon mahimo buligan sia sa paghangop sini nga mga hitabo sa iya kaugalingon. Apang wala sing tingog nga kumawas sa iya mga bibig. Sa unhan, daw nagapalayo kag nagapalayo pa gid ang ila balay. Sa iya palibot, wala sing bisan dahon nga nagakulas. Ang adlaw mataas na kag nagsingkal pa gid ang init. Ang tubig sa suba naglabaab na kag bisan sa handong sang magapa nga lumboy iya mabatyagan ang tagiti sang init. Nagpanihol sia, hampang nga nagapanawag sang hangin, apang bisan ang kakugnan kag mga paklang sing lubi sa pihak sang pangpang wala gid maghulolag. Namubo sia sang pila ka kabu nga tubig. Nabatyagan niya ang daw pag-aso sang iya lawas. Nabugnawan sia kag daw nagpagsik ang iya kalawasan.

Apang sa malip-ot nga mga tinion, daw sa ginahilantan naman sia. Indi mapunggan nga nagabalik ang iya painuino sa madamo nga mga hitabo sa ila pagpangabuhi. Indi na naman sia mahim-os sang iya madumdoman ang pag-agi ni Ramoncito sa ila balay sadtong Domingo sing hapon lamang.

Nagapanilhig sia sa ila ugsaran sang iya mabatian ang lapaklapak kag hangos sang kabayo. Gulpe nga nagdulog ang duha ka kabayo sa sagwa sang ila kudal, upod ang pagtap-ok sang madamol nga yab-ok. Napiyong niya ang iya mga mata sa paglikaw sang puling, kag sang iya pagmuklat, isa ka mabakod nga ulitao ang nagahimutad sa iya. Nagpalayo sia sa daku nga kakugmat. Daw nakuhaan sia pangalibutan. Sang namarasmasan sia, iya namulalongan nga ara na sia sa likod sang ila balay sa may idalom sang kusina. Sa sulod sang balay, halos dalagan ang pagkadto ni Tatay niya sa bentana. Nabatian niya ini nga nagpanawag sa kay Nanay niya. "Tinay, Tinay, ang Senyorito!" Maathag sa iya palamatin-an ang pagdagundagon sang iya amay sa hagdan kag ang pagdalagan sang iya iloy sa bentana.

"May tinagu ka, Tando!" Nabatian niya ang tingog ni Ramoncito nga daw nasadyahan.

"Ang ano, Senyorito?" Ang mahinay nga pamangkot nga may dala nga katingala ni Tatay niya.

"May tinagu ka...!" Ang iya lang nabatian kag naghinay nga daw hutik na lang ang kasugpon. Ano pa wala na niya mabatii.

"Senyorito, indi pa...!" Ang tingog ni Tatay niya halos nagapakitluoy.

"Kon amo, magabalik ako ugaling!" May dala nga pamat-od ang tingog ni Ramoncito.

Nakita niya ang pagsakay liwat sang duha ka lalaki sa ila mga kabayo, ang pagkilan sang botas ni Ramoncito sa silak sang adlaw, ang paglatigo sini sa kabayo kag ang paghuyab sang kabayo nga nagpatap-ok sang yab-ok.

Si Tatay niya halos usdang nga nagpungkuon sa lakaran sang ila kudal. Huyhoy ang abaga nga madugay nakatindog. Sia iya nagpadayon sa pagpanilhig. Wala niya pagdayuna ang tuyo nga mamangkot kay Tatay niya kon ano ang kinahanglan sang mga dumoloaw kay iya nakita ang pagbug-at sang lawas sini. Sang ulihi nagtindog ini kag mahinay nga nagsaka sa balay.

"Ano ang kinahanglan ni Cito?" Ang iya nabatian kay Nanay niya. Apang wala niya mabatii ang sabat ni Tatay niya. Daw wala magsabat ini.

Gintutdan niya ang natumpok nga mga sagbot kag laya nga mga dahon sang pahu kag langka. Nagtawhay ang iya panghunahona kag balatyagon. Apang natublag sia sa iya pagdabok sang pagpanaog ni Tatay niya nga dala ang ginunting sa tagob. Nagpalapit ini sa kasagingan sa kilid sang balay. Madugay nga nagtindog ini sa atubangan sang puno sang saging nga wala hulohambal kag daw naurongan. Kag wala sing ano kag ano, ginabot sang iya amay ang ginunting sa tagob kag gintapas ang isa ka puno nga saging, kag sang matumba, sinaksak nga naglalabog ang mga sinipad sang upas.

Bisan karon diri sa bibi sang suba, iya pa madumdoman nga nagdalagan sia pasaka sa balay nga nagapanawag sa kay Nanay niya. Nagsubsob sia sa abaga sang iya iloy samtang nagatudlo sa kay Tatay niya sa idalom. Nagdalagan panaog ang iya iloy. Nakita niya nga nag-untat na si Tatay niya sa pagsaksak sang saging. Nagpungko ini sa natumpok nga mga pusog kag inuli ang ginunting sa tagob. Ang balhas nagatulolagay apang indi niya mamulalongan kon bala nagahilibion ini. Nakita niya ang iya nga iloy nga nagapamahid sang iya mga mata samtang nagasugilanon kay Tatay niya.

Hapon na sang magsaka ang iya ginikanan. Nakatig-ang na gani sia. Ang kahipos nga naghari sa sulod sang balay nagdulot sa iya balatyagon nga daw ungon. Nagapalangurog ang iya unod, apang kon tungod sa ano indi niya mahangpan kag wala gid sia magpangusisa sa iya ginikanan. Natahap sia magpamangkot sa ila kay iya napamatyagan nga daku kag malahalon nga bagay ang ila ginhambalan, sekreto nga daw indi bagay ibuyagyag sa kay sin-o, hitabo nga ayhan indi man niya mahangpan bisan ipaathag sa iya. Padayon ang paghikot nila ni Nanay niya sang palanyapunon nga wala hulohambal. Sa sagwa, sa diutay nga balatunan, si Tatay niya naghilayhilay sa papag nga kawayan. Madugaydugay, pagtakop sang kahapunanon nabatian nila ang pagpanihol ni Berting kag ni Tomas samtang nagatabog sila sang mga karabaw pasulod sa toril. Ang kalinong nila sa sulod sang balay daw nasat-oman sang kabataan, kay mahipos man ang mga ini nga nagkalaon kag naghilimos pagtulog nga wala pamangkutanon.

Ini nga hitabo nagtublag sang iya kalinong, kag bisan karon nga nagaisahanon sia, indi sia mahimunong. Sina nga gab-i, ginhilas sia. Ginapanan-aw niya ang kaputi sang panit ni Ramoncito, kaputi katulad sang upas. Sang pagkaaga, adlaw na sia magbugtaw, isahanon na lang sia nga nagpamahaw. Sa talamnan na ang iya ginikanan kag ang iya mga manghod nakalakat na sa palahalban. Wala na sa toril ang mga karabaw. Sina nga aga, nasuboan sia sa iya pag-isahanon. Luyag niya kuntani nga may masugiran sia sang iya damgo.

Kumaon sia kag magkadto sa balay ni Tya Semang sa may Sambag-kulob. Naabtan niya si Tya Semang nga manuglakat pa-Iloilo kag nagabantay sang trak sa ila ugsaran. Magaduaw si Tya Semang sa iya panganay nga si Pilar nga nagpalagyo sa Iloilo sang indi sia pagtugtan ni Tya Semang nga magpasimpalad sa siyudad. Si Pilar karon mananahi na sa isa ka dress-shop kag nagaeskuwela sa high school sa gab-i. Nabanga sia sa mga ginsugid ni Tya Semang sa iya natungod sa kay Pilar. Nakunyag sia kag nahisa sa maayo nga kapalaran kag palaabuton ni Pilar.

Samtang nagkuso sia sang linabhan, ginapanan-aw niya si Pilar sa ginaobrahan sini. Ayhan si Pilar may suweldo nga kaugalingon kag madamo na ang mga abyan sa bulothoan. Daw ano bala ang makakadto sa Iloilo? Suno sa sugid sang mga nakakadto na, may dalagko didto nga mga balaligyaan, sinehan, palabugnawan, kalan-an, dalagko nga mga bulothoan, kag nanarisari nga kalingawan. Duawon niya kag pasugilanonon si Tya Semang pag-abot sini halin sa Iloilo.

Natublag ang iya panghandurawan sang kalas kag igot sang kawayanan sa tabok-pangpang. Isa ka karabaw nga dulit sang lunang gikan sa turogban ang naglusot sa likod sang kawayanan. Nagpadulong ini sa pangpang kag naghana nga mainom. Apang daw inumol nga bato ang nagtagubtob sa likod sang apat. Nag-isol ini kag nakabulaog sa buho ang isa ka tiil. Nagakiangkiang nga nagdalagan pakadto sa kalubihan paubay sang talaman. Dungan sa pagkabulahog sang karabaw, may nagharakhak sing mabaskog nga halos nakapuno sang kalinong sang kaudtohanon.

Tinumbok ang iya dughan kag nagpalangurog ang iya kaundan sang iya makilala ang tingog. Nanghulonghulong sia nga kinulbaan. Sa hinali nag-athag ang iya panumdoman. Iya na karon nahangpan ang masubo nga pagsugilanon sang iya nga ginikanan sadtong Domingo sing hapon kag ang ila pagkahipos kag pagduyo sang mga inadlaw nga masunod. Ang gab-i sang iya panghunahona daw ginsanagan sang indi maisip kag nanuhaytohay nga kabituonan nga nagasilak katulad sang badlak sang adlaw. Ang kasanag daw nagapanalupsop sa iya balatyagon, painuino, panghandurawan, kag bilog nga pagkatao. Daw nagtudlo ini sa iya pagkababae. Ang pagbutlak sini nga kasanag sa iya kaugalingon amo karon ang nagtuytoy sang iya panghunahona nga iya ginsunod sa pagbuko kon ano ang iya dapat himuon.

Nanghulonghulong sia. Mahawan ang palibot kag wala sia sing sarang mapanaguan. Apang karon pa nga iya na nahangpan ang tanan, wala na sia magbatyag sing kahadlok. Subong bala nga nahibaluan na niya ang iya pagahimuon. Sa ulounhan sa iya tuo nayon, ang suba madalumdalom sang sa may ginapanglabhan niya. Dalidali sia nga naglusong sa tubig malapit sa may nagasangyad nga sanga sang inyam. Iya na nabatian ang kalas sang botas sa nagkalataktak kag laya nga mga dahon sa banas. Nabatyagan na niya ang paglinupad kag pagalalpas sang nakibot kag napukaw nga mga kapispisan. Ang mga alibangbang kag mga tumbaktombak naglinupad sa pagpangita sing iban nga halapunan. Nakalambot na sa iya igdulongog ang paghaplit kag pagtupa sang latigo sa mga sanga sang kahoy kag mga dahon. Nakita ayhan sia? Ayhan wala sia matalupangdi kay nalipdan sia sang kawayanan. Apang ang pangpang unot kay ang mga hilamon kag mga tanom nautosan gid sang init bisan nagapadulong pa lang sa tingadlaw.

Sang pagkatalupangod niya nga nagabadlak ang botas sa silak sang adlaw sa banas sa kilid sang kawayanan, nagsalom sia. Kon daw ano kadugay sang iya pagsalom wala niya mapakti. Daw malupok ang iya dughan sa wala guloginhawa sa idalom sang tubig. Sang maluya na ang iya pamatyag nagbutwa sia. Madulom ang iya panulok bisan nagasilak sing masili ang adlaw. Sang namaradmadan sia, nakita niya nga nagaisahanon sia. Nagtaklas sia sa pangpang. Nabatyagan niya ang pagtapik sang basa nga bayu sa iya lawas kag ini naghatag kabugnaw sa iya bisan sa initan. Madasig sia nga nagdalagan padulong sa dalan. Pagtakboy niya sa naaspalto nga bahin nagbalikid sia. Malayo kag halos indi na makita ang ila balay. Wala na sia bulobalikid nga nagpanglaktod sa kasiutan pa- tadlong sa Sambag-kulob.

From *Hiligaynon*, November 12, 1969

The Awakening
(Bunyag-Takas)

Lucila V. Hosillos

She felt that her whole body was changing. For about a month now she was feeling this unease about herself. Only now did she feel this way. She gazed at her face in the crystal clear water of the little well she had dug out in the river bank. No, she didn't see any change in her figure although there was something different in her face. She went on washing the clothes of her younger brother and sister and then she rinsed them hurriedly because the heat was getting to be scorching. She had to get home soon to prepare lunch for *Nanay* and *Tatay* who would be coming back from the farm.

She turned her gaze straight ahead of her. In the distance, the roof of their house was a mere haze in the noonday glare. The path from the river to the road was clear, but that which branched off to their house was thick with underbrush. The carabao *Tatay* was using for ploughing the field had not yet been tethered to the mango tree beside their house. So, her parents were not done yet with work on the farm.

It was quiet around her; it seemed the whole barrio had gone to break and turn the field. In the stillness, all those strange feelings and thoughts about herself reigned. She felt lonely. It seemed like her parents, brothers and sisters were drifting farther and farther away from her. It seemed like she couldn't get into their feelings and thoughts. But she could not let them in into hers either.

During those moments she felt greater kinship with the creaking bamboo trees across the river. The butterflies which fluttered close to the the flowers of the *lumboy* where she sought the shade seemed to understand her feelings more. The loud piercing scream of the *tagwati* seemed to plumb the depths of her feelings, probing into her thoughts. Tiny waves that lapped gently over her feet on the sand seemed ready to befriend her, and listen to her talk about her feelings.

The image of her father suddenly appeared before her. Thin but sturdily built. A gentle face and an amiable expression. His mien and expression reflecting a tranquil mind and good will. But it was this kindheartedness coupled with their hard life that led to her parents' frequent quarrels. Because he was too kind, he was unable to bargain with the landlord who grabbed their share of the harvest. If he bargained at all, he would soon back down, cringe and become too timid to talk even with Pablo who was *Don* Ramon's caretaker. How much more when he had to face *Señor* Ramon or *Señorito* Ramoncito. Her father could not refuse any of their demands. He would simply be stricken dumb, not knowing what to say. He would just smile sheepishly and laugh ingratiatingly. He would say "Yes, yes," nodding his head again and again. Because their landlords knew her father's weakness, they would dump on him work for which he went unpaid, cheat him on his share of the harvest and charge unreasonable interest on his debts.

These scenes stuck to her mind and chest. She put much of the blame on her father, and sometimes she would take her mother's side when her parents argued. But when she saw her father's face which bore no shadow of anger, ill-will, or spite, she felt resentful of her mother.

Her father's servility to their landlord caused her heart great fear and distress but it was not yet clear to her immature mind why. Towards their neighbor who listened frequently to her parents' quarrels, she did not feel shame, but anger. She supposed they were secretly pleased to see a family with a more miserable plight. Now, while doing the laundry she felt weary thinking about their lot.

In just one month, she seemed suddenly to have matured. Like something had roused her thoughts and feelings concerning their situation. So suddenly she awakened to the cares of their life.

Was it perhaps because she was getting close to puberty? She couldn't keep still. Her thoughts and feelings could not be put to rest. She kept thinking even when she was busy planting, harvesting, gathering firewood, sometimes even while conversing. Disparate ideas intermingled in her thoughts, images, and dreams.

Along with the unfolding of new realizations about their unrelieved misery, she had begun feeling a transformation in her body and a self-consciousness whenever she noticed someone looking at her. Now she remembered what happened last week when they attended the fiesta at San Rafael. The toastmaster who introduced the queen recited the following lines:

> Inday
> A seed sprouting
> Her face
> A flower blooming.

She fancied that this sweet verse was about her and was dedicated to her. She felt her whole being blossom—her heart, her mind, her body, all things pertaining to her womanhood. For the first time in her life, she became aware of herself. She was, after all, a person that breathed, moved, grew—sprouting and then blossoming.

Since then, she noticed a change in her voice, in her appearance, in the way she moved. She began to be envious of the things she saw in others, and of those who enjoyed a comfortable lifestyle. She knew that she could never find an escape from lease-farming. No matter how much the whole family toiled and exposed themselves to rain and heat, their share of the harvest remained the same. Instead of their debt getting smaller, it got larger.

But if the way she viewed people had changed, so had the way people looked at her. She observed that young men would sometimes stare at her, as on that Wednesday, the town's market day, when she wore a decent dress and looked trim and tidy. But she could not yet understand all these. She was aware, though, that those who watched her noticed how she would avoid their gaze from shyness and self-consciousness.

Now in her aloneness, she felt like screaming at her parents, at their neighbors, at the whole world, to ask them to help her understand this strange newness in herself. But not a sound escaped from her lips. In the distance, their house seemed to recede more and more. Around her, not a single leaf rustled. The sun was high and the heat had become even more intense. The river water had already turned warm and even in the shade of the spreading branches of the *lumboy* she could feel the sun's scorching heat. She whistled, a game she would play to call on the wind, but even the cogon and the coconut trees in the field across the river did not stir. She poured several jugs of water on her body and felt refreshed and energized.

But after a little while, she was feverish once more. She could not stop herself from thinking of the many occurrences in their life. What disturbed her again was the thought of Ramoncito's visit to their house just last Sunday afternoon.

She was sweeping the ground by their gate when she heard the hurried galloping and panting of horses. Two horses came to an abrupt halt just outside of their fence, accompanied by a cloud of dust. She had to close her eyes to avoid getting a mote into her eyes, and when she opened these, she found a sturdy young man already staring at her. She ran away from great fear. It seemed she had fainted briefly. When she came to her senses, she found herself behind the house right below the kitchen. In the house, her father broke into running as he was rushing towards the window. She heard him call to her mother, "Tinay, Tinay, *Señorito* is here!" Even now she could still hear her father's brisk footsteps on the staircase, and her mother running towards the window.

"You're hiding something, *Tiyo* Ando!" Ramoncito sounded pleased.

"Hiding what, *Senorito*?" Puzzled, *Tatay* asked gently.

"You're hiding someone...!" This was all that she heard clearly. The rest seemed to have died down to a whisper; she could no longer hear their voices.

"No, *Señorito*, not yet...!" her father's voice was pleading.

"Then, I shall come back...!" Ramoncito's voice carried an air of resolve.

Then two men climbed up their horses. She saw Ramoncito's boots glistening in the sunshine, his whipping the horse, the horses galloping away in a cloud of dust.

Her father almost fell as he leaned his weight on the stiles of their fence. He sat still for a long time, his shoulders hanging down limply. She for her part went on sweeping. She wanted to ask her father what the guest had wanted but it seemed like something was weighing on him so she did not. Later, he got up and slowly climbed the stairs.

"What did Cito need?" she heard her mother ask. She didn't hear her father answer. It seemed like he hadn't.

She set fire to the heap of rubbish and the dead leaves from the mango and the *langka*. Her mind was more at peace now. But she stopped kindling the fire when her father walked down the stairs carrying a bolo in its scabbard. He walked towards the banana patch at the side of the house. For a long time he stood facing a banana tree without saying a word and looking like he were in a state of shock. And suddenly, without warning, he pulled out the bolo from its sheath and struck at the banana tree. When it fell, he chopped up the trunk with all his strength.

Even now, by the river bank, she could remember how she ran up the stairs quickly, calling out to her mother. She remembered falling into her mother's arms, pointing to her father. Her mother ran down the stairs. She saw that her father had stopped hitting at the trees. Now he was seated on the mound of stalks, his bolo back in its sheath. His sweat was profuse. She could not tell if he was weeping or not; her mother though was wiping her father's eyes as she talked with him.

It was afternoon when her parents came home. In fact, she had already cooked rice. The silence that prevailed in their house was like a splinter stuck on her. Her body was shaking but just why, she couldn't understand. She didn't ask her parents though. She was hesitant to ask them because she perceived they were talking about something of grave importance, a secret not to be revealed to anyone and something she wouldn't understand even if this were explained to her. She and *Nanay* went about preparing dinner without talking to each other. Outside, in their small sala, her father stretched out on the bamboo sofa. A little bit later, near dusk, they heard the whistle of Berting and Tomas as they herded in their carabaos into the pen. It seemed the stillness in the house did not escape the brothers. They took dinner quietly and then promptly got ready for bed without asking a single question.

These incidents disturbed her. Even now that she was alone, she felt listless. She dreamt that night, dreamt of the fairness of Ramoncito's skin. It was as white as a banana stalk.

The following morning she got up late and had to take breakfast by herself. Her parents had already gone to the field and her brothers, to the pasture area. The carabaos were no longer in their pens. Now she felt lonesome being by herself. She wished she could confide her dream to someone.

She took her breakfast and proceeded to look for *Tiya* Semang at Sambag-kulob. She found *Tiya* Semang waiting by their gate for the bus to Iloilo. *Tiya* Semang was going to visit her daughter Pilar who had run away to Iloilo when *Tiya* Semang did not permit her to try her luck in the city. Now she worked as a dressmaker in a shop and attended classes in the evening. What *Tiya* Semang told her about Pilar impressed her. She was excited but also envious of Pilar's good fortune and promising future.

As she washed her clothes, she imagined Pilar working in the shop. Perhaps Pilar drew her own salary and had a lot of friends in school. How would it feel to be in Iloilo? Those who had been there said it had large department stores, moviehouses, refreshment parlors, restaurants, and schools. It offered different kinds of recreation. She was going to visit *Tiya* Semang when she would get back from Iloilo.

But her reverie was broken by the creaking of bamboo trees across the river. A carabao, black and sticky with mud from the rice paddies, slipped out from the clumps of bamboo. It moved towards the river and was about to drink from it. But a stone, the size of a fist, thudded on its back. It stepped backwards, one of its feet sinking into a mudhole. Limping, it ran towards the coconut grove bordering the farm. When the carabao tripped into the mudhole, someone burst into a guffaw so loud that the stillness of noon was broken. Her heart winced, her whole being trembled when she recognized the voice. She looked around nervously. Everything now was suddenly clear to her. Now she understood her parents' dispirited conversation that Sunday afternoon and their silence and gloom in the folloowing days. The darkness of her mind was now illuminated by the countless stars shining as bright as day. The light suffused her feelings, her thoughts, her imagination, her whole being. This light guided her thoughts now and helped her map out what to do.

Again, she looked around for a place to hide. She was in a clearing and there was nowhere she could hide. But now that she understood all, she was no longer afraid. She knew what she had to do. A short distance from her, somewhere to the right, the river was deeper than the place where she was washing her clothes. She dived into the river close to the spot where a branch of an *ingyam* was hanging over the water. She could now hear boots shuffling against the withered leaves on the trail. She could now sense the flight and escape of the birds that had been startled and awakened. The butterflies and the dragonflies had taken wing in search of new perches. Her ears picked up the flicking of the whip and its whacking on the branches and leaves of trees. Did he see her? Perhaps not. The bamboo grove screened her. The river bank was parched though and the grass and plants were already sucked dry by the heat even before summer had come.

When she saw the boots glinting in the sun, she plunged in. As to how long she remained under water she could not guess; her chest seemed ready to burst from holding her breath. When she felt her lungs would give way, she resurfaced. She couldn't see clearly in the sun's glare, but when she recovered her senses, she saw that she was by herself. She climbed up the river bank. Her wet dress was glued to her body, cooling her even in the heat of the sun. Quickly, she ran towards the road. When she stepped on the asphalted road, she looked back. Their home was far away now and hardly visible. Without turning her head, she made her way into the dense undergrowth, the shorter way to Sambag-kulob.

Binyag-Takas

Lucila V. Hosillos

Naramdaman niya ang pagbabago ng kanyang katawan. Mag-iisang buwan na ngayong parang hindi niya maintindihan ang kanyang sarili. Ngayon pa lang siya nakaramdam nito. Tinitigan niya ang kanyang mukha sa malinaw na balun-balonang inuka niya sa pampang ng ilog. Wala siyang napansing pagbabago sa kanyang anyo maliban sa kanyang mukha. Nagpatuloy siya sa paglalaba at dalidali niyang binanlawan ang mga damit ng kanyang nakababatang kapatid, dahil tumitindi na ang init. Kinakailangang makauwi na siya at makapaghanda ng pananghalian ng kanyang Tatay at Nanay na manggagaling sa bukid.

Ibinaling niya ang kanyang paningin sa malayo. Sa unahan, halos hindi maaninag ang kanilang bahay sa nakasisilaw na init. Mahawan ang landas sa tabing-ilog patungo sa kalsada, subalit ang sangang patungo sa kanyang bahay ay masukal. Hindi pa nakatali ang kalabaw ng Tatay niya sa punong-mangga sa gilid ng bahay. Kung gayon, nasa bukid pa sila.

Tahimik ang kanyang paligid. Halos lahat sa baryo ay nag-aararo at bumubungkal ng lupa. Sa katahimikang ito, naghari ang mga damdamin at hagap tungkol sa kanyang sarili na hindi niya maunawaan. Pakiramdam niya nag-iisa siya. Malayo sa kanya ang kanyang magulang at mga kapatid at patuloy pang napapalayo. Parang hindi niya maabot ang kanilang pag-iisip at damdamin. Hindi niya nais ipabatid sa kanila ang kanyang naramdaman at iniisip.

Sa mga sandaling ito, parang mas malapit pa sa kanya ang langitngit ng kawayanan sa kabilang ibayo ng ilog. Parang mas nauunawaan pa ang kanyang mga damdamin ng mga paruparong maghapong lumiligid-ligid sa mga bulaklak ng duhat na kanyang pinalimliman. Ang matinis na huni ng tagwati ay parang humahalungkat ng kanyang damdamin—at nagtatanong kung ano ang kanyang iniisip. Ang tubig na aalun-alon at pasagi-sagi sa kanyang mga paa sa buhangin ay parang nakikipagkaibigan sa kanya at nangungusisa tungkol sa kanyang damdamin.

Biglang lumitaw sa kanyang handurawan ang anyo ng kanyang ama. Payat ngunit matatag ang katawan. Magiliw at maamo. Ang kilos at pagtingin parang salamin ng panatag na damdamin at magandang loob. Subalit ang magandang ugaling ito kasama ng kanilang pagdarahop ang siyang naging sanhi ng malimit na pag-aalitan ng Tatay at Nanay niya. Dahil sa kahinaang loob ng kanyang ama, hindi ito nakikipagtalo sa may-ari ng lupang kanilang inuupahan, kahit na sinasamsam nito ang kanilang parte sa naaning bigas. Kung makipagtalo man ang kanyang ama, agad itong nagpapahinuhod at nahihiyang mangatwiran kahit na ang kaharap lang ay si Pablo, ang katiwala ni Don Ramon. Lalo na kung si senyor o si senyorito na ang kaharap—ang ama niya'y di na makapaliwanag o makatanggi. Parang pipi at hindi na alam kung ano ang sasabihin. Pangiti-ngiti at patawa-tawa na lang. Paoo-oo, pasalu-saludo at patangu-tango. Dahil alam ng Don ang magandang loob ng kanyang ama, tinatambakan ito ng mga gawaing hindi binabayaran, dinadaya sa pagbilang ng bigas, at pinapasobrahan ang kwenta ng kanyang utang at babayaran.

Parang salugsog ang mga pangyayaring ito sa puso't isip niya. Malaki ang paninisi niya sa kanyang ama at kung minsa'y pinapanigan niya ang kanyang Nanay kung ito'y nagagalit sa kanyang bana. Subalit pag nakita niya ang kanyang ama na wala man lang bakas ng poot o paghihiganti, sumasama rin ang loob niya sa kaniyang ina.

Ang pagpapangayupapa sa kanilang mga amo ay pumukaw sa kanyang puso ng matinding pagkabahala at malaking pagkatakot, ngunit hindi pa rin maliwanag sa murang isip niya kung bakit. Sa kanilang mga kapitbahay na malimit nakikinig sa pag-aaway ng kanyang magulang, hindi siya nahihiya kundi nagagalit; alam niyang lihim silang natutuwa dahil may nakikita silang mas gipit pa sa kanila ang kalagayan. Ngayon, habang naglalaba siya, nanghihina ang kanyang katawan at pag-iisip sa kanilang kalagayan.

Sa loob ng isang buwan, bigla siyang tinubuan ng bait. Parang may pumukaw sa kanyang damdamin at pag-iisip tungkol sa kanilang kalagayan. Bigla siyang nagising sa mga suliranin at hapdi ng kanilang pamumuhay. Dahil kaya nagdadalaga siya? Hindi siya mapakali. Hindi mapalagay ang kaniyang pag-iisip at damdamin. Walang tigil ang kanyang pag-iisip kahit na siya'y abala—nagtatanim, nag-aani, nangangahoy—at kung minsan kahit na may kinakausap. Sari-saring bagay at kaisipan ang nangagsabay-sabay sa kanyang isip, handurawan, at panaginip.

Sabay sa bagong pag-unawa na walang-kaibsan ang kanilang gipit na kalagayan, napansin niya ang pag-iiba ng kanyang katawan at ang kanyang pagkahiya kung may naramdaman siyang nakatitig sa kanya. Ngayon naalala niya ang nangyari noong nakalipas na Linggo sa kanilang pagdalo sa piyesta ng San Rafael. Binigkas ng tagapagkilala ng reyna ang mga linyang sumusunod:

Si Inday
Binhing umuusbong
Ang anyo'y bulaklak
Na namumukadkad.

Pakiwari niya ang tamis ng mga katagang ito'y ukol sa kanya at inilaan sa kanya. Naramdaman niya ang pamumukadkad ng kanyang damdamin, ng buo niyang katawan, at ng mga bagay na nauukol sa kanyang pagkababae. Sa buong buhay niya, iyon ang kaunaunahang pagkakataong naramdaman niya ang sariling pagkatao, na siya pala'y humihinga, gumagalaw, tumutubo, umuusbong, at namumulaklak.

Mula noon naramdaman na niya ang pagbabago ng kanyang boses, ng kanyang pagtingin sa buhay, ang pag-iiba ng kanyang itsura at kilos. Pinalitan niya ang pag-aayos ng kanyang buhok, pananamit at paglalakad. Naramdaman niya mula noon ang pagkahili sa mga bagay na nakikita sa iba, at pagkainggit doon sa may maluwag na pamumuhay. Naintindihan na niya na halos walang kaginhawaan silang mararanasan sa pagiging kasama sa pagsasaka. Kahit anong pagsisikap ng buong pamilya, pagbibilad sa init at pagpayangyang sa ulan, hindi mararagdagan ang kanilang inani. Sa halip na mabawasan ang kanilang mga utang, lalo na nga itong nadagdagan.

Ngunit kung nagbago ang paningin niya sa mga tao at mga bagay, nag-iba rin ang paningin sa kanya ng kanyang kapwa-tao. Napuna niyang tinititigan siya ng mga binata. Lalung-lalo na noong Miyerkules. Pamilihang araw iyon sa bayan at nakabihis siya nang maganda at nakapag-ayos. Ngunit hindi pa niya naiintindihan ang kahulugan ng mga bagay na ito. Batid niyang napansin ng kahit sinong nakakakita sa kanya na iniiwasan niya ang kanilang mga titig sa laki ng pagkahiya at pagkawili sa sariling isip at damdamin.

Ngayon sa kanyang pag-iisa, napapasigaw siya sa kanyang mga magulang, sa mga kapitbahay, sa buong mundo na kung maaari ay matulungan siya sa pag-uunawa sa mga nangyayari sa kanyang sarili. Subalit walang tinig na nakawala sa kanyang mga bibig. Sa unahan, waring papalayo nang papalayo pa ang kanilang bahay. Sa kanyang palibot, wala ni isang dahong kumakaluskos. Mataas na ang araw at tumitindi ang init. Maligamgam ang tubig sa ilog at kahit na sa lilim ng mayabong na duhat, naramdaman pa rin niya ang kasukdulan ng init. Sumipol siya, larong tumatawag-pansin sa hangin, subalit ang kakugunan at ang mga dahon ng kaniyugan sa kabilang pangpang ay di man lang tumitinag. Binuhusan niya ang sarili ng ilang tabong tubig. Naramdaman niyang tila umuusok ang kanyang katawan. Napapreskuhan niya ang kanyang sarili at nakaramdam ng panibagong sigla.

Subalit di-nagtagal, parang nilagnat na naman siya. Hindi niya mapigil na bumalik ang kanyang isip sa mga pangyayaring naganap sa kanilang pamumuhay. Hindi na naman siya mapakali nang kanyang maalala ang pagdalaw ni Ramoncito sa kanilang bahay noong hapon ng nakaraang Linggo.

Nagwawalis siya sa may hagdanan nang marinig niya ang kaskas at hingal ng mga kabayo. Biglang tumigil ang dalawang kabayo sa labas ng kanilang kural, sabay ang bugso ng makapal na alikabok. Napapikit siya sa pag-iwas mapuwingan at nang ibinuklat niya ang kanyang mga mata, isa nang matipunong lalaki ang nakamasid sa kanya. Lumayo siya sa laki ng pagkatakot. Parang nawalan siya ng ulirat. Nang mahimasmasan siya, napansin niyang nasa may likuran na siya ng bahay sa may ibaba ng kusina. Sa taas, halos patakbong pumunta ang Tatay niya sa bintana. Narinig niya itong tumawag sa Nanay niya: "Tinay, Tinay, ang sinyorito!" Maliwanag pa sa kanyang pandinig ang mga yabag ng

Tatay niya sa hagdan at ang pagtatakbo ng kanyang ina patungong bintana.

"May tinagu ka, 'Tay Ando!" May kasiyahan sa boses ni Ramoncito.

"Ano, sinyorito?" marahang tanong ni Tatay, dala ang pagtataka.

"May tinagu ka!..." Iyon lang ang kanyang narinig; humina na parang bulong ang karugtong.

"Sinyorito, indi pa...!" nagmamakaawa ang tinig ng Tatay niya.

"Kung ganon, magabalik na lang ako!" Parang desidido ang tinig ni Ramoncito.

Nakita niya ang pagsampa muli ng dalawang lalaki sa kanilang mga kabayo, ang pagkinang ng botas ni Ramoncito sa sikat ng araw, ang paglatigo niya sa kabayo bago kumaskas uli ito ng takbo, sabay pagbugso ng makapal na alikabok. Halos matimbuwang ang Tatay niya sa baranda ng kanilang bakod. Laylay ang mga balikat at matagal na nakatayo na parang wala sa sarili. Nagpatuloy naman siyang magwalis. Hindi na niya tinuloy ang balak na tanungin ang Tatay niya kung ano ang kailangan ng dumalaw dahil nakita niyang parang tumamlay ito. Ilang sandali pa, tumindig ito at marahang umakyat sa bahay.

"Anu ang kailangan ni Cito?" tanong ng Nanay niya. Hindi niya narinig ang sagot ng kanyang Tatay. Parang hindi sumagot ito. Pinaningasan niya ang bunton ng basura at mga layang dahon ng mangga at nangka. Huminahon ang kanyang loob. Subalit nagambala ang kanyang pagniningas nang manaog ang Tatay niya na dala-dala ang balisong sa kuluban nito. Lumapit ito sa sagingan sa may gilid ng bahay. Matagal na nakatindig sa tapat ng puno ng saging na walang kaimik-imik, parang natitigilan. At walang anu-ano, binunot ng kanyang ama ang balisong at pinanggapas ang isang punong-saging. Nang bumagsak ito'y pinagtataga niya ang puno hanggang magliparan ang saha ng saging.

Magsahangga ngayon, sa may pampang ng ilog, naalala niyang tumakbo siyang paakyat sa bahay para tawagin ang kanyang Nanay. Sumubsob siya sa balikat ng kanyang ina, sabay turo sa Tatay niya sa ibaba. Patakbong pumanaog ang kanyang ina. Nakita niyang tumigil na ang Tatay niya sa pagputol ng saging. Naupo ito sa bunton ng pira-pirasong saha ng saging at ibinalik ang balisong sa kaluban. Dumadaloy ang pawis subalit hindi niya matiyak kung umiiyak ito. Nakita niyang pinapahiran ng kanyang Nanay ang mga mata ng ama habang sila'y nag-uusap.

Hapon na nang umakyat ang kanyang mga magulang. Nakapagsaing na nga siya. Ang katahimikang naghari sa buong bahay ay parang salubsob na nanuot sa kanyang kalooban. Nanginig ang kanyang kalamnan, subalit hindi niya maunawaan kung bakit at hindi rin naman siya nangusisa sa kanyang mga magulang. Nag-alinlangan siyang magtanong sa kanila dahil naramdaman niyang mahalaga ang kanilang pinag-uusapan, isang lihim na hindi dapat ibunyag kahit na kanino, isang pangyayaring hindi rin niya mauunawaan sakaling ipaliliwanag ito sa kanya. Patuloy na naghanda ang mag-ina ng hapunan na walang imikan. Sa labas, sa maliit na sala, nag-unat-unat ang Tatay niya sa papag-kawayan. Di naglaon, sa takipsilim, narinig nila ang pagsipol nina Berting at Tomas habang pinagtataboy ang kanilang mga kalabaw sa loob ng koral. Parang nasakyan ng magkakapatid ang katahimikan sa bahay, dahil tahimik silang kumain at naghandang matulog nang hindi man lang nagtatanong.

Bumalabog sa kanyang kapayapaang-loob ang mga pangyayaring ito, at kahit na ngayong nag-iisa siya, hindi siya mapakali. Binangungot siya ng gabing iyon. Parang nakikita niya ang maputing balat ni Ramoncito, kaputiang tulad sa ubod ng saging. Pagkaumaga, tanghali na siyang nagising at nag-iisang nag-almusal. Nasa bukid na ang kanyang mga magulang at nakaalis na ang kanyang mga kapatid sa pastulan. Wala na ang mga kalabaw sa koral. Nalungkot siya sa kanyang pag-iisa. Ibig sana niyang may mapagkwentuhan ng kanyang panaginip.

Kumain siya at nagtungo sa bahay ni Tiya Semang sa may Sambag-kulob. Patungong Iloilo si Tiya Semang at naghihintay ng trak sa may bakuran nila. Dadalaw siya sa panganay niyang si Pilar. Lumayas ito papuntang Iloilo nang hindi siya tinugutan ni Tiya Semang na makipagsapalaran sa lungsod. Mananahi na si Pilar ngayon sa dress shop at nag-aaral sa high school sa gabi. Naaliw siya sa mga kwento ni Tiya Semang tungkol kay Pilar. Hanga siya sa mabuting kapalaran ni Pilar, at sa magandang kinabukasan nito. Hangad din niya ito.

Habang pinagkukusot niya ang labahan, nilalarawan niya si Pilar sa pinagtatrabahuan nito. Marahil may sariling sweldo na siya at may maraming kaibigan sa eskwelahan. Ano kaya ang pakiramdam ng taong nakarating na sa Iloilo? Ayon sa sinabi ng mga galing na roon, may malalaki itong bahay-kalakalan, sinehan, palamigan, kainan, malalaking eskwelahan at sari-saring libangan. Dadalawin niya si Tiya Semang at pasugilanunon pagkagaling nito sa Iloilo.

Natigil ang kanyang paggugunam-gunam dahil sa kaluskos at langitngit ng kawayanan sa ibayo ng ilog. Isang maruming kalabaw na galing sa putikan ang nakalusot sa likod ng kawayanan. Huminto ito sa pampang at umakmang uminom. Subalit parang isang gakamaong bato ang sumalpok sa likod ng hayop. Pumihit ito at ang isang paa'y nabaon sa lusak. Paika-ika itong tumalilis patungo sa kaniyugang humahanay sa taniman. Sabay sa pagkabulabog ng kalabaw may bumulalas na halakhak na halos pumuno sa katahimikan ng katanghalian. Sinundot ang kanyang dibdib at nanginig ang kanyang kalamnan. Nagpalingun-lingon siya, kinakabahan. Biglang lumiwanag ang kanyang pag-iisip. Naunawaan na niya ngayon ang malungkot na pag-uusap ng kanyang mga magulang noong hapon ng Linggo at ang kanilang panlulumbay sa mga araw na sumusunod. Naliwanagan ang kanyang madilim na kaisipan ng di-mabilang at sari-saring bituin na kumikislap tulad ng sikat ng araw. Ang liwanag ay tumagos sa kanyang damdamin, pag-iisip, gunam-gunam, at buong pagkatao. Parang ipinaliwanag nito ang kahulugan ng kanyang pagkababae. Ito ngayon ang namamatnubay sa kanyang pag-iisip at siyang sinusunod niya sa pagpaplano kung ano ang gagawin.

Lumingun-lingon siya. Mahawan ang kanyang paligid, at wala siyang mataguan. Ngunit ngayong naunawaan na niya ang lahat, hindi na siya nakaramdam ng pagkatakot. Para bang alam na niya kung ano ang kanyang gagawin. Sa unahan sa may gawing kanan, mas malalim ang ilog kaysa sa bahaging nilalabhan niya. Dali-dali siyang lumusong sa tubig doon sa may nakasayad na sanga ng inyam. Narinig niya ang mga yabag ng botas sa nangagkalagas at layang dahon sa daan. Napansin din niya ang pagkabulabog at paglipad ng mga mga nagulantang na ibon. Ang mga alibangbang at tutubi ay nagsiliparan sa paghahanap ng ibang mahapunan. Nakarating na sa kanyang pandinig ang haging at hambalos ng latigo sa mga sanga ng kahoy at mga dahon. Nakita kaya siya? Maaring hindi siya napansin dahil natakpan siya ng kawayanan. Subalit tigang ang pampang; napanot na ng init ang mga damo at mga tanim, gayong papasok pa lang ang tag-init.

Nang mapansin niyang may botas na kumikinang sa sikat ng araw, agad siyang sumisid. Hindi niya tiyak kung gaano siya katagal nakalublob. Parang sasabog ang kanyang dibdib sa pagpigil ng hininga sa ilalim ng tubig. Umahon siya nang makaramdam ng lubos na panghihina. Madilim ang kanyang paningin sa sumisikat na araw. Nang mahimasmasan siya nakita niyang nag-iisa na lang siya. Sumampa siya sa pampang. Naramdaman niya ang pagkapit ng basa niyang damit sa kanyang katawan at ang paglamig nito sa init ng araw. Patakbo siyang nagtungo sa daan. Pagkaapak niya sa naaspaltong bahagi nito, lumingon siya. Malayo na ang kanilang bahay at halos hindi na makita. Hindi na siya lumingon-lingon pa habang tinahak ang kasukalang patungo sa Sambag-kulob.

Ang Gaba sang Katubwan

Julius Flores

Nagabugtaw pa si Benigno sang mabatian niya ang pagbayluhanay sang linupok didto ayon sa may ginsang-an sang kalsada pa-Bay-ongan, sa may katubwan. Apang wala sia makibot. Ginapaabot niya ang hitabo nga ini magsulod na sa isa ka simana. Nagahigda sia sa banig sa tupad ni Agueda kag wala sia magbangon. Namati sia sa mga lupok.

Si Agueda, nga mahamuok na ang katulogon, hinali lang nga nakabangon bangod sa kakibot. Daw sa natagban man sia sang espiritu. Mahambal sia kuntani, siguro masiyagit, apang maabtik sia nga nabutong ni Benigno pabalik sa banig. Kumopo si Agueda sa dughan sang bana.

"Benigno, ini na bala?"

"Sssht!" ang pahipos ni Benigno.

"Ginakulbaan ako."

"Maghipos ka. Ini na."

Lumigad ang pila ka minutos. Sang ulihi lumaka kag huminay ang mga linupok kag daw nabatyagan ni Benigno nga nagapabalik na sanday Komander Marcos sa kabukiran sang Bay-ongan nga dala ang kadalag-an. Napat-od niya nga sanday Komander Marcos ang nagdaog. Naplano na nila ang tanan nga mga taktika sa pag-ambos nga ini. Nahisugtan na nila mga isa ka simana na ang nagaligad. Napamatyagan na nila ang mga hulag ni Simeon Arriola kag ang mga eskort nga PC sini.

Nadumdoman ni Benigno nga sang mga apat ka adlaw nga nagligad, tumaklad sia pa-Bay-ongan sa pagdala sang duha ka bulto nga bugas suno sa ila nahisugtan. Ginpasikto sia sang isa sang mga suod nga tinao ni Komander Marcos, si Pitong

Barbasan, natungod sa kamatuoran sang nagalagaw nga balita nga magakampanya si Simeon Arriola sa maabot nga Sabado sa Bay-ongan. Nagtangutango sia. Pagkatapos, dinugangan:

"Nabatian ko mismo nga nagaplano si Mayor—a, si Simeon Arriola—nga mamiting sa Bay-ongan. Didto ako kahapon sa banwa kag nabatian ko sanday Mehor kag Gadata, inang mga polis ni Simeon Arriola, nga nagahambal natungod sini. Maupod man gani kuno sila kay Simeon. Nagainum-inom sila sa kapehan ni Tya Atang kag ara ako nagasandig sa dingding sa ila tupad. Kon sa akon lang daw sa nahuman na gid ang suspetso ni Simeon Arriola sa mga taga-Bay-ongan, gani nagadalikat sa pagpangampanya."

"Sa inyo wala sila naga-suspetso?"

"Nagapanginlaman kami."

"Kag dapat gid. Indi ako luyag nga makalusot ini sa iban, Benigno. Kabiga nga wala kita sing may nahambalan. Indi gid pag-imitlang bisan kay sin-o, bisan kay Agueda. Kay kon matabo nga maguba ang plano sang Komander bangod sa pagkatarantado ninyo, kamo man mismo ang maukpan sang iya kaakig. Kag nahibal-an naman ninyo kon maakig si Komander Marcos."

Apang wala ni Benigno mapunggi ang pagpasat-om kay Agueda sang hinambalan nila ni Pitong Barbasan. Sa gilayon na lang nga pagkatabinas sang iya baba, nahibal-an sang ulihi ni Agueda ang kamatuoran.

"Ipamaba ina Agueda," ang paandam niya "kag kabuhi naton ang pagaluaton ni Komander Marcos. Indi lang kay ang kabuhi naton nga duha, kundi tubtob man ang kabuhi sang duha naton ka anak. Sa idalom kita karon sang gahom sang Komander, sa idalom kita sang iya proteksyon kag pag-inakop, kag diutay nga pagkatabinas—kag makita mo ang wala mo ginapangita."

Wala makasabat si Agueda. Nagmurarat ang iya mga mata. Nagnganga ang iya baba apang wala sing tinaga nga nagwa. Kag hinali sia nga kumopo kay Benigno.

"Mahalin kita diri, Benigno. Mapatay ako siguro kon magpadugay pa kita diri. Mapatay ako." Halos pahutik kag nagakurog ang tingog ni Agueda.

"Mag untat ka, Agueda!"

"Madugay na ang paghambal ko sa imo nga mahalin kita diri. Ikaw ang balasulon kon..."

Nakauntat si Agueda sang itiklod sia ni Benigno sa dingding. Kakugmat kag pakitluoy ang ginahambal sang iya mga mata samtang nagatamod kag nagabantay sa hulag sang iya bana. Nagaduko si Benigno kay Agueda kag ang iya landong naglikop sa asawa. Nakasugahaw si Agueda sang bunoton ni Benigno ang isa ka matalom nga kutsilyo nga nasab-it sa nipa nga dingding.

"Benigno indi, maluoy ka," talangison ni Agueda.

"Mahipos ka ukon indi!"

"Mahipos, Benigno."

"Ipamaba mo sa iban ang nahibal-an mo?"

"Indi."

"Tandai ina!"

"Huo, Benigno."

"Bag-o kita mapatay, Agueda, ni Komander Marcos ikaw anay ang unahon ko patay kay man ikaw ang kabangdanan. Tandai gid ina. Kag pamatii ako: indi kita makahalin diri. Masuspetso ang Komander. Mahibal-an niya nga naghalin kita bangod sa katarantaduhan mo. Kon mahalin kita, masuspetso sia nga nagdangop kita sa PC kag nagpanugid sang ila nahukmongan sa Bay-ongan. Gani mapabilin kita diri tubtob san-o. Sa idalom sang gahom ni Komander Marcos. Tandai ang natabo kanday Merto kag Binang kag Soling sang nagligad nga tuig sang paarakan sila sang bala sang mga badigard ni Simeon Arriola."

"Sanday Komander Marcos ang naghimo sadto."

"Maghipos ka! Sanday Simeon Arriola ang tagatuga sadto, tandai ina. Indi ang Komander. Nagauniporme sila. Ang PC nagauniporme. Gani mga PC sila. Nakit-an mo ang lawas nila? Pulos buhobuho. Sa ulo, sa tiyan, sa dughan. Dugo sa apipingig, sa baba, sa dughan, sa sakang. Nagalubid si Soling, nagakuriit si Binang kag si Merto nagabuloslo ang iya mga mata. Nakit-an mo ang pagbuslo sang mga mata ni Merto? Nakit-an mo, Agueda?"

Matinong na karon ang kagab-ihon. Sa katubwan wala na sang tinimuktimok. Pumakita sing athagon sa kaisipan ni Benigno ang dagway sang mga bangkay nanday Simeon Arriola kag sang mga kaupod sini. Nagapaligo sila sa kaugalingon nga dugo, gintuhogtuhog sang inagyan sang bala ang salaming sang iya dyep. Ang dyep nagabarakang kag nagatakingtaking sa madalom nga kanal.

Subong man nga nakabugtaw ang duha ka kabataan ni Benigno bangod sa hitabo, apang katulad sang ila amay, pinunggan nila ang handom sa pag-usisa kag nagpabilin sila nga nagahay-ad sa banig sa katambi nga hulot. Ang kahadlok nagasigabong sa sulod sang ila dughan. Kag sang ulihi liwat sila nga natulogan.

Tumabog gikan sa utok nanday Benigno kag Agueda ang katuloyhon. Nagahulid sila nga ang isa ka butkon ni Agueda nagahakos sang dughan sang bana, apang nagpabilin sila nga mahipos. Nagatamod si Agueda sa dulom sa diin ayon ara ang dingding: nagapangutana, nagapamalasulon sing likom kon ngaa—ngaa nadalahig nila ang kaugalingon sa gamo nga ini nga ginalikupan sang katalagman ang matag-adlaw nila nga pagpangabuhi. Kon ngaa nabutang nila ang kaugalingon sa tungatonga sang duha ka banas nga indi maghilisanto, nagasalasala, ginakurog, wala sing pagalutsan pakadto sa matam-is nga kahilwayan.

Madumdoman pa ni Agueda nga pagkatapos sang ila kasal ni Benigno napulo ka tuig na ang nagligad, dinala sia sang lalaki sa duog nga ini bangod "diri ang ila kapalaran." Isa ka pidaso sang duta nga ulomhan nga ginhatag sang ila katigulangan. Wala si Agueda sang mahimo kundi ang mag-upod. Nagadala na sia sadto sing apat ka bulan kag wala sia sing labi nga ginapanumdom kundi ang buasdamlag sang ila anak.

Apang napamangkot niya subong ang iya kaugalingon. Diin na ang kapalaran kag buasdamlag? Ano nga sahi sang kapalaran ang ginapa-abot nila sa duog nga ini? Wala. Wala na ang kapalaran. Madugay na ini ginpatay kag ginlubong sang mga tinuga nga wala maskin diutay nga kaluoy kag konsiderasyon sa ila kasingkasing. Wala na ang kapalaran, ang buasdamlag, kag karon wala na sila sing may mahimo kundi ang magpahimunong, magpaulipon sa kagamhanan sang iban kag magbantay sang pagkamusdok nila sa indi masambit nga kamusmosan.

Apang luas sini may labi pa nga ginahinakitan si Agueda. Kun kaisa sa iya mga dalamguhanon, nahunahona niya nga basi sa ulihi mapatay sia nga isahanon, wala ni bisan isa nga magasulod sang iya bangkay sa isa ka desente nga lungon agod mahatagan sang isa ka desente nga lubong. Sanglit wala na si Benigno, wala na ang ila kaanakan.

Ini ang iya panagupnop. Amat-amat sila nga nagahilayo sa balatyagon sang kada isa, ginaanod, ginasagnoy sang indi mapunggan nga mga hitabo. Nahimo sa iya ni Benigno ang pagpahog sang kamatayon kag sa iya bahin naman, nahimo niya ang pagpakitluoy sa kaugalingon nga kabuhi. Gani wala sing rason kon ngaa indi matabo ang iya ginapanagupnop. Ang Benigno subong nga iya ginahakos indi katulad sang Benigno nga iya ginapakaslan sadtong una pa. Liwan na ini nga Benigno. Iya ginahakos apang tuman kalayo katulad sang mga bituon. Makapalaso katulad sang adlaw kag mabugnaw katulad sang hangin nga nagapanalupsop karon sa linang-atan sang ila salog.

Hinali nga ginhukas ni Agueda ang butkon nga nagasablay sa dughan sang bana. Tumalikod sia kag magbarikutot. Nagapilisnguon agod mapautwas ang paghinakit sang balatyagon.

Nabatyagan ni Benigno ang pag-alsa sang butkon ni Agueda gikan sa iya dughan. Makadali niya nga ginbalikid ini. Nabatian niya ang iya nga pagpilisnguon. Wala sila makahulag.

Mabug-at ang kaisipan ni Benigno. Ginapanumdom niya si Komander Marcos, si Agueda kag ang ila mga anak; si Merto kag si Soling kag si Binang; si Simeon Arriola kag ang mga PC; sia, si Benigno nga nagahinamtong sa baryo sang Candelaria kag ang mga binayle sa plasa kon Sabado sang gabi; ang mga matam-is kag hilway nga mga inadlaw nga karon lunsay patay na, napatay kaupod sa pagkadisgrasya sang iya mga ginikanan sa isa ka bus sa pil-as sang Mangampili.

Natublag sia sang mabatyagan ang pagkuhit ni Agueda.

May ginahambal si Agueda: "Pamatii."

Nagahuyop ang hangin nga halin sa kabukiran sang Bay-ongan, nagadala sang maisog nga pagginhawa ni Komander Marcos. Ginaginhawa ni Benigno ang pagginhawa sang Komander. Indi niya makakas ang Komander sa iya kaugalingon. Katulad ini sang sisi nga nagapilit sa bato sa baybayon. Bisan ang hangin nahimo na nga tulogyanan sang Komander sa pagbantay sang ila mga hulag sa oras sang katulogon.

"Nabatian mo?"

"Ang ano?"

"May nagaugayong."

Kag sa tunga sang paglaslas sang hangin, nabatian ni Benigno ang ginatumod sang asawa. Isa ka hungaw kag nagaantos kag duguon nga tingog, halos nagahalin sa isa ka lulobngan. Samtang nagahilapit ang tagiya, nagadako naman ini sa palamatin-an ni Benigno tubtob sang ulihi sa iya pamatyagan ara na ang tag-iya sang tingog sa puno sang ila hagdanan.

"Tan-awon mo Benigno." Nagakurog ang tingog ni Agueda.

"Magtulog ka!"
"Tan-awon mo."
"Magtulog ka!"
"Apang..."
"Agueda?"
"Basi kaupod sang—Komander."

"Indi mahimo nga may lalong ang Komander. Kaupod ina ni Simeon Arriola. Agueda, matulog na kita."

"Indi ako makatulog samtang may nagaugayong sa aton hagdanan. Ara na sia sa gwa sang ganhaan, Benigno. Pamatii. Ang ugayong ara na sa aton hagdanan. Nagapasaka na sia, Benigno. Ginahadlukan ako."

Halos pahutik na ang tingog ni Benigno: "Wala ka sing may nabatian, Agueda. Tandai ina, wala ka sing may nabatian."

Pagkaaga, humog sang diutay nga talithi sang kabugwason ang duta nga gintumbanan ni Benigno. Sang iya nga pagbukas sang ganhaan, suno sa ila ginapaabot, natampad ang dagway sang isa ka bangkay nga nagasukamod sa duta sa tupad sang ila hagdanan. Nadayunan siguro nga napatay bangod sa indi maantos nga kasakit kag tugnaw samtang nagahulatholat sang ginapangita nga bulig.

Wala magsala si Benigno. Bangkay sang soldado ni Simeon Arriola. Nagauniporme ini sang patig. Husto ang iya panagupnop nga sa bahin lang nanday Simeon Arriola ang nalalong.

Apang hinali nga nakadulog si Benigno sa dalayon na lang niya nga paghimutad sa bangkay. Si Agueda, kag ang duha nila ka kabataan nga subong nagatamod sa ganhaan nga ginakugmat, nakabasa sang hinali nga pagbaylo sang nawong ni Benigno. Nagakatinkatin ini sa tupad sang bangkay kag bangod kay indi matandog, ginalingi niya ang nawong sini.

"Wala ka makakita, Agueda?"

"Sang ano, Tay?" ang kamagulangan ang nagsabat.

"Tan-awa, daw sa kaupod ini ni Komander Marcos."

Nakapisik si Agueda sa nabatian. Ginduko niya ang iya ulo agod mausisa sing matul-id ang dagway sang bangkay.

"Kaupod niya ini Agueda. Kilala ko ang iya guya. Nakit-an ko ini sia sa Bay-ongan. Isa sia sang masami nga ginapatiktik sang Komander. Suod sia nga salaligan sang Komander."

Nagakurog ang tingog ni Agueda: "Wala ka magsala?"

Pinukwat ni Benigno ang mga mata kay Agueda nga nagapahangop nga indi mahimo nga magsala sia.

"Benigno...?"

"Ambot! Indi ako pagpamangkuta."

"Magpangamuyo kita, Benigno."

"Wala ina sing kapuslanan."

"Nagsala ka, Benigno."

"Indi ka maghipos? Ano ang mahimo sang pangamuyo kon akig si Komander Marcos? Wala, Agueda, wala! Sa atubangan ni Komander Marcos ka magluhod kag magpangamuyo. Sa iya atubangan, indi sa Diyos!"

"Kon ano gid man ang matabo, ikaw ang may sala, Benigno. Kagab-i ginsingganan ko ikaw nga buksan ang ganhaan sanglit may nagaugayong. Tagumatayon ang tao, Benigno, nagakinahanglan sing bulig, nagapangayo sing bulig, gani tinao sang Kumander ukon indi dapat kuntani naton nga ginbuligan. Kon ikaw ang sa iya bahin."

"Agueda!"

Binalikid ni Agueda ang duha ka kabataan: "Magsunod kamo sa akon. 'Amay namon, yara Ka sa mga langit.'"

"Ambot kon si sin-o ang may kasal-anan. Imol man lang kita, wala sing gahom, wala sing pilak..."

Dungan nga nakadulog ang mag-asawa sang gikan sa ginsang-an sumampot ang isa ka dyep sang mga PC. Dumolog ini sa atubangan sang payagpayag sang mag-asawa.

Gikan sa dyep nanaog ang isa ka tenyente, isa ka gulanggolang nga lalaki nga may masipat sing mga mata. Daku sia kag mabakod. May madasig kag mapintas nga panghulagholag. Tadlong niya nga ginpalapitan ang hagdanan. Nagapaninghawak nga gintamdan ang bangkay. Nagasunod sa iya ang tatlo pa ka mga soldado.

Namunong si Benigno sa iya nahamtangan. Sige pa ang iya nga pagkatinkatin sa tupad sang bangkay. Sang pagsampot sang tenyente, makadali niya nga gintungkaaw ini. Pagkatapos ginlansang niya ang panulok sa bangkay, nagahulatholat sa igahambal sang tenyente. Si Agueda halos ginpauplok ang ulo sa bintana.

"Kilala mo sia," ang hambal sang tenyente kay Benigno.

"Indi."

Namilit: "Kilala mo sia."

Naghipos si Benigno.

"Ikaw," ang tumod kay Agueda. "Magsabat ka!"

"Wa-wala!"

"Nagabinutig kamo! Kilala ninyo sia bilang tinao ni Kumander Marcos. (Nakaangkon sang hinali nga kabaskog ang tingog sang tenyente.) Pamangkuton ko kamo liwat kag luyag ko nga magsugid kamo sing matuod. Mahimo namon kamo mapaagyan sing kusog kon nagapamilit kamo. Kilala ninyo sia!"

Ginkipot sang mag-asawa ang ila baba.

Sa sini nga tion, naglibot ang duha ka soldado sa ila payagpayag. Nanidingsid-ing sila sa kusina kag sa mga buslot sa dingding, pagkatapos sa isa ka puongpuong sa likod sang balay. Ang isa nabilin nga nagasukbit sang thompson.

"Nahibal-an ninyo ang natabo kagab-i? Ang natabo nga paglinuthanganay sa tunga sang guban ni Komander Marcos kag sang iya ni Mayor Arriola?"

"Wala." Si Agueda ang maabtik nga nagsabat. Tinulok sia ni Benigno sing matalom.

Hambal ni Benigno, "Huo, nabatian namon ang linupok. Apang nagpabilin kami sa sulod sang balay."

Ginsaylusaylo sang tenyente ang iya panulok sa mag-asawa. Liwat nga gintumod si Agueda: "Ikaw, ano ang nabatian mo kagab- i?"

Si Benigno ang nagsabat.

"Ginakulbaan sia tenyente. Amo gid ina sia. Nagasalasala. Indi makahibalo sang ginahambal. Tan-awa sia kay nagakurog."

Madugay kag masusi nga gintamdan sang tenyente si Agueda. Tapat ini gani nga nagpauplok sa bintana. Pagkatapos ginbalikid liwat si Benigno: "Kag ano ang ginhimo ninyo?"

"Wala. Bisan magbangon wala."

"Kag ngaa?"

Dumulog si Benigno: "Makalalagam."

"May nahibal-an kamo sa tuyo ni Kumander Marcos nga ambusan si Mayor Arriola kag ang mga kaupod niya? Nakabati kamo sang mga balita?"

"Wala."

"Imposible. Wala ka nagabinutig? Nahibal-an namon nga madamo diri sa inyo ang nagapakigbuylog sa Kumander, gani nakahibalo sang iya mga plano. Mabug-at nga silot ang ginahatag namon sa nagabinutig sa pangulohan."

"Indi kami kabuylog sang Kumander."

"Kon amo kabuylog kamo namon. Nagabuylog kamo sa pangulohan."

Naghipos si Benigno.

"Kon amo, sanglit kabuylog kamo namon, magsugid kamo sing matuod. May padya nga nagahulat kon inyo mahimo."

"Lunsay kamatuoran ang ginsugid namon."

"Liwan kaina ang ginawakal sang asawa mo sang sa imo."

"Nasiling ko na nga ginakulbaan sia."

"Okey. Pamangkuton ko kamo liwat: kilala ninyo ang lalaki nga ini?"

"Indi. Abi ko kaina PC man nga kaupod ninyo."

"Nagabinutig ka!"

Kag ginsinyasan sang tenyente ang mga kaupod nga dalhon ang bangkay sa dyep. Dinuko ni Benigno ang iya ulo. Ginlikawan niya nga makit-an ang pagpahilayo nila sang bangkay. Apang hinali sia nga nakatungkaaw sang hinali lang sia bulakniton sang duha ka soldado sa magtimbang nga abaga. Kag pilit nila sia nga ginuyod sa dyep. Wala makatingog si Agueda. Husto na gid lang sa pagsunod ang ginakugmat niya nga mga mata sa nagapalayo nga likod ni Benigno.

Karon sirom na. Sa mga kakahuyan sa palibot sang balay mabatian ni Agueda ang paghuni sang mga kirikiri. Nagapungko sia sa atangan kag natakpan ang ganhaan sa iya likod. Nagahulat sia— kag ginakugmat—kay Benigno nga ginpahilayo lang wala gid makahambal ni isa ka tinaga sa ila. Indi niya maisip kon ano na ang nagakatabo karon kay Benigno. Ginakulbaan sia sing lakas. Nagapangadi sia nga halos wala sing untat halin pa kaina sing aga.

Ginalansang ni Agueda ang panulok sa buron nga kalsada sa unhan. Paagi sa malus-aw nga silak sang bulan, makit-an niya ang isa ka panong nga nagakubay sa higad sang kalsada—ang katubwan, ang gaba nga katubwan sa diin natabo na ang madamo nga kalalat- an. Nagakilan ang mga dahon sini sa kada paghuyop sang hangin katulad sang mga ginunting nga ginawaswas sang indi makit-an nga mga kaaway.

Sang ulihi pinukwat ni Agueda ang iya nawong sa kalangitan kag ginpaaninaw sa silak sang bulan ang igpat sang mga luha nga nagapunong sa iya mata. Hinaplos niya sang isa ka palad ang luha kag ang inagihan sang balhas sa iya nawong. Tumindog sia.

Tiniklod ang nagaraginit nga ganhaan kag sumolod. Natampad sa iya ang mga kabataan nga nagasikungkong sa salog kag nagadapat sang pighol kag binuro. Tinamdan sila ni Agueda.

"Manyapon na kita, Nay," ang hambal sang kamagulangan.

"Upod lang kami karon ni tatay mo."

"Maabot pa ato si tatay?"

"Maabot pa sia."

Tumalikod si Agueda. Liwat niya nga tinuhoy ang ganhaan. Kag hinali sia nga nakauklo.

Nagahulat sa iya ang duha ka tao sa idalom sang hagdanan. Nagakalo sila sing buri, gani nalipdan gikan sa silak sang bulan ang ila nawong. Mga dalagko kag mabakod sila nga pagkalalaki, ang isa nga nagapaninghawak burangoson. Wala man sila nagauniporme kag daw indi mahimo nga mga kaupod sila ni Kumander Marcos.

"Si Benigno?" ang pamangkot sang burangoson.

Wala ni Agueda mapunggi ang pagkurog: "Wa-wala pa sia."

"Sa diin sia?"

Wala anay si Agueda magsabat. Liwat niya nga sinusi ang pagtamod sa mga tao. Ginbantabanta ang tunay nila nga pagkatao. Giniliwat sang burangoson ang pamangkot. "Wala sia diri," ang sabat ni Agueda.

"Sa diin gani?"

"Am-ambot."

"Wala ka nakahibalo? Wala ka nagabinutig?"

Naglungolungo si Agueda. Kag pinagwa sang upod sang burangoson ang isa ka rebolber nga nasukbit sa iya balikawang. Tadlong nga tinumod si Agueda.

"Ma-maluoy kamo, to-to-to."

"Sa di-in si Benigno?"

"Sa ban-banwa."

Sa sini nga tion, ang mga kabataan nga nakabati sang bag-o nga mga tingog tumopad sa kay Agueda. Apang husto lang sila sa pagpalamuti sang makit-an ang ipit nila nga kahimtangan. Ginpamangkot sang burangoson si Agueda kon nag-ano si Benigno sa banwa. "Maluoy kamo, to-toto," ang iya pakitluoy. "Ma-mapatay ako ko-kon..."

"Nag-ano sia didto sa banwa?"

"Gin-gindala sang mga sol-soldado."

"Para ano? Para imbestigahon? Ano ang ginsugid ni Benigno?"

"Am-ambot. Wala si-sia sing may gin-ginsugid sa amon. Hus...husto na ni..."

"Nagareklamo ka?" kag pinalagatik sang nagakapot sang rebolber ang gatilyo, tuman na agod magpakitlu-oy naman liwat ang babae sang iya kabuhi. "Sabta sing matarong ang pamangkot ko kon amo."

"Ang-ang ano?"

"Kilala mo ang mga soldado?"

"Iya siguro ni-ni Simeon Ar..."

"Si Simeon Arriola? Maano pa si Simeon Arriola kay patay na sia. Indi pag-imitlang liwat ang iya ngalan. Kon himuon mo..." Kag pinataas sang lalaki liwat ang rebolber. Tinumod ang kabataan. "Kamo, sulod! Hala sulod! Ang bangkay diri, diin na ang bangkay?"

"Ang bangkay? Iya ato sang Kumander ang bangkay."

"Nahibal-an namon. Sa diin?"

"Gin-gindala man sang mga sol-soldado."

"Sa banwa? Para anhon? Ipakaon sa heneral?"

"Upod ang bana ko sa bangkay. Indi niya pagpabayaan ang bangkay."

"Si Benigno? He, he he, he. Agueda, patay na si Benigno." Nakasugahaw si Agueda. Tinagpon niya ang isa ka palad sa iya baba. "Kanday sin-o kami Agueda sa panan-awan mo?"

"Ka-kaupod kamo ni Kumander, in-indi ba..."

Bag-o makatapos si Agueda, bumagrong gikan sa katubwan ang bagrong sang dyep dungan sang pagbusaag sang mga suga sini. Dalidali nga nakuob ang duha ka lalaki sa kilid sang payagpayag. "Dira ka sa ganhaan Agueda. Indi ka dira maghalin," ang paandam.

Dumolog ang dyep sa tupad sang payagpayag. Madugaydogay, may nanaog, kag gilayon ini nga nakilal-an ni Agueda nga si Benigno. Tinumbok ang iya dughan sang kalipay sanglit buhi pa si Benigno.

Dalaganon kuntani niya kag hakson apang nadumdoman niya ang paandam sang duha ka lalaki. Mahinay ang paglakat ni Benigno, halos makasangkol, katulad sang nagalakat sa katulogon. Nagatamod sia kay Agueda apang subong sang wala makakita ini.

"Naano ka, Benigno?" ang pahutik nga pasikto ni Agueda.

Madugaydogay, lumakat na ang dyep. Kag gikan sa ila ginpanaguan, gumwa ang duha ka lalaki. Ginatumod sang isa ang rebolber karon kay Benigno.

"Karon, Benigno," hambal sang burangoson, "kay ari ka na, daku nga kasal-anan ang nabuhat mo kay Kumander. Suod niya nga abyan ang napatay sa idalom sang imo hagdanan. Kag karon ginpasugtan mo ang kaugalingon nga pisapisahon sang pamangkot sang mga soldado ni Simeon Arriola."

Kag dungan sini, umoy-oy si Benigno sa ginatindugan katulad sang gintapas nga saha sang saging. Naghurma ang dugo sa dughan sang iya kamiseta. Gilayon nga tumalikod ang duha ka lalaki, apang nakatapak pa gid lang sila sang pila ka tikang sang ginhapay man sila sang mga bala sa duta.

Madugay nga naurongan si Agueda sa tatlo ka bangkay sa iya atubangan nga karon gintilipunan na sang nakauniporme nga mga tinuga. Kag ginsaylo niya ang panulok sa katubwan kag nakit-an niya ini nga nagalakat, nagasulong kag nagawaswas sang ginunting: nagapalapit ang mga kaaway, isa ka panong tanan, nagakilan ang mga ginunting, kag lumosot gikan sa tilaok ni Agueda ang isa ka malawig kag makatilingil nga tiyabaw.

From: *Hiligaynon*, September 11 and 18, 1968

The Curse of the Sugarcane Fields

(Ang Gaba sang Katubwan)

Julius Flores

Benigno was still up when he heard gunshots ringing somewhere at the crossroad to Bay-ongan, by the sugarcane fields. It did not surprise him; for about a week now he had been expecting this. He did not get up from where he was lying on the *banig* beside Agueda. He just listened to the burst of gunfire.

Agueda, who had been sound asleep, jumped up. It was as if a spirit had possessed her. She wanted to say something, even scream, but Benigno held her down. She clung to him.

"Benigno, is this it?"

"Sssht!"

"I'm scared."

"Shut up."

Later, the shots became intermittent and faint. Benigno imagined that Commander Marcos and his followers had now returned to the hills of Bay-ongan, victorious. He was certain they had won. They had planned this ambush since last week. They had monitored the activities of Simeon Arriola and his PC escorts.

Four days before, Benigno had trekked uphill to Bay-ongan, bringing two sacks of rice—as was agreed upon. There, Pitong Barbasan, one of Commander Marcos' most trusted aides, asked him about the rumor that Simeon Arriola was going to campaign in Bay-ongan this Saturday. Benigno nodded.

"The Mayor, Simeon Arriola, will be holding a rally in Bay-ongan. In the town, I was there yesterday—Mehor and Gadata, Arriola's policemen were discussing this. They too will be going. I overheard this from them as they were sipping coffee at *Tiya* Atang's carinderia; I was leaning on a wall beside them. Arriola isn't sure of Bay-ongan's support so he's set on campaigning here."

"You, do you think they suspected you?"

"We've been very careful."

"You should. See that this doesn't slip out to anyone. Don't say we ever talked about this. Don't mention it to anybody, even to Agueda. If the plan falls through because of your silliness, the Commander will blow his top at you. You know him very well."

But Benigno's tongue slipped and Agueda got wind of the plot.

"Tell on this, Agueda," he warned, "and the Commander will kill us. Not only us but the children too. We're now in his control; just one mistake and we'll get what we're not looking for."

Eyes wide open, her mouth agape, Agueda could not say a word.

Then she clung to her husband, saying: "Let's get out of here at once, Benigno! I can't stand this any more. I will die if we stay here any longer." Her voice was soft and tremulous.

"Shut up!"

"I told you a long time ago we should leave this place. You are to blame if...."

Agueda was cut short when Benigno pushed her against the wall. Her eyes held fear and an appeal as Benigno bent towards her, covering her with his shadow. She stared at him, watching his every movement. Suddenly, she let out a shriek: Benigno had pulled out a sharp knife wedged into the nipa wall.

"Benigno, please, have pity," she cried.

"You will shut up. Or else...."

"Yes."

"You will not let this out."

"No."

"Don't forget that."

"Yes, Benigno."

"Before the Commander kills us, I shall get to you first. So don't ever tell this to anyone. And listen, we can't leave this place. If we do, he would suspect we had sided with the PC and squealed on their whereabouts. We'll stay here under his command. Do you remember what happened to Merto, Binang and Soling last year?

How they were peppered with bullets by Simeon Arriola's bodyguards?"

"It was the Commander's men who did that...."

"Those were Arriola's! Get that into your head. They were in uniform. So they were from the PC. Did you see their bodies? Bulletholed. In the head, in the tummy, in the chest. Blood was all over—on their underjaw, mouth, chest, groins. Soling was all twisted, Binang was grimacing, Merto's eyes were popping out. Did you see Merto's eyes? Did you see them Agueda?"

The night was still now. In the sugarcane fields nothing stirred. Then sprung vividly in Benigno's mind the image of the bodies of Simeon Arriola and his men. Bathed in their blood, the jeep athwart the street canal, its windshield riddled with holes.

Benigno's two children were also roused from sleep by the sound of gunfire but they did not ask what it was all about. They lay sprawled on the *banig* in the adjoining room, their hearts thumping with fear. Then they fell asleep again.

But all sleepiness had been banished from Benigno and Agueda. They lay beside each other, her arm wrapped around him. But neither stirred nor spoke a word. Agueda fixed her gaze on the darkness, where the wall was. Reproaching herself, wondering. How did they get themselves into this dilemma, leaving them dazed, trembling and unable to slip into the bliss of freedom? Gloom had cast its shadow on each waking day of their lives.

Agueda recalled that after her wedding to Benigno ten years earlier, he had brought her to this remote place. He had inherited a piece of rice land from his parents and "here, they would find their fortune." So Agueda had followed him. Then four months pregnant, she had nothing else in her mind but the future of their child.

But where had good fortune gone? Where lay the future? What good fortune awaited them in this far away place? Nothing. This had been slain and buried long ago by creatures who did not even have the slightest compassion for their fellowmen. Good fortune had long since gone, the future was empty, and now they had no choice but to play dumb, be enslaved by the mess of other people, and watch themselves sink into utter misery.

Still another thought disturbed Agueda. Sometimes in her dreams, she saw herself alone in death, not having anyone to give her a decent burial. Not even Benigno or her relatives were there. For she and Benigno had drawn apart from each other, carried away by currents they could not control. He had gone to the extent of threatening her with death; she had been reduced to falling on her knees to plead for her life. There was no reason why her forebodings would not come true. The Benigno in her arms was no longer the Benigno she had married. Now in her embrace, yet as distant as the stars. He could be as scorching as the sun's heat and he could also be as cold as the wind that now seeped into the slats of their bamboo floor.

Abruptly, Agueda drew her arm away from her husband. She turned her back on him, hunched herself up, and broke into a sob to ease the pain inside her. Benigno had felt her arm lift from him. He heard her sob, and briefly he turned to look at her. But he did not stir.

So much was weighing down his mind. He thought of the Commander; Agueda and the children; Merto and Soling and Binang; Simeon Arriola and the PC. He remembered how he used to frequent the public dance in Barrio Candelaria each Saturday night. Those days of leisure and freedom had vanished with his parents when their bus had fallen in the ravine at Mangampili.

His thoughts broke off when he felt Agueda whispering something to him: "Listen."

The wind was blowing from the sugarcane field of Bay-ongan. It carried the strong breathing of Commander Marcos. Benigno was taking it in. He could not scrape off the Commander's presence. It clung to him like an oyster stuck to a rock. The wind was the Commander's steward, watching him even in the night.

"Did you hear?"

"Hear what?"

"Someone is moaning."

Even with the wind tearing and ripping, Benigno heard. A feeble voice, like that of someone agonizing and dying. As the wounded man drew near, his voice grew louder and soon, they sensed that the man had already reached their staircase.

"Open the door for him, Benigno," Agueda's voice was shaking.

"Go back to sleep."

"Go, look...."

"I told you, go back to sleep!"

"But...."

"Agueda?"

"He might be one of Commander Marcos' men."

"That's impossible. No one could have been wounded among them. That man is with the group of Simeon Arriola. Let's go go back to sleep."

"I can't fall asleep when someone is groaning. Benigno, listen. He's now going up the stairs. I'm scared."

Benigno's voice had faded into a whisper: "You have not heard anything, Agueda. Mark that. You've heard nothing."

The next morning, the ground Benigno was standing on was moist with the dawn drizzle. He had opened the door and as he had expected, a body lay sprawled by the staircase. Death had overtaken him, it seemed, when no help came and he could no longer bear the pain and the cold.

Benigno was not mistaken. It was one of Simeon Arriola's men; he was in fatigues. The casualties were only on Arriola's side. But suddenly he was taken aback. He had given the body a closer look. Agueda and their two children who were standing by the door, terrified, caught the change in his expression as he squatted by the corpse, peering at its face.

"Don't you see, Agueda?"

"'Tay, what?" It was the eldest who replied.

"He seems to be one of the Commander's men."

Agueda was jolted when she heard this. She too peered at the dead man.

"This is one of his men, Agueda. I recognize his face. I used to see him in Bay-ongan. He often spied for the Commander. He is a trusted aide."

Agueda's voice shook: "You are not mistaken?"

He looked up at Agueda, his eyes hinting that he could not be wrong.

"Benigno...?"

"I don't know. Don't ask me."

"Let's pray, Benigno. Let's plead for God's mercy."

"That's of no use."

"You've made a mistake, Benigno."

"Are you not going to shut up? What can prayers do? Nothing, Agueda. Nothing. Kneel and plead instead to the Commander."

"Whatever happens, it's all your fault, Benigno. Last night I told you to open the door because someone was groaning. The man was dying, he was begging for help. Whether or not he was a follower of the Commander we should have helped him. If you were in his place...."

"Agueda!"

She turned to her children and said: "Repeat after me. 'Our Father who art in heaven....' "

"I don't know who is to blame. We are poor, we have no power, no wealth...."

The couple started when a PC jeep turned from the corner. It pulled over in front of their hut. A middle-aged lieutenant got off. His eyes were alert, his body well-built and sturdy. Brisk and arrogant in mien, he walked straight to the staircase, and with arms akimbo, regarded the dead man closely. Three soldiers trailed behind him.

Benigno froze. He continued to squat beside the body but turned his head up briefly as the lieutenant drew near. Then he nailed his eyes on the dead man, waiting for the lieutenant to speak. Agueda's head shrank completely behind the door.

"You know him," the lieutenant said to Benigno.

"No."

He pressed. Benigno kept mum.

"You." He pointed to Agueda who was now peeping from the window. "Answer me!"

"N-n-no."

"You're lying! You know he's one of Commander Marcos' men."

The lieutenant raised his voice abruptly. "I shall ask you again and I want you to tell me the truth. We shall use force on you if you don't budge. You know him!"

The couple kept their mouths shut.

At this moment, two of the soldiers began to circle the hut. They peered at the kitchen and into the holes of the hut's walls, and then they looked around at the thicket behind it. The third stayed behind, a Thompson slung on his side.

"Did you hear about what happened last night? The gunbattle between the forces of Mayor Arriola and Commander Marcos?"

"No." It was Agueda who quickly answered. Benigno looked at her sharply, adding: "Yes, we heard gunfire but we remained inside the house."

The lieutenant kept shifting his gaze between the couple. Then he turned again to Agueda. "You. What did you hear last night?"

It was Benigno who replied: "She is tense, lieutenant. She gets all mixed up when she's tense. Look, she's trembling."

The lieutenant stared hard at Agueda. She shrank farther back from the window. He turned again to Benigno: "And what did you do?"

"Nothing. Not even get up from bed."

"Why not?"

Benigno paused. "It was dangerous."

"Did you know that Commander Marcos was planning to ambush the mayor? Did this reach your ears before?"

"No."

"Impossible! You're not lying? We know many of you here are his sympathizers, and so you've been let in on his plans. Remember, we punish heavily those who are traitors to the government."

"We don't sympathize with the Commander."

"Then you support the government."

Benigno didn't reply.

"And, since you do, you will tell us the truth. A reward awaits you."

"But we've told you all that we know."

"Your wife was babbling something else."

"I told you she was nervous."

"Okay. Let me ask you again. Do you know this man?"

"I thought a while ago that he was one of you."

"Liar!"

Then the lieutenant waved to his men to haul the corpse into the jeep. Benigno lowered his head to avoid looking at them but he raised it when two soldiers grabbed him by the shoulders. They dragged him towards the jeep. Unable to breathe a word, Agueda could do nothing but follow her husband with terror-struck eyes.

It was dark now. Twilight had fallen. In the thicket around the house, the *kiri-kiri* were chirping. Agueda was sitting on the *atangan*, the topmost step of the bamboo staircase, her back against the door. She was very worried. Benigno had to leave without saying a word to the family. She hated to imagine what was now happening to him. Terrified, she had been waiting and praying without cease since the morning.

She fixed her gaze on the street ahead. It was blurred, but in the faint moonlight she could see rows of sugarcane lining the roadside. The sugarcane field. That accursed field. The scene of so much tragedy. With each gust of wind, its sheaves glistened like bolos being brandished by unseen enemies. She turned her face up to the sky and her tears gleamed in the moonlight. With one palm, she wiped off her tears and the sweat running down her face.

She stood up. Pushed the creaking door and stepped inside. Seated on the floor, their knees folded up, the children were eating lumpfuls of cold rice and *binuro*, or salted fish, with their hands.

"Nanay, let's eat," the eldest said.

"I'll just eat with your father later."

"Is he coming home tonight?"

"Yes."

Agueda turned around and walked back to the door again. She winced. At the foot of the stairs two men were waiting for her. They were wearing *buri* hats, so their faces were screened from the moonlight. Both were burly men. The one with arms akimbo sported a moustache. They were not in uniform, but neither could they be Commander Marcos' men.

"Where's Benigno?" asked the bemoustached man.

"He...he is not here," she was shaking.

"Where is he?"

Agueda did not answer right away. She scrutinized the men, trying to gauge their real identity.

"Where is he?" he asked again.

"He's not here."

"I know. But where is he?"

"I... I don't know."

"Are you sure? Are you not lying?"

Agueda shook her head. The other man pulled out the revolver tucked into his waistband and aimed it at Agueda.

"Wait. Have pity on me, *Toto*."

"Where is Benigno?"

"In...in the town."

At this point, the children who had heard the voices walked up to Agueda. When they sensed the danger they were in, they turned pale. The man asked what Benigno was doing in the town.

"Have pity on me, *Toto*, have pity," she pleaded. "They will kill me if...."

"What's he doing in the town?"

"The, the s-soldiers picked him up."

"For what? To be questioned? What did Benigno tell them?"

"I... I don't, don't know... He hasn't told us anything. Please, please. Enough...."

"Are you complaining?" The other man clicked the trigger, enough to make the woman plead for her life again. "Then answer, answer me properly."

"Wha....t?"

"Do you know those soldiers?"

"Probably Simeon Arriola's."

"Simeon Arriola? What else can he do? He's dead. And don't mention his name again. If you do...."

His companion raised his gun again and this time aimed it at the children. "Get inside! The body here. Where is it?"

"The body. Was that one of the Commander's men?"

"We know. But where is it?"

"The soldiers brought it with them too."

"To the town? To be fed to the general?"

"My husband was with him. He will not leave it alone."

"Benigno? He, he, he, he. Agueda, Benigno is already dead."

Agueda screamed. He gagged Agueda with the palm of his hand.

"On whose side are we, Agueda? What do you think?"

"You, you are the comm... commander's men, aren't you?"

Before Agueda could finish, a jeep zoomed out of the sugarcane fields, flooding the street with its headlights. The two men ran quickly for cover to the side of the hut. Then one of them warned her: "Stand by the door. Don't move."

The jeep pulled up in front of the hut. In a few moments, someone got off. Agueda recognized him. It was Benigno. And her heart jumped with joy to see him still alive. She was about to run into his arms but she remembered the men's warning. Benigno walked slowly, like someone walking in his sleep. His eyes were on Agueda but it seemed like he didn't see her.

"What's wrong with you?" she mumbled to him.

The jeep drove off quickly, and the two men emerged from their hiding place. Now the man was pointing his gun at Benigno.

"Alright, Benigno," said the man with the moustache.

"You've betrayed the Commander. The dead man was close to him. Besides, you have allowed yourself to be grilled by Simeon Arriola's soldiers."

At that very moment, Benigno tottered and fell like a young banana tree being mowed down. Blood stained the t-shirt on his chest. The two men walked away immediately, but they had just taken a few steps when they were also felled by bullets.

For a long while, Agueda stood frozen before the bodies sprawled in front of her. Now she was surrounded by uniformed men. She shifted her gaze to the sugarcane field. The enemy was advancing, closing in on her, threatening her with their glistening scythes. Then burst forth from Agueda's throat, a long, piercing scream.

Ang Gaba sa Tubuhan

Julius Flores

Gising pa si Benigno nang marinig niya ang palitan ng putok sa may sangandaan patungong Bay-ongan, doon sa may tubuhan. Pero hindi siya nagulat. May isang linggo nang inaabangan niya ito. Nakahiga siya sa banig sa tabi ni Agueda at hindi na siya bumangon pa. Nakinig siya sa putukan.

Subalit si Aguedang mahimbing na ang pagkatulog ay nagulantang. Parang nasapian siya ng espiritu. Magsasalita sana siya, nais sanang tumili, nguni't maagap siyang hinila ni Benigno sa banig. Yumakap si Agueda sa dibdib ng asawa.

"Benigno, ini na bala?"

"Pssst!" pinatahimik siya ni Benigno.

"Ginakabahan ako."

"Huwag kang maingay. Ini na."

Lumipas ang ilang minuto. Nang lumaon, dumalang at humina ang mga putukan at parang nalalarawan ni Benigno na pabalik na sina Kumander Marcos sa kabukiran ng Bay-ongan, dala ang tagumpay. Tiyak niya na sina Kumander Marcos ang nanalo. Naplano na nila ang lahat na taktika sa pag-ambus na ito. Napagpasiyahan na nila iyon nang may isang linggo na. Napagmatyagan na nila ang bawat kilos ni Simeon Arriola at ang mga eskort nitong PC.

Naalala ni Benignong may apat na araw na ang nakalipas, umakyat siya papuntang Bay-ongan para magdala ng dalawang sakong bigas ayon sa kanilang pinagkasunduan.

Inusisa siya ng isa sa mga pinagkakatiwalaan na tauhan ni Kumander Marcos, si Pitong Barbasan, kung totoo nga ang kumakalat na balitang nangangampanya si Simeon Arriola sa darating na Sabado sa Bay-ongan. Tumangu-tango siya. Pagkatapos, idinugtong:

"Ako mismo nakarinig nga nagaplano si Mayor—a, si Simeon Arriola—nga magamiting sa Bay-ongan. Nandoon ako kahapon sa bayan at narinig ko, sina Mehor at Gadata, iyong mga pulis ni Simeon Arriola nga naga-usap tungkol dito. Sasama din nga raw sila kay Simeon. Gainum-inom sila sa kapihan ni Tiya Atang at nandoon ako nakasandal sa isang tabi. Sa tingin ko, buo na ang hinala ni Simeon Arriola sa mga taga Bay-ongan, kaya't sumisikap na mangampanya rito."

"Sa inyo indi siya nagasuspetso?"

"Nagaingat kami."

"Dapat gid. Indi ko gustong makalusot ito sa iba, Benigno. Sabihin mong wala tayong ging-usapan. Huwag na huwag mong banggitin ito kahit kanino, kahit kay Agueda. At kung masira ang plano ng Kumander dahil sa katarantaduhan ninyo, kayo na mismo ang mapuputukan ng galit ni Kumander Marcos. Alam niyo naman kung paano magalit si Kumander Marcos."

Ngunit hindi napigil ni Benigno ang magpahiwatig kay Agueda ukol sa pinag-uusapan nila ni Pitong Barbasan. Nadulas na lang ang kanyang dila, at nalaman tuloy ni Agueda ang katotohanan.

"Ipagsabi mo ina, Agueda," ang babala niya "at buhay naton ang kikitilin ni Kumander Marcos. Indi lang buhay naton nga duha kundi pati na rin ng duha naton nga anak. Nasa gahom kita ngayon sang kumander, nasa proteksyon at pananakop niya kita, at pag nadulas tayo nang kaunti, matatagpuan naton ang di naton ginahanap."

Hindi nakasagot si Agueda. Nandilat ang kanyang mga mata. Napanganga ang kanyang bibig subalit walang katagang lumabas. At bigla siyang yumakap kay Benigno.

"Umalis na kita diri, Benigno. Mapatay ako siguro kung tatagal pa kita diri," bulong ni Agueda, ang boses ay nanginginig.

"Tumigil ka, Agueda!"

"Matagal nang ginasabi ko sa iyo na umalis na kita rito. Ikaw ang may kasalanan kung...."

Tumigil si Agueda nang itulak siya ni Benigno sa dingding. Nakalarawan sa kanyang mga mata ang takot at pagmamakaawa habang nakikiramdam at nagbabantay sa kilos ng asawa. Nakayuko si Benigno kay Agueda at tinakpan ito ng kanyang anino. Napasigaw si Agueda nang bunutin ni Benigno ang isang matalim na kutsilyong nakasuksok sa nipang dingding.

"Benigno, indi, maawa ka," ang pagsusumamo ni Agueda.

"Tumahimik ka at kung indi...."

"Tatahimik na, Benigno."

"Ipagsasabi mo sa iban ang nalalaman mo?"

"Indi."

"Tandai ina!"

"Huo, Benigno."

"Bago tayo patyon, Agueda, ni Kumander Marcos, ikaw muna ang uunahin kong patyon dahil ikaw ang dahilan. Tanda-i gid ina. At makinig ka: indi kita makakaalis dito. Magasuspetso si Kumander. Malalaman niyang umalis kita dahil sa kalokohan mo. Magahinala siyang nakisanib tayo sa PC at nagsumbong tungkol sa kanilang pinagtataguan sa Bay-ongan. Kaya't magapaiwan kita dito hanggang kailan man. Sa ilalim ng gahom ni Kumander Marcos. Natandaan mo ang nangyari kina Merto at Binang at Soling nung taong nakalipas? Nang pinaulanan sila ng bala ng mga badigard ni Simeon Arriola?"

"Sila Kumander Marcos ang gumawa nun...."

"Tumahimik ka! Sila Simeon Arriola ang may kagagawan niyon. Indi ang kumander. Nakauniporme sila. Ang PC nakauniporme. Gani mga PC sila. Nakita mo ang mga katawan nila? Butas-butas. Sa ulo, sa tiyan, sa dibdib, sa hita. Nakapilipit si Soling, naka-ngiwi si Binang, at si Berto nangag-usli ang mga mata. Nakita mo ang pag-usli ng mga mata ni Merto? Nakita mo, Agueda?"

Tahimik na ngayon ang gabi. Sa tubuhan wala nang bumubulung-bulong. Malinaw na nalarawan sa isip ni Benigno ang mga bangkay ni Simeon Arriola at mga kasama nito. Naliligo sila sa sariling dugo, tinutuhog ng nagsidaang bala ang salamin ng kanilang dyip. Ang dyip ay nakahalang at nakatingkayad sa malalim na kanal.

Noon din, nagising ang dalawang anak ni Benigno dahil sa nangyari, ngunit katulad ng kanilang ama, pinigil nila ang hangaring mag-usisa at nagpaiwan na lang silang nakahilata sa banig sa tabing kwarto. Kumakabog ang takot sa loob ng kanilang dibdib pero di-nagtagal, nakatulog silang muli.

Lumipas ang pagkaantok ni Benigno at Agueda. Nagsiping sila, ang isang braso ni Agueda, nakayakap sa dibdib sang bana, subalit nanatili silang kapwa walang imik. Nakatitig si Agueda sa dilim, sa may bandang dinding: nagtatanong, naninisi nang lihim kung bakit—bakit nadawit nila ang mga sarili sa gulong ito na tumakip ng panganib sa maaliwalas sana nilang pamumuhay. Kung bakit napagitna sila sa dalawang daan na hindi magkatugma—nakakataranta, nakanginginig dahil walang malulusutan patungong katahimikan.

Naaalala pa ni Agueda na, matapos ang kasal nila ni Benigno, may sampung taon na ang nakalipas, dinala siya ng lalaki sa pook na ito dahil "dito ang kanilang kapalaran." Isang pirasong lupang pansaka na ibinigay ng kanilang mga magulang. Walang magawa si Agueda kundi sumama. Apat na buwan na siyang nagdadalang-tao at wala siyang ibang inisip kundi ang kinabukasan ng kanilang anak.

Subalit natanong niya ngayon ang kanyang sarili. Saan na ang kapalaran at kinabukasan? Anong klaseng kapalaran ang aasahan nila sa pook na ito? Wala. Wala na ang kapalaran. Matagal na itong pinatay at inilibing ng mga manunupil na walang maski kaunting konsiderasyon sa kanilang puso. Wala na ang kapalaran, ang kinabukasan, at ngayon wala na silang magawa kundi ang magwalang-kibo, magpaalipin sa kaguluhan ng iba, at maghintay malugmok sa kawalang-pag-asa.

Subalit bukod dito, mayroon pang kinahihintakutan si Agueda. Kung minsan sa kanyang pagmumuni-muni, napagisip-isip niyang sa darating na panahon, mamamatay siyang nag-iisa, wala maski na sinong maglalagay ng kanyang bangkay sa isang disenteng kabaong. Dahil wala na si Benigno, at wala na rin silang kamag-anak.

Ito ang bumagabag sa kanya. Unti-unting nagkakalayo ang kanilang mga damdamin, inaanod, tinatangay nang hindi mapipigilang pangyayari. Nagawa sa kanya ni Benigno ang pagbanta ng kamatayan at sa kanyang panig naman, nagawa niya ang magmakaaawa para sa sariling buhay. Kaya't walang dahilang hindi magkakatotoo ang kaniyang pinangangambahan. Ang Benignong yakap-yakap niya ngayon ay hindi na ang Benignong pinakasalan niya noon. Kanyang niyayakap subalit kasinglayo na ng mga bituin. Nakakapaso tulad ng araw at malamig tulad ng hanging lumulusot ngayon sa mga puwang ng kanilang sahig.

Tinanggal niyang bigla ang kanyang brasong nakasampay sa dibdib ng kanyang asawa. Tumalikod siya at namaluktot. Humikbi para paginhawain ang hinanakit.

Naramdaman ni Benigno ang pag-alsa ng braso ni Agueda sa kanyang dibdib. Saglit niyang nilingon ito. Narinig niya ang hikbi ng asawa. Subalit hindi siya tuminag.

Mabigat ang iniisip ni Benigno. Si Kumander Marcos, si Agueda at ang kanilang mga anak; si Merto at si Soling at si Binang; si Simeon Arriola at ang mga PC; siya, si Benigno na nakararating sa baryo Candelaria at mga sayawan sa plasa kung Sabado ng gabi. Ang mga matamis at tahimik na araw na ngayon ay patay na, namatay sabay ng kanyang mga magulang sa isang bus sa bangin ng Mangampili.

Napaigtad siya nang maramdaman ang pagkalabit ni Agueda.

May ibinubulong ito. "Pakinggan mo."

Umiihip ang hangin galing sa kabukiran ng Bay-ongan, dala-dala ang malakas na hininga ni Kumander Marcos. Hinihinga ni Benigno ang hininga ni kumander. Hindi niya maikaskas sa sarili ang kumander. Katulad ito ng talabang nakakapit sa bato ng dalampasigan. Kahit na ang hangin ay nagawang luklukan ng kumander para bantayan ang kanilang mga kilos sa oras ng pagtulog.

"Narinig mo?"

"Ang anu?"

"May gahalinghing."

At sa gitna ng hagupit ng hangin, narinig ni Benigno ang tinutukoy ng asawa. Isang tinig—mahugong, nagdurusa, at naghihingalo—parang nanggagaling sa libingan. Habang palapit ang may tinig, lumalakas naman ito sa pandinig ni Benigno hanggang sa huli pakiramdam niya'y naroon na ang tinig sa may puno ng kanilang hagdanan.

"Dungawin mo, Benigno," nagiginig ang tinig ni Agueda.

"Matulog ka na!"

"Dungawin mo."

"Matulog ka na!"

"Subalit..."

"Agueda?"

"Basi kasamahan ni kumander."

"Indi maaring may sugatan sa panig ni kumander. Kasamahan iyan ni Simeon Arriola. Matulog na kita."

"Indi ako makatulog kung may gaalulong sa aton hagdanan. Nandiyan na siya sa may paanan ng hagdanan. Paakyat na siya, Benigno. Natatakot ako."

Halos pabulong na ang tinig ni Benigno. "Wala kang narinig, Agueda. Tandai, wala kang narinig."

Kinaumagahan, mamasa-masa sa kaunting ambon ng madaling araw ang lupang kinatatayuan ni Benigno. Pagbukas niya ng kanyang pinto, tulad ng kanilang inaasahan, nahantad ang anyo ng isang bangkay na nakahandusay sa lupa sa tabi ng kanilang hagdanan. Natuluyan sigurong namatay; hindi natiis ang sakit at lamig sa kahihintay ng inaasahang tulong.

Hindi nagkamali si Benigno. Bangkay ng sundalo ni Simeon Arriola. Nakauniporme ito ng patig. Tama ang kanyang pagpalagay na sa panig lang ni Simeon Arriola ang sugatan.

Subalit biglang natigilan si Benigno matapos mapagmasdang mabuti ang bangkay. Si Agueda at ang dalawa nilang anak na ngayon ay nakatingin sa may pintuan na parang natatakot, nakabasa ng biglang pagbabago sa mukha ni Benigno. Nakatingkayad ito sa may tabi ng bangkay at dahil sa hindi niya ito mahipo, sinilip niya ang mukha nito.

"Indi mo nakita, Agueda?"

"Ang anu, 'Tay?"

"Tingnan mo, daw kasama ini ni Kumander Marcos."

Napaigtad si Agueda sa narinig. Yumuko siya para masuring mabuti ang itsura ng bangkay.

"Kasama niya ini, Agueda. Kilala ko ang kanyang mukha. Isa siya sa mga laging nagasubaybay para kay kumander. Lubos siyang pinagkakatiwalaan ni kumander."

Nanginginig ang tinig ni Agueda: "Indi ka nagkamali?" Ibinaling ni Benigno ang kanyang mga mata kay Agueda, matang nagpapahiwatig na hindi siya maaaring nagkamali.

"Benigno...?"

"Ambot! Huwag mo akong tanungin."

"Manalangin tayo, Benigno."

"Walang kabuluhan iyan."

"Nagkamali ka, Benigno."

"Indi ka titigil?"

"Anu ang maobra sang dasal sa galit ng kumander? Wala, Agueda, wala. Sa harap ni Kumander Marcos ka lumuhod at magdasal. Sa harapan niya, indi sa Diyos!"

"Kung anu man ang mangyayari, ikaw ang may-sala, Benigno. Kagab-i, sinabi ko sa iyong buksan ang pinto dahil may gaalulong. Nag-aagaw buhay ang tao, Benigno, nangangailangan ng tulong; alagad man ni kumander o indi, dapat sana gingtulungan naton siya. Kung ikaw ang sa kanyang lugar...."

"Agueda!"

Nilingon ni Agueda ang dalawang bata. "Sumunod kayo sa akin. Ama namin, sumasalangit ka...."

"Aywan kung sinu-sino ang may kasalanan. Mahirap lang naman tayo, walang gahom, walang pilak...."

Sabay na natigilan ang mag-asawa nang mula sa sangandaan, sumulpot ang isang dyip ng PC. Huminto ito sa tapat ng kubo ng mag-asawa. Mula sa dyip pumanaog ang isang tinyenteng nasa kalagitnaang gulang at may masipat na mata. Malaki siya, matipuno. Maliksi at mapagmataas kumilos. Dumiretso siya sa hagdanan. Nakapamaywang na pinagmasdan ang bangkay. Sumusunod sa kanya ang tatlo pang sundalo.

Nanatili si Benigno sa kanyang kinalalagyan. Nakatingkayad pa rin siya sa tabi ng bangkay. Nang lumapit ang tinyente, madali niyang tiningnan ito. Pagkatapos, ipinako niya ang kanyang paningin sa bangkay habang naghihintay-hintay sa sasabihin ng tinyente. Lalo namang kumubli si Agueda sa may bintana.

"Kilala mo siya," ang sabi ng tinyente kay Benigno.

"Indi."

Namilit: "Kilala mo siya."

Tumahimik si Benigno.

"Ikaw," tinuro niya si Agueda. "Sumagot ka!"

"I-indi!"

"Nagasinungaling kayo! Alam niyong alagad siya ni Kumander Marcos. (Biglang lumakas ang tinig ng tinyente.) Tatanungin ko kayo uli at magsabi kayo sang totoo. Maari namin kayong idaan sa dahas kung magmamatigas kayo. Kilala ninyo siya!"

Itinikom ng mag-asawa ang kanilang bibig.

Sa mga sandaling ito, umikot ang dalawang sundalo sa kubo. Sumilip sila sa kusina at sa mga butas ng dingding, at pagkatapos sa mga talahib sa likuran ng bahay. Ang isa naiwang nakasakbat ng tomson.

"Nabalitaan ninyo ang nangyari kagabi? Ang pagbabarilan ng pangkat ni Kumander Marcos laban sa pangkat ni Simeon Arriola?"

"Indi," si Agueda ang mabilis na sumagot. Tinitigan siya ng matalim ni Benigno.

Ang sabi ni Benigno: "Huo, narinig namin ang barilan. Pero nanatili kami sa loob ng bahay."

Pinalipat-lipat ng tinyente ang kanyang paningin sa mag-asawa. Tinuro uli si Agueda: "Ikaw, ano ang narinig mo kagab-i?"

Si Benigno ang sumagot: "Ginakabahan siya Tinyente. Ganyan talaga siya. Indi alam ang pinagsasabi. Tingnan mo, nanginginig."

Matagal at masusing pinagmasdan ng tinyente si Agueda. Lalo pa nga itong nagpahumpak sa bintana. Pagkatapos, nilingon niya uli si Banigno. "At ano ang ginawa ninyo?"

"Wala. Maski na bumangon, wala."

"At bakit?"

Sandaling tumigil si Benigno: "Mapanganib."

"May nalalaman kayo sa plano ni Kumander Marcos na ambusin si Mayor Arriola at ang mga kasama niya. Nabalitaan ba ninyo?"

"Indi."

"Imposible. Indi ka nagasinungaling? Alam namin na marami dito sa inyo ang nakikipagkutsaba sa Kumander, kaya't nakakaalam ng kanyang mga plano. Mabigat nga parusa ang ginabigay namin sa nagasinungaling sa pamahalaan."

"Indi kami kakampi ni kumander."

"Kung gayon, kakampi namin kayo. Nagakampi kayo sa pamahalaan."

Tumahimik si Benigno.

"Kung gayon, dahil kakampi namin kayo, magasabi kayo sang totoo. May pabuyang naghihintay kung gagawin ninyo iyan."

"Totoo lahat ang sinabi namin."

"Iba kanina ang pinagsasabi ng asawa mo kaysa sa sinasabi mo."

"Sinabi ko nang kinakabahan siya."

"Okey. Tatanungin ko uli kayo. Kilala ninyo ang lalaki nga ini?"

"Indi. Akala ko kanina PC rin tulad ninyo."

"Nagasinungaling ka!"

At sinenyasan ng tinyente ang mga kasama na dalhin ang bangkay sa dyip. Yumuko si Benigno. Iniwasan niyang tingnan ang pagkaladkad nila ng bangkay. Subalit bigla siyang natingala nang sunggaban siya ng dalawang sundalo sa magkabilang balikat. At pilit nilang hinila siya sa dyip. Hindi nakakibo si Agueda. Sapat na lang ang pagsunod ng kanyang nagimbal na mga mata sa papalayong likod ni Benigno.

Takipsilim na. Sa mga kakahuyang palibot ng bahay naririnig ni Agueda ang paghuni ng mga kiri-kiri. Nakaupo siya sa pinakamataas na baitang ng hagdanan at ang kanyang likod ay nakasandal sa may pintuan. Naghihintay siya—at nagigimbal dahil si Benigno'y napalayo nang hindi man lang nakapag-iwan ni isang kataga sa kanila. Hindi niya maisip kung ano na ang nangyayari kay Benigno. Kinakabahan siya nang labis. Nagdarasal siya nang walang tigil magmula pa kaninang umaga.

Ipinako ni Agueda ang kanyang paningin sa madilim-dilim na kalsada sa unahan. Sa banaag ng buwan, nakita niya ang mga nakahanay sa tabi ng kalsada—ang tubuhan, ang gaba ng katubuhan na kung saan naganap ang marami nang trahedya. Kumikinang ang mga dahon nito sa bawat pag-ihip ng hangin, tulad ng mga itak na iwinawasiwas sa hindi nakikitang kaaway.

Di-naglaon, inangat ni Agueda ang kanyang mukha sa kalangitan at naaninag sa liwanag ng buwan ang kislap ng mga luhang pumigta sa kanyang mga mata. Hinaplos niya sa isang palad ang luha at ang pinagtuluan ng pawis sa kanyang mukha. Tumayo siya. Tinulak ang lumalangitngit na pintuan at pumasok. Nakita niya ang mga batang nakasikungkong sa sahig at sumusubo ng bahaw at binurong isda. Pinagmasdan sila ni Agueda.

"Maghapunan na tayo, Nanay," ang sabi ng panganay.

"Sabay na lang kami mamaya ng Tatay mo."

"Darating pa bala si Tatay?"

"Darating pa siya."

Tumalikod si Agueda. Muli siyang tumungo sa pintuan. Pero bigla siyang napaurong.

Dalawang tao ang naghihintay sa kanya sa may hagdanan. Nakasumbrero sila ng buri, kaya't natakpan ang kanilang mga mukha sa liwanag ng buwan. Malalaki at matitipuno silang lalaki, may bigote ang isang nakapamaywang. Hindi sila nakauniporme at hindi rin maaaring kasama sila ni Kumander Marcos.

"Si Benigno?" ang tanong ng may bigote.

Hindi napigil ni Agueda ang panginginig: "Wa-wala pa siya."

"Nasaan siya?"

Hindi muna sumagot si Agueda. Masusi niyang tiningnan muli ang mga tao. Kinikilatis ang tunay nilang pagkatao. Inulit ng may bigote ang kanyang tanong. "Wala siya diri," ang sagot ni Agueda.

"E, nasaan nga siya?'

"Ay-aywan."

"Indi mo alam? Indi ka nagasinungaling?"

Umiling-iling si Agueda. Inilabas ng kasama na may bigote ang rebolber na nakasukbit sa kanyang baywang. Tuwiran niyang tinitigan si Agueda.

"Ma-maawa kayo, 'To-to-to."

"Saan si Benigno?"

"Sa ba-bayan."

Sa mga sandaling ito, ang mga batang nakarinig ng bagong tinig ay tumabi kay Agueda. Subalit lubha silang namutla nang nakita ang kanilang kagipitan. Tinanong ng may bigote si Agueda kung anong ginawa ni Benigno sa bayan. "Maawa kayo, To-to," ang kanyang pagsusumamo. "Ma-mapatay ako ku-kung...."

"Anong ginawa niya roon sa bayan?"

"Gin-gindala ng mga sundalo."

"Para ano? Para imbestigahin? Ano ang ginsumbong ni Benigno?"

"Am-ambot. Wala si-siyang sinabi sa amin. Ta-tama na it...."

"Nagareklamo ka?" at pinalagtik ng isang may tangan na rebolber ang gatilyo nito, sapat na para magmakaawa muli ang babae para sa kanyang buhay.

"Sagutin mo nang maayos ang tanong ko kung gayon."

"Ang-ang ano?"

"Kilala mo ang mga sundalo?"

"Siguro kay, kay Simeon Ar...?"

"Si Simeon Arriola? Ano pa ang gagawin ni Simeon Arriola kung patay na siya? Huwag mong banggitin uli ang kanyang pangalan. Kung gagawin mo...." at inangat uli ng lalaki ang rebolber. Binalingan niya ang mga bata. "Kayo, pasok! Hala pasok! Ang bangkay rito? Saan na ang bangkay?"

"Ang bangkay? Kasamahan iyon ng kumander."

"Alam namin. Nasaan?"

"Gin-gindala din ng mga sundalo."

"Sa bayan? Para anuhin? Ipakaon sa heneral?"

"Kasama ng asawa ko ang bangkay. Indi niya pababayaan iyon."

"Si Benigno? He, he, he, he. Agueda, patay na si Benigno." Napasigaw si Agueda. Tinakpan niya ang bibig ng kanyang palad. "Kanino kami kakampi, Agueda, kanino sa tingin mo?"

"Ka-kasama kayo ni Kumander, i-indi ba...?"

Bago makatapos si Agueda, umugong mula sa katubuhan ang ugong ng dyip sabay sa pagkalat ng ilaw nito. Dalidaling tumago ang dalawang lalaki sa gilid ng kubo. "Diyan ka sa pintuan, Agueda. Huwag ka riyang umalis," ang banta ng isa.

Huminto ang dyip sa tapat ng kubo. Ilang sandali pa, may nanaog at agad itong nakilala ni Agueda na si Benigno.

Tumalon ang kanyang dibdib sa kasiyahan dahil buhay pa pala si Benigno. Susugurin sana niya at yayapusin ito, nguni't naalala niya ang babala ng dalawang lalaki. Mabagal ang paglakad ni Benigno, walang direksyon, tulala tulad nang lumalakad na tulog. Nakatitig siya kay Agueda, subalit animo hindi nakikita ito.

"Napaanu ka, Benigno?" ang pabulong na pabungad ni Agueda.

Ilang sandali pa, umalis na ang dyip. Mula sa kanilang pinagtaguan, lumabas ang dalawang lalaki. Iniumang ngayon ng isa ang baril niya kay Benigno.

"Ngayon, Benigno," sabi ng may bigote. "Ngayong nandito ka na, malaking kasalanan ang naubra mo kay kumander. Matalik niyang kaibigan ang namatay sa paanan ng hagdanan mo. At bukod dito, pinayagan mo pa pala ang sarili mong paikut-ikutin ng tanong ng mga sundalo ni Simeon Arriola."

Sabay nito nabuwal si Benigno sa kanyang kinatatayuan tulad ng ginapas na puno ng saging.

Humugis sa kamiseta ang tinagusan ng dugo sa kanyang dibdib. Agad tumalikod ang dalawang lalaki, subalit katatapak pa lang nila ng ilang hakbang nang ginapas din sila sa lupa ng mga bala.

Matagal na natigilan si Agueda sa harap ng tatlong bangkay na ngayon ay napaliligiran na ng mga unipormeng tao. Inilipat niya ang kanyang paningin sa katubuhan at nakita niya itong lumalakad, sumusulong, at nagwawasiwas ng mga itak: palapit nang palapit ang mga kaaway, isang pangkat ito, kumikislap ang mga itak.

At lumusot sa lalamunan ni Agueda ang isang mahaba at nakabibinging tili.

Ang Hustisya sa Dagat

Leothiny S. Clavel

Hinaboy ni Lucio ang bukog sang bangros sa dagat, pinilo ang dahon sang saging agod putson ang nabilin nga sud-an kag naghambal sa pakaisa, "Kaon na, Perto. Udto na."

"San-o ayhan magtunga ang awa nga ato? Kaina pa sang alas otso kita diri," siling ni Perto samtang ginabuksan ang balon.

Ang mga pulong ni Perto dinagit sang hangin nga sumampok sa ila baroto. Naglinggalingga ang baroto kag sinudlan sang tubig. Kinuha ni Lucio ang kabu nga lata kag nagsag-a. "Panulay nga hangin!" Buyayaw niya.

Nagdako ang mga mata ni Lucio sang may makita sia nga daku nga ikog sang isda nga nag-agi sa idalom sang baroto. "Perto, ato na! Ang lambat, dali!"

Hambal ni Perto sang madula sa pananawon nila ang awa nga may isa ka metro ang **kahabaon**, "Tani, wala na naton pag-isaka ang lambat. Nano abi kay wala na kita maglaom nga matunga sia liwat."

"Maayo pa siguro indi anay kita magpauli. Basi matunga naman sia." Ang tingog ni Lucio daw nagakurog sa pamatin-an ni Perto bangod sang gahod nga himu sang mga balod.

May pumisik sa may likod nayon ni Perto nga nagapungko sa isa ka punta sang baroto. Nakita ini ni Lucio nga nagapungko man sa pihak nga punta. "Tan-awa, ara dira," siling ni Lucio.

Nagbalikid si Perto. "Wala man," pulong niya. "Sa painuino mo lang ato." Kag ginpagwa niya ang isa ka daku nga binangon.

"Anhon mo ina?" pamangkot ni Lucio .

"Kon madakpan naton ang isda, utdon naton ang iya ikog. Pagkatapos, ibalik naton sia sa dagat."

"Ngaa?"

Wala na makasabat si Perto kay daw may nagbutong sang ila lambat paidalom. Hinay-hinay nila nga ginhunos ini. "Mabug-at kaayo," pulong ni Lucio.

Una nga tumonga ang ikog. "Sia matuod," singgit ni Perto.

Nagdalagkó ang mga balod. "Indi bala, malunod ang baroto kon tatlo na kita diri sa ibabaw?" pamangkot ni Lucio.

"Dali-a ang pagbutong," sabat kag sugo ni Perto samtang ginapasulod nila sa baroto ang lambat. Kinahanglan nga mautdan gilayon ang iya ikog; basi sia mapatay."

Sang matakas na ang awa dalidali nga kinuha ni Perto ang binangon agod lab-on ang punta sang ikog sang isda. Pinunggan sang wala nga kamot ni Lucio ang lawas sang isda samtang ang mga tudlo sang tuo niya daw lansang nga gusto maglusot sa mga hasang.

"Pinatay kuno si Indo paagi sa pagkuga," daw nabatian niya karon ang hapon nga balita sadto sang iya ka abyan sa talyer nga iya ginaobrahan sa Panit-an.

"Imposible ina," may kakulba ang iya sabat sadto. "Kaupod pa namon sia nanday Kosme, Susing, Hector kag Polding nga nag-imnanay kagab-i. Didto bala sa tubaan ni Tya Mameng."

"Didto kuno ginkuga si Indo sa sulod sang auditoryum pagkatapos sang binayle. Makaagahon na kuno sang matabo ang krimen. Hamak mo, kahapon lang masako si Indo sa pagbulig sa paghanda sang binayle para sa aton kapistahan diri sa Panit-an. Kag kahapon sa adlaw sang pista tuman kasadya sa iya. Iya na gali ato pamilinbilin."

Wala sia sing hinambal. Nagpadayon ang kahambal: "Ang pulisya natingala man kon ngaa makaabot sia didto samtang hubog sia siling ni Tya Mameng sang maghalin sa iya tindahan."

"A, huo. Natandaan ko na," sabat niya. Pagkatapos namon inom, sinundan namon si Indo nga nauna sa amon magpauli kay maagi pa sia kuno sa awditoryum. Hambal niya may nalimtan sia didto."

Nautod ang pagbalita sang iya abyan sang umabot ang isa ka polis.

"Lucio, puwede bala nga mag-upod ka anay sa akon agod makuhaan ka sang pila ka impormasyon? Daw mabudlay ang kaso nga ini gani kinahanglan namon ang imo bulig."

Madamo ang tao sa departamento sang pulisya. May mga bata kag tigulang, ang tanan naga-usyoso kon ano gid ang natabo. Ato man didto si Kosme, Susing, Hector kag Polding, ang mga kaupod niya sa imnanay sang kaagahon nga matabo ang krimen. Sang magtulok sa iya ang mga ini daw kumorog ang iya mga kaunoran.

"Gusto lang namon mahibal-an kon matuod ang ginasugid sang apat nga ina," pulong sang hepe sang pulisya dayon tudlo kanday Kosme. "Siling nila upod kamo sang mga tinion nga natabo ang pagpatay kay Indo. Sinundan kuno ninyo si Indo sa awditoryum, pero sang wala ninyo sia makita didto nagdayon na lang kuno kamo sa balay ni Kosme agod makainom sang mainit nga kape."

Nakaginhawa sia sing madalom. Pagdumdom niya sia ang ginapamangdan sang apat sa pagpatay kay Indo. Karon, sia pa gani ang ginapamangkot kon tama ang ginsugid sang apat.

Mahambal sia kuntani apang may sumiyagit sa sulod sang selda. Nabatian sang tanan ang isa ka lagapak. Daw paha nga hinanot sa panit sang tao.

Nabatian niya ini kag ang ugayong nga sumonod naghatag sa iya sing kabakod. Kon makabati sia sang ugayong nagabatyag sia sing isa ka kadalag-an nga indi niya mahibal-an kon ano. Basta nalipay sia magpamati sini kag may isa ka hitabo nga nagabalik sa iya painuino. Sa kada kita niya sang isa ka ginasilutan ukon sa kada makabati sia sang nagaugayong, nadumdoman niya si Tatay niya sang buhi pa ini.

Ang Tatay ni Lucio maluyagon magbulang. Ang ila ginakabuhi sadto nga mag-amay amo ang ginakita ni Tatay niya sa bulang. Kay pirme napyerde ini, napilitan si Lucio nga magbakal kag magbaligya sang mga botelya. Amo ini ang iya trabaho hasta sia makaabot sa ikanapulo ka tuig. Nag-untat sia sing pagbaligya sang botelya sang kuhaon sia sang kumpare ni Tatay niya nga kabulig sa talyer sini. Halin sadto daw nag-ayuayo ang ila pangabuhi.

Apang indi ini ang mga hitabo nga nagabalik sa panumdoman ni Lucio sa tinion nga sia makabati sang tingog sang nagaantos. Sang diutay pa sia namatay ang iya iloy kag sia nabilin sa iya mapintas nga amay. Ginhimo niya ang tanan nga nahibaluan agod lamang nga mapalapit sia sa kabubot-on sang iya amay. Pag-abot sini halin sa bulangan, iya ini ginasukaran sang pagkaon. Kag kon mainit ang ulo sini iya ginaulog-ulog paagi sa pahatag sang iya kinitaan sa pagbaligya sang botelya sa adlaw nga ina.

Sa diutay nga sala nga mahimo ni Lucio, sipa, dukol ukon sumbag ang ginabaton niya kay Tatay niya. Sadto nahisa sia sa iya mga kaabyanan. Mabuot sa ila ang ila mga amay. Samtang sia, uhaw sa paghigugma sang iya amay, sang isa ka ginikanan. Maayo pa gani ang manok ni Tatay niya kay nagabaton sang pagtamod ini. Ginahimashimas ini kon aga kag ginasaburan pa pirme sang mais.

Isa ka gab-i sadto, mabaskog ang hangin kag ulan. Nakibot si Lucio sang umabot ang amay nga akig kaayo.

"Lucio ngaa wala mo pag-isaka ang manok? Nakita mo, nagapalangurog sa katugnaw!" Siling sang amay dayon pakita sang manok nga nabasa masyado sang ulan. Ang tingog sang amay daw daguob nga umabot sa pamatin-an ni Lucio.

Wala na makasabat si Lucio sang tumopa ang inumol sa iya suloksulok. Nakahibi sia sa kasakit. Nagpakitluoy sia sa amay: "Nalipat ako, 'Tay. Indi na maliwat ang tanan." Apang wala mamati si Tatay niya kag wala ini mag-untat kastigo sa iya hasta nga indi sia makabangon.

Bisan nga daw wala na sing animo si Lucio, nabatian niya nga may nagtawag sa iya amay.

"Ponso, magpanaog ka!" Singgit liwat sang isa ka tao sa idalom sang wala maghulag si Ponso. Nabatian ni Lucio ang mga tikang sang iya amay pakadto sa kusina kag dumayon ang mga ini sa hagdanan. Pinilit niya nga magtindog apang tama sa iya kaluya.

Ang mabaskog nga ulan wala makalunod sa tugalbong nga naghalin sa silong. Kinulbaan si Lucio sang mapaktan niya nga may mga tao nga nagdinalagan palayo sa ila balay.

Binuno sang talibong ang iya amay sang isa ka grupo nga lalaki. Pulo ang samad sini. Sang gab-i nga ato, wala si Lucio sing mahimo kundi bantayan ang bangkay sang iya amay nga iya napasaka sa balay sa pihak sang iya kaluya. Nag-alagay ang luha sa mga mata niya sang makita ang mga samad sang iya amay.

"Tay, maayo ka pa kay ang mga samad mo nabaton mo sa mga tao nga naakig sa imo. Ang akon nga mga samad nabaton ko sa tao nga pinakamahal ko sa kalibutan."

Sadto nagtilaok ang manok ni Tatay niya. Nakauklo si Lucio. Nagabagrot ang ngipon nga dumalagan sia sa kusina kag sa daku nga kaakig, binali ang liog sang manok. "Ikaw ang may sala sang tanan!" Singgit niya. Nabatyagan ni Lucio nga lumato ang iya mga tudlo sa kaakig.

" 'Si Lucio ang pumatay kay Indo!' Ina ang mga nabatian sang tanan halin sa selda," padayon sang estorya ni Lucio sa iya pangabuhi sang matapos na sila panyapon ni Perto.

"Tumalagsahon gali ang mga hitabo sa imo pangabuhi," siling ni Perto. "Gai ko man nga naurongan ka kaina sang mauyatan mo sa may hasang ang awa."

Nagpadayon sa pagsugilanon si Lucio.

Isa ka tigulang ang tag-iya sang tingog nga naghalin sa selda nga ato. Nakita niya ang labhag sang paha sa panit sang tigulang. Sa una nga kahigayunan nahadlok sia magtan-aw sa panit nga nangalom.

Siling sang tigulang nakita niya sia nga nagadalagan pagwa sa awditoryum sang mabatian niya nga may daw nahulog nga isa ka sako nga humay didto. Masakit ang buot niya nga sia ang ginapabangdan nga nagpatay kay Indo, bangod lamang sa sirkumstansya nga sia ang naabtan sang mga tao nga nagauyat sa liog sang ulitao. Ginpaathag sang tigulang nga nagpalapit sia kay Indo sang makita niya nga wala na ini nagahulag.

"Pero, kaupod namon nga apat si Lucio sang tinion nga natabo ang krimen," pangapin ni Susing. "Imposible nga yara sa duha ka lugar sa isa ka tinion si Lucio."

"Tyo Merto," hambal niya sa tigulang. "May suga pa bala sang makita mo ako nga nagadalagan pagwa sa awditoryum?"

"Huo. Mapawa didto kag nakilala ko gilayon kon sin-o ang tao didto."

"Tyo Merto," padayon niya. "Nakilala mo bala ang babae nga ina? Inang nagapungko dapit sa puwerta?"

Pinapirot ni Tyo Merto ang iya mga mata. Buron sa panulok niya ang guya sang babae nga ginatudlo niya.

"Indi ko makilala. Mahina na ang suga sang akon mata. Halos ko na makilala ang tao kon may mga napulo ka metros ang kalayuon. Tigulang na ako."

"Chief," pulong niya, "ginakasubo ko nga silingon nga ako may importante pa nga kadtuan. Puwede bala nga padayon ninyo ang pagimbestigar sa akon karon sa gab-i? Pero padayunon ninyo ang pag-imbestigar kay Tyo Merto. Halimbawa, mangayo kamo sing paathag kon paano niya ako nakilala, sa iya man mismo nga pagtuad, sa layo nga beinte ka metros, samtang indi niya gani makilala ang iya gumangkon nga babae sa kalayuon nga napulo ka metros."

Nakapiyong si Lucio pagabot sa parte nga ini sang iya sugilanon. Nakabatyag sia sing kahadlok sa mga natabo. Ang tugnaw sang hangin nga naghalin sa baybayon nagdugang sa iya kahadlok. Nagpagot ang iya mga bag-ang, kag wala sa buot nga pinagwa ang iya panyu. "Paano ko makuga sang panyu si Indo? Tigulang na ako kag indi ko sia madaog sa kusog," amo ini ang siling ni Tyo Merto sa imbestigasyon sang gab-i nga ato. Apang ginbuy-an sia sang pulisya sang mapamatud-an nga hubog sia sang tinion nga pinatay si Indo kag wala sing motibo nga nakuha sa iya nga handumon niya ang pagpatay sa abyan. Ang resulta sang imbestigasyon nagpakita man nga sia kaupod nanday Kosme sang matabo ang krimen. "Pero indi bala mahimo nga nalipat si Kosme kon sin-o ang mga ka-upod niya pakadto sa ila balay, bangod sa kahulogbon?" Pamangkot sadto ni Tyo Merto sa hepe sang pulisya.

Pinilo niya ang panyo agod mangin triyangulo ang korte sini. Kinaptan niya ang duha ka punta kag hinabyughabyug ang panyu. Sumablay ang ikatlo nga kanto sini kag nagbalibod sa nabilin nga parte sang panapton.

"Maayo nga nakabakasyon ka diri sa Dumalag," siling ni Perto. "Basi na lang nga malipatan mo ang tanan nga natabo."

Binutongbutong niya ang panyu. Naghulogot ang bunang sang panapton kag daw nanginpisi sa kabakod.

Nakabungkaras si Perto. Wala si Lucio sa higdaan sini.

Dalidali niya nga ginsuksok ang iya *jacket* kag dumalagan pakadto sa baybay. Mga alas tres na sang kaagahon kag ang tunga nga guya sang bulan daw nagabag-id sa maitom nga panganod. Tiniklod niya ang isa ka baroto pakadto sa tubig nga napihak sang agyan sang salakyan.

Nagpalanghugot ang mga maskulo ni Perto sa likod, dughan kag braso sang magbugsay sia. Madasig ang iya pagbugsay, wala pahuway. Kay ang tubig nga tup-an sang iya bugsay daw kristal nga nagkalawas-ag.

"Inutdan ko ang ikog sang awa agod manghina ang panglangoy niya."

"Kon utod na ang iya ikog, mahimo ko na sia malagas sakay sa baroto. Madasig ako magbugsay."

"Ginbalik ko sia sa dagat kay indi ko sia gusto dakpon. Indi ko sia gusto mapatay. Kinahanglan nga may awa ang dagat agod buhi ang tao."

"Halin pa sang akon pagkabata ginhandom ko na nga matultolan ang lugar nga ginabun-agan sang mga bangros. Kon mahibala-an ko ang kondisyon sang tubig kag palibot sa diin ginabun-ag ang mga bangros, puwede ko na madakop ang tanan nga awa nga may bihod kag ibutang sa sangha. Gusto ko makita ang pagbun-ag kag pagdako sang mga bangros."

"Indi ako magdakop sang daku nga awa hasta wala ko pa mahibal-i ang klase sang lugar nga ginabun-agan sang isda nga ina."

Ang mga ini ang sabat ni Perto sa madamo nga pamangkot ni Lucio sang matapos sila panyapon sang pagligad nga gab-i. Gusto mahibal-an sang ulihi kon ngaa wala pag-ipauli ni Perto ang awa nga nadakpan nila kahapon kag ngaa pagkatapos utdan ang ikog sini inuli ang isda sa dagat.

Bisan matugnaw ang kaagahon, wala pahuway ang pag-agay sang balhas sa malapad nga likod ni Perto.

"Indi dapat madakpan ni Lucio ang awa," himulongon niya sa kaugalingon. Nagpadagat sia bangod sa hinambal sa iya ni Lucio kagab-i: "Gusto ko dakpon kag patyon ang awa!"

Sang makita niya nga madasig ang paghulag sang isa ka suga sa dagat, nahibal-an ni Perto nga nakita na ni Lucio ang awa kag ginalagas niya ini.

Inubos ni Perto ang iya kusog sa pagbugsay. Natbutyog ang baroto kag ang madamol nga bula sang tubig amo ang tanda sang iya madasig nga pag-agi.

"Indi pagpatya!" Singgit ni Perto sang makapalapit na sia sa baroto ni Lucio kag makita nga ginahanaan sini sang bangkaw ang isda.

Nakibut si Lucio. Wala niya gilayon madiparahe si Perto. Pinadayon niya ang paghana.

Madali nga nagsaylo si Perto sa baroto sang pakaisa kag pinilit nga agawon ang bangkaw. Nanginpadlos si Lucio. Nalubag ni Perto ang kamot ni Lucio nga nagakapot sang bangkaw. Binuy-an ni Lucio ang bangkaw nga nahulug sa tubig kag lumutaw.

Diri kag nakaptan ni Lucio ang liog ni Perto kag ang iya duha ka kamot nga pinatig-a sang iya pamanday sa Panit-an daw salsalon nga humogot. Wala sing animo nga natumba si Perto sa baroto.

Kinab-ot ni Lucio ang nagalutaw nga bangkaw kag pinangita ang awa. Sang masiplatan niya ini pinalupad niya ang bangkaw. Dinaplisan ang lawas sang awa kag lumogdang ini. "Napatay ko sia!" Singgit ni Lucio.

Lumompat sia sa tubig kag sinalom ang isda apang wala niya ini makit-i. Nagbutwa sia sing makadali agod makakuha sang presko nga hangin. Kinulbaan sia sang makita niya nga malayo na ang nagabugsay nga Perto. Nadumdoman niya ang lahog sa iya ni Perto kagab-i. "Pagnahubog ako basi masugilanon ko sa mga kaupdanan ko ang imo kinabuhi. Mahibal-an sang tanan nga ikaw ang nagpatay kay Indo!"

"Kinahanglan nga maabtan ko sia!" Kag sumakay si Lucio sa nabilin nga baroto. "Basi magtimalos sia sa akon kag isumbong niya sia sa pulisya."

Apang sang magbugsay na lang sia nakit-an naman niya ang awa. Mahinay ini nga nagalangoy palayo sa iya.

Tinulok na lang sang matalom ni Lucio ang isda kag madasig nga ginlagas si Perto. "Kinahanglan nga mapat-od ko nga indi sia makasugid sa pulisya!"

Umontat sa pagbugsay si Lucio sang mag-agi sa kilid sang baroto ang duha nga awa nga parehas kadako sang iya ginbangkaw. Nagdalagko ang iya mga mata. Sang sundan sang panulok niya ang mga ini nalipatan niya si Perto—labi na gid sang magdungan ang duha ka isda sa isa nga iya ginbangkaw. Pinatung-an sang duha ka awa ang nasakit nila nga kaupod kag dungan sila naglangoy palayo kay Lucio. Nasiplatan sang ulitao nga malip-ot ang ikog sang isa sa duha ka awa nga bag-o nag-abot.

"Yatis nga awa ina, a!" Kag liniso ni Lucio ang iya baroto kag linagas ang isda nga may malip-ot sing ikog.

Nakatakas na si Perto sa baybay. Ang iya liog masakit pa gihapon bangod sa pagkuga sang pakaisa. Tumangla sia sa langit. Maka-agahon na apang daw indi magbutlak ang adlaw sina nga aga. Madamo sing gal-om ang langit kag nabatian niya nga nagakinalas ang mga dahon sang lubi bangod sang pagsampok sa ila sang nagabaskog nga hangin.

"May bagyo nga manug-abot," himulongon niya sa kaugalingon samtang ginaasoy ang dalan pauli. Sang malayo na sia, binalikid niya ang dagat sa diin ang awa nga may malip-ot sing ikog amo ang hustisya nga nagasakay sa mga dalagko nga balod.

From: *Hiligaynon*, December 3, 1969

Vengeance in the Sea

(Ang Hustisya sa Dagat)

Leothiny S. Clavel

Lucio flung the milkfish bones into the sea, wrapped the leftover food in banana leaves and turned to his cousin: "Take your lunch now, Perto; it's noontime."

"I wonder when that *awa* would come up again. We've been waiting for it since eight o'clock this morning," Perto said as he unwrapped his lunch. Perto's words were seized by the wind that slammed against their boat. The boat rocked and drew in water. Lucio got a tin can and bailed it out. "Damn this wind," he cursed.

His eyes rolled when he spotted a large fish tail cross beneath the boat. "Perto, it's here! The fish net. Quick!"

When the one-meter-long *awa* disappeared, Perto said: "We shouldn't have put away the net. But then, we didn't expect it to come up again."

"Maybe, we shouldn't go home, yet. It might come up again." Lucio's voice seemed shaky to Perto's ears because of the splashing waves. Something dashed behind Perto's end of the boat. Lucio, who was seated at the other end, saw this: "Look behind you, it's there," he told Perto.

Perto turned. "It's nothing. You were just imagining it." Then he pulled out a large *binangon*.

"What will you do with that?" Lucio asked.

"If we catch the fish, we'll cut its tail. Then, we'll hurl it back into the sea."

"Why?"

Perto couldn't reply because something was tugging at their net. They pulled it up slowly. "It's very heavy," Lucio said.

The tail was the first to surface. "We got it!" Perto yelled.

The waves rose. "Won't the boat keel over if there are three of us here?"

"Pull it up quickly," Perto commanded as they hauled the net into the boat. "We must cut its tail at once; it may die."

As soon as the *awa* surfaced fully, Perto got hold of his long *binangon* to cut its tail. Lucio held the body of the fish with his left hand, and with his right, he gripped its head so hard that his fingers were like nails driving through the gills.

"Indo, they say, was strangled." Lucio could still hear his friend's news that afternoon in the machine shop at Panit-an.

"But that's impossible!" he had answered nervously. "He was with us—Kosme, Susing, Hector and Polding—when we went drinking last night. At *Tiya* Mameng's *tubaan*.

"People say Indo was strangled in the auditorium after the dance. It was early morning, they say when the incident happened. Would you believe, it was only yesterday that Indo was fussing over the preparations for the dance for our fiesta here in Panit-an. And he was very happy. He must have been saying his last goodbye."

Lucio held his tongue. The speaker continued: "The police are also puzzled at how he got there for, according to *Tiya* Mameng, he was drunk when he left her store."

"Ah, now I remember," Lucio answered. "After drinking, Indo went home first. He said he still had to pass by the auditorium because he had forgotten something there."

The account of Lucio's friend was cut short when a policeman came.

"Lucio, could you come with me first? We need some information. We're having a hard time here so you 've got to help."

There were a lot of people, young and old, at the police station. All were curious about what exactly had happened. His drinking companions on the morning of the crime were also there—Kosme, Susing, Hector, and Polding. When they turned to him, he shivered.

"We just want to check if what these four guys were telling us is true," said the police chief, pointing at Kosme and the rest. "They said you were all together at the time Indo was killed. They also say that you followed him to the auditorium, but when you didn't see him there you went on to Kosme's house to drink coffee."

Lucio heaved a sigh of relief. He thought the four had accused him of killing Indo; now it was he being asked to bear out the claims of the four.

He was about to speak when someone shrieked. Everybody heard a whacking. It sounded like a belt being lashed against the bare skin of a body.

Lucio heard this, and the groan which followed excited him. Each time he heard someone groan, he felt some sense of power which he couldn't quite understand. And now a certain incident came back to him. Whenever he saw someone tormented or heard someone groan, he remembered his father.

Lucio's father was fond of cockfighting. Father and son lived on what his father earned from cockfighting. Because he often lost, Lucio was forced to buy and sell used bottles. This was his work until he was ten years old. But he stopped peddling these when his father's *kumpare* took him in as an assistant in his machine shop. Since that time, their life eased up a bit.

But these were not the things that flashed across Lucio's mind whenever he would hear the voice of someone suffering. When he was small, his mother had died and he was left to his cruel father. He did all he could to gain his father's affection. When his father would come home from the cockpit, food would be laid out on the table. And if he was in a bad mood, Lucio would try to calm him by giving him his day's earnings.

But for every little mistake of Lucio, his father would kick him, punch him, or hit him on the head. At that time, he envied his friends whose fathers were affectionate. For his part, he was thirsty for parental love. He felt the fighting cock was better off than he since his father took good care of it. He would stroke the cock each morning and sprinkle corn grits for it on the ground.

One night—when the wind was strong and the rain heavy—Lucio was taken by surprise when his father came home furious.

"Lucio, why didn't you take the rooster inside? See, he's shivering from the cold!" his father said, holding up to him the chicken drenched from the rain. His father's voice sounded like thunder to his ears. Before Lucio could answer, his father's clenched fist landed on his stomach. He cried from the pain. He begged his father for some mercy. "'Tay, it skipped my mind. This will not happen again." But his father did not listen; he continued on beating his son until the boy couldn't get up any more.

Although Lucio was only half-conscious, he heard someone call out loud to his father. "Ponso, come down!" he heard the man shout again from below their house when Ponso did not stir. Lucio heard his father's footsteps going towards the kitchen and then down the staircase. He tried getting up but he was very weak.

Not even the heavy rain could drown out the loud crash which came from beneath the house. Lucio was alarmed when he sensed that some people were running away from the house.

A group of men had stabbed his father with a heavy bolo. He had received ten stab wounds. That night, there was nothing Lucio could do except watch his father's body which he was able to carry up the house despite his weakness. Tears flowed from his eyes when he saw the wounds of his father.

"'Tay, you're luckier than I. You received your wounds from people who were angry with you. While I, I received mine from the person I care for the most in the world."

At that instant, his father's rooster crowed. Lucio jerked up. Gritting his teeth, he ran to the kitchen and, enraged, broke the rooster's neck. "You are to blame for all this!" he shouted. Lucio felt his fingers snap from anger.

" 'It was Lucio who killed Indo!' Everyone heard these words coming from the prison cell," Lucio went on, as he recounted his life story to Perto after dinner.

"You have an unusual life story," Perto said. "So that's why you looked startled this morning when you held the gills of the *awa*."

Lucio continued his story.

The voice from the cell came from an old man. Lucio saw the welts of the whip on the skin of the old man. For the first time he was scared to look at bruised skin.

The old man said he saw Lucio run out of the auditorium about the same time he heard something like a sack of rice fall. He felt really bad that he was accused of killing Indo just because he was caught holding the young man's neck when people came. The old man said that he drew near Indo when he noticed that the young man lay unmoving.

"But Lucio was with us at the time the crime happened," Susing said on behalf of Lucio. "It's impossible for Lucio to be in two places at the same time."

"*Tiyo* Merto," Lucio said to the old man. "Were the lights still on when you saw me running?"

"Yes, it was bright and it was easy to see people there."

"*Tiyo* Merto," he continued, "can you recognize the woman there? The one who's seated by the door?"

Tiyo Merto blinked his eyes. The face of the woman being pointed at looked blurred.

"I can't recognize her. My eyesight is weak. I can hardly see a person ten meters away. I am old."

"Chief," he said, "I'm sorry, I need to go somewhere else now. Could you just put this off till tonight? But go on questioning *Tiyo* Merto. Ask him how he could have recognized me from a distance of twenty meters when he can't even tell it's his niece ten meters away."

Lucio closed his eyes when he reached this part of the story. He was worried at the way things were shaping up. The cold air which blew from the seashore seemed to heighten his fears. He gritted his molars, and without being aware of it, he took out his handkerchief. "How could I have strangled Indo with a handkerchief? I am already old and was of no match to him." That was what *Tiyo* Merto said when he was investigated further that night. The police released Lucio when it was established that he was drunk at the time Indo was killed and had no motive for killing his friend. Their inquiry showed that he was with Kosme at the time of the crime. "But couldn't it be that Kosme didn't notice who had gone with him to the house, being tipsy himself?" *Tiyo* Merto asked the Chief of Police.

Lucio folded his handkerchief into a triangle. Holding it on two ends, he swung it until its third end hung on the rest of the handkerchief and wound around it.

"It's a good thing you've come to Dumalag for a vacation," Perto said. "Maybe, you'll learn to forget everything." Lucio kept on pulling the handkerchief on both ends. Its threads tightened up until it became strong as rope.

Perto jumped up. Lucio was no longer in his bed.

Quickly, he put on his jacket and ran towards the seashore. It was now about 3:00 o'clock in the morning and the half-moon seemed to graze its face on the dark clouds. He pushed his banca towards the water, slicing through it.

Perto's back, chest, and arm muscles grew taut as he rowed. He paddled swiftly, without pause. And the water he paddled through looked like scattered crystal pieces. He remembered what he had said to Lucio.

"I cut the tail of the awa to slow it down."

"If his tail is cut, I can chase him easily with my boat. I row fast."

"I hurled it back into the sea; I don't want to keep him. I don't want him to die. The awa must live to make man live."

"Ever since I was a child, I've always wanted to discover the spawning ground of the milkfish. If I get to know the condition of the water and the surroundings of its spawning ground, I can catch all egg-carrying awa and transfer these in the fishpond. I'd like to see how the milkfish grows and develops."

"I will not catch a big awa until I get to see its spawning ground."

This was Perto's reply to the many questions Lucio had asked him when they finished taking dinner last night. Lucio wanted to know why Perto hadn't brought home the *awa* they had caught yesterday afternoon and why after cutting its tail he had thrown it back into the sea.

Although the morning was cold, perspiration dripped continuously down Perto's wide back.

"Lucio shouldn't catch the *awa*," Perto told himself. He set out to sea quickly because he remembered what Lucio had told him last night: "I want to catch and kill that *awa*."

When he noticed a light flickering in the sea, Perto knew that Lucio had already found the *awa* and was chasing it.

Perto used up all his strength to paddle. The boat zipped through and the bubbles swooshed in its wake.

"Don't kill it!" Perto shouted as he drew close to Lucio's boat and saw that Lucio was aiming his spear at the fish.

Lucio was startled. He had not noticed Perto. He continued aiming.

Perto moved into his cousin's boat and tried to wrench the spear from his hand. Lucio slipped from Perto's grip. But Perto was able to twist Lucio's hand that held on to the spear. Lucio dropped the spear on the water and there it lay floating.

At this instant, Lucio grabbed Perto's neck and his hands, grown strong from working as a smith, were like an iron grip. Perto dropped unconscious in the banca.

Lucio reached for the spear adrift on the water and searched for the *awa*. When his eyes found it, he flung the spear at it, and the *awa* rose to the surface. "I've killed him!" Lucio shouted.

He jumped into the water and dived for the fish but he couldn't find it. He rose to the surface to take a breath of fresh air. When he noticed that Perto was paddling away from him, he got worried. He remembered Perto teasing him last night: "If I get drunk I might get to tell your story to my friends. Everyone will know that you killed Indo!"

"I must get to him!" And Lucio got into his boat. "He might take revenge on me and squeal to the police!"

But when he was just starting to row, he sighted the *awa* again. It was slowly swimming away from him.

Lucio just shot the fish a piercing look and quickly turned to chase Perto. "I must make sure he does not tell on me!"

But Lucio stopped rowing when two *awa* swam up to the side of the boat. They were as big as the previous one he had aimed his spear at. His eyes goggled. As he followed them with his eyes he forgot Perto, more so when the two fish joined the one he had thrown his spear at. The two *awa* swam on each side of their companion and swam away from Lucio. The young man noticed that one of the two *awa* which had just come had a short tail.

"Damn that *awa*!" Lucio swung his boat around to chase the fish with a short tail.

Perto had already gone ashore. His neck still smarted from being gripped by his cousin. He looked up at the sky. It was dawn now but it seemed like the sun wasn't going to rise that day. The sky was heavy with clouds and he heard the wild rustling of the leaves of the coconut trees as the strong wind lashed at them.

"A storm is coming," he told himself as he treaded the path home. When he had gone far, he turned around to the sea where the *awa* with the short tail rode with vengeance on its billowing waves.

Ang Hustisya sa Dagat

Leothiny S. Clavel

Inihagis ni Lucio sa dagat ang gulugod ng bangus, ibinalot sa dahon ng saging ang natirang ulam at sinabi sa kanyang pinsang buo, "Kain na, Perto. Tanghali na."

"Kailan bala lilitaw ang sabalong iyon? Kanina pang alas otso kita diri, " ang sabi ni Perto habang binubuksan ang baon.

Dinagit ang mga salita ni Perto ng hanging sumalpok sa kanilang baroto. Gumiwang-giwang ang baroto at nasidlan ng tubig. Kinuha ni Lucio ang latang kabo at naglimas. "Linti nga hangin ini, a!" mura niya. Nandilat ang mga mata ni Lucio nang makita niya ang malaking buntot ng isdang dumaan sa ilalim ng baroto. "Ayan, Perto! Ang lambat, dalian mo!"

Nang hindi na nila makita ang sabalong may isang metrong kahabaan, sabi ni Perto, "Sana, indi na natin iniligpit ang lambat. Pano kasi indi naman natin akalaing lilitaw siyang muli."

"Mabuti pa siguro huwag na muna kitang umuwi. Baka lilitaw uli siya." Parang nanginginig ang tinig ni Lucio gawa ng malakas na alon.

May tumalsik sa may likuran ni Perto doon sa isang dulo ng baroto. Nakita ito ni Lucio dahil nakaupo siya sa kabilang dulo naman ng baroto. "Tingnan mo, nandiyan banda sa iyo," ang sabi ni Lucio.

Lumingon si Perto. "Wala naman diri," ang sabi niya. "Guniguni mo lang iyon." At inilabas niya ang isang malaking balisong.

"Aanhin mo iyan?" tanong ni Lucio.

"Kung madakop natin ang isda, puputulin natin ang kanyang buntot. Pagkatapos, ibabalik natin siya sa dagat."

"Bakit?"

Hindi na makasagot si Perto dahil may humatak sa kanilang lambat nang paibaba. Dahan-dahan nilang itinaas ito. "Mabigat masyado," ang sabi ni Lucio.

Unang lumitaw ang buntot. "Iyan na nga!" sigaw ni Perto.

Lumaki ang mga alon. "Indi lulubog ang baroto kung tatlo na tayo rito sa itaas?" ang tanong ni Lucio.

"Bilisan mo ang pagbatak," utos ni Perto habang pinapapasok nila ang lambat sa baroto. "Kailangang maputol agad ang iya buntot; baka siya mamatay."

Nang makaahon na ang sabalo, dali-daling kinuha ni Perto ang balisong para tagain ang dulo ng buntot nito. Pinigil ng kaliwang kamay ni Lucio ang katawan ng isda, habang nakadiin na parang pako ang mga daliri ng kanyang kanang kamay sa hasang nito.

"Napatay kuno si Indo. Sinakal!" Parang naririnig pa niya ang balita nang hapong iyon ng kanyang kaibigan sa talyer na pinapasukan sa Panit-an.

"Imposible iyan," may kaba ang kanyang sagot noon. "Kasama pa namin siyang mag-inuman ni Kosme, Susing, Hector at Polding kagabi. Doon bala sa tubaan ni Tiya Mameng."

"Doon kuno gingsakal si Indo sa loob ng oditoryum pagkatapos ng baylehan. Magmamadaling araw na raw nang nangyari ang krimen. Biruin mo, kahapon lang abala si Indong gatulong sa paghahanda sa sayawan para sa pista rito sa Panit-an. At kahapon, araw ng pista, parang ang saya gid niya. Iyon pala, nagapaalam na."

Hindi siya kumibo. Nagpatuloy ang kanyang kausap: "Nagtaka rin ang pulisya kung bakit nakarating siya roon samantalang, ayon kay Tiya Mameng, lasing siya sang umalis sa tindahan."

"A, huo. Natatandaan ko na," sagot niya. "Pagkatapos naming uminom gingsundan namin si Indo na naunang umuwi, dahil dadaan pa raw sa oditoryum. Sabi niya, may nakalimutan siya roon."

Natigil ang pagbabalita ng kanyang kaibigan nang dumating ang isang pulis.

"Lucio, sumama ka muna sa akin para mahingan ka ng ilang impormasyon. Medyo mahirap ang kasong ito kaya't kailangan gid namin ang iyong tulong."

Maraming tao sa presinto ng pulisya. May mga bata at matanda, ang lahat ay nag-uusyoso kung ano ang nangyari. Naroon din sina Kosme, Susing, Hector at Polding na mga kasamahan niya sa inuman noong umaga ng krimen. Nang ibaling nila ang kanilang paningin sa kanya, parang nanginig ang kanyang kalamnan.

"Gusto lang namin malaman kung totoo ang ginasabi ng mga iyan," wika ng hepe sabay turo kina Kosme. "Sabi nila kasama raw kayo noong mga sandaling gingpatay si Indo. Sinundan niyo raw siya sa oditoryum, pero indi niyo siya nakita roon. Natulog na lang daw kayo sa bahay ni Kosme para makainom ng mainit na kape."

Nakaginhawa siya nang malalim. Akala niya siya ang pinagbibintangan ng apat sa pagpatay kay Indo. Ngayon siya pa nga ang tinanong kung tama ang inereport ng apat.

Magsasalita pa sana siya, subalit may tumili sa loob ng selda. Narinig ng lahat ang isang haginit. Parang sinturon ito na nilatigo sa balat ng tao.

Narinig niya rin ito at ang halinghing sumunod ay nagbigay sa kanya ng sigla. Kung nakakarinig siya ng halinghing nakakaramdam siya ng kasiyahang hindi niya maintindihan kung ano. Basta't nasisiyahan siyang makinig dito. May isa ngang pangyayaring bumalik sa kanyang isip. Tuwing makakita siya ng nagdurusa o makarinig ng pananangis, naaalala niya ang kanyang Tatay noong ito'y buhay pa.

Mahilig magsabong ang Tatay ni Lucio. Ang kita sa sabong ang tanging inaasahan nila noon. Dahil malimit matalo ito, napilitan si Luciong bumili't maglako ng bote. Trabaho niya ito hanggang magsampung taon siya. Tumigil siya ng paglalako ng bote nang kunin siya ng kumpare ng kanyang Tatay bilang katulong sa talyer nito. Mula noon, umigi-igi ang kanilang pamumuhay.

Subalit hindi ito ang mga pangyayaring nanumbalik sa isip ni Lucio sa mga sandaling makarinig siya ng tinig ng isang nagdurusa. Maliit pa siya nang namatay ang kaniyang ina at nalwan siya sa kaniyang malupit na ama. Ginawa niya ang lahat niyang nalalaman para mapalapit siya sa kanyang ama. Pagkagaling nito sa sabungan, hinahainan niya ito ng pagkain.

Kung mainit ang ulo nito, kanya itong aamu-amuin at bibigyan ng kanyang kita sa paglalako ng bote sa araw na iyon.

Pero sa kaunting pagkakamali ni Lucio, sipa, batok o suntok ang inaabot niya sa Tatay niya. Noon nainggit siya sa kanyang mga kaibigan. Mabait sa kanila ang kanilang mga ama. Samantalang siya, uhaw sa pagmamahal ng kanyang ama, ng isang magulang. Mabuti pa nga ang manok ng Tatay niya at nakakatanggap ng paglingap. Hinihimas-himas ito ng kanyang ama tuwing umaga, at lagi pang sinasabugan ng mais.

Isang gabing malakas ang hangin at ulan, nagulat na lamang si Lucio nang dumating ang kanyang Tatay na galit na galit.

"Lucio, bakit indi mo ipinanhik ang manok? Tingnan mo, nanginginig sa lamig!" sabi ng ama, sabay pakita sa manok na basang basa ng ulan. Ang tinig ng ama parang kulog na umabot sa pandinig ni Lucio.

Hindi nakasagot si Lucio dahil lumagpak na ang isang suntok sa kanyang sikmura. Naiyak siya sa sakit. Nagmakaawa siya sa ama: "Nalimtan ko 'Tay. Indi na ma-ma-uulit ang lahat." Subalit hindi nakinig ang Tatay niya sa kanya, at patuloy itong kinastigo hanggang hindi na makabangon.

Halos walang-malay na si Lucio, pero narinig niyang may tumawag sa kanyang ama.

"Ponso, manaog ka!" sigaw uli ng isang tao nang hindi tuminag si Ponso. Narinig ni Lucio ang mga yabag ng kanyang ama patungong kusina at papanaog sa hagdanan. Pinilit niyang tumayo subalit lubha siyang mahina.

Malakas ang ulan pero hindi nalunod dito ang lagabog na nanggaling sa silong. Kinabahan si Lucio nang maramdaman niyang may mga taong nangagsitakbong palayo sa bahay.

Pinagsasaksak ng itak ang kanyang ama ng isang grupo ng lalaki. Sampu ang sugat nito. Nang gabing iyon walang nagawa si Lucio kundi bantayan ang bangkay ng kanyang ama; naiakyat niya ito sa bahay sa kabila ng kanyang panghihina. Tumulo ang luha sa mga mata niya nang makita ang sugat ng kanyang ama.

" 'Tay, mabuti ka pa imo at ang mga sugat mo, natanggap mo sa mga taong galit sa iyo. Itong mga sugat ko natanggap ko sa taong pinakamamahal ko sa mundo."

Sa saglit na iyon, tumilaok ang manok ng Tatay niya. Natigilan si Lucio. Lumalangitngit ang mga ipin, tumakbo siya sa kusina at sa laki ng galit, binali niya ang liig ng manok. "Ikaw ang may kasalanan ng lahat!" sigaw niya. Naramdaman ni Luciong lumagutok ang kanyang mga daliri sa galit.

" 'Si Lucio ang pumatay kay Indo!' Iyan ang mga katagang galing sa selda na narinig ng lahat," patuloy ang pagkukuwento ni Lucio ng kanyang buhay matapos silang nanghapunan ni Perto.

"Kakaiba gali ang buhay mo," sabi ni Perto. "Kaya pala daw natigilan ka kanina nang hawak-hawak mo ang hasang ng sabalo."

Nagpatuloy pang magkuwento si Lucio.

Nagmula sa isang matanda ang boses sa seldang iyon. Nakita niya ang mga latay ng sinturon sa balat ng matanda. Sa unang pagkakataon, natakot siyang tumingin sa pasa sa balat.

Nakita raw siyang palabas ng oditoryum nang marinig ng matanda na parang may isang sakong bigas na bumagsak. Masama ang loob niya na siya ang pinagbintangang pumatay kay Indo, dahil lamang sa pangyayaring naabutan siyang hawak-hawak ang liig ng binata. Ipinaliwanag ng matanda na lumapit lang siya kay Indo nang makita niyang hindi na ito gumagalaw.

"Pero, kasama naming apat si Lucio sa sandaling naganap ang krimen," katig ni Susing. "Imposibleng nasa dalawang lugar si Lucio sa iisang panahon."

"Tiyo Merto," sabi niya sa matanda, "May ilaw pa bala nang makita mo akong tumakbo palabas sa oditoryum?"

"Huo. Maliwanag doon at nakilala ko agad kung sino ang tao doon."

"Tiyo Merto," ang patuloy niya. "Nakikilala mo ba ang babaing iyan? Iyang nakaupo sa may pintuan?"

Pinakurap ni Tiyo Merto ang kanyang mga mata. Malabo sa kanya ang mukha ng babaing tinuturo sa kanya.

"Indi ko makilala. Mahina na ang aking mga mata. Halos indi ko na makilala ang tao kung may sampung metro ang layo niya. Matanda na ako."

"Tsip," sabi niya, "may mahalagang lakad pa ako. Puede bala mamayang gabi niyo na lang ipagpatuloy ang pag-iimbestiga sa akin? Pero imbestigahin niyo si Tiyo Merto. Tanungin niyo, halimbawa, kung paano niya akong nakilala, sa layo ng dalawampung metro, samantalang indi nga niya makilala ang kanyang pamangkin na babae sa layo lang ng sampung metro."

Napapikit si Lucio pagsapit sa bahaging ito ng kanyang kwento. Nakaramdam siya ng pangamba sa pangyayari.

Nagpatindi rito ang lamig ng hanging galing sa tabing-dagat. Lumangutngut ang kanyang mga bagang at wala sa loob na pinalabas niya ang kanyang panyo. "Paano ko masakal sang panyo si Indo? Matanda na ako at indi ko masukatan ang lakas niya?" iyon ang sabi ni Tiyo Merto sa imbestigasyon ng gabing iyon. Ngunit pinakawalan si Lucio ng pulis nang mapatunayang lasing siya sa mga sandaling pinatay si Indo at walang motibong napagtiyak sa kanyang pagpatay sa kaibigan. Ayon din sa resulta ng imbestigasyon, kasama siya nina Kosme nang mangyari ang krimen. "Pero indi ba puedeng makalimutan ni Kosme kung sin-o ang mga kasama niya patungo sa kanyang bahay dahil sa kalasingan?" tanong noon ni Merto sa hepe ng pulisya.

Tinupi ni Lucio ang panyo para maging anyong tatsulok ito. Hinawakan niya ito sa magkabilang dulo at pinainda-indayog. Sumabit ang ikatlong dulo at pumulupot sa naiwang parte ng panyo.

"Mabuti't nakapagbakasyon ka diri sa Dumalag," sabi ni Perto. "Baka sakaling malimtan mo ang lahat na nangyari." Binanat-banat niya ang panyo. Nabanat ang hibla ng tela at naging malapisi ang tibay nito.

Napabalikwas si Perto. Wala si Lucio sa higaan nito. Dalidali niyang isinuot ang kanyang *jacket* at tumakbo patungong tabing-dagat. Mga alas-tres na ng umaga at ang kalahating buwan parang kumikiskis sa maitim na ulap. Tinulak niya ang isang baroto sa tubig na nahiwa sa bakas ng sasakyan.

Nanikip ang mga kalamnan ni Perto sa likod, sa dibdib at sa braso nang nagsagwan siya. Matulin ang kanyang pagsagwan, walang patid. At ang tubig na tinatamaan ng kanyang sagwan parang kristal na nangagsisabog. Naalala niya ang kanyang sinabi kay Lucio.

"Ginputulan ko ng buntot ang sabalo para bumagal siyang lumangoy."

"Kung putol na ang kanyang buntot, maari ko na siyang habulin sa aking baroto. Mabilis ako magsagwan."

"Gingbalik ko siya sa dagat dahil indi ko siya ibig hulihin. Indi ko siya gustong patayin. Kailangang may sabalo ang dagat para mabuhay ang mga tao."

"Mula pa sa aking pagkabata, hinangad ko nang matunton ang lugar na pinangigitlugan ng mga bangus. Kung malaman

ko ang kondisyon ng tubig at ang kapaligiran ng pinangingitlugan ng bangus, puede ko nang madakop ang lahat nga sabalo na may itlog at ilagay sa palaisdaan. Ibig kong makita kung paano pinanganganak at tumutubo ang bangus."

"Ayokong dumakip ng malaking sabalo hangga't di ko malalaman kung saang uri ng lugar ito pinanganganak."

Mga sagot ito ni Perto sa maraming tanong ni Lucio matapos silang maghapunan nang nakaraang gabi. Gustong malaman nito kung bakit hindi inuwi ni Perto ang sabalong nadakip nila kahapon at kung bakit matapos pinutol ang buntot nito inihagis uli ito sa dagat.

"Indi dapat madakop ni Lucio ang awa," bulong niya sa sarili.

Nang makita niya ang mabilis na paggalaw ng ilaw sa dagat, natiyak ni Pertong nakita na ni Lucio ang awa at hinahabol na ito.

Ginamit ni Perto ang buong lakas sa pagsagwan. Pinatulin niya ang baroto; umalimbukay ang tubig, tanda ng pagdaan niyang mabilis.

"Huwag mong patayin!" sigaw ni Perto nang mapalapit na siya sa baroto ni Lucio at makitang tinututukan nito ng sibat ang isda.

Nagulat si Lucio. Hindi niya agad napansin si Perto. Ipinagpatuloy niya ang pagtutok.

Dali-daling lumipat si Perto sa baroto ng pinsan at nagpumilit agawin ang sibat. Kumalas si Lucio.

Pinilipit ni Perto ang kamay ni Lucio na may tangan ng sibat. Nabitiwan ni Lucio ang sibat, nahulog ito at lumutang.

Sinunggaban ni Lucio ang liig ni Perto. Parang bakal ang pag-ipit ng kanyang dalawang kamay na pinatibay ng kanyang pamamanday sa Panit-an. Nabuwal si Perto sa baroto, nawalan ng malay.

Inabot ni Lucio ang lumulutang na sibat at hinanap ang awa. Nang matanaw niya ito, pinalipad niya ang sibat. Nadaplisan ang katawan ng sabalo at lumubog ito. "Napatay ko siya!" sigaw ni Lucio.

Tumalon siya sa tubig at sinisid ang isda pero hindi niya ito nakita. Pumaibabaw siya nang manandali para makasagap ng sariwang hangin. Kinabahan siya nang makitang malayo na ang nagsasagwang si Perto. Naalala niya ang biro ni Perto sa kanya kagabi: "Kung malasing ako baka maikuwento ko sa mga kasama ko ang iyong nakaraan. Malalaman ng lahat nga ikaw ang pumatay kay Indo."

"Kailangang maabutan ko siya!" At sumakay si Lucio sa iniwang baroto. "Baka maghiganti siya sa akin at isuplong ako sa pulis!"

Subalit nang magsagwan siya nakita na naman niya ang sabalo.

Dahan-dahang lumangoy itong palayo sa kanya. Tinitigan na lang ni Lucio nang matalas ang isda at mabilis na hinabol si Perto. "Kailangan kong siguraduhing indi siya makakapagsumbong sa pulisya!"

Tumigil si Lucio ng pagsagwan nang dumaan sa gilid ng baroto ang dalawang sabalong sinlaki ng kanyang sinibat. Nandilat ang kanyang mga mata. Nang sundan ng paningin niya ang mga ito, nakalimutan na niya si Perto—lalo na nang sinabayan ng dalawang sabalo ang isang nasibat na niya. Pinagitnaan nila ang sugatang kasama at sabay lumangoy palayo kay Lucio. Napansin ng binata na mas maiksi ang buntot ng isa sa dalawang sabalong kararating lamang.

"Buwisit nga sabalo ini!" Pinihit ni Lucio ang baroto at hinabol ang isdang maikli ang buntot.

Nakaahon na si Perto sa tabing-dagat. Masakit pa ang kanyang liig sa pananakal ng pinsan. Tumingala siya sa langit. Madaling araw na subalit parang hindi sisikat ang araw nang umagang iyon. Makapal ang ulap sa langit at narinig niyang kumakaluskos ang mga dahon ng niyog dala ng pagsampok dito ng malakas na hangin.

"May bagyo nga nagapalapit," bulong niya sa sarili habang tinatahak ang daang pauwi. Nang malayo na siya, nilingon niya ang dagat. Sa malalaking alon nito nakasakay ang sabalong may maikling buntot—ang hustisya sa dagat.

Sa Lawod sang Pangabuhi

Ismaelita Floro-Luza

Madugay nga nagtindog si Lorna sa iya atubangan. Waay nagahulag. Nakadulog si Dardo sa pag-uba sang iya sapatos kag tinulok ang nawong sang asawa. Nagatamod gihapon ini sa pito ka panid nga bentihon nga tinunghol niya. Suweldo yadto ni Dardo para sa isa ka kinsena. Kag sa nawong ni Lorna, amat-amat niya nga namasnahan ang pagkulap sang gal-om.

"Ini lang?" nabatian niya nga hambal ni Lorna nga naladlad sa gihapon ang kamot.

"Siyento kuwarinta na lang ina," waay sa buot nga balos ni Dardo nga pinadayon ang pag-uba sang sapatos. "Binuhinan ko sing bale kuwarinta. Beinte sa alamutan namon sa bangkete ni Mr. Velasco (si Mr. Velasco isa ka kaupod ni Dardo sa opisina nga manugretiro na sa palangakuan), napulo para sa regalo namon sa iya kag ang napulo binayad ko sa utang ko sa kantina sang opisina."

Larawan sang isa ka lutos nga nakapungko si Lorna sa kaatubang nga sopa. Daw indi gihapon makapati! Nagakurinot ang agtang. "Ano sa banta mo ang matabo sa aton sa siyento kuwarenta nga ini, Dardo?"

"O," nakapukwat si Dardo.

"Ang kuwarta mo!" hilmunon na ang pagkabasag sang tingog ni Lorna. "Aba, Dardo! Ano sa laom mo ang buhaton ko diri? Sa plete sa balay... kuwarenta...suga, otso...tubig, lima ka pisos...sa utang sa tindahan, beinte singko na tanan. Bugas...sud-an! Ang sapatos pa nga ginapangayo ni Dandoy mo para sa boy eskauting, pamasahe mo kag panigarilyo! Maayo kon indi *blue seal*. Aba, pisos siguro ang kaha kag isa ka maghapon mo lang nga suyop!"

"Ara ka naman! Buwisit nga...," hinali nga tumindog si Dardo. "Gumwa naman ang litaniya nga ina. Ano ka bala?"

"Ano ka bala?" balik nga binghal ni Lorna. "Anhon ko ining kuwarta mo?"

"Di, paiguon mo bisan pa ano!"

"Paiguon? Nahibaluan mo bala nga magalitik naman ang ulo sing paiguigo sini? Aba, ang badyet ko, bisan anhon ko na sing unat indi na gid mahimo! Duha pa abi ang nagagatas sa mga anak mo!"

"Mahimo bala?" pugong ang pagbungat ni Dardo. "Karon na ina. Ginagutom ako!"

"Maayo ka imo kay..."

"Indi ka bala mag-untat?" pasinggit na nga balikid ni Dardo.

"Indi! Ngaa indi mo bala luyag mabatian ang kamatuoran nga kulang ang pamilya mo?"

Apang ang kasingki sang panalabton ni Lorna, hinali nga nauntat. Hinulikap niya ang iya nawong nga hinali nga uminit bangod sa tupa sang kamot ni Dardo. Masakit! Mabinhod!

"Tinampa mo ako?"

"Nagapamilit ka!" hinali nga tumalikod si Dardo nga daw sadto lamang makabugtaw sa kamatuoran nga natup-an niya sing kamot ang tiayon. Apang nalimot sia sa kaugalingon. Sa una nga kahigayunan sa iya kabuhi, sadto lamang niya natup-an sing kamot si Lorna. Waay na sia makapugong sa kaugalingon.

Naghibi si Lorna. Masinakiton. Ginhimulatan ni Dardo ang magbalikid sa asawa nga sadto naganguyngoy sa sopa, apang indi niya mahimo. May kon ano nga gahom ang nagapugong sa iya. Kag sa baylo, nasapwan na lamang ni Dardo ang kaugalingon nga nagasuksok liwat sang iya kamisadentro nga nagakabit sa salandigan sa pulongkoan. Kag madasig na nga nanaog.

Sumakay si Dardo sa naglabay nga dyep. Ginpakamaayo niya nga sa isa ka restawran na lamang manyaga.

Naka-order na si Dardo sing pagkaon, apang nagapabilin gihapon nga daw nagaalimbukay ang sulod sang iya dughan. Bation gihapon sa iya ang paglinagumba sang kaakig nga kaina pumogad didto. Kag ang kainit sang nawong ni Lorna, ara gihapon sa iya mga palad. Kinuom niya. Masakit panumdomon nga nagamitan niya sing kamot ang tiayon. Ini ang isa ka butang nga ginlikawan niya buhaton sugod pa sadto. Apang sumonod sa talaksan ang iya kaalipungot. Kag nalimtan niya ang tanan. Wala na sia sing itugot pa. Napilasan ang iya balatyagon sa wala sing panabitabi nga mga pinanghambal ni Lorna.

Napulo ka tuig na karon nga sila nakasal ni Lorna. Kag lima ka bilog na ang nanginbunga sang ila paghigugmaanay. Si Lorna, nakatapos sing pagkamanunodlo sang kaslon sila. Apang waay niya ini pagpatudloa. Luyag niya nga magapabilin lamang ang tiayon sa sulod sang balay agod magtatap sang iya mga kinahanglanon sa amat amat nagadamo nila nga mga anak. Ang ginabaton ni Dardo nga tatlo ka gatos kag kalim-an tuman na agod makasabat sang ila pang-adlaw-adlaw nga kinahanglanon. Apang sang magdamo na ang ila kabataan kag ang kamagulangan nagabutho na, amat-amat man nga nabatyagan ni Dardo ang pagpiot sang ila pagsinalayo. Amat-amat nga nagdako ang galastuhan. Butang nga amo ang masunson sandigan sang ila balaison ni Lorna.

Nakahulag si Dardo sang ibutang sang tag-alagad ang iya inorder nga pagkaon. Sinugoran na niya ang paghungit. Apang nabatyagan niya nga nadula na ang kaina kagutom nga naglikos sa iya. Nadulaan sia sing gana. Uminom na lamang si Dardo sing tubig kag liwat nga tinawag ang tag-alagad. Binayaran ang nakaon kag madasig nga tinultol ang ganhaan paggwa.

Sa opisina magderetso si Dardo sina nga udto. Waay na sia magbalik sa ila balay. Luyag niya nga palipason ang kaalipungot nga sadto nagaamat-amat naman sing hupa sa sulod sang iya dughan. Kag sa iya pag-isahanon sa atubangan sang iya latok sa talatapan, wala man sia sing naaputan nga buhaton. Igu man lang magduhongan. Si Lorna gihapon ang larawan nga nagahampang sa iya painuino. Ngaa nadapatan niya si Lorna sing kamot? Ngaa nabuhat niya ang subong sa tinuga nga mahal kaayo sa iya? Ang napulo ka tuig, isa gayod ka malip-ot nga panahon para sa iya agod manginlab-as sa handurawan ang nagliligad sa ila ni Lorna. Indi sa paghakwat sang kaugalingon nga bangko. Apang may angkon si Dardo nga kaambong. Kag indi maisip ang mga babae nga napangakuan niya sing paghigugma. Mga babae nga waay naman sia pagpaslawa. Apang sa kadamuon sang natipon niya nga mga kahagugma, si Lorna ang iya pinakasalan. Indi matahom si Lorna kon nawong ang pagahambalan. Kasarangan lang. May hitsura man. Diutay. Pero natun-an niya ini nga higugmaon sing himpit. Kay Lorna lamang sia magtuad sing paghigugma nga upod ang iya kasingkasing. Siling pa sang iya mga kaabyanan sadto, nakuha kuno sia ni Lorna sa angkon sini nga kaalam. Ginaako niya. Maalam matuod si Lorna. Balediktoryan sang magtapos sa hayskol kag *Magna Cum Laude* sang magtapos sa kolehiyo sa kurso sang pagkamanunodlo. Ginapabugal niya ang kinaadman nga ini ni Lorna sa iya kapareho nga lalaki. Mapalaron sia!

Ang matam-is nga handurawan sang nagliligad, lubos nga nakapalimot sang iya kaakig. Gani sang maggwa si Dardo gikan sa opisina sina nga hapon, mamag-an na kaayo ang iya pamatyag. Waay sia pagbugnoha ni Lorna sang magsampot sia sa balay. Pat-od ni Dardo nga naghinakit sing kapin sa iya ang tiayon. Kag pati na ang ila mga anak nga ayhan nakahangop na sang nasaksihan nga natabo sa ila nga duha, waay na nagaginahod katulad sang kinaandan.

Sa ila paghigda sina nga gab-i, nagapabilin gihapon nga wala sing tingog si Lorna. Nagatakilid ini sa pihak nayon sang kama. Nakabatyag si Dardo sing kahuya apang yadto ginpilit niya nga pakigsumpongan. Kinahanglan nga magbugnohanay sila ni Lorna. Kinahanglan nga makapangayo sia sing pasaylo.

"Ling?" mahinay ang tingog nga kinaptan niya sa butkon ang tiayon. Waay ini maghulag.

"Pasayluhon mo kuntani ako sa natabo kaina. Pero magpati ka kutani nga indi ko hungod nga buhaton yadto sa imo. Nalimot lamang ako sa kaugalingon. Napuno lang ako!"

Kalinong. Waay gihapon nagahulag si Lorna.

"Ling? Please..."

Wala gihapon sing sabat. Nakaginhawa sing madalom si Dardo nga piniyong ang mga mata. Nahibaluan niya nga nagabugtaw si Lorna kag nabatian sini ang tanan niya nga ginpanghambal. Apang nagapakunokuno lamang nga nagakatulog.

Mataas na ang adlaw sang magbugtaw si Dardo sang sumonod nga aga. Katulad sang kinaandan, nagahulat sa latok ang iya pamahaw. Humigop lamang sia sing kape. Kag sang magpaalam sa tiayon, isa ka mahinay nga "huo" ang pinakawas ni Lorna.

Madamo pa nga mga inadlaw ang madasig nga napupo sa pungango sang panahon. Kag sa sulod sang panahon nga ina, nagbalik naman ang daan nga katawhay sa sulod sang panimalay nanday Dardo kag Lorna. Apang namutikan ni Dardo nga sugod sadtong hitabo nga nadapatan niya sing kamot ang tiayon, nanginmahipos na ini. Kag isa ka aga, amo na lamang ang kakibot ni Dardo sang mabugtawan nga nakailis ang tiayon.

"May laktan ka?" pasikto niya.

"Huo," sabat ni Lorna. "Nalipatan ko gali nga silingon sa imo. Nakasulod na ako bilang manunodlo sa *Holy Ghost* (isa ka kolehiyo nga ginadumalahan sang mga madre ang tinumod ni Lorna) kag karon nga adlaw ako maumpisa."

Nakanganga si Dardo.

"Ang pamahaw mo ara na sa latok. Kag ginbilin ko naman kay Talia ang mga kinahanglanon mo."

Nakapanagitlon si Dardo. Nahinalian sia. Apang nakahalin lamang si Lorna, waay na sia makatindog pa. Madugay sia nga naurongan. Sa sulod sing iya kasingkasing, may kon ano nga kahapdi ang hinali nga tumohil. Pilit niya nga pinaligad yadto. Ginbawibawi. Ayhan may katarungan man si Lorna sa nanginpamat-od sini.

Kag ang sumonod pa nga mga inadlaw amo ang nagsaksi sang kamag-o sa ila pangabuhi. Nadula na ang kinaandan nga pag-imbestigar ni Lorna sa denintimos nga madula sa iya suweldo kada kinsena nga mag-entrega sia. Kag nahibaluan ni Dardo nga daku man ang ginabaton sang tiayon sa ginatudloan sini. Kamag-o sa pamatasan ni Lorna nga umabot sa hitabo nga waay na gani sini ginasuknai ang bana kon hungdon nga indi mag-entrega ukon malipat man. Kag sining ulihi pa gid nga mga inadlaw, natukiban na lamang ni Dardo nga luas sa ginabaton ni Lorna sa bulothoan, naga *tutor* pa gali ini sa duha ka anak ni Mrs. Sales nga amo ang kabangdanan kon ngaa masunson nga magab-ihan ang tiayon sa pagpauli.

Ang gumontang nahanungod sa kuwarta, nadayunan na nga nadula sa ila pagsinalayo. Halog na ang ila pagginawi sa pilak. Kag nakapamakal naman sila sing mga panapot para sa mga kabataan kag pila ka kasangkapan sa sulod sang balay. Apang ang tanan nga ato, ang tanan nga kapinasahi, may kon ano nga kasakit nga nadulot sa pagkatao ni Dardo. Nabatyagan niya nga may daku nga kakulangan. Kag ang kakulangan nga ina amo ang ginapilit niya nga laghapon sa tanan nga adlaw. Masaw-a batunon ang kamatuoran. Apang ginapangita niya ang litaniya sang utang nga ginapresentar sa iya ni Lorna. Ang mga gumontang nahanungod sang kinahanglanon sang mga kabataan. Mga butang yadto nga nakapabatyag sa iya sang iya kamalahalon sa iya panimalay. Nga sia ang sandigan sa ila paglangoy sa pangabuhi. Ginakapyutan sang iya mga mahal sa kabuhi. Kag sa pamatyag ni Dardo, padayon nga nagalakat ang mga inadlaw kag padayon man nga nagakadula ang iya kapuslanan bilang amay. Sa tinion nga magentrega sia sing suweldo, waay sa buot nga batunon lamang yadto ni Lorna kag taguon. Ni waay na ginaisipa sa iya atubangan katulad sang kinaandan. Daw wala na sing kapuslanan ang nanginbayad sang iya pagpabalhas kag paghimulat. Subong bala nga daw ginapabatyag sa iya ni Lorna nga bisan indi na sia magpangita, masarangan sini nga padalaganon sing tayuyon ang ila pangabuhi. Ano na lamang abi ang iya pulos bilang amay? Ano?

Bag-o nga suweldo si Dardo sina nga hapon. Mapagsik ang iya lawas sang sumampot sa ila balay sanglit luas sa kinaandan niya nga ginabaton may dugang pa yadto nga bale siyento singkuwenta nga bonus. Pinangita niya dayon ang tiayon nga sadto masako sa mga hilikuton sa kusina. Tinunghol niya ang nagabaknal nga sobre.

"Ano ini?"

"Suweldo ko," may pagpabugal sa tingog. "Kag may dugang pa ina nga bonus." Pilit nga ginbasa ni Dardo sa nawong sang asawa ang ginapaabot nga kalipay. Apang nakabatyag sia sing kapaslawan sang makita nga waay magbag-o ang nawong ni Lorna.

"A," hagyu lamang nga nagyuhom si Lorna. Pinadayon sini ang ginahikot. "Ilihog lang gani tungtong dira sa altar kay tapuson ko lang ining ginaluto ko. Nakapamahaw ka na bala?"

Waay magsabat si Dardo. Nabatyagan niya nga daw hinali nga nagpalanguy-oy ang iya mga tuhod. Masakit kaayo ang iya pamatyag. Kag laragway sang isa ka lutos nga tinuhoy niya ang ila hulot. Pahaboy nga binutang didto ang sobre sa ibabaw sang altar.

Nakapanyapon na sila sina nga gab-i kag nagapahunayhonay na sila nga mag-asawa sa salas sang balay sang maghambal si Dardo.

"Nagahinakit ka pa bala sa akon, Ling?"

Nakapukwat si Lorna. "Ngaa nakahambal ka sing subong sina, Dardo?"

"Sanglit nabatyagan ko. Amat-amat na nga nadula ang akon kapuslanan bilang amay sa puloy-an nga ini. Sa mga problema sa pangabuhi, waay mo na ako ginahilabti! Subong bala nga...nga..."

"Ginapangita mo ang daan naton nga pagsinalayo?" may katingala sa tingog si Lorna.

Nagtango si Dardo. "Namutikan ko, sugod sang dapatan ko ikaw sing kamot, nagbag-o ka pa tubtob karon."

"Nalimtan ko na ang nahanungod didto, Dardo," balos ni Lorna. "Ang buot mo silingon," may tunay nga igpat sa mata ni Lorna, "ginapangita mo ang litaniya sang utang nga masunson ko ginapresentar sa imo? Ang akon baba?"

"Didto ko lamang nabatyagan nga malahalon ako sa imo...kag sa aton mga anak, Lorna," may kapait sa tingog ni Dardo.

"Kon nahibaluan mo lamang nga ginhinulsolan ko sing kapin ang mga pamatasan ko sadto, Dardo," hambal ni Lorna. "Ang kalainan sadto sa aton pagpangabuhi kag sa aton mga anak nga amat-amat na nga nakakilala sang kamatuoran. Nakabugtaw lamang ako sa kamatuoran nga indi ko dapat buhaton ang pamatasan nga ato sa imo sang dapatan mo ako sing kamot. Nakamaradmad ako sa kamatuoran nga indi ko makuha ang mga problema naton sa pangabuhi paagi sa baba. Nalipat ako sa akon tinun-an, Dardo. Kag sugod sadto ginpangako ko na sa kaugalingon ang pagbag-o. Huo, mahal ko ikaw, Dardo. Mahal ka namon. Kag sa lawod nga ini sang pangabuhi, indi kami mahimo nga makatabok kon wa-ay ka," may luha sa mga mata ni Lorna.

From: *Hiligaynon*, April 27, 1966

In the Sea of Life

(Sa Lawod sang Pangabuhi)

Ismaelita Floro-Luza

For some moments, Lorna stood before him. She did not move. Dardo stopped taking off his shoes and looked up at his wife. She was still staring at the twenty-peso bills he had handed over to her. This was Dardo's take-home pay for half a month. He noticed a pall gradually settling on Lorna's face.

"Just this?" he heard Lorna ask, her palms still wide open.

"For now, it's only P140," Dardo replied nonchalantly and resumed taking off his shoes. "I took out about P40—P20 as contribution for the banquet for Mr. Velasco (Mr. Velasco was Dardo's co-employee who was retiring), P10 for our gift to him, and P10 as payment to our canteen in the office."

Lorna's face fell as she sat down on the sofa before her. Like she couldn't understand what this was all about. She frowned. "How far do you suppose we can go with this, Dardo?"

"*O*," Dardo didn't know whether to stand up or sit.

"Your money!" her voice hoarsened. "Dardo, what do you think we can do with this? House rent—P40, light—P8, water—P5, payment for what we owe the *sari-sari* store—P25, rice, food! The shoes Dandoy is asking for, his boy scout uniform, your fare, and your cigarette allowance. Good, if it were not blue seal. This must be P1 per pack now and you finish smoking it in just one day."

"There you go, again! Damn it!" Dardo stood up quickly. "Coming out with that litany. What's happening to you?"

"What's happening to you?" Lorna retorted. "What can I do with your money?"

"Then make do with it!"

"Make do with it? Do you know that I'll have to break my head again trying to make both ends meet? But our income, no matter how I figure out the budget, isn't enough. Just think, we still have two children feeding on milk!"

"Do you mind?" Dardo controlled himself. "Let's talk about that later. I'm very hungry."

"You're lucky you don't...."

"Aren't you going to shut up?" Nardo shouted as he turned to his wife.

"No! Why? Don't you want to hear the truth—that your family can't make both ends meet?"

But Lorna's sharp retort was cut short. She touched her face; it felt hot from the blow that had just flown from Dado's hands. It hurt at first. And then it felt numb.

"You slapped me?"

"You forced me to!" Dardo turned away from his wife as if realizing only now that he had hit her. He had forgotten himself. For the first time in his life he had to lay his hand on Lorna. He had lost control.

Lorna wept. Wept very hard. Dardo wanted to turn to his wife as she cried in the sofa, but he couldn't. Some force was holding him back. Instead, he found himself getting back into the shirt he had hung on the chair. Then he dashed downstairs.

Dardo got into a passing jeepney. He thought it best just to take his lunch in a restaurant.

Even after he had ordered his food from the menu, he continued to seethe. He could still hear the tumult raging within his chest and his hand still smarted from the hotness of Lorna's cheeks. He clenched it. This was the very thing he had always avoided.

But his patience had reached its limits. He could not take anything more from her. Lorna's tongue was sharp and she had wounded his feelings.

They had been married for ten years, their love now blessed with five children. Lorna had already gotten her education degree when they got married. But he did not let her teach. He wanted his wife to stay home so she could take care of the needs of his growing family. At first, Dardo's salary of P350 was enough to meet their needs. But when they had more children and the eldest started schooling, Dardo began to feel their tight financial situation. Expenses rose, causing his frequent quarrels with Lorna. Dardo's thoughts broke off when the waiter served the food he had ordered. He started to eat, but the hunger which had gripped him a while ago was gone. He had lost his appetite. He just drank water and called the waiter back. He paid for his food and quickly headed for the exit.

Dardo went straight to his office that afternoon. There, he wanted to soothe his anger; it was now subsiding slowly. But he could not settle down to work as he sat in front of his table. Certain thoughts lingered. And it was Lorna's image which continued to play in his mind. Why had he used force on Lorna? Why had he done this to someone so dear to him? Ten years was a short time; the past flashed across his mind. Modesty aside, he was an attractive man. There were countless women he had proposed to. But not one of them really got to discover this secret. Among the girlfriends he had collected, it was Lorna he married. She wasn't that pretty—just a bit. But she was very intelligent so he learned to love her truly. It was Lorna alone he gave his heart to. At that time, his friends said that Lorna had won his heart because of her intelligence. Yes, that was true. Lorna was bright. She graduated valedictorian from high school and *magna cum laude* from college. He used to boast of Lorna's intelligence among his fellow males. He was fortunate.

These sweet memories made him forget his anger. So, when Dardo left the office that afternoon, he felt light-hearted. Lorna ignored him when he came home. Dardo knew she was still resentful of him. And even the children, who must have understood what was going on between their parents, did not make their usual noise.

When they went to bed that night, Lorna remained silent. She lay on her side at one side of the bed. Dardo was ashamed to approach her but he made an effort to fight this. He would have to apologize to her.

" 'Ling?" he whispered, touching her arm. She did not stir.

"I'm sorry for what happened this morning. Believe me, I didn't do it on purpose. I just forgot myself. I felt pushed to the wall."

Silence. Lorna continued lying still.

" 'Ling. Please ...."

No reply came. Dardo took a deep breath and closed his eyes. He knew Lorna was awake and had heard all that he had said, but she pretended to be asleep.

The sun was at its peak. It was almost noon when Dardo woke up the following morning. As usual, his breakfast was ready but he just sipped the coffee. When he bid his wife goodbye, Lorna let go a soft "yes."

Many more days were plucked from the stem of time. And during that time, peace and harmony returned to their home.

But Dardo observed that ever since that incident, his wife had turned reticent. Upon waking up one morning, Dardo was surprised to see Lorna already dressed up.

"Are you going somewhere?" he asked her.

"Yes," Lorna replied. "I forgot to tell you—I've been hired to teach at Holy Ghost (a college managed by nuns) and today is my first day to teach."

Dardo could only gape at her.

"Your breakfast is ready, and I have told Talia to take care of your needs."

Dardo swallowed hard. He was taken by surprise. Lorna had left, and he had not said a word. He was stupefied. Something seared through his heart although he made an effort not to mind it. He tried to soothe himself. Perhaps, Lorna was right in her decision.

In the following days, their lifestyle changed. Lorna no longer bothered to check if his salary was short of this or that amount. Dardo knew that his wife was receiving a comfortable salary at the college. But he wasn't used to Lorna's not asking for his salary. In the past few days, Dardo also discovered that other than her teaching job, she was tutoring Mrs. Sales' two children. That was why his wife would often come home late.

The discussions over money stopped. Now they could spend with more ease. They were able to buy clothes for the children and some things for the house. But the changes disturbed Dardo. He felt a great absence. It was this he was trying to understand all this time. It was loathsome to accept the truth. Now he was waiting for Lorna to bring up the usual litany of debts. He missed the discussions regarding the needs of the children. These made him feel important in the household. That they depended on him in their journey through the sea of life. That his dear ones were dependent on him. But it seemed to him that as days wore on, his role as father of the house was becoming less and less important. Whenever he would give his salary to Lorna she accepted it nonchalantly, then set it aside promptly. She would not even count the bills in front of him as she used to. She did not seem to value his efforts at all. Lorna seemed to be making him feel that even if he did not earn, she would be able to support the family comfortably. Of what use was he now as a father? Of what use?

That morning Dardo had just received his pay. He was in high spirits when he reached home because other than his usual take-home pay he had received a P150 bonus. Immediately, he looked for his wife who was busy in the kitchen. He handed a well-stuffed envelope to her.

"What's this?"

"My pay," he said with some pride. Dardo searched for some hint of appreciation in her face. But he was disappointed; Lorna's face remained impassive.

"Ah," Lorna smiled slightly. She went on working. "Please just put it on the altar; I've got to finish cooking. Have you taken your merienda yet?"

Dardo did not reply. He felt his knees suddenly go wobbly. It seemed he was falling ill. The picture of frustration, he threw the envelope on the altar.

The family had already taken dinner and the couple were relaxing in the sala when Dardo spoke.

"Are you still mad at me 'Ling?"

Lorna was startled.

"Why do you say that, Dardo?"

"It's just that I feel I'm becoming useless as head of the family. As to our our day-to-day problems you don't seek my help any more. You know, like I were, I were...."

"Do you miss the way we used to treat each other?" Lorna sounded puzzled.

Dardo nodded. "I noticed that since that incident, you've changed. You still resent me."

"I don't think of that at all, Dardo," Lorna assured him. "You mean to say," there was amusement in Lorna's eyes, "you are expecting me to present you with a litany of accounts as I used to? My nagging mouth?"

"That was the only time I felt important to you and our children, Lorna," Dardo sounded bitter.

"If you only knew, I am really sorry I acted that way, Dardo," Lorna said, teary-eyed. "It had a bad effect on our life and on our children who are now beginning to understand the facts of life. I realized I shouldn't have done that to you; we can't solve our problems with my big mouth. I forgot what they taught me in school, Dardo. And since that time I promised myself I would change. I love you, Dardo. You are dear to us. And the sea of life we can't cross without you," said Lorna, teary-eyed.

Sa Dagat ng Buhay

Ismaelita Floro-Luza

Matagal nakatayo si Lorna sa harap niya. Hindi tumitinag. Napahinto si Dardo sa paghubad ng kanyang sapatos at tiningnan ang mukha ng asawa. Nakatungo pa rin ito sa pitong tigbebeinte na iniabot niya. Suweldo iyon ni Dardo para sa kalahating buwan. At napansin niyang unti-unti nang nabalot sa dilim ang mukha ni Lorna.

"Ito lang?" wika ni Lorna na nakaladlad pa rin ang kamay.

"Siyento kuwarinta na lang iyan," wala sa loob na sagot ni Dardo at ipinagpatuloy uli ang paghuhubad ng sapatos. "Binawasan ko ng bale ba kwarinta. Beinte bilang ambag namin sa bangkete para kay G. Velasco (kasamahan ni Dardo sa opisina si G. Velasco at ito'y magreretiro na), sampu para sa regalo namin sa kanya at sampu para pambayad sa utang ko sa kantina ng opisina."

Anyong natalo si Lorna nang napaupo sa sopang nasa tapat nila. Parang hindi pa rin makapaniwala. Nakakunot ang noo. "Ano sa tingin mo ang mangyayari sa siyento kwarintang ito, Dardo?"

"O," nagitla si Dardo.

"Ang kwarta mo!" basag na ang tinig ni Lorna sa inis. "Aba, Dardo! Ano bala ang maobra ko sini? Sa upa ng bahay—kwarinta, sa ilaw—otso, sa tubig—lima, sa utang sa tindahan—beinte singko, bigas...ulam! Ang sapatos pa na hinihingi ni Dandoy para sa boyskawting, pamasahe mo at panigarilyo. Mabuti kung indi *blue seal*. Aba, piso siguro ang isang kaha niyan a, at maghapon mo lang ginahithit!"

"Andiyan ka na naman! Buwisit nga!" biglang tumindig si Dardo. "Lumabas na naman ang litanyang iyan. Ano ka ba?"

"Ano ka ba?" balik-singhal ni Lorna. "Anhon ko itong kuwarta mo?"

"Di pagkasiyahin mo maski na papano!"

"Pagkasiyahin? Alam mo ba nga nagaputok na ang ulo ko sa kaiisip kung paano pagkasiyahin ito? Aba, ang badyet natin, maski paanong unat ko indi gid puede! Dalawa pa kasi sa mga anak mo ang gainom ng gatas!"

"Puede bala?" pigil na pigil ang pagsalita ni Dardo. "Saka na iyan. Ginagutom na ako!"

"Mabuti ka nga at...."

"Indi ka ba titigil?" pasigaw na liningon siya ni Dardo.

"Indi! Bakit? Ayaw mo bang pakinggan ang katotohanang ginakapos ang pamilya mo?"

Subalit biglang napigil ang masakit na pananalita ni Lorna. Hinipo niya ang kaniyang mukha na biglang nang-init sa tama ng kamay ni Dardo. Makirot! Namamanhid!

"Sinampal mo ako?"

"Mapilit ka!" biglang tumalikod si Dardo na parang noon lang nagising sa katotohanang napagbuhatan pala niya ng kamay ang asawa. Subalit nakalimot siya sa kanyang sarili. Sa kaunaunahang pagkakataon napagbuhatan niya ng kamay ang tiayon. Hindi siya nakapagtimpi ng sarili.

Umiyak si Lorna. Malungkot. Sinikap ni Dardong balingan ang asawang ngumunguyngoy sa sopa, nguni't hindi niya magawa. May kung anong gahom ang pumipigil sa kanya. Sa halip, napansin na lang niya ang sariling nagsusuot uli ng kamisedentrong nakasabit sa sandalan ng upuan. At mabilis siyang pumanaog. Sumakay si Dardo sa dumaang dyip. Minabuti niyang mananghalian na lang sa isang restawran.

Nakaorder na si Dardo ng pagkain, subalit parang kumukulo pa rin sa galit ang kanyang dibdib. Naririnig pa rin niya ang silakbo na pumugad doon kanina. Naramdaman pa rin niya sa kanyang mga palad ang init ng mukha ni Lorna. Kinuyom niya ito. Kaysakit isipin na nagamitan niya ng kamay ang asawa. Isang bagay itong iniiwasan niya magmula noon pa. Subalit umapaw na sa takalan ang kanyang pagkapoot. At nalimutan niya ang lahat. Hindi na siya nakatiis. Nasugatan ang kanyang damdamin sa walang-pasintabing pagsasalita ni Lorna.

Sampung taon na silang kasal ni Lorna. At lima na ang naging bunga ng kanilang pagmamahalan. Tapos sa kursong pagtuturo si Lorna nang ikasal sila. Subalit hindi niya ito pinayagang magturo. Ibig niyang manatili na lamang ang asawa sa bahay para asikasuhin ang mga kailangan ng kanilang dumadaming anak. Sapat na ang P350 na tinatanggap ni Dardo para sa kanilang pang-araw-araw na pangangailangan. Subalit nang dumami na ang kanilang mga anak at ang panganay ay nagsimula nang mag-aral, naramdaman ni Dardo ang paggigipit ng kanilang pamumuhay. Dumami ang pagkakagastusan. Bagay na iyon ang malimit na pinagsisimulan ng alitan nila ni Lorna.

Napaudlot si Dardo nang ilagay ng serbidor ang kanyang inorder na pagkain. Sinimulan niya ang pagsubo. Ngunit naramdaman niyang wala na ang pagkagutom na dumaklot sa kanya kanina. Nawalan siya ng gana. Uminom na lamang siya ng tubig at muling tinawag ang tagapagsilbi. Binayaran niya ang kinain at mabilis na tinunton ang pintuan palabas.

Sa opisina tumuloy si Dardo nang tanghaling iyon. Hindi na siya bumalik sa kanilang bahay. Ibig niyang palipasin ang galit na unti-unti nang humuhupa. Subalit sa kanyang pag-iisa sa harap ng kanyang mesa, wala rin naman siyang nagawa. Parang nagpalipas lang siya ng panahon. Si Lorna pa rin ang naglalaro sa kanyang isip. Bakit niya napagbuhatan ng kamay si Lorna? Bakit niya nagawa iyon sa nilalang minamahal niyang labis?

Kay ikli ng sampung taon; sariwa pa rin sa kanyang alaala ang kahapon nila ni Lorna. Hindi sa nagbubuhat siya ng sariling bangko. Makisig siya. At hindi mabilang ang mga babaing napangakuan niya ng kanyang pagmamahal. Hindi naman siya ibinunyag ng mga ito. At sa maraming kasintahang kanyang naipon, si Lorna ang kanyang pinakasalan. Hindi siya maganda kung mukha ang pag- uusapan. Katamtaman lang. May itsura rin naman, kaunti. Pero natutuhan niyang mahalin ito. Kay Lorna lamang siya nagtapat ng pag-ibig ng buong puso. Sabi pa nga ng mga kaibigan niya noon, nakuha raw siya ni Lorna dahil sa talino nito. Inamin niya. Matalino si Lorna. Balediktoryan ito nang magtapos sa kursong pagtuturo sa kolehiyo. Ipinagmamayabang niya ang dunong ni Lorna sa kapareho niyang lalaki.

Dahil sa matamis na alaalang ito, lumipas ang kanyang galit. Kaya't nang lumabas si Dardo sa opisina nang hapong iyon, maluwag na ang kanyang pakiramdam. Hindi siya binati ni Lorna pagsapit niya sa bahay. Tiyak ni Dardong labis na naghinakit ang kanyang asawa. Maging ang mga bata na marahil nakaintindi na sa nasaksihan nilang nangyari sa mga magulang ay hindi nagsiingay tulad ng kanilang nakagawian.

Pagkahiga nila nang gabing iyon, nanatiling walang imik si Lorna. Nakatagilid ito sa isang tabi ng kama. Nakaramdam si Nardo ng pagkahiya, ngunit pinilit niyang labanan iyon. Kailangang magkabati sila ni Lorna. Kailangang makahingi siya ng tawad dito.

" 'Ling?" mahina ang kanyang tinig, at hinawakan niya sa braso ang asawa. Hindi ito tuminag.

"Patawarin mo sana ako sa nangyari kanina. Talaga, indi ko sinasadya. Nakalimot lang ako sa sarili. Napuno lang ako."

Katahimikan. Hindi pa rin kumikibo si Lorna.

" 'Ling? *Please*...."

Hindi pa rin sumagot. Nagbuntong-hininga si Dardo at pinikit ang mga mata. Alam niyang gising si Lorna at dinig nito ang lahat na kanyang sinasabi, pero nagkunwaring tulog.

Mataas na ang araw nang magising si Dardo. Tulad ng kinaugalian, naghihintay na sa mesa ang kanyang almusal. Uminom lamang siya ng kape. At nang magpaalam sa asawa, isang mahinang "huo" ang pinakawalan ni Lorna.

Maraming araw pa ang mabilis na napitas sa tangkay ng panahon. Bumalik ang katahimikan sa kanilang pamamahay. Subalit napansin ni Dardo na magmula noong napagbuhatan niya ng kamay si Lorna, naging tahimik na ito. Isang araw nagulat na lamang si Dardo nang magisnang bihis na ang kanyang asawa.

"May pupuntahan ka?" tanong niya.

"Huo," sagot ni Lorna. "Nakalimutan ko palang sabihin sa iyo. Natanggap akong magturo sa Holy Ghost (isang kolehiyong pinamamahalaan ng mga madre ang tinutukoy ni Lorna), at ngayon ako maga-umpisa."

Napanganga si Dardo.

"Nandiyan na sa lamisa ang almusal mo. At ginbilin ko na rin kay Talia ang mga kailangan mo."

Napalunok si Dardo. Nabigla siya. Ngunit nakaalis na lamang si Lorna, hindi pa siya nakaimik. Matagal siyang natigilan. May kung anong hapding gumuhit sa kanyang puso. Pilit niyang pinalampas iyon. Nangatwiran. Siguro may dahilan naman si Lorna sa kanyang desisyon.

Maraming naging pagbabago sa kanilang pamumuhay nang mga sumunod na araw. Nawala na ang gawi ni Lornang mag-imbestiga sa sisentimong nawawala sa kanyang suweldo tuwing kinsenas. Napagalaman ni Dardong malaki ang tinatanggap ng asawa sa pinagtuturuan nito. Hindi na rin humihingi ng paliwanag si Lorna kung sinadya niyang di mag-entrega ng suweldo o di kaya'y sadyaing hindi magbigay nito. Natuklasan din ni Dardo nitong mga huling araw na bukod sa pagtuturo ni Lorna sa eskwela, *nagtu-tutor* din ito sa dalawang anak ni Gng. Sales na dahilan kung bakit malimit gabi na kung umuwi ang asawa.

Ang alitan tungkol sa kwarta ay tuluyan nang nawala sa kanilang pagsasama. Hindi na sila hirap. Nakapamili na sila ng mga damit para sa mga bata at ng ilang kasangkapan sa loob ng bahay. Subalit ang lahat na mga pangyayaring iyon ay nagdulot ng kung anong kirot sa pagkatao ni Dardo. Nakaramdam siya ng malaking kakulangan. Parang may hinahanap-hanap siya sa bawat araw. Mahirap tanggapin ang katotohanan. Ngunit hinahanap-hanap niya ang paglilitanya ni Lorna ng mga utang. Ang alitan tungkol sa mga kailangan ng mga bata. Mga bagay iyong nagparamdam sa kanyang mahalaga siya sa bahay. Na siya ang tagaalalay sa kanilang paglalangoy sa buhay. Kinakapitan ng kanyang mga minamahal. Sa pakiramdam ni Dardo, habang lumalakad ang mga araw patuloy ring nawawala ang kanyang kabuluhan bilang ama. Tuwing mag-eentrega siya ng suweldo, parang wala lang na tatanggapin ito ni Lorna at itatago. Ni hindi man lang binibilang sa kanyang harapan tulad noon. Parang hindi na kailangan ang naging bayad ng kanyang pawis at hirap. Parang ipinahihiwatig ni Lornang kahit na hindi siya maghanapbuhay, kaya nitong mapatakbo ang kanilang pamumuhay. Ano na lang ang kanyang kabuluhan bilang ama? Ano?

Bagong suweldo si Dardo noong hapong iyon. Masigla siya dahil bukod sa kanyang suweldo, may bonus pa siyang bale siyento singkwenta. Hinanap niya agad ang asawa. Abalang abala ito sa kusina. Inabot niya ang nakaumbok na sobre ng suweldo.

"Anu ini?"

"Suweldo ko," may pagmamalaki sa kanyang tinig. "At may dagdag pa iyan na bonus." Hinanap-hanap ni Dardo sa mukha ng asawa ang inaasahang kasiyahan. Subalit nalungkot siya nang makitang wala man lang pagbabago sa mukha nito.

"A," bahagyang ngumiti si Lorna at nagpatuloy sa kanyang ginagawa. "Pakitungtong nga lang dira sa altar at tatapusin ko lang ining ginaluto ko. Nakameryenda ka na?"

Hindi sumagot si Dardo. Bigla siyang nanlambot. Nangatog ang kanyang mga tuhod. Masamang-masama ang loob. Larawan ng isang nabigo, tinunton niya ang kanyang kwarto at inihagis ang sobre sa ibabaw ng altar.

Nakapaghapunan na sila ng gabing iyon at nagpapahingalay silang mag-asawa sa salas nang magsalita si Dardo.

"May hinanakit ka pa bala sa akin, 'Ling?"

Nagitla si Lorna. "Ba't ka nagsalita nang ganyan, Dardo?"

"Paano kasi, parang nawawala na ang kabuluhan ko sa balay nga ito. Sa mga problema natin hindi mo na hinihingi ang aking tulong. Para bang...parang...."

"Ginahanap mo ang dati nating pagsasama?" may pagtataka sa tinig ni Lorna.

Tumango si Dardo. "Napansin ko, magmula nang mapagbuhatan kita ng kamay, nagbago ka na sa akin. May sama ng loob ka pa hanggang ngayon."

"Nakalimutan ko na iyon, Dardo," sagot ni Lorna. "Ang ibig mong sabihin," may kakaibang kislap sa mga mata ni Lorna, "ginahanap mo ang litanya sang utang nga lagi kong inihaharap sa iyo? Ang aking bibig?"

"Doon lang ako nakaramdam nga mahalaga ako sa iyo...at sa ating mga anak, Lorna," may kapaitan sa tinig ni Dardo.

"Kung nalalaman mo lang, pinagsisisihan kong labis ang gin-asal ko noon, Dardo," sabi ni Lorna. "Ang kasamaang dulot niyon sa ating mga anak nga unti-unti nang namumulat sa katotohanan. Nagising lamang ako sa katotohanang indi dapat ganoon ang naging asal ko sa imo sang mapagbuhatan mo ako sang kamay. Indi pala malulutas ang problema sa paggamit ng bibig lamang. Nalimutan ko ang aking pinag-aralan, Dardo. At mula noon ipinangako ko na sa aking sarili na magbago. Mahal ka namin. At sa dagat sang buhay, indi kami maaaring makatawid kung wala ka." May luha sa mga mata ni Lorna.

Matapok ang Tambis

Elizabeth Batiduan

Sa tanan nga adlaw ang Sabado ang akon ginakaugtan. Kay man wala ako sing klase kag wala man sing klase si Manang. Kon sa bagay luyag ko man gani nga wala sing klase apang magpundo man lang ako sa balay nga ginaguwardyahan ni Manang, maayo pa nga magmantener na lang ako sa eskwelahan. Tama kasabad kay Manang. Kon yara ako sa ibabaw ginapapanaog niya ako, kon yara ako sa idalom ginapasaka niya ako. Indi ako makapalayo sa balay kag dayon singgitan. Anuano man ang sirbato sang City Hall kon alas dose man. Pati pagkaon ko iya nga ginabantayan. Indi ako makahambal kon nagamual ako kag indi mapalagtik ang akon kutsara kag pinggan. Bisan ang pagtig-ab ko iya pa nga ginamuno.

Katulad karon, Sabado nga adlaw. Una nga nakatapos sing pamahaw si Tatay. Sumonod nga tumindog si Nanay.

"Manghimos kamo diri, Didi," bilin ni Nanay, "manindahan lang ako."

Sa handom ko nga makahalin man dayon, ginus-ab ko na lang ang lima ka bilog nga pandesal kag padalundonan sang kape. Kumadlaw si Manang. Nagahapuhapo ako nga tumolok sa iya.

"Daw sa ginamadyik mo lang ba."

Wala ako magsabat. Tumindog ako agod maggwa.

"Hep, hep, diin ka makadto? Wala pa ako makatapos."

"Ay ti kon san-o ka imo makatapos amo man ang tungatonga ko sa imo?"

"Basta magpungko ka dira. Mabudlay na karon ang magsinggitan kon mangindulaan ka naman."

Wala na ako magsuay bisan batok pa sa akon buot. Kalaba sang mga kuko ni Manang, isa pa wala si nanay nga mangapin sa akon. Gani wala ako sing mahimo kundi bantayan sia sa iya de-numero nga pangaon. Kag daw ginasunlog gid niya ako kay tapat pa gani nga ginapahinay niya ang pagkaon. Daw sa ginapamangkot pa niya ang pandesal kon bala usangon niya ukon indi.

Sang ulihi nakatapos gid man sia. Ginsampaw niya ang mga pinggan kag tinungtong diri ang mga baso.

"Trapuhan mo ang lamisa kay manghugas ako. Pagkatapos manilhig ka didto sa idalom. Kon makatapos ka didto sumaka ka diri kag buligan mo ako sa paglampaso sang salog."

Wala gilayon ako makatingog sa daw ora pro nobis kasako nga mandar ni Manang. Aba sobra na ini. Gali kay grade to lang ako patam-an ya ba. Kinahanglan mapautwas ko ang akon rason.

"Siling ni mis indi kuno mag-obra ang magagmay nga mga kabataan kay indi na magdako."

Masulod tani sa kusina si Manang apang bumalik sia sang mabatian ang akon siniling.

"Gago! Pagmis mis mo karon. Isa ka dosena na ang kabataan sang maestra mo mis pa gihapon? Hoy, Ricarido! Indi ka magsagad pangatarungan ha? Ang obra nga ina ang masami ko iparte sa imo, karon mareklamo ka? Indi ako gaga agod ipaobra sa imo ang indi mo masarangan. Gamay pa kuno sia. Dugaydogay mataas ka pa sa akon, a."

"Kay putot ka man mo," himulongon ko kag dayon dakpon ang trapo. Yudipongkol nga pangabuhi. Kadamo ang magulang sa kalibutan kon ngaa amo gid ini ang akon natup-an nga daw sa masinggan ang baba. Maayo lang kon may kinahanglan sia sa akon kay si Ric ang tawag niya sa akon. Kon wala gani ginapalagsak lang niya ang Ricarido nga kalaw-ay pamatian p'ro.

Maayo gid sa akon si Manang kon magbisita sa balay ang nagapangaluyag sa iya. Si Manang indi tuman katahom kag indi man tuman kalaw-ay. Apang sa banta ko wala sia sing naluyagan sa mga nagapangaluyag sa iya. Kay man indi niya ako pagpahalinon sa iya tupad kag makita ko gid nga ginapadiwalan niya ang mga ini kon wala nagaluluk sa iya. Tanan sila may salawayon sa iya panulok. Pareho kay Tony. Panawag niya diri si brotsa. Kay man may bigote si Tony kag daw sa senador pa kuno kay pirme lang nagadekuwatro kon magpungko.

Sa mga nagapangaluyag kay Manang, si Maning ang akon nagustohan. Mabuot si Maning kag may dala sia pirme nga mga dulse kag sokolate kon magkadto sia sa balay. Ang diperensya lang kay piang sing diutay si Maning. Ambot kon naano. Naugot gid si Manang sa iya. Kon kaisa ginapanghaboy niya ang dala sini nga mga dulse. Kag kon wala na si Maning dayon niya sundon ang panglakat sini nga piniang. Kag kaangayan gid kay Manang kon magpapiangpiang.

Isa ka adlaw may nagsaylo sa tupad sang amon balay nga madugay na nga wala sing tao. Bag-o lang ako mag-abot halin sa eskuwelahan kag dayon ko panaog kag magtan-aw samtang ginapasaka nila ang ila mga gamit. Pinalapitan ko ang lalaki nga nagatindog kag nagapamahid sang iya balhas.

"Diri na kamo maestar?" pamangkot ko sa iya.

"Huo," sabat niya kag nagyuhom pa.

"Kami diri lang," tinudlo ko ang amon balay.

"Magkasilingan gali kita. Ano ang ngalan mo?"

"Si Ric ako," sabat ko.

"Si Jerry naman ako," sabat niya.

Nakabatyag ako dayon sing kahamuot kay Jerry. Mainabyanon gali sia kag ginatratar niya ako nga daw kasubong sang iya panuigon.

"Sanday Tatay kag Nanay mo ina?" tinudlo ko ang gulanggolang na nga lalaki kag babae nga nagatudlo sa duha ka tao sa pagpasaka sang ila mga gamit.

"Huo."

May ipamangkot pa tani ako apang may nanitsit sa balay. Nagbalikid ako. Nagbalikid man si Jerry. Nakita ko si Manang nga nagapamaypay sa bintana.

"Mapauli na ako, Jerry. Basi manyaga na kami," kag dayon ko dalagan pauli.

Sang magpauli ako pagkahapon halin sa eskuwelahan nakita ko si Jerry nga nagamakinilya sa may bintana. Pagkakita niya sa akon ginpasaka niya ako. Dayon ko man saka kag magtan-aw sang iya ginabuhat. Kadasig sa iya magmakinilya. Daw nagapiri lang ang iya mga tudlo.

"Ano ang ginamakinilya mo?"

"Sugilanon."

"Sugilanon sa ano?"

"Sugilanon para sa *Hiligaynon*."

"Manunolat ka gali?"

"Medyo," kag nagyuhom si Jerry. "May ipamangkot gali ako sa imo, Ric. Sin-o yadtong namaypay sa imo kaina sa bintana?"

"Si Manang yadto."

"Ano ang ngalan ni Manang mo?"

"Marieta. Ang iya hayu Didi."

"Suplada si Manang mo?"

"Kon kis-a suplada. Kon kis-a indi man."

Nagkadlaw si Jerry. "May nobyo na sia?"

"Wala," kag ginsugiran ko sia parte sang nagapangaluyag kay Manang. Sa pamatyag ko interesado gid sia sa ginapanugid ko kay gin-untatan gid niya ang pagmakinilya. "Ngaa mangaluyag ka man bala kay Manang?"

"Indi. Basi pati ako hikayan ni Manang mo."

"Indi niya ikaw paghikayan kay guwapo ikaw kag indi piang pareho kay Maning."

Wala magsabat si Jerry. Nagyuhom lang sia kag magpadayon sa pagmakinilya.

Isa ka Domingo, nagsimba kami ni Manang. Nasugata namon si Jerry sang nagapauli na kami.

"Hoy, Jerry," malayo pa nagsinggit na ako, "Diin ka makadto?"

"Dira lang," nagyuhom sia sa akon. "Mapauli ka na?"

"Huo. Nagsimba kami ni Manang."

"Ti dira ka lang anay. May kadtuan pa ako," kag dayon niya talikod.

"Sin-o ato?" pamangkot ni Manang samtang nagadulot ang iya mata kay Jerry.

"Si Jerry ato. Amo ato sila ang nagsaylo sa balay nanday Tya Rosa sa aton tupad. Amigo ko sia."

"Sugod karon indi na ako maluyag nga makig-abyan ka sa tao nga ina. Makita ko gani ikaw, orasan mo gid."

"Pero, Manang, kabuot kay Jerry."

"Kabuot! Wala sing urbanidad! Bastos! Ni magtulok sa akon wala gid. Ano ang pagdumdom niya sa akon, taotao sang humay?"

Wala na ako magbais kay Manang. May salimao siguro sia. Sang una ginaaway niya ang tao kay ginatulok sia kuno kag ginapanihulan. Ano sia kuno, idu? Karon kay wala sia pagsapaka ni Jerry naakig man.

Sugod sadto daw nagsuplada na gid si Manang. Kon kaisa naham-ot man ako sa iya ginabuhat. Kon maglabay gani si Jerry sa amon ugsaran dayon gid niya pangyam-id kag magsilin sang 'tse!' Kag kon magdungan sila sing pamintana dayon niya isira ang bintana kag dasunan ina dayon sang linagabong sa iya sulot. Apang patka sina kay pirme ko sia madakpan nga nagalingling kay Jerry sa diutay nga buho sa dingding.

Apang likom kay Manang pirme man ako gihapon nagakadto kay Jerry. Kag sia pirme ang topiko sang amon sugilanon. Ginsugiran ko si Jerry nga akig si Manang kay wala niya pagsapaka. Apang makadlaw lang ini kag magsiling nga matak-an gid sa ulihi si Manang.

Apang isa ka adlaw naabtan gid ako ni Manang nga naghambaro kay Jerry sa ila balkon. Nagmulodlo ang iya mga mata sang matanglaan niya ako.

"Magpanaog ka dira! Ricarido! Dali!" nagapaninghawak pa nga sugo ni Manang. "Nagsiling ako nga indi ka makig-upod sa mga tao nga kuwan."

Tapat. Nagapangita pa ako sing inugrason sang maghambal si Jerry.

"Mga tao nga ano, Miss?"

"Indi ikaw ang ginahambal ko. Wala ka sing labot," maisog nga sabat ni Manang.

"Apang may ginatumod ka. Ngaa indi mo pag-ihambal ang luyag mo silingon?" hambal ni Jerry.

"Luyag mo gid mahibalan? Puwes, mga tao nga bastos ang buot ko silingon. O, ano karon?"

"May bastos matuod diri. Apang indi ako ukon si Ric."

"Kag sin-o sa banta mo?"

"Sin-o bala haw?" nagyuhom pa si Jerry.

Nakahangop si Manang. Nadugangan ang iya kaakig.

"Bastos! Magpanaog ka dira!" ako naman ang iya inatubang. Daliii...!"

Nanaog ako apang dumalagan ako kay Nanay nga sadto nagaluto sang amon panyapon. Linagas ako ni Manang apang nagpalipod ako kay Nanay. "'Nay, 'Nay, ara si Manang hu, 'Nay!"

"Ano bala ina, Didi?" natak-an nga hambal ni Nanay.

Nagdulog si Manang. Naghulat ako nga isugid niya ako kay Nanay apang wala niya pagbuhata. Siguro indi maluyag nga mahibal-an ni Nanay nga nakig-away sia kay Jerry. Humalin sia nga nagapamulogso.

"Andaman mo lang karon nga bata ka," kumod ni Manang.

Pila ka adlaw ako nga nagapangalihid kay Manang. Apang isa ka adlaw tinawag ako ni Manang nga manaka kuno kami sing tambis kanday Tiya Cheding. Nalimtan siguro niya nga akig sia sa akon. Dayon ko man kuhaon sang alat kag mag-upod sa iya. Madamo ang puno sa laguwerta ni Tiyay Cheding. Tunga sa kilometro ang kalayuon halin sa amon.

Madamo na ang mga luto kag makaluloyag tulokon sa nagaagaw- agaw nga pula kag rosa nga duag. Nagpalumba kami ni Manang sing saka sa isa ka puno nga nagapulagang sang bunga. "Ric, magpanguyapot ka sing maayo," paandam ni Manang. "Katapok baya sining mga sanga sang tambis. Mahulog ka gani, ambot sa imo."

Igu lang sia makatapos sa paghambal sang magragamak ang sanga nga iya ginatungtongan.

"Manang, mahulog ka!" apang ulihi na. Humagpaas sa idalom kaupod sang sanga nga nabali.

"Aragoy..." uraroy ni Manang.

Dalidali ako nga nanaog. Binuligan ko sia nga makatindog apang humogsoy sia liwat.

"Indi ako makatindog," kuriit ni Manang. "Nabali siguro ang tiil ko. Kasakit gid."

"Ti ano na lang ang pagpauli mo? Indi ako makasarang maghakwat sa imo."

"Pauli to anay sa balay kag tawga si Nanay. Dali ka!"

"Huo," dayon ko man huyab. Nakibot si Jerry nga sadto nagamakinilya sa ila balkon sang nagahuganas ako nga umabot.

"Naano ka, Ric?" singgit niya sa akon.

"Si Manang nahulog sa tambis. Indi na makatindog," singgit ko man nga sabat kag dayon saka sa ibabaw. Tinawag ko kag pinangita sa bug-os nga balay si Nanay. Apang wala sia. Nanaog ako liwat agod pangitaon tani sa iban nga balay si Nanay kay siling ko basi nakighambaro lang sa amon kasilingan. Apang nakita ko ang likod ni Jerry nga nagadalagan pakadto sa katambisan, gani nagsunod na lang ako sa iya. Nagadalagan lang ako apang natingala ako sa mga hulag ni Jerry. Abi ko wala gid sia nagasapak kay Manang. Apang ngaa madasig pa sia sa tren sang mabatian nga nahulog sa tambis si Manang?

Una nga nakaabot si Jerry sa nahamtangan ni Manang. Apang nakapreno ako sa pagdalagan sang mabatian ko ang akig nga tingog ni Manang.

"Maano ka diri? Layas dira!"

Sadya ini karon. Dayon ko palipod sa madabong nga tanom. Mabudlay na nga makita ako ni Manang. Patod nga akig sia kay ginsugiran ko si Jerry.

"Ikaw pa ang buligan ikaw pa ang maakig," sabat ni Jerry.

"Indi ko kinahanglan ang bulig mo. Masarangan ko ang maglakat nga mag-isa."

Ginsid-ing ko sila. Nagatindog si Jerry sa atubangan ni Manang. Nakita ko nga nanghawid anay sa puno sang tambis si Manang kag magtindog. Nagtikang. Isa...duha...kag hinali natumba. Didto gid sia tumopa sa butkon ni Jerry. Kag halos nagmulodlo ang akon mga mata sang hinali halukan sia ni Jerry. Nagpalak si Manang. Apang sang ulihi nagpahimunong sia kag nakita ko nga naglikos ang iya butkon sa liog ni Jerry. Ginkisapkisap ko ang akon mga mata kay daw indi ako makapati sa akon nasaksihan. Sang sid-ingon ko sila liwat, ginakugos na ni Jerry si Manang. Kag indi na ini akig. Nagayuhom pa sia kay Jerry. Nagasunod lang ako sa ila apang nagakatol ang akon tingkoy. Gatod nga pangabuhi! Indi ko gid ubos maisip ang matabo nga daw kahinali lang kag indi ko mahangpan.

From: *Hiligaynon*, 1966

The Branch Is Still Brittle

(Matapok ang Tambis)

Elizabeth Batiduan

Of all the days in the week, it's Saturday I hate most. That's because I've got no classes, nor does *Manang*. Actually I like it when there are no classes but if I have to stay at home with *Manang* poking her nose at everything I do, I'd rather hang around at school. I really hate her! If I am upstairs, she asks me to come down; if downstairs, she asks me to go up. I take one step out of the house and she yells at me. No, not even the City Hall whistle at 12:00 noon can match up to her voice. She nitpicks even on the way I eat. I should not speak when my mouth is full, my spoon should not clink against the plate. Even my belching she grumbles about.

Like this Saturday. The first to finish eating breakfast was *Tatay*. Then *Nanay*.

"Clean up the house, Didi," *Nanay* told my sister. I'm just going to market."

In my rush to go, I stuffed my mouth full with five pieces of *pan de sal* one after the other, washing them down with coffee. *Manang* laughed. Gasping for breath, I looked at her.

"Whew, like magic!"

I didn't say a word. I got up and headed straight for the door.

"Hey, hey, hey! Where are you going? I'm not through with you yet."

"Why, should I hang on to to your skirt till I don't know when?"

"Just sit there, okay? I don't like having to yell when you're nowhere to be found."

I kept my mouth shut, but I gritted my teeth. *Manang* grew her nails long; besides, *Nanay* was nowhere around to back me up. So I could do nothing but watch her eat with measured bites. I think she was bent on teasing me because she slowed down her eating even more. Like she was asking the *pan de sal* if it would allow her to chew it or not.

She finished eating, finally. She piled the plates onto each other and placed the drinking glasses on top.

"Wipe the table; I've got to wash the dishes. Then sweep the ground under the house. When you're finished, come up again and help me mop the floor." My sister recited her commands like the *ora pro nobis.* What could I say? Really, she's too much. Just because I'm only in the second grade, she thinks she can push me around. I'll show her.

"Miss said children shouldn't be made to work or else they won't grow tall."

Manang was about to go into the kitchen but she turned around when she caught what I said.

"Miss, miss! Stupid! Don't you know your teacher already has twelve kids? Stupid! *Hoy*, Ricarido! Don't keep on arguing with me. I always ask you to do these. How come you're grumbling now? I'm not so stupid as to let you do things you can't do! Hmm...so he says he's still short. Watch. In a little while, you may shoot up and even get to be taller than I."

"'Cause you're really short, that's why," I mumbled to myself and grabbed the rag. *Yudipongol*! This life! There are so many elder sisters in the world; why did I get stuck with this one who keeps on yakking like a machine gun? It's nice when she needs something from me 'cause she calls me Ric. But when she doesn't, she throws around the name Ricarido just like that. I hate listening to her!

Manang is extra nice to me when someone visits her at home. She isn't pretty nor ugly. But I think there's no one she likes among her suitors. 'Cause she won't let me leave her side when they come; I even catch her sticking out her tongue at them when they're not looking. To her, each one has one defect or the other. Like Tony—she calls him *brotsa* or brush 'cause he's got a moustache and sits with crossed legs like some senator.

But among *Manang*'s suitors, it's Maning I like best. Maning is kind, he gives me candies and chocolates when he comes to the house. Trouble is, Maning limps a bit. I don't know why. And *Manang* simply can't stand him. Sometimes, she even throws these candies right in front of him. And soon as he leaves, she starts to ape his limping. And wow, is she awfully good at it!

One day, some people moved into the house just beside ours; this has long been vacant. I had just come home from school and right away I rushed downstairs to watch them bring up their stuff. I stepped up near the guy who was standing and wiping off his sweat.

"You're staying here now?" I asked him.

"Yes," he answered, and even smiled.

"That's where we live," I said, pointing to our house.

"So, we are neighbors. What's your name?"

"Ric," I replied.

"Jerry, here," he introduced himself.

I took to Jerry at once. He was very friendly; and he treated me like I was his age.

"Are they your *Tatay* and *Nanay*?" I pointed to the middle-aged man and woman who where directing two men bringing up their things into the house.

"Yes."

I would have asked him more questions but I heard someone hiss at me. I turned around. Jerry did, too. I saw *Manang* waving at me from one of our windows.

"I've got to go, Jerry. I think it's time for lunch." And at once, I ran home.

On my way home from school that afternoon I saw Jerry typing by the window. When he saw me, he invited me to come up. Right then, I went up and watched what he was doing. He typed very fast. It seemed his fingers were just flying.

"What are you typing?"

"A story."

"About what?"

"A story for the *Hiligaynon*."

"So you're a writer."

"Somewhat." And then he smiled. "Oh, by the way, let me ask you, Ric. Who was it waving at you this noon?"

"That was *Manang*."

"What's your *Manang*'s name?"

"Marieta. Her nickname is Didi."

"Is your *Manang* a snob?"

"Sometimes, yes; sometimes, not."

Jerry laughed. "Does she already have a boyfriend?"

"None." And then I told him about *Manang*'s suitors. I think he was really interested because he stopped typing. "Why? Are you thinking of courting her too?"

"No. She might also find fault with me."

"She won't find fault with you 'cause you're handsome and not limping like Maning."

Jerry didn't answer. He simply smiled.

One Sunday, *Manang* and I went to Mass. We met Jerry on our way home.

"*Hoy*, Jerry." He was still some distance but I hollered. "Where are you going?"

"Oh, just there," he smiled at me. "Are you going home now?"

"Yes. *Manang* and I have just been to Mass."

"Okay, I'll get going now. I've got to go somewhere else." And then he turned around at once.

"Who was that?" *Manang* asked, her sharp eyes following Jerry.

"That's Jerry. They're the ones who moved into *Tiya* Rosa's just beside our house. He's my friend."

"From now on, I don't want to see you with that guy again. If you do, better watch out."

"But *Manang*, Jerry is so nice."

"Nice? He's got no manners! How rude! He didn't even give me one glance! What does he think of me—some scarecrow in the field?"

I didn't argue with *Manang* any more. I guess she was in a bad mood. She would get mad whenever somebody stared or whistled at her. What was she? she asked. A dog? But now that Jerry ignored her, she was mad too.

From that time on, *Manang* became even more haughty. Sometimes I was kind of amused at the way she acted. Whenever Jerry would pass by our gate, she would immediately frown and let out a "*Tse!*" And when they happened to look out of the window at the same time, she'd close ours quickly, then bang at something in her room. But don't be fooled; I would often catch her peeping at Jerry through a hole in our wall.

Without her knowing though, I still went to see Jerry. And she was always the topic of our conversation. I told Jerry that *Manang* was mad that he didn't pay her any attention. Then he would just laugh and tell me that *Manang* would sooner or later get fed up acting the way she did.

But one day, *Manang* caught me chatting with Jerry in their verandah.

"Ricarido! Come down, quick!" *Manang* commanded me, her arms akimbo. "Didn't I tell you not to go with such people?"

That was it! I was still thinking of what reason to give her when Jerry butted in.

"People like what, Miss?"

"I'm not talking to you. Will you mind your own business?" came *Manang*'s fierce reply.

"But you're referring to someone. Why don't you say what you want to say?" Jerry continued.

"You really want to know who? Well, rude people! That's whom....So what?"

"Yes, there are rude people around here, but it's neither I nor Ric."

"And who do you think they are?"

"Well, who do you think?" Jerry smiled.

Manang understood now. And how she blew her top!

"Wh...Shame on you! Come down the stairs!" Now she had turned to me. "Quick."

I ran down but I went straight to my mother who was then cooking our dinner. *Manang* chased me but I hid behind *Nanay*'s back. " 'Nay, 'Nay, *Manang*'s after me."

"What's the matter, Didi?" *Nanay* sounded peeved. *Manang* backed off. I waited for her to tell on me, but she didn't. Maybe, she didn't want *Nanay* to know that she had quarreled with Jerry. Grumbling, she let go off me, but she mumbled, "Watch out, you kid!"

For days I was careful not to offend *Manang*. But one day, she called me, and said we were to pick *tambis* from *Tiyu* Cheding's orchard. She must have forgotten that she was mad at me. Anyway, I grabbed the fruit basket at once and went off with her.

There are so many *tambis* trees in *Tiya* Cheding's orchard. This was about half a kilometer from us.

A lot of fruits were ripe now and it was fun to see the reddish pink flowers of the *tambis* tree just about to turn red. *Manang* and I raced up one of these trees. "Ric, hold on tight," *Manang* warned me, "the branches of the *tambis* are brittle. If you fall, I don't know what we're going to do with you."

She had just said these words when the branch she was stepping on, snapped.

"*Manang*, watch out, you'll fall!" Too late. She tumbled onto the ground with the broken branch.

"Ooouch!" *Manang* groaned.

I hurried down quickly. I helped her get up but she fell on her back again.

"I can't...I can't stand up...." *Manang*'s face was screwed up. "I think my foot is broken. Ooooh, it really hurts...."

"How can you go home? I can't carry you."

"Go and call *Nanay*. Hurry!"

"Okay." And at once, I ran off. Jerry who was then typing in their balcony was surprised to see me running breathlessly.

"Ric! What's happened to you?" he shouted at me.

"*Manang*! She fell from the *tambis* tree! She can't stand up," I shouted back, as I ran up our stairs. I called out to *Nanay* and looked for her throughout the house. But she was nowhere to be found. I rushed down again to look for *Nanay* among our neighbors 'cause she might be just chatting with them. I caught Jerry's retreating back; he was already running towards the orchard, so I just followed him. As I ran, I wondered why Jerry was acting this way. I thought he was ignoring *Manang*. But why did he move faster than a train when he found out *Manang* had fallen from the *tambis*?

Jerry reached the spot where *Manang* had fallen before I did. But I stopped short when I heard *Manang*'s angry voice.

"What are you doing here? Go away!"

This was going to be fun. Quickly, I hid behind the thick bushes. *Manang* shouldn't see me. For sure she would be sore that I had told Jerry.

"Here I come rushing to help you, and what do I get?" Jerry replied.

"I don't need your help. I can walk by myself."

I peeped. I saw *Manang* grasp the *tambis* trunk; then, she stood up. She took a step. One...two...and then...She fell straight into Jerry's arms. And my eyes almost popped out when Jerry suddenly kissed her. *Manang* kicked and flayed. But later she calmed down and I saw her slip her arm round Jerry's neck. I kept blinking because I couldn't believe what I was seeing. When I peeped again, Jerry was already carrying *Manang* in his arms. And she was not mad anymore. She was even smiling at Jerry. I followed them, scratching my nape. What was happening? I hadn't expected this and I simply couldn't understand why.

Marupok ang Macopa

Elizabeth Batiduan

Sa lahat ng araw, pinakaayaw ko ang Sabado. Paano kasi, wala akong klase at wala ring klase si Manang. Kung sa bagay gusto ko sanang walang klase pero kung titigil lang naman ako sa bahay na ginuguwardiyahan ni Manang, mabuti pang magtiyaga na lang ako sa eskuwelahan. Talagang nakakasuya itong si Manang. Kung nasa bahay ako, pinabababa niya ako; kung nasa silong, pinapapanhik. Hindi pa nga ako makalayo sa bahay at nandiyan na, naninigaw. Ano na ba ang silbato ng City Hall kung ihahambing sa kanya. Pati pagkain ko binabantayan. Hindi ako dapat magsalita kung namumualan at hindi magpalagitik ng aking kutsara at pinggan. Pati ang pagdighay ko kanyang pinupuna.

Katulad ngayong Sabado. Unang nakatapos ng almusal si Tatay. Sumunod tumayo si Nanay.

"Magligpit kamo diri, Didi," bilin ni Nanay, "mamalengke lang ako."

Sa hangad kong makaalis rin agad, nilunok ko na lang ang limang pan de sal at sinundan ng pantulak na kape. Tumawa si Manang. Humihingal akong tumingin sa kanya.

"Parang minadyik mo lang, ba."

Hindi ako sumagot. Tumayo ako para lumabas.

"Hep, hep, saan ka pupunta? Indi pa ako tapos."

"E, kung hanggang kailan ka ba matatapos tutunga-tunganga lang ako sa iyo?"

"Basta umupo ka lang diyan. Mahirap ang magsigawan tayo mamaya kung mawawala ka na naman."

Hindi ako sumuway kahit laban pa sa aking loob. Mahahaba ang mga kuko ni Manang; isa pa, wala si Inay na kakampi sa akin.

Kaya wala akong nagawa kundi pagmasdan ang kanyang de-numerong pagkain. Parang nanunukso, lalo nga niyang pinabagalan ang kanyang pagkain. Para bang tinatanong pa niya ang pan de sal kung ngunguyain niya ito o hindi. Sa wakas, natapos rin siya. Pinagsapawsapaw ang mga pinggan at ipinatong ang mga baso sa taas nito.

"Punasan mo ang misa at magahugas pa ako. Pagkatapos, magwalis ka doon sa silong. Matapos doon, umakyat ka dito at tulungan mo akong maglampaso sa sahig."

Hindi agad ako nakakibo dahil sing bilis ng *ora pro nobis* ang utos ni Manang. Aba, sumusobra na siya. Porke ba greyd tu lang ako pinasosobrahan na lang niya ako. Kailangang mangatuwiran.

"Sabi ni 'Mis indi daw dapat magtrabaho ang mga batang maliliit at baka indi na sila tataas."

Papasok na sana sa kusina si Manang pero bumalik siya nang marinig ang aking sinabi.

"Gago! Mismisin kita diyan. Isang dosena na ang anak sang titser mo, mis pa rin? Huwag ka ngang laging mangangatuwiran, ha? Parati kong pinagagawa iyan sa iyo, at ngayon nagareklamo ka pa? Indi ako gaga nga magpapagawa sa iyo sang indi mo kaya. Maliit pa raw siya. Mayamaya mas mataas ka pa sa akin, a."

"Paano, pandak ka," bulong ko na sabay sunggab ng pamunas. Yoditupang buhay ito, oo. Ang daming ate sa buong daigdig, kung bakit itong parang masinggan ang bibig ang nabagsakan ko. Mabuti lang kung may kailangan siya sa akin at Ric ang tawag niya. Kung wala naman, e parang ipinalalagapak lang niya ang Ricarido na kay sagwang pakinggan.

Mabait talaga si Manang sa akin kung bumibisita sa bahay ang mga manliligaw niya. Si Manang hindi gaanong maganda pero hindi rin namang gaanong pangit. Pero sa tingin ko wala siyang nagugustuhan sa mga manliligaw niya. Paano, ayaw niya akong paalisin sa tabi niya at nakikita ko talagang pinandidilaan niya ang mga ito kung hindi nakatingin. Lahat sila ay may kapintasan sa kanyang paningin. Tulad ni Tony. Tawag niya dito *brotsa*. Kasi may bigote si Tony at parang senador pa raw dahil pirmeng nakadekwatro kung umupo.

Sa mga nanliligaw kay Manang, si Maning ang gusto ko. Mabait siya at pirmeng me dalang kendi at tsokolate kung pumunta sa bahay. Ang deperensya nga lang pilay nang kaunti si Maning. Ewan kung napaano. Kung minsan, pinagtatapon ni

Manang ang dala nitong kendi. At kung wala na si Maning, agad niyang ginagaya ang paglakad nitong pilay. Kuhang-kuha niya!

Isang araw, may lumipat sa gilid namin, sa bahay na matagal na ring walang tao. Bagong dating lang ako sa eskuwelahan. Agad akong nanaog at nanood habang iniaakyat nila ang kanilang mga gamit. Nilapitan ko ang isang lalaking nakatayo at nagpupunas ng kanyang pawis.

"Dito kayo titira?" tanong ko sa kanya.

"Huo," sagot niya na nakangiti pa.

"Kami, diyan lang," sabay turo sa aming bahay.

"Magkapitbahay pala tayo. Anong pangalan mo?"

"Ric," sabat ko.

"Si Jerry ako," sagot niya.

Nakagaangang loob ko agad si Jerry. Magiliw pala siya, at itinuturing niya ako na parang kasing-edad niya.

"Sila ba ang Tatay at Nanay mo?" tinuro ko ang may katamtamang-gulang na lalaki at babae. Nakaturo naman sila sa dalawang taong dala-dala ang kanilang mga gamit.

"Huo."

May tatanungin pa sana ako nang may sumitsit sa bahay. Lumingon ako. Lumingon rin si Jerry. Nakita kong kumakaway si Manang sa bintana.

"Uuwi na ako, Jerry. Baka mananaghalian na kami," at tumalilis akong pauwi.

Nang umuwi ako noong hapong iyon, nakita ko si Jerry na nagmamakinilya sa may bintana. Pagkakita niya sa akin, pinapanhik niya ako. Agad naman akong pumanhik at nanood sa kanyang ginagawa. Ang bilis niyang magmakinilya. Parang pinalilipad lang ang kanyang mga daliri.

"Ano ang minamakinilya mo?"

"Sugilanon."

"Sugilanon sa ano?"

"Sugilanon para sa *Hiligaynon*."

"Manunulat ka gali?"

"Medyo," at ngumiti si Jerry. "May tatanungin pala ako sa iyo, Ric. Sino iyong kumaway sa iyo kanina sa bintana?"

"Si Manang iyon."

"Ano ang pangalan ng Manang mo?"

"Marieta. Ang kanyang palayaw, Didi."

"Suplada ang Manang mo, ano?'

"Kung minsan, suplada. Kung minsan, indi naman."

Tumawa si Jerry. "May nobyo na siya?"

"Wala," at isinaysay ko sa kanya ang tungkol sa mga manliligaw ni Manang. Sa pakiramdam ko, talagang interesado siya sa mga sinusumbong ko sa kanya dahil tinigil niya ang pagmamakinilya. "Bakit, magaligaw ka man kay Manang?"

"Indi. Basi pintasan niya ako."

"Indi siya magapamintas sa iyo. Gwapo ka, e. At indi pilay, tulad ni Maning."

Hindi sumagot si Jerry. Ngumiti lang siya at nagpatuloy magmakinilya.

Isang Linggo, nagsimba kami ni Manang. Nasalubong namin si Jerry nang pauwi na kami.

"Hoy, Jerry," malayo pa, sumigaw na ako. "Saan ka pupunta?"

"Diyan lang," ngumiti siya sa akin. "Uuwi ka na?"

"Huo. Nagsimba kami ni Manang."

"E, diyan ka na muna. May pupuntahan pa ako," at agad siyang tumalikod.

"Sino iyon?" ang tanong ni Manang habang sinusundan ng matalim na tingin si Jerry.

"Si Jerry iyon. Sila ang lumipat sa bahay ni Aling Rosa, sa gilid natin. Kaibigan ko siya."

"Magsimula ngayon, ayoko nang makipagkaibigan ka sa taong iyan. Makita ko lang nga kasama mo siya, bantayan mo gid."

"Pero Manang. Ang bait ni Jerry."

"Mabait! Walang urbanidad. Bastos! Ni tumingin sa akin, indi man lang. Anong tingin niya sa akin, tao-tao sa palayan?"

Hindi na ako nakipagtalo kay Manang. Siguro may sumpong siya. Noon, inaaway niya ang tao dahil tumitingin sa kanya at naninihol. Ano raw siya, aso? Ngayon na hindi siya pinansin ni Jerry, nagagalit rin.

Mula noon, parang lalong nagsuplada si Manang. Kung minsan, natatawa rin ako sa kanyang mga kilos. Kung dumadaan si Jerry sa may hagdanan namin, agad siyang umiirap at nagsasabi ng "Tse!" At kung sabay silang dumungaw, agad niyang sinasara ang bintana at pinasusundan ito ng isang lagapak sa kanyang kwarto. Pero ano ka, pirme ko siyang nahuhuling sumisilip kay Jerry mula sa maliit na butas ng dinding.

Hindi alam ni Manang na pirme pa rin akong pumupunta kina Jerry. At siya parati ang paksa ng aming sugilanon. Sinumbong ko kay Jerry na galit si Manang dahil hindi niya ito pinansin. Pero tumatawa lang ito at nagsabing magsasawa rin si Manang.

Pero isang araw naabutan ako ni Manang na nakikipag-usap kay Jerry sa kanilang balkon. Nanlaki ang kanyang mga mata nang makita niya ako.

"Manaog ka diyan! Ricarido! Dalian mo!" nakapamaywang pa na inutos sa akin ni Manang. "Sinabi ko sa imo nga huwag kang sumama sa mga taong 'kwan."

Lagot! Nag-iisip pa ako ng maidadahilan nang magsalita si Jerry.

"Mga tao nga ano, Miss?"

"Indi ikaw ang kausap ko. Wala kang pakialam," ang marahas na sagot ni Manang.

"Ngunit may pinatatamaan ka, a. Ba't indi mo sabihin kung sino ang tinutukoy mo?" tanong ni Jerry.

"Gusto mo talagang malaman? Puwes ang mga taong bastos ang aking tinutukoy. O, ano ngayon?"

"May bastos nga rito pero indi ako o si Ric."

"At sin-o bala ang ginatukoy mo?"

"Sin-o nga ba?" ngumiti si Jerry.

Nakaintindi si Manang. At lalong nadagdagan ang kanyang galit. "Bastos! Pumanaog ka diyan!" ako naman ang kanyang binalingan. "Daliiii...!"

Pumanaog ako pero tumakbo ako kay Nanay na noon nagluluto ng hapunan. Hinabol ako ni Manang pero tumago ako sa likuran ni Nanay. " 'Nay, 'Nay, si Manang, o, 'Nay!"

"Ano ina, Didi?" may halong yamot ang pag-usisa ni Nanay.

Tumigil siya. Hinintay kong isumbong niya ako kay Nanay pero hindi niya ginawa ito. Siguro, hindi niya gustong malaman ni Nanay ang pag-aaway nila ni Jerry. Umalis siyang nagdadabog.

"Mag-ingat ka, bata ka," bulong ni Manang.

Ilang araw akong nag-iilag kay Manang. Pero isang araw, tinawag niya ako at aakyat daw kami sa macopa ni Aling Cheding. Nakalimutan na niya yatang galit siya sa akin. Agad naman akong kumuha ng basket at sumama sa kanya. Maraming punong macopa sa lagwerta ni Aling Cheding. Mga kalahating kilometro ang layo nito sa amin.

Marami na ang mga hinog na bunga at kaygandang tingnan ang pag-aagaw ng kulay na pula at rosas. Unahan kami nang akyat ni Manang sa isang punong namumula sa bunga.

"Ric, kumapit ka nang mabuti," pinaingat ako ni Manang. "Marurupok itong mga sanga ng macopa. Kung mahulog ka diyan, ambot na lang kung anung gagawin ko sa iyo."

Katatapos lang niyang magsalita nang lumagutok ang sanga ng kanyang kinatatayuan.

"Manang, mahulog ka!" Pero huli na. Lumagapak siya sa lupang kasama ang sangang nabali.

"Araay...!" daing ni Manang.

Dalidali akong nanaog. Tinulungan ko siyang makatayo ngunit nabuwal siya uli.

"Hindi ako makatayo," nakangiwi si Manang. "Nabalian siguro ako sa paa. Napakasakit."

"E, paano ka makauwi? Indi kita kayang buhatin."

"Umuwi ka muna sa bahay at tawagin si Nanay. Dalian mo!"

"Huo." At tumalilis ako ng takbo.

Nagulat si Jerry na noon nagmamakinilya sa kanilang balkon nang humahagibis akong dumating.

"Anong nangyari sa iyo, Ric?" sigaw niya sa akin.

"Si Manang, nahulog sa macopa. Indi na makatayo!" pasigaw ko ring sagot na sabay akyat sa bahay. Tinawag ko si Nanay at hinanap sa buong bahay, pero wala siya. Pumanaog ako uli para hanapin sana siya sa aming mga kapitbahay. Kako baka nakikipag-tsismisan siya. Ngunit nakita ko ang likod ni Jerry na tumatakbong patungo sa lagwerta ng macopa. Tumakbo rin ako pero nagtaka ako sa mga kilos ni Jerry. Akala ko ba hindi niya pinapansin si Manang. Pero ba't mas mabilis pa siya sa tren nang marinig niyang nahulog sa macopa si Manang?

Unang nakarating si Jerry sa kinahantungan ni Manang. Pero nagpreno ako ng pagtakbo nang marinig kong galit ang boses ni Manang.

"Anong ginagawa mo rito? Alis diyan!"

Masaya ito. Agad akong tumago sa mayabong na tanim. Mahirap na kung makita ako ni Manang. Siguradong magagalit siya at binalitaan ko si Jerry.

"Ikaw pa ang tutulungan, ikaw pa ang galit," sagot ni Jerry.

"Hindi ko kailangan ang tulong mo. Kaya kong lumakad nang mag-isa."

Sinilip ko sila. Nakatayo si Jerry sa harap ni Manang. Nakita ko na kumapit muna si Manang sa puno ng macopa at tumayo. Humakbang. Isa...dalawa...at biglang bumagsak uli. Doon talaga siya tumama sa braso ni Jerry. At nandilat ang aking mga mata nang bigla siyang hinalikan ni Jerry. Humulagpos si Manang. Pero matapos ang ilang sandali huminahon siya at nakita ko na lang na nakapalibot ang kanyang braso sa liig ni Jerry. Kumurapkurap ang aking mga mata dahil hindi ako makapaniwala sa aking nakita. Nang silipin ko sila uli, pinapangko na ni Jerry si Manang at hindi na ito galit. Nakangiti pa nga siya kay Jerry. Sumunod ako sa kanila, pero talagang kumati ang aking buntot-maya.

Buwisit na buhay ito, oo! Naguluhan talaga ako sa nangyari. Nakakabigla at hindi ko pa rin maintindihan.

Ang Pagbalik

Julius Flores

Gab-i na sang magwa ang lalaki sa sinehan. Makadali nga pumondo sia sa masanag nga lobby. Ginaling-an sia, nagapamulpog ang mabug-at nga sakit sa pagtimbang niya nga agtang.

Sa pamuno nagatamod sia sa sanag gikan sa mga salakyan sa kalsada. Sang ulihi sinaylo niya ang iya panulok sa manipulon nga taknaan sa ibabaw sang takilya, kag pagkatapos sa relo sa iya butkon, 8:33.

Kag hinali niya nga nadiparahan nga nadugayan sia gali sing mga lima ka oras sa sulod sang sinehan. Natulogan. Indi niya mapunggan ang katuloyhon. Karon gab-i na. Nabatyagan niya ang pagdapya sang diutay nga hangin gikan sa pantalan sa unhan.

Matinong kag halos wala sing unod ang sinehan. Kag dugangan nga mabugnaw ini, makadali sia nga natulogan. Wala sia matulogi sing duha ka gab-i nga nagligad sa bapor bangod sa galong sang makina kag subong man sa basa nga teheras. Bangod sa kagutok sang bapor, nakatupa sia sa pasilyo ayon sa andamyo nga indi kuntani bagay hamtangan sang isa ka nagabayad nga pasahero. Apang wala sia sing mahimo. Sang gab-i luas sa mabaskog kag mabugnaw nga hangin nga nagalapdos sa iya nawong, nagadapya man ang balod, nagasampok sa kilid sang bapor kag nagaalyak sa gutok nga pasilyo.

Apang sa pagkamatuod, indi lang kay ini ang tunay nga mga kabandanan. May iban pa. Nagaut-ot ini sa iya painuino, sa iya pagkatao. Nahatagan gid lang sia sing diutay kag makadali nga katawhayan sa sulod sang sinehan, bangod siguro sa kalaka sang mga tao diri kag subong man kay sa liwan na ini nga lugar.

Pagkatapos sang duha ka adlaw kag duha ka gab-i nga pagbiyahe, nakaabot sia sa sini nga siyudad nga liwan ang mga talan-awon, liwan ang mga kalye, liwan ang pulong nga iya nabatian.

Nakabugtaw sia makis-a sa iya katulogon bangod sa kakibot. Nakasiyagit ang pila ka mga kolehiyala sa iya likod. Sa telon, nakit-an niya nga ginalikupan sang nakasuot sing itom kag nakakalo sing itom nga mga tinuga ang bida nga babae. Ginpakita sing makadali ang ginakugmat nga nawong sang babae, dason ang nagadalagan sini nga mga bati-is, dason ang mga *black-hooded* nga tinuga, dason ang dugo sa palad sang bida bangod sa pagkaligpit sa mga balagon. Nagapalapit nga nagapalapit sa iya ang mga maligno tubtob sang ulihi.

Piniyong niya ang iya mga mata. Kag sa telon sang kaugalingon niya nga kaisipan nagpakita ang dagway sang isa ka babae. Nagahaplay ini sa salog kag nagatakilid apang sa apipingig athagon ang pag-agay sang preska nga dugo. Sa kamot ara pa ang isa ka rebolber, isa ka Colt, bag-o pa kag nagabadlak sa kasarangan nga silak sang isa ka bombilya.

Karon nagatindog na sia sa kilid sang kalsada, nagahulat sa pagbaylo sang trapiko agod makatabok. Nagatangla sia sa otel sa pihak sang kalsada. Madulom sa nakandaduhan niya nga hulot.

Gikan sa iya likod, hinali lang nga dumapya ang mahumot kag mahagpok nga alisbong sang mainit pa nga pinirito nga mani. Kag daw sa hinali man sia nga nakabatyag sing gutom. Nabatyagan niya ang pagdaguok sang mabugnaw niya nga kasudlan. Nadumdoman niya nga wala gali sia makapanyaga. Sang pagbaylo sang trapiko, sumonod sia sa mga nagatalabok kag tinultol ang isa ka makitid nga restawran.

Daw isa lang ini ka giha sa kilid sang isa ka daku kag daan nga balay nga semento. Kahapon sing hapon nanerbesa sia diri. Malaka ang mga tao sa sulod sang restawran, kalabanan mga lalaki—gani kabangdanan kon ngaa gilayon niya nga naluyagan ini sa nahauna nga iya pagkakita.

Sang iya pagsulod nagtokar ang *jukebox* sa tupad sang ganhaan. *Massachusetts.* Nalumos ang iban nga kagalong sa galong sang musika. Pinili ang isa ka lamisa nga nagasandig sa dingding, ayon sa likod kag malapit sa kusina. Pumongko sia nga nagatalikod sa ganhaan. Umorder sang isa ka dagaya nga panyapon, may lukon kag *ice-cold* nga serbesa. Sang pagbalikid niya sa despatsadora agod mapamangkot ang bill sang kinaon, pagkatapos, hinali nga nasiplatan sang iya mga mata ang babae, isa ka nakabayo sing puraw itom nga· babae, nagapalipod sa ganhaan kag hagyu nga nalipdan sang *jukebox*, nagatamod sa iya. Gilayon ini nga tumalikod kag ang iya bayhon—ang bida sa sine? Apang imposible. Indi mahimo. Hinali nga nagkubakoba ang iya dughan.

Tumindog sia sa tuyo kuntani nga sundon ang babae. Nakit-an niya ini nga nagatabok sa kalsada, padulong sa sinehan. Nahagil-ot sa mga tao kag sang ulihi nangindulaan.

Pagkaligad sang pila ka minutos, nagapasaka na sia sa madulom nga hagdanan sang otel. Ang otel nagaukopar sang ikaduha kag ikatlo nga panalgan kag nagatamwa sa sinehan sa idalom. Baratuhon. Sang nagligad nga sunog nga nag-upos sang merkado publiko nasakam pati ang ikatlo nga panalgan sini. Gani karon ang ikaduha nga panalgan na lang ang ginaserbisyuhan. Daw subong lang sang atop ang ikatlo nga panalgan.

Sang iya pag-abot diri nagabitbit sia sang isa ka mamag-an nga maleta. Isa ka makatilingala nga panulok ang ginsugata sa iya sang *desk clerk* samtang ginasulat niya ang iya ngalan sa libro nga tinunghol sini. May isa ka sahi ang panulok sang clerk nga naghambal sa iya nga indi pagsaligan ini. Pagkadaho sang yabi gilayon niya nga tinultol ang kaugalingon nga hulot. Kinandaduhan sang makasulod na kag sang matungtong na niya ang maleta sa ibabaw sang isa ka lamisa, inuba niya ang sapatos kag pabugtoy nga humay-ad sa kama.

Sang hapon tumawag sia sa telepono kay Alfred. Daku ang katingala ni Alfred, apang luas sa pagkatingala napamatyagan niya ang pagpangduhadoha sa tingog sang abyan. Daw subong sang nagbalhin si Alfred. "Mahapit lang ako dira," ang iya pasaan bag-o iuli ang awditibo.

Nagakatulog pa si Alfred sang iya pag-abot kahapon. Humolat sia anay sa salas, nagbasabasa sang mga magasin, samtang ginpukaw pa sang isa ka suloguon si Alfred. Matiuntion gumwa ini nga ginahimashimas ang gumon nga buhok kag nagapalamula pa ang mga mata.

"Wala gid magpahibalo nga maabot ka gali. Kuntani nasugat ko ikaw sa pantalan," ang hambal ni Alfred. Madalom ang panulok sa iya ni Alfred, nagapanurisok, nagapangutana, nagapangduhadoha. Nahibal-an niya nga nabasahan na ni Alfred ang natabo sa pamantala-an. Si Alfred gid lang ang solo nga nakahibalo sang kaangtanan nila ni Nina.

"Nagapati ka...?" ang pasikto niya sang ulihi sa isa ka manubo nga tingog. Nagpabilin nga mahipos si Alfred. "Alfred...."

"Ikaw ang naghimo...?"

Ginlungolungo niya ang iya ulo.

"Kag si sin-o?"

"Sia...patihon mo ako. Sia ang nag-utas sang kaugalingon niya nga kabuhi."

"Ang rebolber."

"Ambot...ambot...."

Tumindog sia. Nagapalanglingin ang iya bagol. Nagapamulpog ang dugo sa iya apipingig. Sa iya atubangan hipos nga nagatamod si Alfred. Ginahatukhatok sia sang panulok sini.

Kag pumaibabaw ang tingog ni Alfred: "Nagabinutig ka!"

Lumigad sia sa duha ka hulot nga may mga suga na. Luas sa ordinaryo nga ganhaan, may habyughabyog ini nga ganhaan katulad sa mga opisina. Nabatian niya ang diutay nga tingog sang mga kabataan gikan sa isa ka hulot. Sa pasilyo nasugata niya ang isa ka magasawa: nagasandig sila sa balkonahe kag nagatan-aw sang nagkalainlain nga mga sugang-kilas. Ginatudlo sang lalaki ang iban nga mga bahin sang siyudad.

Sang ulihi naabot niya ang kaugalingon nga hulot. Pumondo sia sa atubangan sang ganhaan. Ginhisapo sang isa niya ka kamot ang yabi sa bulsa sang iya pantalon. Wala madugayi mahinay na niya nga ginatiklod ang ganhaan. Sang makasulod, liwat niya nga ginkandaduhan ini. Sa tunga sang dulom, inuba niya ang iya kamisadentro apang hinali lang sia nga nakadulog. Subong sang nagadapya ang init sang pagginhawa sang isa ka tinuga sa iya dulonggan, subong sang nabatyagan niya ang maid-id sini nga pagtamod sa iya. Amat-amat sia nga umisol sa dingding. Nagpanglaghap ang isa niya ka kamot sang *switch* samtang ang isa naman nagahanda sa pagpangapin sa kaugalingon. Apang wala sia sing may nahikapan nga *switch*; wala na ini sa kilid sang ganhaan.

Kag sa isa ka pamusod hinali nga sumiga ang *table lamp*.

Dungan sa pagsiga sang suga tumohaw ang mahinay nga kaladlawon sang babae. Nagahigda ini sa kama sa tupad sang dingding, apang subong amat-amat na ini nga nagbangon kag nagsandig sa isa ka ulonan. Manipulon ang korte sang malus-aw nga iwag gani diutay lang nga bahin sang hulot ang ginasanagan. Sa dulom ang nawong sang babae kag indi athagon ang bug-os nga dagway.

"Nakibot ka?" hambal sang babae.

Bag-uhanon ang tingog sa iya palamatin-an. Mahinay. Tuman kahinay. Masiling nga ginadapya sang hangin gikan sa kon diin. Apang wala sapayan sa iya kahinayon, may tuno ini sang pagpangganyat, gani ang nahauna nga nagsulod sa iya kaisipan nga isa ini ka babae nga may lawasnon nga kinahanglan. Apang nagpabilin pa sa gihapon sa iya balatyagon ang pagpangduhadoha kag kahanawa; nagapangduhadoha sia sa maarumiraw nga silak sang suga kag—paano nakasulod ang babae sa iya hulot samtang nakandaduhan naman ini?

"Gaano ka di?" ang sambit niya sang ulihi.

Kumadlaw sing mahinay ang babae. "Nagahulat," ang malip-ot nga sabat, "sa imo."

"Nagsala ka. Kapoy ako. Magbalik ka lang diri sa iban nga adlaw."

Naghipos ang babae.

"Magwa ka na. Ginakapoy ako."

"Ikaw ang ginahulat ko."

"Nasiling ko na nga kapoy ako. Gwa! Gwa! Basi gusto mo pa nga tawgan ko ikaw sing polis?"

Humipos ang babae. Humolag. "Ang bayu ko," hambal sini.

"Sa diin? Kag magwa ka na dayon."

"Sa tupad sang lamisa."

Nahulog ang iya mga mata sa pulongkoan nga ginatumod sang babae. Kag hinali sia nga nakaisol. Nagasablay sa iya ang puraw itom nga mga panapton. Ang babae sa restawran...ang bida sa sinehan...ang bangkay....Kumorog ang iya kalawasan. Daw linansang sia sa iya tinindugan. Amat-amat sia nga ginapamahulay. Gintinguhaan niya nga sipaton ang nawong sang babae apang daw hungod niya ini nga ginatago sa dulom.

"Ang bayo ko," ang sulit sang babae.

Kag nakatikab gid man sia sang ulihi. "Sin-o ka!"

"Si Nina," ang malip-ot nga sabat. "Nina."

"Nagabinutig ka. Indi ikaw si Nina. Nakilal-an ko ikaw."

Subong sang nakibot nga nagkadlaw liwat ang babae.

"Ambot," ang sabat sang babae. "Ambot kon nakilal-an mo ako. Basta ini pa lang ang kahigayunan nga nag-atubangay kita. Isugid ko na gid lang, nakit-an ko ikaw kaina sa restawran kag kahapon, sa *lobby* sang sinehan. Ambot kon nakit-an mo man ako basta nakit-an ko ikaw."

Humolag ang babae sa tuyo kuntani nga ipakita sa sanag ang kaugalingon apang pinunggan niya. "Indi! Indi ka dira maghalin!"

"Kag ngaa?" ang makahulogan nga pamangkot sang babae. Sang wala man lang sia magsabat: "Okey. Indi ako diri maghalin kon gusto mo. May kilala ako sang una. Halos pareho kamo sang itsura, kadakuon, kagulangon, kaambungon. Daw kapid gid kamo. Amigo ko sia, steady na kami ugaling...napatay. Aksidente sa salakyan. Sia ang ginalutohan ko subong."

"Indi!"

Pumadayon ang babae subong sang wala makabati sang iya hinambal. "*Really*, sia daw ikaw gid. Sang nahauna niya nga pagdala sa akon sa iya apartment, sia ang gin-abot sang kordam. Nagakurog, nagatindog katulad mo, sagad lang tamod sa akon; indi makahulag, indi makahambal, ambot kon ano ang nakit-an niya sa akon nawong."

"Ano ang makit-an ninyo nga mga lalaki sa akon nawong? A, indi ka gali makakita sang akon nawong. Ipalapit ang suga. *C'mon*."

"Ipalapit ang suga sa akon nawong."

"Mag-untat ka!"

"*C'mon*! Ipalapit... ipalapit...."

Kag sa isa ka pisok binuklas niya ang solo nga suga sa sulod sang hulot. Ginwaswas ini sa babae kag sa tunga sang paghinurongkadol sang mga pagkabutang pumaibabaw ang isa ka tiyabaw.

Sang mabuksan ang hulot, natampad sa panulok sang mga nagtugpa—ang *desk clerk*, mag-asawa kag tatlo ka boy sang otel—ang dagway sang lalaki nga nagasukamod sa dingding. Nagatalikod ini gikan sa kon ano nga dimakit-an nga kaaway, nagahapuhapo, ginapamahulay. Sa salog naglinapta ang buong nga bombilya. Kag, sa siya, nakit-an nila ang nagisi nga tipik sang bayu nga itom.

From *Hiligaynon,* October 23, 1968

The Apparition
(Ang Pagbalik)

Julius Flores

It was already dark when the man left the moviehouse. He stopped for a while in the well-lit lobby. He was trembling, both temples pounding.

At first, he watched the headlights from the vehicles in the street. Later, he shifted his gaze to the round wall clock above the ticket counter, and then to his wristwatch. It was 8:33.

He realized he had stayed too long inside the moviehouse—five hours. He had drifted to sleep, just couldn't fight it. Now it was late. He felt the breeze blowing gently from the harbor up ahead.

It was quiet in the moviehouse; there was hardly anyone there. It was also cool, so it was easy to fall asleep. For the past two nights, he could not sleep because the engine kept on droning and his cot had gotten wet. The ship was crowded so he had to settle for a space in the passageway by the gangplank where no paying passengers should have been. But he had no choice. At night, aside from the cold wind that bit into his face, the waves lashed out at the ship's hull, splashing water onto the crowded passageway.

But these were not the only reasons why he could not sleep; there were others. And these gnawed into his thoughts, into his whole being. He was given a brief respite inside the moviehouse, perhaps because the moviegoers were few, and the place was new. After two days and two nights of traveling, he had reached this city where the scenery, the streets and the language were different.

He was roused from his sleep. A number of college girls had let out a scream. Some men clothed in black and wearing black hats were closing in on the leading character. Scenes were flashing one after the other: the woman's terror-stricken face, her legs as she scampered to escape, the black-hooded intruders, and her hands bloody from the pressure of the rope that had bound them. The evil men advanced towards her, closer and closer, until....

He closed his eyes. And in the screen of his own mind flashed the image of a woman. She was on the floor, lying on her side, fresh blood oozing from her jaw. Still in her hand was a revolver, a new Colt which glistened in the light of the bedroom lamp.

He was standing now by the sidewalk waiting for the traffic lights to turn green so he could cross. He looked up at the hotel on the other side of the street. It was dark in the room he had locked up.

From behind him floated suddenly the pungent smell of newly fried peanuts. And just as suddenly, he felt hungry. He heard the growling of his empty stomach. He realized he had not taken his lunch yet. When the light changed, he followed the flow of pedestrians and headed for a small restaurant.

This stood on what looked like an alley beside a large cement house. Yesterday afternoon, he had drunk beer here. Customers had been few, mostly men, and so he had liked the place the moment he had seen it.

The jukebox by the door was blaring *Massachusetts*, when he got in. All noise was drowned out by the din of the music. He chose a table beside the wall farthest from the door and close to the kitchen. With his back turned to the door, he sat and ordered a heavy meal, which included prawns and beer. As he turned to the waitress to ask for his bill, he caught sight of a woman dressed completely in black, leaning against the door and partly screened by the jukebox. She was watching him from the distance. She turned her back quickly. The star in the movie? That was impossible. That couldn't be. But his heart was suddenly beating wildly.

He stood up, thinking of following her. He saw her cross the street towards the moviehouse, mingling with the crowd, then disappearing.

In a few minutes, he was on his way up the dark staircase of the hotel. These occupied the second and third floors of the building overlooking the moviehouse. A cheap hotel. In a recent fire that had gutted the public market, even the third floor of the hotel had been razed. So today, only the second floor was in use; the third floor served as a roof.

When he reached this place yesterday, he was carrying a light suitcase. The desk clerk gave him a perplexed look as he wrote his name in the registry handed to him. The look told him he couldn't trust the clerk. When he got the key, he headed for his room immediately. He fastened the door as soon as he got in and after dropping his suitcase on the table, took his shoes off. Then he lay down on the bed.

That afternoon, he called up Alfred. Alfred sounded surprised, but other than this he sensed some hesitation in the tone of his friend. Had Alfred changed? "I'll drop by," he had told his friend before replacing the receiver.

Alfred was still taking a nap. He had to wait in the sala where he skimmed through a few magazines, while a maid woke Alfred up. In a little while, his friend came out from his room, ruffling his unkempt hair, his eyes still flushed from sleep.

"Why didn't you let me know you were coming? I would have picked you up in the pier," Alfred told him. But Alfred was looking at him deeply, probing, wondering, doubting. Now he was sure that Alfred had already read about what had happened in the papers. Only Alfred knew of his affair with Nina.

"So you think it's true...?" he asked his friend softly. Alfred remained silent. "Alfred...."

"You did it...?"

He shook his head.

"And who else?"

"It was she...believe me. She took her own life."

"The gun."

"I don't...I don't know."

He stood up. He felt dizzy. Blood throbbed in his nape.

Then Alfred raised his voice: "You're lying!"

He passed by two rooms whose lights were already turned on. Aside from the usual door, each room had a swinging door, like those found in offices. He heard the tiny voices of children in one of the rooms. He met a couple in the corridor: they were standing by the balcony looking at the many neon lights. The man was showing her the different parts of the city.

Finally he reached his own room. He stopped by its door. He felt for his key in his pants. In a short time, he was slowly pushing the door open. When he got in, he locked the door again. In the darkness, he took off his shirt, but something gave him a start. He felt the warm breath of some creature on his ears, sensed it watching him closely. Slowly, he turned towards the wall. With one hand, he groped for the switch while with the other, he made ready to protect himself. But he couldn't find it; it was not by the side of the door any more.

And then suddenly, from one corner, a table lamp turned on.

Along with this, came the soft laughter of a woman. She lay on the bed beside the wall, but now she got up slowly and leaned against the pillow. The bulb was round and so its light was faint and only a small part of the room could be lighted. Since the woman's face was turned towards the dark only a part of her whole figure could be seen.

"Did I startle you?" the woman asked.

The voice was new to him. Soft. Very soft. It seemed wafted from somewhere by the wind. But other than this softness, the voice had a seductive tone, and so, the first thing that crossed his mind was that the woman was a prostitute. But something both worried and puzzled him; in the faint light he wondered—how did this woman get into his room when it was locked?

"What are you doing here?" he said at last.

The woman laughed. And she replied: "Waiting, waiting for you."

"You've made a mistake. I'm tired. Just come back some other day."

The woman kept silent.

"Go away. I am tired."

"I've been waiting for you."

"I've told you I am tired. Get out! Get out of here! Or, shall I call the police?"

Again she did not reply. But now, she was starting to move. "My dress," she said.

"Where is it? So you can get out."

"On the chair, beside the table."

His eyes fell on the chair the woman pointed at. He stepped back abruptly. A pure black dress hung on the chair. The woman in the restaurant...the actress in the moviehouse...the corpse.... His whole body was trembling. He seemed nailed to the spot on which he stood. Slowly, his body broke into a cold sweat. He tried to get a glimpse of the woman's face but she seemed to be hiding it in the dark on purpose.

"My dress," the woman asked again.

And at last, he managed to open his mouth: "Who are you?"

"Nina," was the brief reply. "Nina."

"You are lying! You're not Nina. I know you."

As if startled, the woman laughed once again.

"I don't—I don't know if you know me. This is the first time we've come face to face. But let me tell you—I saw you this noon at the restaurant and yesterday at the lobby of the moviehouse. I'm not sure if you noticed me, but I saw you."

The woman moved, apparently to show herself fully in the light. "No! No! Don't move!"

"And why not?" the woman asked somewhat knowingly. "Okay. I shall not budge from here, if you wish. I knew someone before. He looked just like you, the same face, built, age, attractiveness. He was my friend, we were going steady...but he died. A car accident. It's he I'm mourning for now."

"No!"

The woman went on like she didn't hear what he had said: "Really he was just like you. The first time he brought me to his apartment, it was he who got nervous. He was trembling, frozen, like you now: he couldn't move, he couldn't utter a word. I don't know what he'd seen in my face."

"What do you guys see in my face? Oh, but you can't see my face. Bring in the lamp. Bring it close to my face."

"Stop it!"

"C'mon! Bring it to me. Come nearer!"

In a second, he seized the lone lamp in the room. He beat the woman with it and in the midst of the confusion a loud scream was heard.

The room was forced open. Before the eyes of those who gathered there—the desk clerk, the couple and the three hotel boys—was the figure of a man sprawled against the wall. It seemed to be turning away from some invisible enemy; it was panting, sweating. On the floor were scattered the broken pieces of the bulb. And on the chair—a piece torn from the black dress.

Ang Pagbabalik

Julius Flores

Gabi na nang lumabas ang lalaki sa sinehan. Saglit siyang huminto sa maliwanag na *lobby*. Nahihilo siya. Parang pinupukpok sa matinding sakit ang magkabilang bahagi ng kanyang noo.

Nang umpisa, nakamasid siya sa sinag ng mga sasakyan sa kalsada. Matapos ang ilang sandali, inilipat niya ang kanyang paningin sa bilog na orasan sa ibabaw ng takilya, at pagkatapos, sa relos na nasa kanyang pulsuhan—8:33.

Bigla niyang napansin na natagalan pala siya nang limang oras sa loob ng sinehan. Nakatulog. Hindi niya napigil ang kanyang pagkaantok. Ngayon, gabi na. Naramdaman niya ang dapya ng kaunting hangin mula sa pantalan sa may unahan.

Tahimik at halos walang tao sa sinehan. Malamig din, kaya't madali siyang nakatulog. Nang dalawang gabing nakalipas, hindi siya nakatulog dahil sa ugong ng makina ng bapor at dahil din sa basa niyang teheras. Masikip sa bapor, kaya't nalagay siya sa pasilyong nasa may andamyo na di dapat sanang paglagyan ng mga pasaherong bumabayad. Subalit wala siyang magawa. Noong gabi, bukod sa malakas at maginaw na hangin na nanampal sa kanyang mukha, nangadapya rin ang alon, sumasalpok sa gilid ng bapor at sumasaboy ng tubig sa masikip na pasilyo.

Pero sa totoo, hindi lang ito ang naging dahilan ng di niya pagkaidlip. May iba pa. Ngumangatngat ito sa kanyang pag-iisip, sa kanyang pagkatao. Nakaramdam siya nang kaunti at madaliang katahimikan sa loob ng sinehan. Marahil, dala ng kakaunting tao at naiibang lugar. Matapos ang dalawang araw at dalawang gabing pagbibiyahe, narating niya ang siyudad na ito na kakaiba ang tanawin, ang mga kalye at ang wika.

Gumulantang sa kanya ang mga tili ng mga kolehiyala sa may likuran niya. Sa telon, nakita niyang pinagsasalikupan ng mga taong nakasuot-itim at nakasombrerong itim ang bidang babae. Manandaling ipinakita ang nasisindak na mukha ng babae, sunod ang kanyang tumatalilis na mga paa, sunod ang mga *black-hooded* na tao, at ang kanyang mga palad na nagdurugo sa pagkagapos. Papalapit nang papalapit ang masasamang tao hanggang sa....

Ipinikit niya ang kanyang mga mata. At sa telon ng sarili niyang handurawan, nagpakita ang anyo ng isang babae. Nakahiga itong patakilid at sariwang dugo ang dumadaloy sa kanyang baba. Sa kaniyang kāmay, nariyan pa ang isang baril, isang Colt—bago, at kumikislap sa ilaw ng isang bombilya.

Ngayon, nakatayo na siya sa gilid ng kalsada, naghihintay sa pagpalit ng trapiko para makatawid. Tumingala siya sa otel sa tapat. Madilim sa kanyang nakakandadong silid. Sa may likuran niya bigla lamang dumapyo ang mabango at sariwang samyo ng pinipritong mani. At dagli rin siyang nakaramdam ng pagkagutom. Naramdaman niya ang pag-aangil ng kanyang sikmurang walang-laman. Naalala niyang hindi pa pala siya nakapananghalian. Pagpalit ng trapiko, sumunod na siya sa mga nangagsitawid at tinunton ang isang makitid na restawran. Nasa maliit na puwang ito sa gilid ng isang malaking bahay na semento. Kahapon ng hapon, nagbeer siya rito. Kaunti ang tao sa restawran, karamihan ay mga lalaki—dahilan kung bakit nagustuhan niya ito sa unang tingin pa lang.

Pagpasok niya tumutugtug ang *jukebox* sa tabi ng pintuan. *Massachusetts*. Nalunod ang ibang ugong sa lakas ng musika. Pinili niya ang isang mesang nakasandal sa dingding sa may bandang likuran na malapit sa kusina. Umupo siyang nakatalikod sa pintuan. Umorder ng isang saganang hapunan, may sugpo pa at *ice-cold* na beer. Nang liningon niya ang waytres para kunin ang bill, natanaw niya ang isang babaing nakadamit-itim, nakatalikod sa pintuan at bahagyang natakpan ng *jukebox*—nakamasid sa kanya. Agad itong tumalikod, at ang kanyang itsura—siya ba ang bida sa sine? Imposible. Hindi maaari. Bigla siyang kinabahan. Tumibok ng malakas ang kanyang puso.

Tumayo siya para sana sundan ang babae. Nakita niya itong tumawid ng kalsada, patungong sinehan. Subalit nakihalo sa mga tao at nawala sa kakapalan nito.

Pagkalipas ng ilang minuto, paakyat na siya sa madilim na hagdanan ng otel. Saklaw ng otel ang ikalawa at ikatlong palapag na kung saan tanaw ang sinehan sa ibaba. Mumurahin. Sa nakaraang sunog na tumupok sa pamilihang bayan, natupok pati ang ikatlong palapag nito. Kaya ngayon, ang ikalawang palapag lang ang nagagamit. Ang ikatlong palapag ang nagsisilbing atip.

Nang dumating siya rito kahapon, bitbit niya ang isang magaan na maleta. Masusi siyang tiningnan ng *desk clerk*, habang sinusulat niya ang kanyang pangalan sa librong inabot nito. May uring pagtingin ang klerk na nagsasabing hindi siya dapat magtiwala rito. Pagkabigay ng susi, agad niyang hinanap ang sariling kuwarto. Kinandaduhan niya ang pintuan sa sandaling nakapasok siya, inilapag ang maleta sa ibabaw ng mesa, inalis ang sapatos at mabagal na tumihaya sa kama.

Noong hapon, tumawag siya kay Alfred. Nagulat si Alfred. Pero liban sa pagkagulat, napansin niya ang pag-aalinlangan sa boses ng kaibigan. Parang umiba na si Alfred. "Dadaan ako riyan," ang paalam niya bago isara ang awditibo.

Natutulog pa si Alfred nang dumating siya kahapon. Naghintay muna siya sa salas, nagbasa-basa ng magasin, habang ginigising si Alfred ng katulong. Matapos ang ilang sandali, lumabas ito na pahimas-himas ng kanyang magulong buhok at namumula ang mga mata.

"Indi ka man lang nagpasabing darating ka gali. Di sana nasundo kita sa pier," ang sabi ni Alfred. Tinitigan siya nang malalim ni Alfred, nanunuri, nang-uusisa, nandududa. Marahil nabasa na ni Alfred sa diyaryo ang nangyari. Si Alfred lang ang may alam tungkol sa kaugnayan nila ni Nina.

"Naniniwala ka...?" mahinang tanong niya. Nanatiling walang-imik si Alfred. "Alfred...."

"Ginawa mo...?"

Umiling-iling siya.

"E, sino?"

"Siya...maniwala ka. Siya ang kumitil ng kanyang sariling buhay."

"Ang baril."

"Ambot...ambot...."

Tumayo siya. Nahihilo. Walang-imik na nakamasid si Alfred. Parang nakatutusok ang kanyang paningin.

At pumaibabaw ang tinig ni Alfred: "Nagasinungaling ka!"

Lumagpas siya sa dalawang kwartong may ilaw na. Maliban sa ordinaryong pintuan, may isa pang paimbay-imbay tulad ng nakikita sa mga opisina. Narinig niya ang maliliit na tinig ng mga bata mula sa kwarto. Sa pasilyo, may nasalubong siyang mag-asawa: nakasandal sila sa balkonahe at nanonood ng sari-saring kislap-ilaw. Ipinakikita ng lalaki ang iba't ibang parte ng siyudad.

Narating niya ang kaniyang kwarto. Tumigil siya sa tapat ng pintuan. Kinapkap ng isa niyang kamay ang susi sa pantalon. Di-nagtagal, marahan na niyang itinulak ang pintuan. Nang siya'y nakapasok, muli niyang kinandaduhan ito. Inalis niya ang kanyang kamisedentro, subalit bigla siyang natigilan. Parang may dumapyong init ng hininga ng kung sinong nilalang sa kanyang tainga, at parang naramdaman niya ang masusing pagmasid nito sa kanya. Dahan-dahan siyang umurong sa dingding. Nangapa ng *switch* ang isa niyang kamay, habang ang isa naman ay akmang ipagtatanggol ang kanyang sarili. Subalit wala siyang nakapang *switch*; wala na ito sa gilid ng pintuan.

Sa isang sulok, biglang sumindi ang *table lamp*.

Sabay sa pagbukas ng ilaw, narinig niya ang mahinang pagtawa ng isang babae. Nakahiga ito sa kama sa may tabi ng dingding, ngunit ngayon, dahan-dahan itong bumangon at sumandal sa unan. Bilog ang korte ng malamlam na ilaw kaya't bahagya lang ang nailawan sa kwarto. Nasa dilim ang mukha ng babae, at hindi nakikitang mabuti ang itsura nito.

"Nagulat ka?" tanong ng babae.

Ngayon lang niya narinig ang tinig na ito. Mahina. Labis na mahina. Parang tangay ng hangin mula sa kung saan. Ngunit kahit na mahina, may tono itong nang-aakit kaya't naisip niya agad na ito'y babaing may pangangailangang pangkatawan. Ngunit nanatili pa rin siyang nagdududa, nangangamba sa malamlam na sinag ng ilaw: paano nakapasok ang babaing ito sa kanyang kwarto samantalang nakakandado naman ito?

"Naga-ano ka di?" natanong din niya.

Tumawa nang mahina ang babae. "Gahintay," ang siyang maikling sagot, "sa imo."

"Nagakamali ka. Pagod ako. Bumalik ka na lang sa ibang araw."

Hindi kumibo ang babae.

"Umalis ka na. Pagod ako."

"Ginahintay kita."

"Sinabi ko nang pagod ako. Umalis ka na! Alis! Baka gusto mong tumawag ako ng pulis?"

Tumahimik ang babae. Tuminag. "Ang damit ko," ang sabi nito.

"Saan? Para makaalis ka na ngayon din."

"Sa silya, sa tabi sang mesa."

Natapat ang kanyang mga mata sa silyang itinuro ng babae. Napaurong siya. Nakasampay sa silya ang purong itim na damit. Ang babae sa restawran...ang bida sa sinehan...ang bangkay...nanginig ang buo niyang katawan. Parang pinako siya sa kanyang kinatitindigan. Unti-unti siyang pinawisan nang malamig. Sinikap niyang masulyapan ang mukha ng babae, subalit parang sadya niya itong itinatago sa dilim.

"Ang damit ko," inulit ng babae.

Nabuksan niya ang kanyang bibig. "Sin-o ikaw!"

"Si Nina," ang maikling sagot. "Nina."

"Nagasinungaling ka. Indi ikaw si Nina. Kilala kita."

Parang nagulat na tumawa uli ang babae.

"Ambot," ang sagot ng babae. "Ambot kung nakikilala mo ako. Pero ito pa lang ang unang pagkakataong makaharap kita. Sasabihin ko na lang, nakita kita kanina sa restawran at kahapon sa *lobby* ng sinehan. Ambot kung nakita mo ako, pero ikaw, nakita ko."

Kumilos ang babae para sana ipakita sa liwanag ang kanyang sarili, subalit pinigil niya ito. "Huwag! Huwag kang umalis diyan."

"At bakit?" may makahulugang tono ang pagtanong ng babae. Nang hindi siya sinagot, nagpatuloy siya: "Okey, indi ako aalis dito kung iyan ang gusto mo. May kilala ako noon. Halos pareho kayo ng itsura, katawan, edad at pagkakisig. Parang kambal gid kayo. Kaibigan ko siya, *steady* na kami...pero namatay. Aksidente sa sasakyan. Siya ang pinagluluksahan ko ngayon."

"Indi!"

Nagpatuloy ang babae na parang walang narinig. "*Really*, parang ikaw talaga. Nang una niya akong dalhin sa kanyang *apartment*, siya ang inabot ng nerbiyos. Nanginginig, nakatayo tulad mo, nakatitig sa akin; indi tumitinag, indi makasalita, indi ko alam kung ano ang nakita niya sa aking mukha."

"Anu ang nakikita niyo nga mga lalaki sa aking mukha? A, indi mo nga pala nakikita ang aking mukha. Ilapit mo ang ilaw. *C'mon*, ilapit mo ang ilaw sa aking mukha!"

"Tumigil ka!"

"*C'mon*! Ilapit...Ilapit mo...."

Sa isang iglap, sinunggaban ng lalaki ang solong ilaw sa kwarto. Inihampas niya ito sa babae. At sa gitna nitong lagapakan, pumaibabaw ang isang tili.

Nang mabuksan ang kwarto, natapat sa paningin ng mga sumaklolo—ang *desk clerk*, ang mag-asawa, at ang tatlong boy sa otel—ang anyo ng isang lalaking nakasubasob sa dingding. Parang may iniiwasang kung anong di-nakikitang kaaway, humihingal, pinagpapawisan nang malamig. Sa sahig, nakakalat ang basag na bombilya. At sa silya may isang punit na damit—kulay-itim.

Si Montor

Anghel M. Magahum

Ikapulo nga takna sang kagab-ihon kag tumaliwan sa baybayon sang Silay, Negros nga Nakatundan ang lorsa "Caridad" nga matabuk pa Ilong-ilong.

Masanag ang bulan, nangisapkisap ang kabituunan, mahawan ang langit, mabugnaw kag mahanahay ang hangin nga nagahuyup gikan sa naaminhan, wala sing pamalud kag matulin ang dalagan sang sakayan.

Sa sulod sang kamarote, may tatlo ka sumalakay nga amu si Ramon nga nagahigda kag si Julian nga iya abyan nga nagapanghuy-ab kag nagaduka sa iya ginapungkuan, kag si Andres nga nagahigda kag daw nagakatulug sa luyu nga nayon.

Si Ramon tumindog kag hinampak sing mabaskug sang iya kamut ang abaga ni Julian nga nakibut kag nadula ang iya katuyu.

"Dili na kita magtulog kay kaagahon na ini kag malapit na lamang ang Ilong-ilong," ang pulong ni Ramon.

"Nakalabao na ayhan kita sang katunga sang aton talabukon?" nakiana si Julian.

"Sa banta ko nga laban na, kay madasig ang dalagan sang aton sakayan, matulin, wala sing pamalud kag mabaskug ang lasagas sang amihan nga nagatulud sa aton.

"Agud nga malingaw kita nga dili pagtuyhon, sugiran ta sadtong moros nga si Montor nga ginbitay sa patag sang banwang Salog kag nagbilin sing makakulugmat nga handumanan sa mga banwang natakas sang probinsiang Ilong-ilong.

Nagkilalahay kami kag nagabyanay ni Montor sa kombento sa Villa de Arevalo, sang nagatilipon kami didto nga nagapakigaway sa idalum sang pagpangulo ni Heneral Angel Corteza batok sa mga tropang Kastila ni Heneral Diego de los Rios nga nagpangalig-on sa banwang Parian kag ginadumalahan ni Koronel Brandais.

Sang pagabut sa Villa ni Heneral Leandro Fullon kag sang iya mga tropa gikan sa Antike sa pagbulig kay Heneral Corteza, dala niya si Montor.

Si Heneral Fullon, si Montor kag ang iban niya nga mga opisyal, sa kombento man magdayon kag si Montor kon magkaon walis kag kon kis-a kon magipingay kami sa lamisa nagasapdingay ang duha namon ka butkon.

'Anu ang mga moros kon magkaon pulus mga walis?' siling ko sa iya.

Bumalikid sia sa akon, kumadlaw kag magsiling: 'Ang walis matanda nga magluthang sa pagpatay kay Rios kag maayo nga maglabu sa pagutud sang ulo ni Brandais.'

Sang isa sina ka hapon nga ginabombardeo kami sa Villa sang mga kanyon kag mga pusil sang duha ka bapor sang mga katsila, nga nagabalikbalik, ang isa mahalin sa baybayon sang Parian pa Ogtong kag ang isa mahalin sa Ogtong pa Tigbawan, nabatian ko nga daw lumupuk sa hulut ni Montor sa kombento. Nagdumdum ako nga si Montor amu ang nagpalupuk sang iya rebolber, amu kag sumulud aku gilayon sa amu nga hulut kag wala ko makita si Montor kay dumalagan sa baybay sa pagbantay sa mga katsila kon tumakas. Nasayuran ko, nga yadtong daw sa lupuk ang katunog sa hulut ni Montor, amu ang bala sang pusil nga mauser sang mga katsila nga tumupa kag lumapus sa dingding nga tapi sang amu nga hulut.

Sunu sa ginpanugiron sa akon ni Montor nga sia nagalagad anay nga suluguon ni Heneral Rios. Ginbunyagan sia sa pagkakristohanon kag si Heneral Rios amu ang nanganak sa iya. Sang ulihe nahimo sia nga soldado kag sang nagasukut na ang ribok sa bug-os nga kapudud-an, nalagyo sia sa mga tropang katsila kag umimpon sa mga manriribok nga pilipinhon. Si Montor kasubong sang iban nga tanan nga mga pilipinhon nga nahagugma sang kaluasan sang patubuan, nakigaway sa pagapin sa iya kauturan kag kasubong sang kasingkal sang dugu sang iya kaliwatan sa pagkamoros, maisug kag mabangis subong sang sapat nga talunanon. Sang ulihe, bumulag sa iya bunghay nga mga manriribuk, nagpain sa pagdumala sang mga nagsulunud sa iya, kumadto sa mga banwang natakas kag nagbilin sing makakulugmat nga buhat sa mga banwa nga iya maagihan sa pagpangawat kag pagpamatay tubtub nga nadakup sia sang mga punuan kag binitay sa tunga sang patag sa Salog. Sang pagsaka niya sa hagdan sang bitayan nadulaan sing kaisug kay napukao, napunaw kag dugay naumpawan."

From: "Si Montor," *Hinugpong nga mga Sugilanon*
(Iloilo: La Panayana, 1935)

Montor
(Si Montor)

Anghel M. Magahum

It was ten o'clock in the evening when the ferry "Caridad" sailed from the shore of Nakatundan in Silay, Negros for Iloilo.

The moon was shining bright, the stars were twinkling and the sky was clear. It was cool; a gentle breeze was blowing from the northeast. The sea was calm and the boat was sailing swiftly.

Inside the cabin, there were three passengers: Ramon, Julian, and Andres. Ramon was lying down; Julian, who was seated, was yawning and nodding from drowsiness; and Andres, who was also lying beside them, appeared to be asleep.

Ramon stood up and hit Julian hard on the shoulders, jolting him and banishing his sleepiness.

"Let's not sleep any more. It's early morning and Iloilo is quite close," Ramon said.

"Do you think we're more than halfway now?" asked Julian.

"I think so. Our boat is going fast, the water is calm, and the southwest wind driving us is strong."

"To amuse ourselves and not fall asleep, let me tell you the story of the Moro named Montor, who was executed in the valley of Salog town, leaving a tragic memory among the people of the inland towns of Iloilo.

Montor and I knew each other; we became friends in the convent of Villa de Arevalo when the soldiers encamped there. Under the leadership of General Angel Certeza, we fought the Spanish troops of General Diego de los Rios who dug in at the town of Parian commanded by General Brandais. When General

Leandro Fullon and his troops from Antique arrived at the villa to help General Certeza, he brought Montor with him.

General Fullon, Montor and other officials stayed at the convent. Montor would sit to my left beside the table, our elbows grazing sometimes.

'Do Moros always eat with their left hand?' I asked him.

'This left-hander was the one that gave the shot which felled Rios and the stroke that cut Brandais' head.'

That afternoon, when cannon and guns from the Spanish warships bombarded the villa repeatedly, and bullets crisscrossed from two directions—one from the shore of Parian to Ogtong, the other from Ogtong to Tigbawan—I heard an explosion from Montor's room in the convent. I thought it was Montor who had fired his gun, so I rushed into his room but I didn't see him there. It seems that earlier he had run to the shore to watch Spanish soldiers who were attempting to escape. I learned that the sound was that of a bullet from the Spaniards' mauser which had penetrated the wooden wall of the room.

According to Montor's account, he worked as a messenger for General Rios. He was christened a Catholic, General Rios being his godfather. Later he enlisted as a soldier and when the revolution was raging all over the Philippines, he deserted the Spanish troops and joined the Filipino revolutionaries. Montor, like all the revolutionaries who loved their native land, fought in defense of his country with the hot-bloodedness of his race and with the courage and ferocity of a jungle animal. But later, he deserted his division and abandoned the responsibilty to lead his troops. He went into each liberated town, becoming its scourge as he set the towns on fire, robbed and killed, until finally he was hanged in the plains of Salog. As he went up the stairs of the scaffold, he lost heart, it seemed, for he collapsed and fainted. It was quite sometime before he gained consciousness."

Si Montor

Anghel M. Magahum

Ikasampu ng gabi nang tumulak ang lantsang "Caridad" sa baybay ng Nakatundan sa Silay, Negros. Patawid ito sa Iloilo.

Maliwanag ang buwan, kumikislap ang mga bituin, mahawan ang langit, malamig at banayad ang amihang umihip. Kalma ang dagat at matulin ang takbo ng sasakyan.

May tatlong pasahero sa kamarote: kabilang dito si Ramon na nakahiga, si Julian, ang kanyang kaibigan, na humihikab na at nakatukatok sa kanyang inuupuan, at si Andres na nakahiga sa may tabi nila at anyong natutulog na rin.

Tumayo si Ramon at hinampas nang malakas ang balikat ni Julian; nagulat ito kaya't pinawian ng pagkaantok.

"Dili na kita matulog; maga-madaling araw na at malapit na ang Iloilo," sabi ni Ramon.

"Nakakalahati na kaya tayo?" tanong ni Julian.

"Sa tingin ko, lampas na, dahil matulin ang sasakyan, tahimik ang dagat, at malakas ang amihang gatulak sa aton."

"Para maaliw tayo kag indi aantukin, kukuwentuhan ko kayo tungkol kay Montor na binitay sa patag ng bayang Salog at nag-iwan ng nakagigimbal na alaala sa mga nakalayang bayan sa Iloilo.

Nagkakilala kami at naging magkaibigan ni Montor sa Villa de Arevalo. Doon nagkatipun-tipon ang mga sundalo ni Heneral Angel Corteza. Kalaban namin ang mga tropang Kastila ni Heneral Diego de los Rios na nagkampo sa bayang Parian na nasa ilalim noon ng pamamahala ni Koronel Brandais.

Sa tulong ni Heneral Certeza dumating si Heneral Leandro Fullon at ang kanyang mga tropa mula sa Antike. Kasama nila si Montor.

Tumuloy sa kombento si Heneral Fullon, si Montor, at iba pang mga opisyal. Kaliweteng kumain si Montor at kung minsan kung nagkakatabi kami sa mesa, sumasagi pa ang aming mga braso.

'Ang mga Moros, kaliwete gid bala kumaon?' ang tanong ko sa kanya.

Lumingon siya sa akin, tumawa at sumagot: 'Ang kahusayan ng kaliweteng ito ang bumaril· kay Rios at pumugot ng ulo ni Brandais.'

Noong isang hapong binomba kami ng mga kanyon at baril mula sa dalawang bapor ng Kastila, at pabalik-balik ang mga bala mula sa baybayin ng Parian hanggang Ogtong at mula naman sa Ogtong hanggang Tigbawan, narinig kong may pumutok sa kuwarto ni Montor sa kombento. Akala ko si Montor ang nagapaputok kaya pumasok ako agad sa kanyang kwarto pero wala siya; tumakbo pala siya sa baybayin para magbantay ng mga Kastilang aahon. Natuklasan kong ang pumutok sa kuwarto ni Montor ay nanggaling sa Mauser ng mga Kastila. Nakalusot ito sa dingding na kahoy ng kwarto.

Ayon kay Montor, nagsilbi muna siyang utusan ni Heneral Rios. Bininyagan siya at si Heneral Rios ang ninong. Pagkatapos pumasok si Montor bilang sundalo. Nang sumiklab na ang rebolusyon sa buong kapuluan, tinakasan niya ang mga tropang Kastila para sumapi sa mga rebolusyonaryong Pilipino. Tulad ng kanyang kapuwa Pilipino, mahal ni Montor ang lupang tinubuan; nakipaglaban siya para sa kanyang mga kapatid nang may sidhi at init na likas sa lahing Moro. Kasing-tapang at kasing-bangis siya ng mga hayop sa gubat.

Nguni't sa dakong huli, tumiwalag si Montor sa mga rebolusyonaryo at binitiwan ang pamumuno ng kanyang pangkat ng sundalo. Tumuloy siya sa mga bayang nakalaya, at kumalat didto sang lagim—nansunog, nagnakaw, at pumatay—hanggang sa siya'y dinakip at binitay ng mga alagad ng batas sa kapatagan ng Salog. Nang umakyat si Montor sa hagdan ng bibitayan, maliwanag na nawalan ito ng loob, pagka't siya'y nabuwal, nahimatay, at matagal bago nagkamalay uli."

Pagpanumbalik

Leovigildo Gonzaga

Nabatyagan ni Tiyo Inso ang pagliso sang asawa. Napat-od niya nga wala pagdapui sang katuyo ini. Husto lang pagbulubaliswa si Tiya Biana sa banig. Matiuntion pa nabatian ni Tiyo Inso ang ginahimunggan nga pagpisngo. Ini sinundan sang pag-urahab.

Daw wala sang mahibal-an nga buhaton si Tiyo Inso. Nahangpan niya kung ano ang balatyagon nga nagapugad sa dughan sang asawa. Sia amo man ang ginabatyag kung ngaa hindi man siya matulugan.

Makatalandog ang pag-urahab ni Tiya Biana.

"Uy...uy...hindi man pagpatama...."

Labi lamang ang pagurahab ni Tiya Biana sang mahibal-an nga nakamata pa gali si Tiyo Inso.

Nagbangon si Tiyo Inso. Tinamdam ang asawa nga ang mga kamot nagatakop sa nawong.

"Ngaa?" ang mahinay nga pagusisa sang tigulang nga lalaki. Hinapulas niya ang likod sang asawa.

Isa ka madalom nga hibubon-ot ang pinakawas ni Tya Biana.

"Man...inang mga anak ko...matapos naton padakuon bayaan na lang kita. Wala sila sing pag-ulikid...wala... Daw indi kita ila mga ginikanan...iban nga tao na kita!"

May kapait ang pagpautwas sang mga tinaga kag indi malikawan ni Tyo Inso ang pagbatyag. Ginkagat niya ang mga bibig.

"Pati na si...Luisa...Sia pa naman ang...Ay, Inso...."

Natinguhaan ni Tyo Inso nga ipahamtang ang balatyagon. "May bana na sia," paglingaw ni Tyo Inso. "May kinamatarong na ang bana sa pagdala sa iya bisan diin. May kaugalingon na sila nga pangabuhi nga dapat atubangon."

"Apang kinahanglan pa bala nila ang magbulag?" pangatarungan ni Tya Biana. "Ginsiling ko naman sa ila nga indi ako magpahilabot sa ila pangabuhi, a."

"Batunon na naton ang kamatuoran nga ang ila ginbuhat subong man sang ginbuhat naton sang una. Sa kabangdanan nga indi matamay."

Nakadulog sa pagpisngo si Tya Biana.

"Natandaan mo bala? Ina man ang nasiling sa aton nanday Nanay kag Tatay sang aton ipabutyag sa ila ang buko sa pagtuhay sa ila. Wala man kita mapunggi. Luyag ko sadto nga magkaugalingon kita sa gilayon. Luyag ko sadto nga makaugalingon ko ang mga katungdanan nga dapat tungdan sang isa ka bana. Luyag ko nga ang paglipay sa imo matigayon sa akon nga pagtinguha lamang kag ang mahatag mo nga kalipayan sa akon kaugalingon mo nga pagtinguha. Nahangpan mo ina sadto, indi bala?"

Wala makasabat si Tya Biana. Nagapilisnguon lang sia.

"Nahibal-an ko nga nahangpan mo ang balatyagon sang mga anak mo ugaling ara ka sa kahimtangan nga subong sangsa ila ni Nanay sadto."

"I-ikaw...wala ka bala pagbatyag?" inusisa ni Tya Biana ang bana.

Nakakadlaw si Tyo Inso.

"Nagabatyag man," sabat sini.

"Apang sa pihak sina, nagabatyag man ako sing bugal. Wala magsayop sa pagpili sing palaman-on ang mga anak mo nga babae. Kag wala man magsayop ang mga anak mo nga lalaki sa pagpamat-od nga magbulag sa aton sang sila magpinangasawa. Sila katulad man naton, indi bala?"

Wala magsabat si Tya Biana.

"Kag nangin-malipayon ako. Kag ikaw malipayon man...indi bala?"

Wala sing tinaga nga nagkawas sa mga bibig ni Tya Biana. Hinakos lang niya ang may kaanuman kag lima ka tuig nga bana kag magpadayon sa paghibi sa dughan sini.

Liwat ginhapulas ni Tyo Inso ang likod sang asawa. Ang pag-uyog sang mga abaga ni Tya Biana amat-amat nga naglaka tubtob nga magmaaliwanay ang balatyagon sini.

"Matulog na kita," tugda ni Tyo Inso. "Buas...aton ang tanan nga hilikuton sa balay."

Liwat nga nakahibi si Tya Biana.

"Ngaa?"

"Na-nahadlok ako," ang sabat sang asawa. "Basi...basi indi ko na mabuhat ang ginbuhat ko."

Nakaurok si Tyo Inso. Nakatulok sing maturirok sa guya sang may kan-uman ka tuig na nga asawa. Hinali man nga hinakop sang katahap ang iya kasingkasing. Basi indi man sia makahatag sing kasadyahan kay Tya Biana katulad sadto.

"A...matulog na gani kita," ang nasiling na lamang ni Tyo Inso.

Apang wala pagdapui si Tyo Inso sang katuyo. Samtang nagahigda indi niya matapna ang pagpanumbalik sang mga handumanan. Sadtong diutay pa ang ila kabataan, nagtimbanganay sila sa pagtuytoy sang mga ini. Ang mga anak nila nga mga babae gintudloan ni Tya Biana sang mga katungdanan sang mga babae sa balay: pagpangluto, pagpanglaba, pagpamalansa, pagpanursi, kag pagpanglimpyo sa sulod sang balay. Sia naman ang nagtudlo sa anak nga mga lalaki sa mga hilikuton sang lalaki: pagpanguma, pagpamisak sing inuggatong, pag-atop sang balay, pagpanag-ob, kag pagkaayo sang guba nga mga kudal. Sang magdalagko na ang mga anak, naagyan nila ang mga tinuig nga halos wala na sila sing mahikot kay ang mga anak na nila ang nagtatap sang tanan sa sulod sang balay kag sa uma. Ang ginbuhat na lamang nila amo ang pagtulotimbang sa mga anak. Apang karon minyu na ang tanan kag nagtuhay sa ila. Nabilin sila nga duha. Kag lunsay may katahap nga nagapugad sa ila mga dughan.

Nakabangon sing hinali si Tyo Inso. Kinuso niya ang mga mata. Natulogan gid man gali sia. Wala na sa iya luyo si Tya Biana. Nadunggan niya ang pagsirit sang ginaprito sa ila diligamuhan.

Nanaog si Tyo Inso. Sinugalaw sia sang mabugnaw nga hangin samtang nagapanaog sa ila hagdanan. Nakakurog sia.

Madulomdulom pa. Pinangita ni Tyo Inso ang wasay kag parakol nga ara nasab-it sa siklat sang ila balay nayon sa idalom sang ganhaan.

Sang makita niya ang mga gamit dayon niya palapit sa hinantal nga kahoy nga nautod niya sang lagari sadtong pila ka adlaw na ang nakaligad.

Sinandig niya ang wasay kag parakol sa hinantal nga kahoy. Umonat siya. Inumol ang mga kamot kag magaksyon subong sang isa ka boksidor nga nagapakigsumpong sa ibabaw sang ring.

Nakayuhom si Tyo Inso sang matiuntion. Kinuha niya ang isa ka utod nga kahoy. Tinungtong ang isa ka punta sini sa nagahigda nga daku nga inutod nga nagakalasup-ak na kay ginagamit nga dalat-ulan.

Kinaptan niya ang wasay. Hagyon nga gindat-on sa punta sang bilialon, hinayaw niya sang wasay kag ihanot sa inutod nga kahoy nga nabiak gid sa duha ka bahin.

Nasadyahan si Tyo Inso. Matanda pa gali sia mag-uyat sang wasay.

Matiun-tion pa, mataas na gawa ang tinumpokan sang iya binial. Basa man sia sang balhas.

"Inso, husto na anay ina," nabatian niya nga panawag sang asawa.

Nakaliso si Tyo Inso sa ginhalinan sang tingog. Nakita niya nga malapit na gid sa iya likuran si Tia Biana.

"Nakasukad na ako," pahibalo ni Tya Biana. May dala ini nga tualya kag iya ginpahiran ang balhas sang bana. "Indi ka anay magpatama, basi magulpihan ka."

"Sus, ina lang!" may pagpabugal pa nga sabat ni Tyo Inso.

"Wala pa gani ako paghapua, a. Medyo nakapuykapoyan lang apang tan-awa bala kon pirme na ang akon pag-uyat sang wasay?" Nakita niya nga nagakilan sa kalipay ang mga mata sang asawa.

Madasig ang paghungit ni Tyo Inso sang kan-on. Gutom gid sia. Apang nakadulog sia sang ulihi sa pagkaon sang matalupangdan nga wala pagkaon si Tya Biana kundi nagatulok lang nga nagatulok sa iya.

"Ngaa indi ka pa magkaon?"

"Ginatan-aw ko lang kon...kon...."

"Kon naluyagan ko ang imo linutoan? Aba...nakita mo na gid nga wala'y pahuway ang akong pagdapal, a. Paborito ko nga pagkaon ining ginluto mo abi. Kalukalo, estrelyado nga itlog, sinugba nga pinakas kag tahu. Aba...indi ako maharaw kon amo ini ang akon pamahaw!"

"Paborito mo gani...apang...ang pagluto ko?"

Nagkadlaw si Tyo Inso. "Ining babae nga ini, huo. Daw nadulaan ka na sing pagsalig sa imo ikasarang! Wala paglubad ina!"

Ginpadayon ni Tyo Inso ang pagkaon. Sang liwat niya pasiplatan ang asawa nakita niya nga nagayuhom ini apang may mga luha nga nagapunong sa mga mata.

"Manamit ang akon linuto? Katulad sadto?" ang mahinay nga pamangkot ni Tya Biana nga daw luyag pa gid pasaligon sang bana.

"Amo gid, wala paglubad," pasalig ni Tyo Inso. "Wala sing kinalis...subong man sadto nga ginanamitan gid ako sang imo linutoan."

"Manilhig pa gali ako karon matapos makakaon kag magtuob sang pahu," nahambal ni Tya Biana nga nagsugod na sa paghungit sang kan-on.

"Kag manag-ob man ako," sugpon man ni Tyo Inso.

"Daw si Luisa ining nagapadulong, a. Si Luisa matuod!"

Nakita ni Tyo Inso nga nagtalikod sa bintana si Tya Biana. Gumwa ini agod sugaton ang anak.

"Nakapamasyar ka?" ang hambal ni Tya Biana sang mag-atubangay sila sa balkon sang balay kag matapos makabisa si Luisa.

Naghulat si Tyo Inso sang igasabat sang kamanghuran nga anak.

"Ka-kamusta kamo ni Tatay diri?" ang pamangkot ni Luisa bilang sabat sa iloy.

Nagsulod ang duha ka babae. Nagbisa si Luisa sa amay.

"Indi gid ako aramon," hambal ni Luisa. "Basi siling ko nga...nga...."

"Nga ano?" turasok ni Tya Biana. "Nga basi nga indi na kami makatatap sang amon kaugalingon?"

"Nahibal-an ko, Nay, nga nagahinakit gid kamo sa ginbuhat namon nga pagtuhay ni Fidel." Nadayunan nga nangurog ang tingog ni Luisa. Daw luyag na ini maghibi.

"Aba... wala. Wala."

"Gani nga nagduaw ako agod makita ko ang kahimtangan ninyo kag kon ano ang akon mabuhat. Siling ko...basi nga kinahanglan nga...."

"Aba si Fidel ang tatapon mo. Masarangan ko ang pagtatap pa kay Tatay ninyo!"

"Nay?"

Nakadlaw sing matunog si Tyo Inso. Napat-od niya nga wala maghangpanay ang duha. Si Luisa may pagpati nga nagahinakit gid ang iya iloy samtang minatuod naman ang hambal ni Tya Biana nga dapat nga si Fidel ang tatapon ni Luisa.

"Wala mo mahangpi si Nanay mo, Luisa," hambal ni Tyo Inso. Nakatulok sa tigulang nga lalaki ang anak. Amo man si Tya Biana. "Husto ang iya ginahambal. Si Fidel na anay ang tatapon mo kay makasarang pa naman sia magtatap sa akon kag sa balay."

Daw wala masanagi si Luisa. Nagakunot pa ang agtang sa kabulong.

"Wala kami sing kaakig sa inyo, Luisa," pabutyag ni Tyo Inso, "bangod kay kamo nagtuhay."

Apang indi nila mapapati si Luisa. Nagasalangisag pa ang balatyagon sini. Daw luyag nga maghibi.

"Mabudlay mo mapatihan matuod nga wala kami paghupot sing aligutgot sa inyo," padayon ni Tyo Inso. "Ang maayo nga magbalik ka sa Domingo kaupod ni Fidel. Pahibal-on ko man ang iban mo nga mga utod nga magkari sa amo nga adlaw upod ang imo mga bayaw. Diri kamo manyaga tanan. Si Nanay ninyo ang magaluto sang panyaga."

Nakatulok si Luisa sing masusi sa iloy.

"Ngaa, Luisa, nagdumdom ka bala nga nalimtan ko na ang pagpangluto?"

"A-aba, wala, Nay," maabtik nga sabat ni Luisa nga nagnayanaya ang guya. "Mabalik kami sa Domingo, diri kami magapanyaga. Makakaon naman gali kami sang linutoan ni Nanay."

Gin-agbayan ni Tyo Inso si Tya Biana kag ang isa ka kamot ni Tya Biana nagalikos sa hawak sang bana samtang nagatindog sila sa luyo sang gawahan kag nagalantaw sa nagapalayo nga Luisa. Nagbalikid si Luisa kag namaypay sa mga ginikanan. Namaypay man ang duha ka tigulang.

"Ang anak mo," may kaham-ot ang tingog ni Tya Biana. "Daw nalipat siguro nga ako ang nagtudlo sa ila sa pagluto. Nagahunahona siguro nga pagutman ko ikaw."

Wala masugpon si Tyo Inso. Husto lang ini magkadlaw.

"Hoy, manag-ob ka gani. Wala na sing tubig ang aton tadyaw didto sa pantaw. Maayo kay wala maisipi ni Luisa nga linglingon ato. Kon nalinglingan niya ato, basi silingon si Fidel nga sag-uban kita," may hagyon sang pagsunlog ang tingog ni Tya Biana.

"Sobra ka abi ka buraska sa tubig, mo!"

Nakigkadlaw man si Tya Biana sa bana. Kamalipayon sa ila. Subong man sadto, sang bag-o lang sila makasal.

From: *Hiligaynon*, January 10, 1973

Remembrances

(Pagpanumbalik)

Leovigildo Gonzaga

Tiyo Inso felt his wife turn. He sensed that sleep had not yet come to her. She just kept tossing in her bed. In a little while, he started hearing some stifled sobs. Soon, she broke into a loud weeping.

Tiyo Inso wasn't sure what to do. He understood the feelings nesting in her chest. These also bothered him, that's why he, too, couldn't sleep.

Tiya Biana's weeping touched him.

"Now, now, don't work yourself up."

But she wailed even more now that she knew *Tiyo* Inso was still awake.

Tiyo Inso got up. He stood watching his wife covering her face with her hands.

"What's wrong?" he asked her gently. He stroked his wife's back.

Tiya Biana gave out a deep sigh.

"Our children...after we raise them, they just turn their backs on us. Like we're not their parents...like we're strangers to them."

There was bitterness in the way she let out these words and *Tiyo* Inso could not help being pained. He bit his lips.

"Even Luisa...she, whom we...oh, Inso...."

Tiyo Inso managed to express his feelings. "She's married now," *Tiyo* Inso soothed her. "Her husband has the right to bring her anywhere he wishes. They have their own life to live."

"But must they live apart from us?" she argued. "I gave them my word I wouldn't meddle in their life."

"Biana, we'll just have to face up to the fact that what they've done is the same thing we did before for reasons no one can belittle."

Tiya Biana stopped sobbing.

"Do you remember? That was the same thing *Nanay* and *Tatay* told us when we let them know of our plan to live apart from them. Nothing could stop us. It was my wish then to live on our own the moment we got married. I wanted to take on the responsibilities a husband should. I wanted to make you happy from out of my own sweat and you to make me happy on your own. You understood that before, didn't you?"

Tiya Biana didn't answer. She just continued sobbing.

"I'm sure you know the feelings of your children except that now you're in the situation that *Nanay* was in."

"You...you...are you not hurt?"

Tiyo Inso laughed.

"Of course, I am," he answered. "But I also feel proud that your daughters did not make a mistake in choosing their husbands. Nor were your sons mistaken when they decided to live apart from us when they got married. They're like us, aren't they?"

Tiya Biana kept silent.

"And I was happy. And you were too...weren't you?"

Not a word escaped from *Tiya* Biana's mouth. She just embraced her sixty-five-year-old husband and went on crying on his bosom. Gradually, the shaking of her shoulders eased and soon, she calmed down.

"Let's go to sleep," *Tiyo* Inso broke in. "Tomorrow, we'll have to do all the household chores."

Tiya Biana started crying again.

"What's wrong now?"

"I'm scared. I might not...not be able to do what I used to...."

Tiyo Inso trembled. He gazed intently at the face of his sixty-year-old wife. Fear had also seized his heart. He wasn't sure he could make *Tiya* Biana happy like he used to.

"Ahh... let's just go to sleep." That was all *Tiyo* Inso could say.

But sleep didn't come easily to *Tiyo* Inso. Lying there, he couldn't shake off memories flitting into his mind. They had helped each other raise the kids. *Tiya* Biana had taught their daughters the chores girls were supposed to know—cooking, washing, ironing, sewing, and house cleaning. For his part, he had taught the boys men's chores—farming, chopping firewood, putting up the roof for the house, drawing water from the well, fixing the broken fence. There came a time when the couple no longer had to work because the children who had grown up took over managing the house and the farm. The only thing they did was to straighten out conflicts among the children. But now they were all married and living apart from their parents. Really, the couple were apprehensive about the future.

Tiyo Inso jumped up from his bed. He rubbed his eyes. He had fallen asleep after all. *Tiya* Biana was not by his side any more. He could hear the hiss of frying in the kitchen.

Tiyo Inso went downstairs. A cool wind met him on his way down. He trembled from the cold.

It was still a bit dark. *Tiyo* Inso looked for the *wasay* and the *parakol* wedged in the bamboo slats directly below the door.

As soon as he got his tools, he went at once to the pile of wood he had cut with his saw a few days ago. He leaned the axes against the pile of wood. He stretched. Then he clenched his fists and shadow-boxed.

In a short while, *Tiyo* Inso was smiling. He took a piece of wood. Fitted one end onto a big block of wood now coming apart from frequent use as a wood-chop support. He swung the *wasay*, the axe with the longer handle, against the edge of the wood piece, raised it, and with one stroke, cut the block sharply into half.

He was delighted. So he could still make his mark with the axe. In a short time he had stacked a pile of wood. He was sweating.

"Inso, that's enough already," he heard his wife call. Inso turned in the direction of the voise. *Tiya* Biana was approaching closely behind him.

"The rice is ladled out now," *Tiya* Biana let him know. She had a towel with her and she wiped the sweat off her husband. "Don't work too hard; this may be too much for now."

"*Sus*! Only this?" There was a tinge of boasting in *Tiyo* Inso's reply. "I'm not even out of breath yet. I'm just a bit tired, but look, do you see how I can hold the axe steady?" She saw that her husband's eyes were shining with pleasure.

Tiyo Inso dug in with his hands and gobbled up the rice. He was really starved. After a little while, he stopped when he noticed that *Tiya* Biana was not eating, but just gazing at him.

"Why are you not eating yet?"

"I'm just watching if...if...."

"If I still enjoy what you cooked? Well, see. See how my hands move non-stop? You've prepared my favorites. Fried rice, eggs sunnyside up, broiled *pinakas* and *tahu*... Really...if this is the kind of breakfast I'll get I won't ever get feeble."

"Your favorite food, yes...but what about the way I cook?"

Tiyo Inso laughed. "Oh, my lady, really. Have you lost confidence in what you can do? That hasn't faded one bit."

Tiyo Inso went on eating. When he next glanced at his wife, he saw that she was smiling, but there were tears in her eyes.

"I still cook well? Just like before?" *Tiya* Biana asked softly as if looking for further assurance from her husband.

"Really, it's unfading," *Tiyo* Inso assured her. "Not a grain leveled from the *gantangan*....just like before, I love your cooking."

"By the way, I'll go sweep the yard, then set fire on the rubbish to smudge the mango tree," *Tiya* Biana said, as she started putting food into her mouth.

"And I'll go fetch water," *Tiyo* Inso added.

"This looks like Luisa drawing near. Yes, it's Luisa." *Tiyo* Inso saw that *Tiya* Biana had turned away from the window to go out and meet their daughter.

"You've dropped by?" *Tiya* Biana asked when they stood facing each other in the balcony and Luisa had raised her mother's hand to her forehead.

Tiyo Inso waited for the reply of the youngest daughter.

"How...how are you and Tatay getting along here?" Luisa asked in reply to her mother.

The two women entered the house. Luisa raised her father's hand to her forehead.

"I couldn't feel at ease," Luisa said. "I told myself you might...might not...."

"What?" *Tiya* Biana interrupted her. "That we might not be able to take care of ourselves?"

"*Nanay*, I know that you were really hurt that Fidel and I decided to live on our own." Luisa's voice broke now. She seemed on the verge of crying.

"Oh, no. Not at all."

"So I've come to visit to see how you're doing and what I can do to help. I told myself...you might need...."

"But really, it's Fidel you must look after. I can still take care of your father."

" '*Nay*?"

Tiyo Inso broke into a loud laughter. He realized the two had misunderstood one another. Luisa thought that she had hurt her mother's feelings while *Tiya* Biana had really meant it when she said Luisa should take care of Fidel.

"You did not understand your mother, Luisa," *Tiyo* Inso said. The daughter was looking at the old man. So was *Tiya* Biana.

"That's right. You must take care of Fidel first because she can still look after me and our household."

Luisa was unable to catch what they meant. Her brows remained knitted.

"No, we don't hold any ill-feelings against you Luisa," *Tiyo* Inso clarified for her, "for deciding to live apart from us."

But they could not convince Luisa. She was still confused. She looked like she wanted to cry.

"You can't believe we don't resent you," *Tiyo* Inso continued. "Why don't you come back on Sunday with Fidel? I'll ask your brothers and sisters to come along with their spouses. You'll all take your lunch here. Your mother will prepare lunch."

Luisa looked intently at her mother.

"Why, Luisa, do you think I can't cook any more?"

"No...no, *Inay*," Luisa answered quickly, her face lighting up. "We'll come back on Sunday; we'll take lunch here. We can taste *Nanay*'s cooking again."

Tiyo Inso put an arm round *Tiya* Biana's shoulder and she put hers round his waist while they stood by the door watching Luisa walk away. Luisa turned back and waved at her parents. The old couple waved back.

"Your child," *Tiya* Biana sounded amused. "Perhaps she has forgotten I was the one who taught them how to cook. She's thinking perhaps I'd let you starve."

Tiyo Inso didn't say anything more. He just laughed.

"*Hoy*, go fetch some water. The jar in the *pantaw* is empty. It's a good thing Luisa didn't think of going to our kitchen balcony. If she had, she might have peered into the jar there and told Fidel to fetch water for us," *Tiya* Biana said in a jesting tone.

"That's because you're so wasteful with water."

Tiya Biana and her husband laughed. They were very happy. Just like the time when they were newly married.

Pagpanumbalik

Leovigildo Gonzaga

Naramdaman ni Tiyo Insong pumihit ang asawa. Batid niyang hindi pa ito dinapuan ng pagkaantok. Pabiling-biling si Tiya Biana sa banig. Ilang sandali pa, narinig ni Tiyo Inso ang pinipigil na hikbi. Sumunod ang hagulhol.

Parang hindi alam ni Tiyo Inso ang gagawin. Naintindihan niya ang pumupugad na damdamin sa dibdib ng asawa. Naramdaman niya iyon, kaya't hindi rin siya makatulog.

Makababagbag-damdamin ang hagulhol ni Tiya Biana.

"O...tahan na, indi ka magpasobra...."

Lalong tumindi ang paghagulhol ni Tiya Biana nang malamang gising pa pala si Tiyo Inso.

Bumangon si Tiyo Inso. Minasdan ang asawang nakatakip ang mga kamay sa mukha.

"Bakit?" ang malumanay na pang-usisa ng matandang lalaki. Hinaplos niya ang likod ng asawa.

Isang malalim na buntong-hininga ang pinalabas ni Tiya Biana. "Kasi...ang mga anak ko...matapos natin silang palakihin, pababayaan na lang tayo. Indi sila marunong lumingon ...wala...parang indi nila tayo magulang...ibang tao tayo...!"

May pait ang pagbitiw nitong mga kataga at hindi naiwasan ni Tiyo Insong masaktan din. Kinagat niya ang kanyang mga labi.

"Pati na si...Luisa...siya pa naman ang...ay, Inso...."

Sinikap ni Tiyo Insong mapahinahon ang damdamin, "May bana na si Luisa," inalualo siya ni Tiyo Inso. "May karapatan na ang asawa niyang dalhin siya kahit saan. May sarili na silang buhay na haharapin."

"Bakit kailangan pa bala nila ang magbukod?" ang tanong ni Tiya Biana. "Sinabi ko naman sa kanilang indi ako makikialam sa kanilang buhay, a."

"Ti tanggapin na natin ang katotohanang ang gin-obra nila siya ring ginawa natin noong una. Sa dahilang indi puwede hamakin."

Natigil ang paghihikbi ni Tiya Biana.

"Natandaan mo bala? Amo man ang sinabi sa atin sang Nanay at Tatay nang pinaalam natin sa kanila ang balak nating bumukod. Indi rin tayo napigil. Ibig ko noong magsarili sa lalong madaling panahon. Ibig kong masarili ang mga pananagutang dapat tupdin ng isang bana. At mapaligaya ka sa sarili kong pagsisikap lamang, at mapaligaya mo din ako sa sarili mong pagsisikap. Naintindihan mo iyan noon, di bala?"

Hindi nakasagot si Tiya Biana. Humikbi uli siya.

"Alam ko nga naiintindihan mo ang damdamin sang mga anak mo pero ang kalagayan mo ngayon ay tulad sa kalagayan nina Nanay noon."

"I-ikaw...indi ka bala nagahinakit?"

Napatawa si Tiyo Inso.

"Nagahinakit din," sagot nito. "Pero nakakaramdam din ako ng pagmamalaki. Indi nagkamaling pumili sang banahon ang mga anak mong babae. At indi rin nagkamali ang mga anak mong lalaki sa pagpasiyang bumukod sila sa atin sang sila'y nag-asawa. Katulad din natin sila, di bala?"

Hindi kumibo si Tiya Biana.

"At naging maligaya ako. At ikaw din...di bala?"

Walang katagang nakalabas sa mga bibig ni Tiya Biana. Niyapos lang niya ang banang may animnapu't limang taong gulang, at nagpatuloy umiyak sa dibdib nito.

Hinaplos uli ni Tiyo Inso ang likod ng asawa. Ang panginginig ng mga balikat ni Tiya Biana unti-unting nabawasan hanggang umaliwalas ang damdamin niya.

"Matulog na kita," sabat ni Tiyo Inso. "Bukas...atin na lahat ang gawain sa bahay."

Muling umiyak si Tiya Biana.

"Bakit?"

"Na-natatakot ako," sagot ng asawa. "Baka...baka hindi ko na kayang gawin ang ginawa ko noon."

Nanginig si Tiyo Inso. Masidhing tinitigan ang mukha ng may animnapung taong gulang na asawa. Bigla ring inangkin ng pangangamba ang kanyang puso. Baka hindi niya madulutan ng kasiyahan si Tiya Biana nang tulad noon.

"A...matulog na gani kita," ang nasabi na lang ni Tiyo Inso.

Subalit hindi nadapuan si Tiyo Inso ng pagkaantok. Habang nakahiga ito hindi naiwaglit ang ilang alaala. Noong maliit pa ang kanilang anak, nagtulungan silang mag-asawang pumatnubay sa mga ito. Ang mga babae ay tinuruan ni Tiya Biana ng mga gawaing pambahay: pagluluto, paglalaba, pamamalantsa, panunursi at paglinis sa loob ng bahay. Siya naman ang nagturo sa mga anak na lalaki ng gawaing panlalaki: pagsasaka, pagsibak ng panggatong, pag-atip ng bahay, pag-igib at pag-ayos sa mga sirang bakod. Nang lumaki na ang kanilang mga anak, may mga taong halos wala ng gawain ang mag-asawa dahil anak na nila ang namahala sa bahay at sa sakahan. Ang tanging gawa nila ay ang makisama sa mga anak. Subalit ngayon may asawa na silang lahat at nakabukod. Naiwan silang dalawa. At lubos ang pangambang namumugad sa kanilang mga dibdib.

Biglang bumangon si Tiyo Inso. Kinuskos niya ang kanyang mga mata. Nakatulog din pala siya. Wala na sa tabi niya si Tiya Biana. Narinig niya ang pagsitsit ng pinirito sa kanilang kusina.

Nanaog si Tiyo Inso. Sinalubong siya ng malamig na hangin habang papanaog sa hagdanan. Nanginig siya.

Madilim-dilim pa. Hinanap niya ang dalawang palakol na nakasabit sa dingding sa gawing ilalim ng pintuan.

Nang makita niya ang mga gamit, agad niyang nilapitan ang bunton ang mga kahoy na kanyang nilagare ilang araw na ang nakalipas.

Isinandal niya ang palakol sa talaksan ng kahoy. Umunat siya. Kinuyum ang mga kamay at kumilos nang tulad ng isang boksidor na nakikipaglaban sa ibabaw ng ring.

Sandaling napangiti si Tiyo Inso. Kinuha niya ang kaputol na kahoy. Itinuntong niya ang dulo nito sa isang malaking pirasong kahoy na nangakaskas na sa sobrang gamit bilang sangkalan.

Hinawakan niya ang palakol. Idiniin ito sa dulo ng bibiyaking kahoy, inilangat at inihampas; nabiyak sa dalawang bahagi ang pirasong kahoy.

Nasiyahan si Tiyo Inso.

Eksakto pa pala siyang humawak ng palakol.

Di naglaon, mataas na ang tumpok ng kanyang sinibak na kahoy. Basa na rin siya ng pawis.

"Inso, tama na muna iyan," narinig niyang tumawag ang asawa.

Napapihit si Tiyo Inso sa pinanggalingan ng tinig. Nasa may likuran na pala niya si Tiya Biana.

"Nakahain na ako," ang sabi sa kanya ni Tiya Biana. May dala itong tuwalya at kanyang pinahiran ng pawis ang asawa. "Indi ka magpasobra; baka mabigla ka."

"Sus, amo lang na!" may pagmamalaki pang sagot ni Tiyo Inso. "Indi pa nga ako humihingal, a. Medyo napapagod lang, pero tingnan mo. Matatag pa ang aking pagtangan ng palakol, di bala?" Nakita ni Tiya Bianang na may ningning sa mata ng asawa.

Mabilis ang pagsubo ni Tiyo Inso ng kanin. Gutom na gutom siya. Pero di-nagluwat, nahinto siyang kumain nang mapansing di kumakain si Tiya Biana at nakatitig lang ito sa kanya.

"Ba't indi ka pa nagakaon?"

"Tinitingnan ko lang kung...kung...."

"Kung nagustuhan ko ang iyong niluto? Aba...nakita mo naman na walang-patid ang aking subo. Paborito ko kasi itong mga niluto mo. Sinangag, estrelyado na itlog, inihaw na daing at tahu. Aba...indi ako mamamayat kung ito ang aking almusal."

"Paborito mo nga...pero...ang pagluto ko?"

Tumawa si Tiyo Inso. "Ang babaing ito, huo. Parang nawalan ka na sang tiwala sa iyong kayang gawin! Wala pagkupas ina!"

Itinuloy ni Tiyo Inso ang pagkain. Nang muli niyang masulyapan ang asawa, nakangiti na ito subalit may mga luhang natitipon sa mga mata.

"Masarap ang gingluto ko? Tulad din noon?" ang marahang tanong ni Tiya Biana na parang ibig pang kunin ang tiwala ng asawa.

"Amo gid," tiniyak ni Tiyo Inso sa kanya. "Walang kaltas...tulad din noong nasarapan ako sa iyong luto."

"Magawalis muna ako matapos kumain at pasusuubin ko ang mangga," sabi ni Tiya Biana na nagsimula nang sumubo ng kanin.

"At maga-igib naman ako," dugtong ni Tiyo Inso.

"Parang si Luisa itong papalapit, a. Aba, si Luisa gid!"

Nakita ni Tiyo Inso na pumihit sa bintana si Tiya Biana. Lumabas ito para salubungin ang anak.

"Napasyal ka?" sabi ni Tiya Biana nang magkaharap na sila sa balkon ng bahay at nakamano na si Luisa.

Hinintay ni Tiyo Inso ang isasagot ng bunsong anak.

"Ku-kumusta kayo ni Tatay rito?" ang tanong ni Luisa bilang pagsagot sa ina.

Pumasok ang dalawang babae. Nagmano si Luisa sa ama.

"Indi ako mapakali," wika ni Luisa. "Sabi ko baka...ba...."

"Baka ano?" ang sabat ni Tiya Biana. "Na baka hindi na namin kayang alagaan ang sarili?"

"Alam ko, 'Nay, na masama gid ang loob mo sa pagbukod namin ni Fidel." Natuluyan nang nanginig ang boses ni Luisa. Parang ibig itong umiyak.

"Aba...wala. Wala."

"Kaya't dumalaw ako para makita ang inyong kalagayan at kung anong maitutulong ko. Kako...baka...kailangan na...."

"Aba si Fidel ang intindiha. Kaya ko pang asikasuhin ang Tatay niyo."

"'Nay?"

Napatawa nang malakas si Tiyo Inso. Alam niyang hindi nagkakaintindihan ang dalawa. Sigurado si Luisang masama ang loob ng kanyang ina, pero totoo rin naman ang sinabi ni Tiya Biana na si Fidel ang dapat asikasuhin ni Luisa.

"Indi mo naiintindihan ang Nanay mo, Luisa," sabi ni Tiyo Inso. Nakatingin sa matandang lalaki ang anak. Ganoon din si Tiya Biana. "Tama ang kanyang sinasabi. Si Fidel na muna ang intindiha dahil kaya pa naman niyang asikasuhin ako at ang bahay."

Hindi pa rin naliwanagan si Luisa. Nakakunot pa ang kanyang noo.

"Indi kami galit sa inyo, Luisa," diniin ni Tiyo Inso, "sa inyong pagbukod."

Subalit hindi nila makumbinse si Luisa. Nalilito pa rin ito. Wari'y gustong umiyak.

"Sadyang mahirap mong paniwalaang indi kami gakimkim sang sama ng loob sa inyo," pagpatuloy ni Tiyo Inso. "Ang mabuti, bumalik ka sa Linggo na kasama si Fidel. Sasabihin ko rin sa iba mong kapatid nga pumunta rito sa araw na iyon kasama rin ang iyong mga bayaw. Dito kayo mananaghaliang lahat. Si Nanay ninyo ang magahanda ng pananaghalian."

Masusing napatingin si Luisa sa ina.

"Bakit, Luisa, sa tingin mo bala nakalimutan ko nang magluto?"

"A, aba, indi, 'Nay," mabilis na sagot ni Luisa, masaya ang mukha. "Mabalik kami sa Linggo, diri kami mananaghalian. Makakakain na naman gali kami sang niluto ni Nanay."

Inakbayan ni Tiyo Inso si Tiya Biana at pinaikot ni Tiya Biana ang kanyang kamay sa baywang ng asawa. Nakatayo sila sa tabi ng bintana at nakatanaw sa palayo nang si Luisa. Lumingon ito at kumaway sa mga magulang. Kumaway rin ang dalawang matanda.

"Ang anak mo," may halong pagtatwa ang tinig ni Tiya Biana. "Nalimutan na niya sigurong ako ang nagturo sa kanilang magluto. Akala niya gugutumin na kita."

Hindi na dumugtong pa si Tiyo Inso. Sapat nang ito'y tumawa.

"Hoy, mag-igib ka na nga. Wala na sang tubig ang ating tapayan doon sa batalan. Mabuti na lang na indi naisip ni Luisang silipin iyon. Baka sasabihan pa niya si Fidel na igiban tayo," may himig panunukso ang tinig ni Tiya Biana.

"Sobrang aksaya ka kasi sa tubig mo!"

Napatawa na rin si Tiya Biana. Ang saya nila. Tulad din noon nang sila'y bagong kasal pa lamang.

Tig-alani

Antonio H. Joquiño

Magulugal-om sang hapon sina. May diutay nga tulotalithi nga natupa pag-abot sang kasisidmon. Wala man lang dugay. Naghuyophuyop ang hangin. Amat-amat nga naghawan ang nawong sang langit kag pumakita ang masanag nga bulan kag ang madamo nga mga bituon.

Nagapungko si Esang sa luyo sang bintana, nga nawangwang sing diutay. Makita niya ang pagsabwag sang kasanag sang bulan sa palibot sa mga kahilamunan nga ginbasa sang talithi. Sa unhan nagagarhom ang nagakalub-asan na nga humay sa mahanayap nga kapatagan. Nagadangat sa iya igsilimhot ang alisbong sang nagagulang na nga humay upod sa mayami nga dapya sang hangin. Sa indi madugay magapalayo na ang gutom sa ila ganhaan, nahimulongon niya sa kaugalingon.

Ang iya iloy nagahuragok na sa hiligdaan nila. Pagkatapos gid nila kaina panyapon dayon sini hinimos ang ila hiligdaan kag magbarikutot. Bangod sa katugnaw kanami matuod ang magpainakop sa kaalabaab nga ginatanyag sang hiligdaan.

Namalo ang sulog nga manok sa unhan. Ayhan gab-i na gid. Nanguy-ab sia. Una nga panguy-ab. Ayhan inugtolog na gid man.

Daw ginaguyod na sia sang kaluyag sa paghisapo sang kaalabaab sang hiligdaan sa tupad sang iya iloy. Sang buhi pa ang iya amay isahanon lang sia nga nagatulog diri. Apang sang mapatay na ang iya amay, nahadlok na sia magtulog diri nga isahanon. Gani ginhingyo niya ang iloy nga magbuylog na sila sa pagtulog.

Matalikod na sia tani sa luyo sang bintana sang malawag ang iya igtalupangod sang kutingkoting sang gitara. Daw ara lang sa idalom sang iya bintana nagahalin. Matiuntion pa nangibabaw ang isa ka masubo nga ambahanon sang isa ka lalaki. Sinid-ing niya sa giha sang bintana. Si Narding. Mahapos niya ini nakilala sanglit masanag ang bulan. Nagaisahanon lang ini.

Matahom sing tingog si Narding. Bisan sin-o sa ila baryo nakahibalo sini. Sampaton man si Narding maglanton sang gitara. Daw nagapisngo ang mga kuwerdas sa iya mga tudlo.

Daw ahat lang nga pinahid ang katuloyhon nga buot na magaangkon sa iya. Wala na sia maghalin sa luyo sang bintana. Apang wala sia magpahilom sa ulitao nga ara sia nagapamati. Wala sia sing tuyo nga gawahon ang nagaharana. Buko niya pabayaan ini nga mag-amba nga mag-amba tubtob nga matak-an ini kag maghalin.

Ayhan kapin sa isa ka takna ang pag-amba ni Narding. Sa katapusan isa ka makatalandog nga salambiton ang ginpabati sini sa iya:

"Ginahandom ko ikaw, Esang.
Ginapung-aw ako kon indi ka makit-an.
Matugon lamang ang akon kahidlaw.
Kon imo ako kaluoyan.
Ihulog sa akon ang imo kaluoy.
Pamati kag dungga ining panganduhoy.
Manginmatam-is ang kamatayon.
Kon ako imo sikwayon.
Pananglit itugot ka sang kapalaran.
Sing pagpakamahal ikaw ang halaran.
Palanggaon ko ikaw sing walay langan.
Tubtob ining lawas angkunon sang lulobngan...."

Nagpabilin pa sing pila ka tion sa pagtindugon si Narding nga nagatangla sa bintana. Subong bala nga nagahulat ini nga gawahon niya. Daw luyag niya ang magkadlaw. Ang dagway ni Narding daw makalulooy nga idu nga nagahulat habuyan sing tul-an.

Nakita niya nga maluya nga naghalin si Narding. Ginsunod pa ini sang iya panulok tubtob na linamon ini sang kadulom didto sa kipawkipawon nga unhan.

Nag-igham ang iya iloy sang magbalik sia sa katre. Nagabugtaw pa gali ang tigulang.

"Abi ko anay nahamuokan ka na gid, Nay," siling ni Esang kag maghigda sa luyo sang tigulang. "Katunog na sang huragok mo kaina."

"Nakabugtaw ako sang mabatian ko nga may harana," balos sang iloy. "Abi ko anay nagadalamguhanon lang ako. Sin-o ato?"

"Ang laon bala."

"Si Narding...?"

"Sia matuod, Nay."

"Gingawa mo bala?" pakiana sang tigulang.

"Wala."

"Indi maayo ina, anak," kag magpanagutsot ang iloy. "Kaakigan ikaw sang tao."

"Maakig man sia kon maakig," kag magkadlaw si Esang. "Wala man ako magsiling sa iya nga magharana sia. Maanad lang ina kon sapakon mo. Nagaawat lang sang tulog naton."

"Payaon ka gid matuod," kag magginhawa sing madalom ang tigulang.

"Kag sia tigulang na. Kuntani ang parehas man niya nga laon ang haranahan niya," puyas ni Esang.

"Indi pa gid man tigulang si Narding. Ayhan duha ka pulo kag pito pa lang ina. Sa isa ka lalaki, bagay gid ina nga panuigon sa pagpangasawa."

"Ginatugpo mo bala sia sa akon, Nay?" pakiana ni Esang.

"Aba, baynte siy ·te kontra disisais. Indi ako."

"Kon sa bagay maayo nga pamanahon inang si Narding," pabutyag sang tigulang. "Mapisan kag wala sing entrada. Wala nagapanabako. Wala nagapahubog tulad sa iban diri nga mga pamatan-on sa baryo."

"Bisan pa, Nay. Indi ako."

"Aba, Esang, wala ko man ikaw ginasugo nga pamanahon mo sia, a," sabdong sang tigulang.

Nagakadlaw nga kinup-an ni Esang ang iya iloy. "Matulog na kita, Nay," siling niya.

Subong sang kinaandan, sa pagabot sang banagbanag sa bulotlakan, ginaguyod na niya ang ila isa ka bilog nga karabaw pakadto sa bakante nga bakulod nga katambi sang ila ulomhan. May dala sia nga alat. Tuyo niya nga maulayhon sing ulotanon

Ginalawig niya ang karabaw. Pagkatapos, mahidaiton nga nagpanglantawlantaw sia sa palibot. May manipis nga alipuop nga nagakulap sa kapatagan. Ang langit sa sidlangan abuabohon. May patimaan sang isa ka maayo nga panahon. Gikan sa iya nahamtangan ginatamdan niya ang diutay nila nga agsa. Nagakalub-asan na ang humay. Nagadul-ay ang bunga. May kalipay sia nga nabatyagan sa pagpanumdon nga maginmaayo karon ang panubason.

Sa unhan makita niya ang bulothoan sang baryo. Natungtong sa ibabaw sang bakulod kag nalibutan sang pila ka puno nga mga kahoy. Makita man niya ang mga bumolutho nga nagakatay sa pagpakadto sa bulothoan sipit ang ila mga tulon-an. May kasubo nga lumabay sa iya balatyagon. Kuntani kon buhi lang ang iya amay wala mauntat ang iya pagbutho. Apang wala sia sing utod. Kon magbutho sia wala sing kabulig ang iya iloy. Waay labot sina, wala gid sing galastuhon sa iya pagbutho. Ang mabahin nila sa ila patubas iguigo gid lang sa ila kinahanglanon sa matag-adlaw. Daw halos na gani sia makabakal sing maayuayo nga bayu.

Ginsugoran na niya ang pagdulhog sa kalbangan. Daw halos sia magtumban sa duta. Kayami sang tun-og nga nagabasa sang kahilamunan. Ginwahigwahig niya ang mga humay sa higad sang kahon diin madamo nga mga lupo kag apat-apat ang nagatubo. Nangutan sia. May pila ka nahot nga tangkong sia nga ginakutol kag mga alum-alom. Kanamit sini kon masubakan sing ginamos.

Wala lang mahibal-i kag mapuno ang iya alat. Amo pa lang sia makatungkaaw kag makamarasmas mga mataas na gali ang adlaw. Mapauli na sia. Apang daw tinumbok ang iya dughan sang matalupangdan nga wala na ang karabaw sa iya sini ginalawigan. Dalidali nga pinalapitan niya ang duog nga ginlawigan. Nakita niya nabugto ang kalat. Nanghulonghulong sia sa palibot. Wala ang hayop. Halos padalagan pinangita niya ini.

Nakita gid man niya ang hayop. Nabangot na ini sa puno sang isa ka aghu. Natingala sia. Sin-o ayhan ang nagbangot diri sang iya karabaw? Nakibot na lang sia sang mabatian ang tingog sang lalaki gikan sa iya likod nayon.

"Sa wala mo pa makuha ang imo karabaw kinahanglan gawaron mo anay," siling sang lalaki.

"Ngaa?" pakiana niya.

"Tan-awa bala," kag gintudlo ni Narding ang malapad nga hinarban sang karabaw sa iya nagakalub-asan nga humay. "Ginapabayaan mo lang ang imo karabaw. Ginhalitan niya ang akon humay. Kinahanglan bayaran mo ina."

"Huo, bayaran ko. Pila?" pasugot niya.

"Indi kuwarta ang kinahanglan ko," kag pumalapit sa iya si Narding.

Ginpadayon ni Esang ang paghubad sang iya karabaw sa ginhigtan.

"Ikaw ang kinahanglan ko, Esang," halos daw hutik nga pabutyag sang ulitao nga gin-uyatan ang mga kamot ni Esang agod punggan ini sa paghubad sang kalat sang karabaw.

Gintinguhaan ni Esang nga butongon ang iya kamot. Apang hugot kaayo ang pag-uyat ni Narding.

"Kinahanglan ko gid ikaw, Esang," padayon ni Narding. "Madugay na nga gintulotandaan ko ikaw. Halin pa sang una mo nga pagpamukadkad. Katahom mo gid, Esang. Naluyag gid ako sa imo. Kon but-on mo lang ako, mapakasal kita dayon. Palanggaon ko ikaw. Pahalipayon ko ikaw Magpati ka sa akon, Esang. Ikaw pa lang ang una nga babae nga nakapabatyag sing paghigugma sa akon kasingkasing. Ikaw ang una kag manginkatapusan nga babae nga akon pagahigugmaon. Ginasumpa ko, Esang."

"Buy-i ang kamot ko," gios ni Esang.

Hinalukan sia ni Narding. Sa pisngi. Sa bibig. Daw namakumako nga ginhibo sia sing halok ni Narding. Masingkal nga mga halok. Sa kadali sang hitabo nga wala gid niya pagaabuta. Wala sia makapanginlaman. Wala sia makalikaw. Igu mamarasmasan sia, tapos na. Ang kamatuoran daw makalilisang nga lupok nga pumansal sa iya isip. Hinalukan sia. Nahalukan na sia. Ini indi sa dalamguhanon lamang. Matuod gid nga natabo. Namag-o sia. Nangidlis. Indi ini matu-od. Indi....

Nagadalagan nga nagahibi sia. Subong sang may kalahadlukan sa duog nga ato nga luyag niya palagyuhan. Pagsampot sa ila ugsaran, daw wala sa kaugalingon nga pumongko sia sa halintang sang hagdanan. Indi sia mahim-os. Masingki ang iya balatyagon. Akig sia. Indi niya mahibal-an kon sin-o ang iya ginakaakigan. Daw luyag niya gan-iton ang iya buhok. Sang ulihi dumolhog sia sa tuboran kag magpaligo.

Sa pagligad pa sang pila ka adlaw, ang mga kapatagan nga sang wala pa lang madugay nagalagtom kon lantawon, karon nagbalhin na sang duag. Ang mga humay gulang na, nagapula na. Handa na nga anihon ukon garabon.

Madamo ang mangangani. Ang hanayap nga kapatagan sa liwat nagakibo sing kabuhi. Ang mga kabalayan kon gab-i nagasinabtanay sa pagpalagpok sang ila mga lusong sa pagpamilipig. Nagalanog tubtob magnagob ang gab-i ang tunog sang hal-o kag lusong. Maaninaw ang tagsa ka pamilya nga nagatilipon sa tupad sang lusong. May nagahiraha sang humay sa kalaha. May nagabayo sang humay nga bag-o nahiraha. Kag may nagatahop sang binayo gikan sa lusong. Ang katugnaw sang kagab-ihon indi na mabatyagan. Ang kaalabaab, ang kalipay, amo ang nagaluntad sa dughan sang tagsatagsa samtang nagapamasaw sang una nga pagkalitaw sang bunga sang ila kinabudlayan.

Nagapamahaw gid ang magiloy sina nga aga sang mabatian nila ang panagbalay sang isa ka lalaki. Gilayon sinid-ing ni Esang kon sin-o ang dumoloaw. Daw tinumbok ang iya dughan sang makita si Narding didto sa ila ugsaran. Gilayon hinakwat niya ang iya pinggan kag maggwa sa pantaw. Wala na sia matalupangdi sang iloy bangod ini na ang nagkadto sa ganhaan agod sug-alawon ang nagapanagbalay.

"Magsaka ka, Narding. Magdayon ka," nabatian ni Esang nga sug-alaw sang iya iloy sa bag-o magsampot nga ulitao.

Nabatian man niya ang paghatag sing maayong aga ni Narding sa iya iloy, samtang nagapasaka ini.

"Nakapasyar ka, Narding," nabatian niya nga pakiana sang iloy sa ulitao.

"May dala ako diri, Tya Gonda," balos ni Narding. "Baye-baye kag pilipig."

"Ay sus, ngaa nagpalibog ka pa nga bata ka. Ti, madamo gid nga salamat. Nagapamahaw gid kami subong. Magpanghinaw ka na didto sa pantaw kag magsalo," agda sang tigulang.

Dalidali nga inubos ni Esang ang unod sang iya tulanhan. Pagkatapos dayon tinusmog ang iya pinggan sa labador nga may tubi kag wala na makainom nga dumalandan panaog. Ayhan natingala gid ang iya iloy sang matalupangdan nga wala na sia sa kalan-an. Nagpangliutliot sia sa kasagingan sa likod sang ila balay kag didto magpaligad sing tinion. Kadugay gid sang iya paghukbo didto. Kadugay kay Narding magpanaog. Ginbantayan niya nga nalumbos ini ugaling magbalik sa ibabaw paagi sa pantaw nga iya man ginpanaugan kaina.

Naabtan niya nga nagakaon ang iya iloy sing baye-baye.

"Sa diin ka magkadto man, Esang?" pakiana sang iya iloy.

Wala niya pagsabta ato.

"Bag-o lang nalumbos si Narding. Gindalhan niya kita sing baye-baye. O, magkaon ka. Para gid man ini sa imo," kag magkadlaw ang tigulang.

"Basi may lumay ini," napautwas niya samtang kumohà sing baye-baye kag magkaon.

"Kon ako lang ang dalaga, indi na kinahanglan nga lumayon pa ni Narding," kag liwat magkadlaw ang tigulang. "Mapalaron ang isa ka babae nga makapamana sa iya."

Naglamho si Esang.

"Sa pamatyag ko daw may huyog sa imo si Narding," padayon sang iloy samtang padayon man ang pagkaon sing bayebaye. "Igapabugal ko nga manginumagad sia."

"Indi ako, Nay," naglungolungo si Esang.

Napundok na ang inani nga humay. Ginapalayalaya pa ini sa initan ugaling ang paglinas. Mahapos uyason ang uhay kon mapakaging ini sa initan.

Isa sina ka gab-i umolan sang mamunog. Sangiit matugnaw, maaga pa magtulog ang mag-iloy. Mga tungang gab-i na sang makabugtaw si Esang. Nakibot sia sang mabatyagan ang pag-alipasa sang mga manok sa idalom sang ila balay. Nanilag sia kag wala madugayi naathagan niya ang nagadaludo nga tubi sa silong. May baha. Nagasalangisag nga pinukaw niya ang iloy. Buylog sila nga lumantaw sa bintana. Ang mga wayang nasul-ob na sang tubi. Daw baybayon ini nga nagaputi.

Gilayon nanaog si Esang nga ginsulay ang nagabagusbos gihapon nga ulan.

"Diin ka makadto?" pakiana sang iloy.

"Ang aton inani, Nay. Takdan ko ang karusa kag hakuton sa takas." Kag nangindulaan si Esang sa nagabagusbos nga ulan. Makahaladlok ang unos. Ang tubig nagadugang sa pagdalom. Manaog man tani si Tya Gonda apang napamatyagan niya nga daw makusog sia sa katugnaw. Gani ginpakamaayo na lang niya nga magpabilin. Kuntani punggan niya si Esang. Nahangawa sia basi mahamak pa ini. Apang malayo na ang lin-ay nga nagasakay sa karusa.

Gintultol ni Esang ang tinumpihan sang ila inani nga humay. Wala na sia sing tinumpokan nga nakita. Puro tubig na lang ang makita niya sa ila ulomhan. Kon amo ulihi na sia. Inanod na sang baha ang ila inani. Wala niya mapunggi ang paghibi.

"Ang amon humay... ang amon humay...," panalambiton niya sa daku nga paghinakit.

Nakatungkaaw sia sang matalupangdan ang nagagarhom nga landong nga umolhot gikan sa takas. Nagsakay ini sa karabaw nga may ginaguyod nga karusa. Wala niya ini makilala gilayon kon wala ini magdulog sa iya nahamtangan kag magpanaog gikan sa likod sang karabaw. Si Narding.

"Ikaw gali, Esang," nakibot nga tamyaw sang ulitao.

"Tapos na ang amon tumpi," may paghinakit nga nasambit niya.

"Wala maano ang inyo tumpi, Esang," pasayod ni Narding. "Naurot ko gid man hakot sa takas ugaling magdalom ang tubig."

"Ginhakot mo, Narding?" daw indi makapati nga napautwas niya. "Ang sa inyo tumpi?"

"Una ko nga ginhakot ang amon. Sang mabatyagan ko nga daw nagadugay ang ulan, gilayon gintakdan ko ang karusa kag sugoran ang paghakot. Pagkatapos sang amon gindason ko ang sa inyo. Sanglit nahibal-an ko nga wala kamo sing masaligan nga magahakot, ako na ang nagmatumato," panaysayon ni Narding.

Indi na niya nabungat ang kadaku sang nabatyagan niya nga pagpasalamat. Sang hingyuon sia ni Narding nga magpasilong sila anay sa isa ka payag nga wala sing tao, mahipos nga nagpasugot sia. Ginhukasan nila ang ila mga karabaw kag ibangot sa puno sang kamunsil nga yara sa luyo sang payag. Pareho sila nga nagakurog sa katugnaw.

"Esang," siling ni Narding matiuntion sang yara na sila sa sulod sang payag. "Luyag ko nga manginkabulig ninyo sang imo iloy tubtob san-o. Mapakasal kita, Esang."

"Indi ako," mahinay niya nga sabat.

Nabatyagan niya ang pagtupa sang kamot ni Narding sa iya abaga.

"Ginatugnawan ka, Narding," nabungat niya nga nagasako ang pagkubakoba sang dughan. "Maayo pa magpauli na kita agod makailis ka."

"Indi ulos ang kinahanglan ko," balos ni Narding samtang ginaamat sia sing hakos. "Ikaw ang kinahanglan ko, Esang. Agod makabatyag man sing kaalabaab ining akon dughan."

"Indi, Narding, indi...," nabungat niya sang mabatyagan nga nagapanginsapo na ang mga bibig ni Narding.

Apang wala man sia magtinguha nga maglikaw. Nahibaloan niya nga ang iya balatyagon wala nagapamatok.

From: *Hiligaynon,* March 22, 1972

Harvest Time

(Tig-alani)

Antonio H. Joquiño

It was a little cloudy that afternoon. At twilight, it drizzled lightly. But just for a short while. A gentle breeze blew now and then. Slowly, the sky cleared, and then shone forth the bright moon and the many stars.

Esang was sitting by the slightly open window. She saw the light cast by the moon all around her, on the grass now moistened by the shower. In the distance, stalks of ripened grain cast their shadow upon the vast ricefields. The cool wind wafted the fragrance of mature grain. In no time, hunger should be leaving the barrio threshold, she told herself.

Her mother was already snoring in their bed. Soon after dinner, she had prepared their beddings and now she was all curled up. It was a cool evening and yielding to the bed's warmth was truly pleasant.

A rooster crowed. Ah, the night was far gone. She yawned. Yes, it was time to sleep. The warmth of her mother's bedside was luring her now. When her father was alive, she would sleep by herself in another room. But when he died, she was afraid to be there by herself. So she asked her mother if she could sleep by her side.

She was about to turn away when she caught the soft strumming of a guitar. In a little while rose the plaintive voice of a man. She peered through a small hole in the window. It was Narding. It was easy to recognize him because the moon was bright. He was alone.

Narding could sing well. Everyone in their barrio knew this. And he could play the guitar so skillfully that the strings seemed to weep as he plucked them.

Now her sleepiness was wiped away. She continued sitting by the window, but she did not let the serenader know that she was there listening. She had no intention of letting him in. She meant to have him sing away until he got so tired that he would leave.

Narding must have serenaded her for about an hour. In the end, he dedicated to her this touching love song:

"I long for you Esang.
I feel lonely when I don't see you
For my loneliness
Only your love will suffice.
Bestow your kindness on me
And listen to my plea.
Only death shall I want
If my love for you is spurned.
Should fortune favor,
My love to you I shall offer.
A love that shall only end
When this body the grave shall claim."

Narding stood a few more moments, his face lifted to the window, as if he was expecting an invitation to come into the house. But Esang just felt like laughing. His face was like that of a pitiable dog waiting for bones to be thrown to him.

She saw that Narding looked weary. She watched him walk away until he was swallowed up in the dimness ahead.

Esang's mother hemmed slightly as her daughter made ready for bed. The old woman was still up, after all.

"I thought you were already sound asleep, 'Nay," Esang said as she lay down beside her mother. "You were snoring very loudly a while ago."

"I woke up when I heard someone serenading," answered her mother. "I thought at first I was just dreaming. Who was it?"

"Oh, the old batch."

"Narding...?"

"Yes 'Nay."

"Did you look out of the window?" the old woman asked.

"No."

"Ch! Ch! That was unkind, my daughter. You shouldn't have done that. He will get mad at you."

"Let him!" Then she laughed. "No one told him to serenade me. If you mind him, he might get into this habit and keep us awake late into the night."

"Aah, you're really young," sighed the old woman.

"And he's old. He should serenade a spinster like himself."

"Narding is not old. He must be only about 27. For a man that's the best time to get married."

"Are you pushing me to accept him, 'Nay? What, twenty-seven against sixteen! I won't hear of that."

"Come to think of it, Narding is a fine young man to marry," her mother reflected. "He's hardworking and has no vices. He doesn't smoke or drink too much unlike many young men in this barrio."

"So what, 'Nay. I just don't like him!"

"Don't get me wrong, Esang. I'm not forcing you to like him," she made this clear to her daughter.

As she was wont to do at daybreak, Esang was now dragging their only carabao up the hill adjacent to their farm. She was carrying a basket for the vegetables she would gather. Leisurely, she looked around her. There was a thin fog that veiled the field. The sky in the east was a greyish white. A sign of good weather. From where she was standing, she viewed the small farm they were leasing. Rice stalks were bent low with clusters of ripened grain. She was pleased to think that the harvest would be abundant.

On top of another hill across her stood the barrio elementary school surrounded by trees. Schoolchildren were filing towards the building, clasping their schoolthings under their armpits. Sadness flitted through her. If only her father were alive, she wouldn't have stopped schooling. But she was the only child. If she went to school, there'd be no one to help her mother. Besides, they had nothing at all to spend for schooling. Their share in the harvest was just enough for their daily needs. In fact, she could barely buy decent clothes.

She started walking downhill. She could hardly step on the grass; it was cold from the dew. She drew aside the rice stalks by the mound of earth enclosing the ricefield. A lot of *lupo* and *apat-apat* grew on this patch. She gathered a few stalks of *kangkong* and *alum-alom*. These would taste good with *bagoong*.

She filled up her basket with these, and before she realized it, the sun had fully risen. She had to go. But something ran through her heart when she noticed that her carabao was no longer where she had tethered it. She hurried to the spot and found that the leash had snapped. She looked about her but the carabao was nowhere to be found.

When finally she caught sight of the animal, it was already tied to an *aghu* tree. She was puzzled. Who could have done this? Just then, a voice from behind startled her.

"You can't just get back your carabao; you've got to redeem it first," the man told her.

"Why?"

"See," Narding showed her a wide swathe the carabao had sliced off from his rice bed. "You leave it to roam around. He has spoiled my palay, and you must pay for that."

"Okay, how much?"

"It's not money I need," Narding said as he drew close to her.

"It's you I need, Esang," the man whispered softly as he stopped her from unhitching the animal. She tried to pull her arm away, but he held her tight.

"I need you, Esang," Narding continued. "Ever since you blossomed into a woman, I've set my eyes on you. You're so beautiful. I'm very fond of you. If you'll only accept my love, we shall get married right away. I will try very much to make you happy. Trust me. You're the first and the last woman I shall love."

"Keep your hands off me," Esang brushed him away.

But Narding kissed her—with burning passion. On the cheek. On the mouth. Smothered her with kisses. It all happened so quickly, she was caught unaware and was unable to dodge him. Before she could get her bearings, it was all over. The reality was like an explosion that resonated in her ears. He had kissed her. She had been kissed. This wasn't just a dream. She was aghast.

Crying, she ran off. As if there was something terrifying from which she wanted to flee. When she reached their house, she sat on the staircase, dazed. She was mad but she didn't know what she was mad about. She felt like pulling her hair. Later, she walked down to the spring and took a bath.

The ricefields which just shortly before were dark green have now changed colors. Fully mature, the palay has turned red. It is ready to be harvested with the rice-cutter or the sickle. Many turn out for the harvest and the vast field has come alive again. The households resound with the pounding of *pilipig*. Each family gathers around a huge mortar and pestle till late at night. Some members roast rice in the big *kalaha*; others pound this roasted rice; still others shift the chaff from the pounded grain. No one feels the coldness of the night, only the warmth and the joy of savoring the first fruits of labor.

Esang and her mother were taking breakfast when someone called out. At once, Esang peeped out to check on who had dropped by. Narding was standing by the staircase. Something twinged in her chest. She took her plate from the table and walked out to the *pantaw*, the kitchen balcony. Her mother had gotten up to open the door and didn't notice her leave.

"Come on up, Narding," Esang heard her say to the man. She heard him greet her mother too.

"You've dropped in, Narding?"

"I've brought you something, *Tiya* Gonda. *Baye-baye* and *pilipig* for breakfast."

"*Ay, sus*, you didn't have to bother. Come, join us. Go wash your hands in the *pantaw*."

When Esang heard this, she gobbled up her food from the bowl. Then quickly, she dunked it in the wash basin and without taking a drink, she dashed down the stairs. Her mother must have been wondering now where she had gone. She threaded her way through the grove of banana trees behind the house and stayed there for a while, killing time. Narding took so long. It was quite a while before she could go up to the *pantaw* again.

Her mother was eating *baye-baye*. "Where have you been, Esang?"

She did not answer.

"Narding has just left. Come on, have some of these. These are really for you, I know." The old woman laughed.

"He might have put some love potion in here," Esang said as she took some *baye-baye*.

"If I were the woman, Narding wouldn't have to use a love potion on me. The woman who gets to marry him is lucky."

Esang suppressed a giggle.

"He's trying to woo you. I'll be proud to have him as a son-in-law."

"But 'Nay, I don't like him."

The rice has now been collected into heaps. It is to be dried in the sun before treading. It would be easy to thresh out the chaff from the grain if the palay were dry.

One night, there was a heavy downpour. Because it was cold, Esang and her mother had gone to bed early. By midnight Esang was awakened by the bustling of their chicken under the house. She jumped up, looked out of the window, and in just a few moments, she made out water rising on the ground. They were getting flooded! Frantic, she woke her mother up. When both looked out, the field was like a glimmering sea. Esang scurried down the stairs to brave the pounding rain.

"Where are you going?" her mother asked.

"Our harvest, Mother. I'll hitch the cart to the carabao to haul up our harvest to high ground."

Esang disappeared quickly in the rain. The current was frightening, and the water continued to rise. *Tiya* Gonda wanted to follow but she was shivering from the cold. She thought of holding back her daughter for she was worried about what may happen to her. But the young girl had already wheeled off.

All that Esang could see was water. So, she had come too late. The flood had already swept their harvest away. She could not stop herself from crying.

"Our rice...our rice...."

But she raised her head when she noticed a figure looming on the high ground. It was riding astride a carabao pulling a cart. She couldn't make out who it was until it was right by her. Narding.

"So it's you, Esang." He looked surprised to see her.

"Our rice..., our rice is gone," she moaned.

"Nothing happened to your rice. Your rice is safe, Esang. I carted it up to high ground before water could rise."

"You did, Narding?" she asked in disbelief.

"When I sensed that the rain would drag on, I tied the cart to our carabao at once and started hauling. First, our rice and then yours. I know you have no one to bring your rice up to dry ground so I did it myself."

Esang was so grateful, she couldn't say anything. When Narding asked her to take shelter in a vacant hut nearby she followed him meekly. They unhitched the carts from their carabaos and tied them to the *kamunsil* tree. They were both trembling from the cold.

"Esang," Narding said just after they had gone into the hut. "I'd like to be of help to you and your mother always. I want to marry you, Esang."

"No," Esang whispered softly.

She felt Narding's hands fall on her shoulders.

"You are cold, Narding," she managed to say, her heart beating very fast. "We'd better go home so you can change."

"It's not clothes I need," Narding answered while slowly he took her in his arms. "It is you I need, Esang."

"No, Narding, no...." She felt Narding's urgent lips.

But she did not draw back. She knew now that she no longer loathed him.

Tag-ani

Antonio H. Joquiño

May pagkamaulap nang hapong iyon. Umambon nang kaunti pagdating ng takipsilim. Saglit lang. Umihip-ihip ang hangin. Unti-unting nahawan ang langit at nagpakita ang maliwanag na buwan at maraming bituin.

Nakaupo si Esang sa tabi ng bintanang bahagyang bukas. Nakita niya ang sinag ng buwan sa palibot, sa mga damong nabasa ng ambon. Sa unahan, sa malawak na kapatagan, dumidilim na halos ang mga magulang na palay. Nalanghap niya ang halimuyak ng gumugulang na palay, sabay ng dapyo ng malamig na hangin. Hindi tatagal, lalayo na ang gutom sa kanilang mga pintuan, naibulong niya sa sarili.

Humihilik na ang kanyang ina sa higaan nila. Pagkatapos lang nilang maghapunan, agad itong naghanda ng kanilang higaan at namaluktot. Dahil sa kalamigan, masarap ang magpasakop sa init na alok ng higaan. Tumilaok ang tandang na manok sa unahan. Ay naku, gabi na! Humikab siya. Unang hikab. Siguro, oras nang matulog. Parang may humahatak sa kanyang lasapin ang init ng higaan sa tabi ng kanyang ina. Nang buhay pa ang kanyang ama, mag-isa lang siyang natutulog dito. Subalit nang mamatay na ito, natakot siyang matulog dito nang mag-isa. Kaya't pinakiusapan niya ang kanyang ina na magkasama na silang matulog.

Tatalikuran na sana niya ang bintana nang tinawag ang kanyang pansin ng pagkalabit ng gitara. Parang sa may ibaba lang ng kanyang bintana. Ilang sandali pa, nangibabaw ang malungkot na awitin ng isang lalaki. Sumilip siya sa pagitan ng bintana. Si Narding. Agad niya itong nakilala dahil maliwanag ang buwan. Nag-iisa siya.

Maganda ang boses ni Narding. Kahit sino sa kanilang baryo ay alam ito. Mahusay rin si Narding na tumugtog ng gitara. Tila humihikbi ang mga kwerdas sa kaniyang daliri.

Parang pilit lang na napahid ang antok na tangkang umangkin sa kanya. Hindi na siya umalis sa tabi ng bintana. Ngunit hindi niya ipinahalata sa binatang nakikinig siya. Wala siyang balak dungawin ang naghaharana. Balak niyang pabayaan itong umawit nang umawit hanggang magsawa at umalis.

May isang oras ding nagharana si Narding. Sa katapusan, isang makabagbag-pusong awit ang ipinarinig sa kanya:

"Nanabik ako sa iyo Esang,
Nalulumbay ako kung di kita makita.
Itong pangungulila, matutugon lang,
Kung ako'y iyong kahabagan.
Ihulog mo sa akin ang iyong awa.
Pakinggan mo at pansinin itong pusong nagsusumamo.
Kamataya'y maging mas matamis pa
Kung ikaw'y tumanggi.
Kung sakaling sa akin idulot ka ng kapalaran
Ang pagmamahal sa iyo'y ihahandog ko.
Mamahalin kita nang walang hanggan
Hanggang buhay ko'y angkinin ng libingan."

Nanatiling nakatingala si Narding sa bintana ng may ilang sandali pa. Para bang naghihintay na dungawin siya. Ang mukha niya'y parang kawawang asong naghihintay hagisan ng buto.

Nakita niyang matamlay na umalis si Narding. Sinundan niya ito ng tingin hanggang malamon sa kalamlaman sa unahan. Tumikhim ang kanyang ina nang bumalik si Esang sa kama. Gising pa pala ang matanda.

"Abi ko mahimbing na gid ang tulog mo, 'Nay," sabi ni Esang at humiga sa tabi ng matanda. "Malakas na ang hilik mo kanina."

"Nagising ako nang maulinigan kong may naghaharana," ang tugon ng ina. "Akala ko nang una, nananaginip lang ako. Sin-o iyon?"

"E, ang laon bala."

"Si Narding?"

"Iyon na nga, 'Nay."

"Dinungaw mo ba?"

"Indi."

"Indi mabuti iyan, anak, " at umiling ang ina. "Magagalit sa iyo ang tao."

"Magalit siya kung magalit," at tumawa si Esang. "Indi ko naman siya sinabihang magharana sa akin. Masasanay lang iyan kung papansinin ko. Makakaabala lang sa tulog naton."

"Bata ka pa gid ya," at huminga nang malalim ang matanda.

"At siya'y matanda na. Sana, katulad din niyang laon ang haranahin niya," pamimintas ni Esang.

"Indi pa naman matanda si Narding. Siguro may dalawampu't pitong taon lang iyan. Sa isang lalaki, tamang-tamang edad ina sa pagpangasawa."

"Ginaparis mo bala siya sa akon, 'Nay?" tanong ni Esang. "Aba, beinte-siete kontra disesais? Indi ako."

"Kung sa bagay mabuting mapamanahon ina si Narding," pagtatapat ng matanda. "Masipag at walang bisyo. Hindi nananabako o naglalasing tulad ng ibang kabataan sa baryo."

"Kahit na, Inay. Indi ako."

"Aba, Esang, indi naman kita ginautusang pamanahun siya, a," pinagsabihan siya ng matanda.

Tumatawang niyakap ni Esang ang kanyang ina. "Matulog na tayo, 'Nay," sabi niya.

Tulad nang kinaugalian, sa pagbanaag ng liwanag sa silangan, hinihila na ni Esang ang kanilang kalabaw patungo sa bakanteng burol na karatig ng lupang kanilang sinasakahan. May dala siyang buslo. Ibig niyang mamitas ng gulay.

Itinali niya ang kalabaw. Pagkatapos, masaya niyang tinanaw ang kanyang palibot. Natakpan ng manipis na ulap ang kapatagan. Parang abo ang langit sa silangan. Nagpapahiwatig ng magandang panahon. Mula sa kanyang kinatatayuan, minasdan niya ang maliit nilang inuupahan. Magulang na ang mga palay. Hutok ang mga palay sa bunga. Nakaramdam siya ng kasiyahan sa pag-iisip na sagana ngayon ang ani.

Sa unahan, nakita niya ang paaralan ng baryo. Nakatuntung ito sa isang burol at nalilibutan ng ilang punungkahoy. Nakita rin niya ang ilang mag-aaral na nakahanay nang papasok sa paaralan, ipit-ipit ang kanilang mga libro. Nakadama siya ng panandaliang lungkot. Kung buhay lang ang kanyang ama, hindi sana natigil ang kanyang pag-aaral. Subalit wala siyang kapatid. Kung mag-aaral siya, walang katulong ang kanyang ina. Bukod pa rito, talagang wala silang pantustos sa kanyang pag-aaral. Tamang-tama lang ang parte nila sa kanilang ani sa pang-araw-araw na pangangailangan. Halos hindi na nga siya makabili ng maayos-ayos na damit.

Nagsimula na siyang bumaba sa daan. Halos hindi siya makahakbang. Kaylamig ng hamog na bumasa sa damuhan. Hinabi niya ang mga palay sa gilid ng mga kahon na kung saan maraming lupo at apat-apat na nangagsitubo. Namitas siya ng panggulay. May ilang pirasong kangkong at alom-alom siyang napitas. Ang sasarap nito kung malahukan ng bagoong. Hindi niya napansing puno na pala ang kanyang buslo. Nang tumingala siya, mataas na ang araw. Uuwi na siya. Subalit sinundot ang kanyang dibdib nang mapansin niyang wala na ang kalabaw roon sa kanyang pinagtalian. Dali-dali niyang tinungo iyon. Patid na ang tali. Minalas niya ang kanyang palibot. Wala ang hayop. Halos patakbong hinanap niya ito.

Nakita na rin niya ang hayop. Nakatali na ito sa puno ng aghu. Nagtaka siya. Sino kaya ang nagtali rito ng kanyang kalabaw? Nagulat na lamang siya nang marinig ang tinig ng lalaki sa may likuran niya.

"Indi mo pa makukuha ang iyong kalabaw, kailangang tubusin mo muna," ang sabi ng lalaki.

"Bakit?" tanong niya.

"Tingnan mo, o," at itinuro ni Narding ang malapad na inukaban nito sa kanyang magulang na palay. "Ginapabayaan mo ang kalabaw mo. Nilaruan niya ang aking palay. Kailangang bayaran mo ina."

"Huo, bayaran ko. Magkano?" pagsang-ayon niya.

"Esang, indi kuwarta ang kailangan ko," at lumapit sa kanya si Narding.

Itinuloy ni Esang ang pagkalas sa kalabaw.

"Ikaw ang kailangan ko, Esang," halos pabulong na ipinagtapat sa kanya ng binata. Hinawakan nito ang mga kamay ni Esang at pinigil ang pagkalas sa kalabaw.

Sinikap ni Esang na hatakin ang kanyang mga kamay. Subalit napakahigpit ang pagkahawak ni Narding.

"Kailangan gid kita, Esang," dagdag ni Narding. "Matagal na kitang napapansin. Mula't sapol pa ng iyong unang pamumukadkad. Napakaganda mo, Esang. Gustung-gusto kita.

Kung iibigin mo lang ako, magapakasal kita agad. Palanggaon kita. Paliligayahin. Magtiwala ka sa akin, Esang. Ikaw ang unang babaing nakapagpatibok sa aking puso. Ikaw ang una at kahuli-hulihang babaing aking iibigin. Isinusumpa ko, Esang."

"Bitiwan mo ang kamay ko," pagtabig ni Esang.

Hinalikan siya ni Narding. Sa pisngi. Sa bibig. Parang sabik na sabik na hinagod siya ng halik ni Narding. Maalab na halik. Napakadali ng pangyayari; hindi niya inaasahan. Hindi siya nakapag-ingat. Hindi siya nakaiwas. Nang siya'y nahinahunan na, tapos na ang lahat. Ang katotohanan na parang nakakalitong putok na gumulo sa kanyang isip. Hinalikan siya. Nahalikan siya. Hindi ito panaginip lamang. Talagang totoo ang nangyari. Nanibago siya. Nanhilakbot. Hindi ito totoo. Hindi...hindi....

Tumakbo siya, mangiyak-ngiyak. Parang may kinatatakutan sa lugar na iyon na ibig niyang iwasan. Pagdating sa kanila, wala sa loob na umupo siya sa paanan ng kanilang hagdanan. Hindi siya mapakali. Mainit ang kanyang pakiramdam. Galit siya. Hindi niya alam kung sino ang kanyang kinagagalitan. Parang ibig niyang bunutin ang kanyang buhok. Matapos ang ilang sandali pumunta siya sa paliguan at naligo.

Pagkalipas pa ng ilang araw, ang kapatagan na kamakailan lang ay berdeng matingkad, umiba na ang kulay. Magulang na ang mga palay, nangagsipula. Handa nang anihin o gapasin.

Marami ang mang-aani. Ang malawak na kapatagan ay tumitibok uli ng buhay. Kung gabi, nagsasagutan ang mga bahay sa paglagapak ng kani-kanilang lusong sa pagpipinipig. Tumutunog hanggang kalaliman ng gabi ang halo at lusong. Maaninag ang bawat pamilyang nangagtitipon sa tabi ng lusong. May naghahalo ng palay sa kawali. May nagbabayo ng palay na bagong halo. At may nagbibistay ng binayo sa lusong. Hindi na naramdaman ang lamig ng gabi. Ang kasiglahan, ang kasiyahan—iyon ang namayani sa puso ng bawa't isa habang lumalasap ng unang bunga ng kanilang pinaghirapan.

Nag-aalmusal ang mag-ina nang marinig nila ang pagta-taopo ng isang lalaki. Agad sinilip ni Esang kung sino ang dumalaw. Parang sinundot ang kanyang dibdib nang makita si Narding sa kanilang ugsaran. Agad niyang iniligpit ang kanyang pinggan at lumabas sa batalan. Hindi na siya napansin ng kanyang ina dahil ito na ang pumunta sa pintuan para tanggapin ang nagpataopo.

"Umakyat ka, Narding. Tuloy," narinig ni Esang ang pagtanggap ng kanyang ina sa kararating lang na binata.

Narinig din niya ang pagbati ng magandang umaga ni Narding habang ito'y umaakyat.

"Nagpasyal ka, Narding," narinig niyang tanong ng kanyang ina sa binata.

"May dala ako diri, Tiya Gonda," sagot ni Narding. "Baye-baye at pinipig."

"Ay, sus, ngaa ka pa nag-abala, bata ka. Ti, maraming salamat na lang. Hustung-husto sa almusal. Hugasan mong kamay mo sa pantaw at makisalo," ang paanyaya ng matanda.

Dali-daling inubos ni Esang ang pagkain sa kanyang pinggan. Pagkatapos sinawsaw ito sa palangganang may tubig at tumakbong panaog nang di na nakainom. Siguro nagtaka talaga ang kanyang ina nang mapunang wala siya sa mesa. Nagpasikut-sikot siya sa kasagingan sa likuran ng kanilang bahay, at doon nagpalipas ng panahon. Matagal siyang nagtago .roon. Kaytagal manaog ni Narding. Hinintay niyang umalis ito bago bumalik sa itaas padaan sa batalan na pinanaugan niya kanina.

Nadatnan niyang kumakain ang ina ng baye-baye.

"Saan ka man pumunta, Esang?" tanong ng kanyang ina.

Hindi niya sinagot ito.

"Kaalis lang ni Narding. Gingdalhan niya tayo ng baye-baye. O, kain na. Sa iyo naman talaga ito," at tumawa ang matanda.

"Baka may gayuma ito," inihinga niya ang pangamba habang kumuha ng baye-baye.

"Kung ako lang ang dalaga, indi na ako kailangan pang gayumahin ni Narding," at muling tumawa ang matanda. "Mapalad ang babaing mapapangasawa niya."

Humagikgik si Esang.

"Sa tingin ko, may gusto sa iyo si Narding," patuloy ng ina habang patuloy rin ang pagnguya ng baye-baye. "Maipagmamalaki ko siyang manugang."

"Indi ako, 'Nay," iiling-iling si Esang.

Naitumpik na ang naaning palay. Pinapatuyu-tuyo pa ito sa initan bago ibistay. Madaling matanggal ang ipa kung napatuyo na ang palay sa initan.

Isang gabi, bumuhos ang ulan. Dahil maginaw, maaga pang natulog ang mag-ina. Bandang hatinggabi na nang magising si Esang. Nagulat siya nang maramdaman ang pag-iingay ng mga manok sa ilalim ng kanilang bahay. Nagmatyag siya at di nagtagal nakita niya ang tumataas na tubig sa silong. Bumabaha. Litung-lito na ginising niya ang kanyang ina. Sabay silang dumungaw sa bintana. Nalubog na ang mga bakanteng lupa. Parang dagat itong kumikinang.

Agad pumanaog si Esang at sinalubong ang bumubuhos pa ring ulan.

"Saan ka pupunta?" tanong ng ina.

"Ang ating inani, 'Nay. Ikakabit ko ang karosa at hahakutin ang palay sa taas." At nawala si Esang sa bumubuhos na ulan. Palalim nang palalim ang tubig. Mananaog din sana si Tiya Gonda, pero naramdaman niyang parang nanginginig siya sa ginaw. Kaya't minabuti na niyang magpaiwan. Sana pipigilin niya si Esang. Nangangamba siyang baka mapahamak ito. Ngunit malayo na ang dalagang nakasakay sa karosa.

Hinanap ni Esang ang pinagtumpukan ng kanilang inaning palay. Hindi na niya makita ang kanilang mandala. Puro tubig na lang ang kanilang sakahan. Kung gayon, huli na siya. Inanod na ng baha ang kanilang inani. Hindi niya napigilang umiyak.

"Ang aming palay...ang aming palay...," ang panambitan niya sa laki ng panghihinayang.

Napatingala siya nang mapansin ang madilim na aninong sumulpot sa dakong itaas. Nakasakay ito sa kalabaw na may hinihilang karosa. Hindi niya ito nakilala kung hindi lumapit sa kanyang kinatatayuan at umibis sa kalabaw. Si Narding.

"Ikaw gali, Esang," gulat na binati siya ng binata.

"Wala na ang aming mandala," nasambit niyang masama ang loob.

"Walang nangyari sa mandala niyo, Esang," ipinabatid sa kanya ni Narding. "Nahakot ko silang lahat paitaas bago lumalim ang tubig."

"Ginhakot mo, Narding?" nasabi niya na parang hindi makapaniwala. "Ang sa inyo?"

"Una ko ginghakot ang amin. Nang maramdaman kong talagal ang ulan, agad kong ikinabit ang karosa at nag-umpisang maghakot. Pagkatapos ng sa amin, sinunod ko ang sa inyo. Alam kong wala kayong inaasahan, kaya't ako na ang nagkusa," ang kwento ni Narding.

Hindi na niya nakuhang masabi ang kaylaki niyang pasasalamat. Nang hiniling ni Narding na magpasilong sila muna sa isang bakanteng kubo, tahimik siyang sumunod. Kinalas nila ang kanilang kalabaw at itinali ang mga ito sa punong-kamatsile sa tabi ng kubo. Kapwa silang nanginginig sa ginaw.

"Esang," ang sabi ni Narding matapos ang ilang sandali sa kubo. "Ibig kong laging makatulong sa inyong mag-ina. Magpakasal na tayo, Esang."

"Indi ako," marahan siyang sumagot.

Naramdaman niya ang kamay ni Narding sa kanyang balikat.

"Giniginaw ka, Narding," nasabi niyang matindi ang kaba ng kanyang dibdib. "Mabuti pa umuwi na tayo para makapagbihis ka."

"Indi damit ang kailangan ko," sagot ni Narding habang dahan-dahan siyang niyayakap. "Ikaw ang kailangan ko, Esang. Para makaramdam din ng init itong aking dibdib."

"Indi, Narding, indi...," nasabi niya nang maramdaman niyang nagmamadali na ang mga labi ni Narding.

Ngunit hindi naman siya nagpumilit umiwas. Alam niya, hindi na tutol ngayon ang kanyang puso.

Appendix

Selected Bibliography of Materials Relating to Translation in Hiligaynon

The following list includes translated works into and from Hiligaynon as well as tools for translation like dictionaries and grammar books. Bilingual materials are likewise included. Corridos in Hiligaynon are listed here as translations, with the rationale explained in Chapter 3. The corrido entries are those available at the University of the Philippines in the Visayas (UPV). About seventy-eight (78) more are found in the H.H. Bartlett Collection of the American Philosophical Library in Philadelphia (available in microfilm at the University of the Philippines, Diliman, UPD) but these will be dealt with in my forthcoming book, *Siday*: Hiligaynon *Folk Poetry* to be published by the Ateneo University Press. Most of the entries published during the Spanish period are taken from Doris Varner Walsh's *Checklist of Philippine Linguistics in the Newberry Library*, Chicago, Illinois, 1950 and *A Catalogue of Printed Materials Relating to the Philippine Islands* 1519-1900 *at the Newberry Library* (Chicago, Illinois: Newberry Library, 1959) (NBL). The library where each entry may be found is indicated by an abbreviation at the end of each entry. A good number of works are found in the U.P. Visayas in Iloilo (UPV). There are various other sources, though: Henry Otley Beyer's Philippine Ethnographic Series' volumes on Bisaya (BEY-UPD/Yale/ Harvard), Encarnacion Gonzaga's thesis on Bisayan Literature done in 1917 at the U.P.(Gon.), the C.R. Boxer Collection at Indiana University at Bloomington, Indiana (IU), E.A. Manuel's *Philippine Folklore Bibliography. A Preliminary Survey* Philippine Folklore Society, 1965 (EAM-U.P.), Isagani R. Medina, comp. and ed. *Filipiniana Materials in the National Library*, (Quezon City: University of the Philippines Press, 1971) NL. The sugilanons translated from Tagalog to Hiligaynon in the period 1936-1938 are found in the collection of *Hiligaynon* in the library of Liwayway Publishing, Inc. in Pasong Tamo, Makati, Philippines (LW). The initials above will be used to indicate the location of the entry.

I. Religious Works

Alvarez, Jose, 1804-1853. Devocion cag trisagio sa iloy sang Dios nga nalapuip sa Puente Celestial sang M.R.P. Fr. Jose Alvarez. Manila: Amigos del Pais, 1882, 15 pp. (NBL)

______________. Escalera del cielo. En idioma Panayano por el M.R.P. 3rd ed. Manila: Amigos del Pais, 1883, 19 pp. (NBL)

Alvarez, Lorenzo. Pagtolon-an sang mga Cristianos nga guinquinatchila ni Padre Lorenzo Alvarez habilitado sini nga obispado cag guinpaimprenta sang Leandro Arrue, Tambobong, 1893, 74 pp. (NBL)

Ang Daan nga Katipan. Manila: Philippine Agency-American Bible Society, 1914, 1125 pp. (NBL)

Ang Bag-ong Katipan Sang Aton Ginoong Jesucristo. Manila: Philippine Agency-American Bible Society, 1914. (NBL)

Avanceña, Anselmo, 1809-1882. Novena ni Señor San Roque, nga guinbinisaya sa pulong nga Hiligaynon ni Padre Anselmo Avancena. Manila: Amigo del Pais, 1882, 16 pp. (NBL)

______________. Novena sang mahimayaon nga bantog nga Virgen cag martir Santa Filomena nga guinbinisaya sa pulong nga Hiligaynon ni D. Anselmo Avanceña. Manila: Amigos del Pais, 1883, 31 pp. (NBL)

Butiña, Francisco, 1834-. Quinabuhi ni Santa Zita, criada o hinuptan. Guinbuhat sa quinachila ni Padre Francisco Butiña, cag guinbinisaya ni Mariano Perfecto. Manila: Imprenta de Sta. Cruz, 1886, 30 pp. (NBL)

Claret y Clara, Antonio Maria abp., 1807-1870. Mga maximas nga espirituhanon con talamdan sang mga pamatan-on sing sang Cristianos nga matuud, guinsulat ni Antonio Maria Claret cag ginbinisaya ni Mariano Perfecto. Manila: Imprenta D. Esteban Balbas, 1890, 64 pp. (NBL)

Cuartero y Medina, Mariano, 1813-1884. Arte del idioma Bisaya-Hiligaino que se habla en Panay y en algunas islas adjacentes. Guadalupe: Asilo de Huerfanos, 1890. (NBL)

Da-igon sa Noche Buena o Natividad sang Niño Jesus. Manila: Imprenta de Santa Cruz, 1885, 32 pp. (NBL, NL)

Gayacao, Juan. Nuevo vocabulario y guia de conversaciones Español-Panayano, 2nd ed. Manila: Plana y C. a, 1879. (First ed. in 1875)? (NBL)

Goles, Isidro, trans. Novena ni Sta. Isabel nga hari sa Ungria, mananabang sa obispado sa Salog. Hinuad sa binisaya nga panayanon sang presbitero Isidro Goles. Manila: Sto. Tomas, 1875, 36 pp. (NL)

Istoria ni Sta Isabela sa ginharian sa Portugal. Guinbinisaya ni N.P. de P. Iloilo City: La Panayana, n.d. 24 pp. In verse. (UPV)

Lara, Fernando de, 1705-1733? Novena sa pagtahud con Jesus, Maria y Josef Trinidad dinhi sa duta, nga among ginatauag sang masunsun nga gayud sang tanan nga mga Cristianos. Binuhat sang Fernando de Lara cag guinbinisaya ni Mariano Perfecto. Manila: Amigos del Pais, 1884. (NL, NBL)

Loyola, Ignacio de, San 1497-1556. Manga ejercicios espirituales sa pulong nga Hiligaynon nga binanggui sang isa ca sacerdote sa manga guinsulat ni San Ignacio de Loyola cag iban pa nga maayo nga libro, cag guinbinicol niya tungud sa pagbuut sang Francisco Gainza cag nian giunhulog sa pulong nga Hiligaynon ni Mariano Perfecto, Manila. Amigos del Pais, 1880, 227 pp. (NBL)

Lozano y Mejia, Raymundo, 1826-1897. Cursos de la lengua Panayana. Manila: Colegio de Santo Tomas, 1876, 231 pp. A second edition of this book appeared in 1892 with the title, Gramatica Hispana-Visaya-Panayana. (NBL)

______________. Palapucao nga umalagda sa mga dalaga, cag catundanan sa mga niño cag iloy. Nga binuhat cag guinbinisaya ni Padre Lozano, 3rd ed. Manila: Amigos del Pais, 1883, 144 pp. (NBL)

Mentrida, Alonso de 1559-1637. Arte de la lengua Bisaya Hiliguayna de la Isla de Panay. Manila: Imprenta del Manual [?] Memye por Don Anastacio Gonzaga 1818. First ed., Manila 1618? "De las letras de la lengua Bisaya," p. 244-45. (NBL)

Milagro o catingalahan nga binuhat sang Santisimo Sacramento sa Altar cay Santa Liduisia cag sa isa ca ido; cag naupdan sing Estacion Mayor, cag pagdu-ao sa Santisimo Sacramento con patente o dayag. Sacado de varios libros, y traducido del Castellano al Bisaya. Manila: Amigos del Pais, 1882. (NBL)

Mirasol, Dionisio M. Vocabulario o manual de dialogos en Espanol y Bisaya. Primera parte. Manila: Chofre y Comp. 1894, 184 pp. (NBL)

Nipon, trans. Mga laygay sa bag-ong nacasal agud sila maginbulahan. Guinbinisaya ni Nipon. Mandurriao, Iloilo: La Panayana, 1927, 24pp. (UPV)

Perez, Pedro. Cahologan sang confesion general nga guinbinisaya cag guinpaimprenta ni D. Pedro Perez. Manila: Amigo del Pais, 1884, 203 pp. (NBL)

Perfecto, Mariano, 1858-. Ang tungud sang dacu nga capuslanan sang tauo sa pagbasa sang mga matarung nga libro nga guinbinisaya ni Mariano Perfecto. Manila: Amigos del Pais, 1881, 16 pp. (NBL)

______________. Buluhaton sa oras sang pagtinga nga labing mahapos cag labing quinahanglan guid sa mga tanan, sanglet pa cay guintugon gani sang usa ca Santo Papa sa usa nia ca Camarero, nga amo ang buhaton con magtinga na sia. Guinbinisaya ni Mariano Perfecto. Manila: Imprenta de Santa Cruz, 1885. 16 pp. (NBL)

______________. Calantahon nga tacus mapamalandongan sang mga casaquit sa purgatorio cag novena sa mga calag nga may matahum nga mga ejemplo sa tagsa ca adlao; decenario nga casaquit ni Jesus cag ang versos ni San Gregorio Papa nga may maramu nga indulgencias nga guinsulat cag ang iban guinbinisaya ni Mariano Perfecto. Manila: Amigos del Pais, 1882. 64 pp. (NBL)

______________. Matahum nga bida ni Sta. Maria Magdalena, ni San Lazaro, kag Santa Marta, Part I. 2nd ed. Iloilo: La Panayana, 1950, 33 pp. A lengthy narrative adapted from "Martin sa Golgota." (NBL)

______________. Novena sa mahimayaon nga Principe, San Rafael Arcangel, guinahingalanan nga bulong sang Dios, cag mananabang gayud sa mga palalacat. Guinbinisaya ni Mariano Perfecto.. Manila: Imprenta de Santa Cruz, 1886, 24 pp. (NBL)

______________. Novena sa mahimayaon nga Sta. Monica, iloy ni San Agustin. Guinbinisaya ni Mariano Perfecto. Manila: Colegio de Santo Tomas, 1885, 72 pp. (NBL)

______________. Quinabuhi ni San Martin, Obispo sa Tours. Guinbinisaya ni Mariano Perfecto sa pangayo sang M.R.P Fr. Angel Abasolo. Manila: La Industrial, 1886, 16 pp. (NBL)

______________. Quinabuhi kag Pasion ni Jesucristo nga aton Ginuo. Iloilo City: La Panayana, n.d., 167 pp. Includes lamentation and prayers in Latin and Spanish. In verse. (UPV)

Rosillo, Pedro Ignacio. Novena sa mahimayaon nga patriarca Sto. Domingo de Guzman, fundador sang orden de Predicadores. Guinbuhat sa quinachila sang Bachiller D. Pedro Ignacio Rosillo. Guinbinisaya cag guinpaimprenta ni Mariano Perfecto. Manila: Amigos del Pais, 1885, 22 pp. (NBL)

Solinap, Simeon, trans. Novena sa pagtahud, cag pagpasidungug sang santos nga tuud nga Cruz sang aton guinoo, nga sarang mahimo sa tatlo nia ca fiesta, cag bisan sa ano nga quinahanglan. Guinbinisaya sa pulong nga Hiligaynon sang presbitero D. Simeon Solinap. Manila: Imprenta de Santa Cruz, 1886, 16 pp. (NBL)

Schuster, I. Historia sagrada. Tilburg, Netherlands, Drukkeriz A. Reynin, n.d., 302 pp. (A trans. in Hiligaynon of the Old and the New Testaments). (UPV)

Tiangson, Pedro Ma. trans. Nobena kay S. Diego de Alcala. Iloilo City: La Panayana, 1949, 145 pp. (UPV)

II. Corridos

Anonymous. Doce Pares sa Pransia nga sakup sang emperador Carlo Magno. Ikaduha nga bahin. Iloilo City: La Panayana, n.d. (UPV)

Anonymous. Kabuhi nga nadangat sang makalolooy nga mag-utod nga si Juan kag Maria. Una kag ikaduha nga bahin, Sta. Barbara, Iloilo: Doming Press, n.d. 65 pp. (UPV)

Anonymous. Makahanuklog nga kabuhi ni Rosa Blanca Flor kag ni Prinsipe Floristo sa guinharian sa Gran Cairo. Ikaduha nga bahin. Iloilo City: La Panayana, 1950, 25 pp.(UPV)

Anonymous. Macatingala nga cabuhi ni Trobador cag ni Trabiata sa guinharian sa Espana, Iloilo City: La Panayana, 1941, 31 pp. (UPV)

Anonymous. Vida ni Padre Juan cag ni Beata Maria cag sang ila anac nga si Papa Silvestre, Iloilo City: La Panayana, 1927, 20 pp. (UPV)

Anonymous. Cabuhi nga guinagui-aguihan sang Háring Solomon nga anak sang profeta cag hari nga si David. Part I and Part II. 2 vols. n.p., n.d. (UPV)

Anonymous. Ang kabuhi nga guinagui-aguihan sang Prinsesa Flosenda sa guinharian sang Hungria. Una nga bahin, 26 pp. Iloilo City: n.d. (UPV)

Anonymous. Kinabuhi ni Prinsipe Igmedio kag ni Prinsesa Cloriana. Iloilo City: La Panayana, n.d. (UPV)

Macahanuclog nga vida ni don Felizardo cag ni Dona Rogeria. Iloilo City: La Panayana, n.d. 35 pp. (UPV)

Perfecto, Mariano. Bukaw kag Maya. Iloilo: La Panayana, n.d. (Dignadice's thesis: Silliman and NL)

Perfecto, Nicolasa trans. Kinabuhi sang pitong infantes nga mga anak ni Busto de Lara. Iloilo City: La Panayana, n.d. (UPV)

Yorim, trans. Ang makahanuclog nga kinabuhi ni Haring Villarba Reyna D. a Maria kag sang tatlo nila ka anak D. Pedro, D. Juan kag D. Pedro, kag D. Isabela sa ginharian sa Teruel. Iloilo City: La Panayana, 1950. (UPV)

_______________. Ang makatingala nga natabu sang kabuhi ni Aladino sang pagkuha niya sang lampara maravellosa kag ang iya pagpangasawa sa princesa sa Tsina. Bahin I, II, III. Iloilo City: La Panayana, n.d. 119 pp. Adaptation. (UPV)

Zaragoza, Artemio. Don Juan Tiñoso, n.p. 1936. Adaptation based on a pamphlet published by La Panayana. (UPV)

III. Essays/Letters

Lopez-Jaena, Graciano. Sa Kadungganan Sang Mga Artista Luna kag Resurreccion Hidalgo (Pamulungpulong nga ginhambal ni Don Graciano Lopez-Jaena sa isa ka Bangkete sang tuig 1884). Trans. by Magdalena Jalandoni. (UPV)

Rizal, Jose. Sulat sa mga dalaga sa Malolos ni Jose Rizal, sa mga maanyag kag magayun nga kababaihan nga Pilipinhon kag kinabuhi ni Juan Luna. Trans. by Graciano Lopez Jaena. Iloilo City: Makinaugalingon, 1934, 29 pp. (UPV)

Rizal, Jose and Lopez-Jaena, Graciano. Handumanan nanday Rizal kag Lopez-Jaena; mga binalaybay nga ginlubad sining duha ka walay kamatayan nga baganihan, 1963. Trans. by Magdalena Jalandoni. (UPV)

Rizal, Jose. Ang pagtulun-an sa Pilipinas. Ilong-ilong: Makinaugalingon, n.d., 26 pp. Translator unknown. (UPV)

IV. Plays

Crisostomo, Jose. *Lucivar*. Natividad, Tibiao: Antique, n.d. A comedia adapted from a European play. Handwritten. (UPV)

Damaso, Jimeno. "It Withered and Revived." A translation of Jimeno Damaso's zarzuela, "Nalaya cag Manalingsing." In Consuelo Damaso, et al. *Philippine Drama: Twelve Plays in Six Philippine Languages*. Quezon City: NSTA-Assisted UPS Integrated Research Program A, 1987, pp. 667-826.

France, Anatole. "Ang Nangasawa Sang Apa." A translation by Evelyn Ballesta of Anatole France's "The Man Who Married a Dumb Wife." Typescript. n.p. n.d., 11pp. (UPV)

Magno, Salvador. *Extravagance and Excesses*. (A translation by Rosario Lucero of Salvador Magno's, *Kaudha kag Kalakasan*, a zarzuela in two acts, 1936). In Ma. Rosario Lucero. "The Zarzuelas of Salvador C. Magno: Conventions, Imitations, and Originality." Unpublished Master's Thesis, Diliman, Quezon City: University of the Philippines, April, 1980.

Rodrigo, Francisco. *Sa Pula Sa Puti*. (A translation by Manuel Tondares Sr. of Francisco Rodrigo's play with the same title), n.p. n.d. (UPV)

Shakespeare, William. *Ang Komerciante Sang Venecia.* A translation of William Shakespeare's *Merchant of Venice* by Recaredo Ho. Mandurriao, Iloilo: La Panayana, Libreria y Encuadernacion, 1933, 39 pp. (UPV)

Torre, Nestor. "Mga Tingog sa Kadudulman." A translation by Francisco Villanueva of Nestor Torre's "Voices of Laughter." Typescript. n.p. n.d. 17pp. (UPV)

V. Novels

A. Following is a list of novels translated from Tagalog to Hiligaynon which were serialized in *Hiligaynon Magazine.* These include the earliest novels translated into Hiligaynon as well as some which were published in 1966 and 1968; these are within the period covered by this study. These are arranged by year in the order in which the novels appeared in *Hiligaynon*. We note that in the earliest translations, the name of the translator was indicated, but not so in the later period. Also listed are the novels in komiks form (K).

1937

Galauran, Fausto J. *Likum Sang Kumpisalan*. Ginbinisaya ni Abe S. Gonzales.

Reyes, Pedrito. *Kulafu. Ang Daku nga Amu, Ang Hari sa Katalunan*. Manugbisaya Anon.

Galauran Fausto. *Balaan nga Panaad*. Linubad ni Prax S. Villaluz.

Francisco, Lazaro. *Waay Pa Magsalup ang Adlaw*. Linubad ni Ulises M. Vadlit.

Virrey, Teodoro at Gregorio Coching. *Via Crucis*. Ginbinisaya ni Abe S. Gonzales.

1938

Caravana, Nemesio E. *Maria Makiling*. Linubad ni Ramon L. Muzones.

Galauran,Fausto J. *Kamot nga Salsalon*. Linubad ni Abe S. Gonzales.

Coching, Gregorio. *Krus nga Likum.*. Linubad ni Ulises M. Vadlit.

Galauran, Fausto J. *Pamatbat Sang Langit*. Linubad ni Abe S. Gonzales.

De Guzman, Susana at Aguinaldo Rosalia. *Pating nga Bukay*. Linubad ni Abe S. Gonzales.

Cruz, Jose Esperanza. *Mutya Sang Dagat*. Linubad ni Ulises M. Vadlit.

Galauran Fausto J. *Gisi nga Hayahay*. Linubad ni Ulises M. Vadlit.

1966

Ramirez, Manuel. *Hulot Isip 711*.

Galauran, Fausto J. *Mahuyang nga Batungdaan*.

Caravana, Nemesio. *Ang Magkabugto Sang Sinukuan*.

Ravelo, Mars. *Yawa nga Lais* (K).

______________. *Babaeng Talunanon* (K).

Del Mundo, Clodualdo. *Apat Ka Espada*.

Gomez, Pablo. *Baga sa Dagami*.

Caravana, Nemesio. *Daraga sa Mayon*.

Galauran, Fausto. *Isa ka Hakop nga Humay*

Del Mundo, Clodualdo. *May Pagkabuhawi* (K).

Ravelo, Mars. *Si Boboy*.

Caravana, Nemesio. *Mutya sa Taal*.

Coching, Francisco V. *Bantilingon*.

Caravana, Nemesio. *Ang Lin-ay sa Bulkan Apo*(K).

1968

Galauran, Fausto J. *Silak sa Altar*.

Caravana, Nemesio. *Pito Ka Espada sang Castilla*.

______________. *Makatalanghaga nga Trumpeta*.

Galauran, Fausto J. *Kamandag sa Akon Dugo*.

1969

Tiburcio, Mar. *Alimpulos sa Ting-adlaw* (K).

Nadres, Orlando. *Dutang Tinuboan* (K)

B. Other Novels Translated from and into Hiligaynon

Jalandoni, Magdalena.*The Lady in the Market*. (A translation by Edward Defensor of Magdalena Jalandoni's *Ang Dalaga sa Tindahan*). Typescript. Iloilo City, 1976, 77 pp. (UPV)

_______________. *Vigil in the Graveyard*. (A translation by Yolanda Velasco of Magdalena Jalandoni's *Ang Bantay Sa Patio*). In Yolanda Velasco. "A Critical Study of Magdalena Jalandoni as a Novelist with Special Reference to *Ang Bantay Sa Patio*." Unpublished Master's Thesis, University of the Philippines, 1952.

Muzones, Ramon. *Margosatubig*. (A translation by Edward Defensor of Ramon Muzones' novel of the same title). Typescript. Iloilo City, 1979, 442 pp. (UPV)

Norada, Conrado. *Wild Flower*. (A translation by Noemi Morales of Conrado Norada's *Bulak nga Ilahas*, 1955. In Noemi Morales. "The Novels of Conrado J. Norada." Unpublished Master's Thesis. Diliman, Quezon City: University of the Philippines, July, 1980.

Ortiga, Ramon. Nimia ang gugma sang isa ka ati nga babae, bahin iv. (Nobela ni Ramon Ortiga nga guinbinisaya ni Anghel Magahum). Mandurriao, Iloilo: La Panayana, 1922, 210 pp. (UPV)

Rizal, Jose. *Noli Me Tangere*. (Ulpiano Vergara's translation into Hiligaynon of Jose Rizal's novel of the same title). Iloilo: Makinaugalingon, 1928, 449 pp. (UPV)

_______________. *El Filibusterismo*. (Ulpiano Vergara and Rosendo Mejica's translation into Hiligaynon of Jose Rizal's novel of the same title). Iloilo: Makinaugalingon, 1933, 332 pp. (UPV)

Zola, Emil. *Ang Utud Sang Mga Imul*. Nobela ni Emile Zola nga guinbinisaya ni Anghel Magahum. Iloilo: Makinaugalingon, 1929, 31 pp. (UPV)

VI. Selected Short Prose Translations

A. These sugilanon translated from Tagalog into Hiligaynon were published in the *Hiligaynon* from 1937-1938.

1937

Vasquez, Francisco M. "Nangindi sa Umay." Linubad ni Uldemuva (May 4).

Bugarin Juan C. "Ang Baganihan nga Nagkasala." Linubad ni Uldemuva (May 11).

Labog, Hilaria. "Patis Lamang." Linubad ni Uldemuva (May 18).

Arcega, Simeon P. "Ang Anak sa Unang Asawa." Linubad ni Uldemuva (May 25).

Vasquez, Francisco M. "Agalon Kag Ulipon." Linubad ni Prax S. Villaluz (June 1).

Alvarez, Epifania. "Pilak Kag Kahagugma." Linubad ni Prax S. Villaluz (June 15).

Santiago, Gervasio. "Josefina." Linubad ni Prax S. Villaluz (June 22).

Santos, Teodorico. "Rata-igo." Linubad ni Prax S. Villaluz (June 29).

Santiago, Belen Manalo. "Lunsay Indi." Linubad ni Prax S. Villaluz (July 6).

Cruz, Victoria Corpus. "Duha ang Asawa." Linubad ni Prax S. Villaluz (July 13).

De Guzman, Susana. "Mga Sulat nga Walay Lagda." Linubad ni Prax S. Villaluz (July 27).

Aguinaldo, Rosalia. "Tubig nga Malinong." Linubad ni Prax S. Villaluz (August 3).

Medina, Buenaventura. "Ang Hutik Sang Kalag." Linubad ni Prax S. Villaluz (August 10).

Arcega, Simeon P. "Pahunan kag Pagabudlay." Linubad ni Prax S. Villaluz (August 10).

Santiago, Belen Manalo. "Nagyuhum ang Bituon." Linubad ni Prax S. Villaluz (August 24).

1938

Alvarez, Epifania. "Namatuk Maghara." Linubad ni Ramon L. Muzones (January 4).

Labog, Hilaria. "Gugma Nga Nag-away." Linubad ni Ramon L. Muzones (January 4).

Santiago, Gervasio B. "Naghatag Sang Dalan." Linubad ni Ramon L. Muzones (January 25).

Santiago, Belen Manalo. "Bangod sa Isang Amba." Linubad ni Ramon L. Muzones (February 1).

Cainglet, G.F. "Ang Daan nga Biolin." Linubad ni Ramon L. Muzones (February 8).

Santiago, Belen Manalo. "Ihambal Mo Lamang." Linubad ni Ramon L. Muzones (February 22).

Villanueva, Pedro Reyes. "Napangitaan Sang Tambal." Linubad ni Ramon L. Muzones (March 1).

Sauco, Teofilo. "Dalamguhanon Lamang." Linubad ni Ramon L. Muzones (March 8).

Arcega, Simeon P. "Doctor del Mar." Linubad ni Ramon L. Muzones (March 22).

Asistio, Narciso. "Pagsalig." Linubad ni Ramon L. Muzones (March 29).

Alvarez, Epifania. "Ang Nabang-awan nga Daya." Linubad ni Ramon L. Muzones April 5).

Santiago, Belen Manalo. "Pamasul Sang Lawas." Linubad ni Ramon L. Muzones (April 12).

Villaroman, Porfirio. "Celia Mahirup." Linubad ni Ramon L. Muzones (April 26).

Santiago, Belen Manalo. "Sa Mga Tapak Mo." Linubad ni Ramon L. Muzones (May 3).

Santiago, Belen Manalo. "Ako, Ang Imo Iloy." Linubad ni Ramon L. Muzones (May 10).

Arcega, Simeon P. "Wala Kamatayon." Linubad ni Ramon L. Muzones (May 17).

Villaroman, Porfirio V. "Ilang-Ilang." Linubad ni Ramon L. Muzones (May 24).

Santiago, Gervasio B. "Hikug Sang Lanubo." Linubad ni Ramon L. Muzones (May 31).

Cruz, Jose Esperanza. "Mutya Sang Dagat." Linubad ni Ulises M. Vadlit (May 31).

Labog, Hilaria. "Hinigugma Ko." Linubad ni Ramon L. Muzones (June 7).

Santos, Teodorico. "Pagbutlak Sang Adlaw." Linubad ni Ramon L. Muzones (June 14).

Alvarez, Epifania. "Tatlo Ka Gatus Ka Pisus." Linubad ni Ramon L. Muzones (June 21).

B. Other Short Prose Translations

Jalandoni, Magdalena. "The Singer on the Raft". (A translation by Edward Defensor of Jalandoni's "Ang Mangagamba sa Balsa"). Iloilo City, 1976.

Lucero, Rosario. *Sugilanon*. (A translation of selected sugilanon into Filipino). Quezon City: Ateneo de Manila University Press, 1990.

VII. Poetry

Hosillos, Lucila V. trans. Three Bathala Poems (A translation from Hiligaynon into English). In "Christian Elements in Early Poetry in Hiligaynon" in Lucila V. Hosillos, *Originality as Vengeance*, Quezon City: New Day Publishers, 1984, pp. 42- 47.

Bonifacio, Andres. "Paghigugma sa Tinubuang Banwa." (A translation by Lucila V. Hosillos of Andres Bonifacio's "Pag-ibig sa Tinubuang Bayan.") In "Notes on Translation."
1976-1977.

______________. "Gugma Sa Punsod". (A translation by Santiago Mulato of Andres Bonifacio's "Pag-ibig Sa Tinubuang Bayan"). *Hiligaynon*, December 4, 1936.

Fernandez, Doreen G. "Ten Hiligaynon Poems: Translation and an Introduction." *Philippine Studies* (21), 1973.

Rizal, Jose. "Ang Katapusan Ko Nga Paalam kag ang Akon Palahilwayan." Mga linubad ni Magdalena Jalandoni sa binisayang Hiligaynon gikan sa walay kamatayon nga mga binalaybay ni Jose Rizal nga "Mi Ultimo Adios" kag "Mi Retiro." (UPV)

Lopez-Jaena, Graciano. "Paghimandag kay Luna Tuhoy sa Iya Kuadro 'La Batalia de Lepanto.' " Pamulungpulong nga ginhambal ni Don Graciano Lopez Jaena sang tuig 1887 sang bangkete nga nahalad sa kadungganan sang napurongan nga pintor nga Pilipinhon cag guinbinisaya ni Magdalena Jalandoni, n.p. n.d. (UPV)

______________. Ang Pilipinas sa Kinalibutan nga Pasundayang sa Barcelona. Pamulungpulong nga ginhambal ni Graciano Lopez-Jaena sa Ateneo, Barcelona sang ika-25 sa Febrero sang 1889 cag guinbinisaya ni Magdalena Jalandoni, n.p. n.d. (UPV)

VIII. Dictionaries/Grammar Books

Aparico, Jose. Arte de la lengua Bisaya-Hiligueino de la Isla de Panay. Corregido y aumentado por Jose Aparico. Tambobong: Asilo de Huerfanos, 1894, 270 pp. "De las letras de la lengua Bisaya," p. 248. (NBL)

"Data Vocabulario Visaya." Pertenece al Aparador dentro de la Pared. Caxon No 19, Legajo 11. C.R. Boxer Collection (IU)

Jonkergouiw, Hubert, comp. English-Visayan Dictionary. ed. by Rev. William Mauerhofer, MHM. San Jose, Antique, 1971, iv, 446 pp. (UPV)

Lozano y Mejia, Raymundo, 1826-1897: O.E.S.A. Gramatica Hispania-Visaya-Panayana. Villadolid, 1892, 278 pp. (NBL)

Maroma, Eladio. Hiligaynon-English Dictionary. Cabatuan, Iloilo, 1973, 2v. 1,019 pp. Typescript. A dictionary of Hiligaynon words which are spelled according to the Amoran rules of spelling. (UPV)

Martin, Julian, 1784-1857: O.E.S.A. *Diccionario Hispano-Bisaya.* Manila, 1842, 461-827 pp. Part 2 of Mentrida's *Diccionario de la lengua Bisaya, Hilegueina y Haraya*, 1841. (NBL)

Maxfield, Charles L. comp. with Visayan students and scholars. *English-Visayan Dictionary.* Iloilo: Philippine Baptist Mission Press, 1913, 162 pp. (UPD, NBL)

Mentrida, Alonso de, 1559-1637: O.E.S.A. *Diccionario de la Lengua Bisaya Hilegueina y Haraya de la Isla de Panay.* Manila, 1841, 460 pp. First printed in 1637. (NBL)

Yap, Jose E. English-Visayan Dictionary (Kapulungan-Iningles-Binisaya) n.p, n.d. 320 pp. Photocopy. Contains more than sixteen thousand English words with their respective equivalents and shades of meaning in Hiligaynon and Hiniray-a dialects. (UPV)

IX. Folklore

History of the first datos who came from Borneo and peopled these islands. From an old manuscript found in the town of Jaiuay, in 1858, and trans. into Spanish by Tomas Santaren. Trans. into English by Pedro L. Tupas and Pedro Suavedes, 1917, 25 pp. (BEY)

Narboneta, Ma. Luisa M. "Hiligaynon Folklore from Negros Occidental," Unpublished Master's Thesis. Manila: Philippine Women's University, 1959.

Monteclaro, Pedro. "Maragtas" (1907). A translation into English by Encarnacion J. Gonzaga, Natividad Rosado, Ramon Locsin and Ismael Golez, 1916, 62pp. (BEY)

______________. "Maragtas" (1907). A translation into English by Manuel L. Carreon, assisted by G.Santiago-Cino and Catalia S. Mieten, Manila, 1943, 82 pp. (UPD)

Dignadice, Fe Java. "A Critical Study of Folklore in the Western Visayas." Unpublished Master's Thesis. Dumaguete City: Silliman University, March 1955. (Silliman and NL)

Clavel, Leothiny. "Oral Literature of Capiz." Unpublished Master's Thesis. Diliman, Quezon City: University of the Philippines, 1972.

Gonzalez, Milagros. "Folktales in Bacolod, Negros Occidental." Manila, January 1925. (BEY)

______________. "Legends from Bacolod, Negros Occidental, February 1925, 6 pp. (BEY)

Millington, W.H and Maxfield, Merton L. "Visayan Folktales." *Journal of American Folklore*, (19): 97-112 and (20): 89-103; 311-18, (1906-1907).

Siscar, Hernando L. "A Study of Some Ilongo Folktales, Songs, Poems, Legends, and Proverbs." Unpublished Master's Thesis. Manila: Philippine Normal College, 1959.

Soncuya, Jose. "The Island of Panay" and the "History of the Bisayas, Manila, 1917. Translations into English by various students in U.P., 1918, 222 pp. (BEY)

Taylor, Hagel Clark and Marovilla-Seva, and Vicente Garcia, "Bisayan Folklore" (Collection and Translation) 1917, 90 pp. (BEY)

X. History

Alcina, Francisco Ignacio. The Muñoz text of Alcina's *History of the Bisayan Islands*. Part 1, Book 3. Preliminary translation by Paul S. Lietz, Philippine Studies Program, University of Chicago, 1960, 373 leaves.(EAM)

Ignacio, Rebecca P. An annotated translation of the Povedano manuscript (1578). Transcript No. 3, Philippine Studies Program, Dept. of Anthropology, Univ. of Chicago, 1954. (EAM)

Santaren, Fr. Tomas, Recorder. Bisayan accounts of early Bornean settlements in the Philippines. Translation from Spanish by Enriqueta Fox, Philippine Studies Program, Dept. of Anthropology, University of Chicago, 1954. (EAM)

A Selected Bibliography of Sugilanon

The following sugilanon were published in *Hiligaynon*.

1937

Achurria, Jesus Roxas. "Umanhon nga Bulak," May 18.

Flor, Trinidad P. "Bili Ang Manggad sa Alon," June 8.

Gabio, Felix T. "Nabanhaw ang Kalisud," August 17.

Ginete, Antonio C. "Maluib nga Walay Sala," August 10.

Janovar, Consolacion J. "Mapait nga Panalambiton," July 6.

Jara, Lilia. "Ang Bunga Sing Pag-antus," June 1.

Jereza, Felicidad J. "Sa Gihapon Handa," May 25.

Sola, Santiago M. "Sang Pagbutlak Sang Bulan," July 13.

Taleon, Federico. "Masubong Balita," July 20.

Ybañez, Benjamin A. "Matam-is nga Likum," June 29.

1938

Carillo, Angeles. "Iloy Sang Akon Anak," June 28.

Chua, Nieves Singson. "Ang Granada," July 12.

Jereza, Felicidad J. "Ang Natagu sa Lulubngan," November 1.

Manoso, Rosario T. "Tunok Sang Isa ka Bulak," October 18.

Muzones, Ramon L. "Hara!" June 28.

______________. "Pagnasnas Sang Kaagahon," July 5.

______________. "Pagbalik Sang Talawan," July 12.

______________. "Kapawa," July 19.

______________. "Pagbihag Sang Gintaipan," August 9.

______________. "Kuntani," August 16.

______________. "Tatlo Ka Adlaw Sa Langit," August 23.

______________. "Maragtas Sang Akon Kabuhi," August 30.

Paguntalan, Augurio A. "Unod Sang Tulun-an," August 31.

1966

Baterna, Quirino. "Ang Guinahulat," June 29.

Cordova, Gerardo G. "Nagapudpod ang Gahom," March 9.

Defante, Raymundo Jr. "Naglagpok nga Inumol," March 16.

______________. "May mga Pakpak nga Pilak," August 31.

______________. "Isa Ka Dulot Sang Hitabo," September 7.

De La Merced, Israel. "Madulom nga Banagbanag," July 27.

Floro-Luza, Ismaelita. "Ang Sikoholiya ni Cherry," August 24.

______________. "Sa Pagkabanhaw Sang Paglaom," November 9.

Mecenas, Leo. "Pagtilaw," November 9.

Mixdon, Manuel A. "Maanyag Pa ang Palibot," September 7.

Naranjo, Teodulfo A. "Kon Wala Niya Pagbudhii," March 16.

Tuclaud, Epifanio. "Ginahakitan ang Pag-abot," March 9.

Yap, Jose. "Nahadlok Mapanaksihon," October 26.

1967

Berdugo, Mary Beth. "Makadlaw Ka Ukon Hindi," March 1.

Defante, Raymundo Jr. "May Katihan ang Kamatayon," March 8.

_______________. "Ang Tsuper kag ang Senyorito," January 11.

Floro-Luza, Ismaelita. "Takya," April 12.

Gargaritano, Nicolas G. "Ginpatalupangod ang Palaabuton," January 11.

Janagap, Clarita. "Naghibi ang Langit," March 15.

Mecenas, Leo. "Ang Tunay na Kriminal," March 8.

Prudente, Reynaldo. "Maryones, Guripat Kon Guripat," February 21.

Roullo, Romeo. "Sa Kadulom May Kasanag," January 4.

Salas, Allyn Joey. "Hangkat Sang Ipalatugsiling," March 22.

Villanueva, Jose. "Kailis Sang Iya Anak," April 12.

1968

Deano, Edith L. "Nangaluyag sa Akon ang Tamawo," March 6.

Defante, Ma. Luisa S. "Kinahanglan Pa Nga Padamguhon," April 17.

Floro-Luza, Ismaelita. "Isa Ka Estratehiya," March 20.

Flora, Leopoldo. "Dalagko nga Kamot," September 4.

Fulo, Nunilon E. Jr. "Sa Punta Sang Dalan," September 25.

Magan, Hernani. "Ang Mga Aswang," December 11.

Nallos, Ma. Linda. "Oh Bernie, Bernie," March 13.

Ramos, Faustino M. "Ang Pihak nga Aritos," October 9.

Salas, Allyn Joey. "Salaluhan sa Paskua," December 18.

Sobrevega, Isabelo S. "Talikala Sang Kahapon," October 23.

1969

Arceo, Hernando. "Ang Ginang sa Telefono," November 26.

Barcebal, Bernardo M. "Pasimpalad ni Boy Crisanto," March 19.

______________. "Ano ang Imo Dulot?" December 17.

Bautista, Nenita S. "Sala nga Pagkilala," July 23.

Castronueva, Norberto S. "Sang Magsiruhana si Nanay Maria," October 1.

Defante, Luisa S. "Nagdramatik Entrans si Batoy," March 5.

______________. "Si Lola Ko kag si Lolo Niya," April 23.

Defante, Raymundo S. Jr. "Ang Taknaan," March 19.

______________. "Dupoydupoy sa Ulot sang Inumol," July 9.

Deferia, Desiderio T. "Davidica," September 10.

______________. "Dialogo," March 26.

Docdocil, Emilo. "Abono sa Suloksulok," August 20.

Echevarria, Ariston. "Pagsulit," December 3.

______________. "Gikan sa Balikutok Padulong sa Bacolod," December 17.

Floro-Luza, Ismaelita. "Lagson Pa Ang Balangaw," March 12.

______________. "Ginahandom nga Bituon," April 2.

______________. "May Iban Pa nga Duag ang Pagpakamahal," December 3.

Floro, Leopoldo P. "Si Shirley, Ang Dalagita," July 23.

Fulo, Nunilon E. "Vidas Miserables," March 5.

________. "Paatras ang Ila Martsa," April 2.

Gargaritano, Nicolas G. "Wala Ginabaylo ang Panghigugma," May 21.

________. "Baylo sang Isa Ka Puna nga Duta," July 9.

Gatpatan, Benito Jr. "Ang Tomboy nga si Liday," April 30.

Gesulgon, Ray Gra. "Amor Patriae," December 17.

________. "Nagaulang Ang Isa Ka Puno Nga Kawayan," December 31.

Gonzalez, Ramon G. "Hilibion Lamang Ang Sabat," March 26.

________. "Kadaygan Nga Wala Nagalubad," April 30.

Javellana, Ernesto F. "Mahamuok Pa Ang Katulogan," July 2.

Joquiño, Antonio H. "Nagailis na ang Dahon," August 6.

Maestrecampo, Angelino G. "Ang Tatlo Ka Kriminal," April 23.

Magallanes, Nenita M. "Akon Anak," April 2.

________. "Ikaw Isa Ka Babae," December 24.

Palanog, Faustino T. "Ang Milagro sa Puong-Puong," July 16.

Pamonag, Nilo Par. "Miliminas: Tuig 0069," March 26.

Roullo, Romeo Jr. "Maalam Magpili," March 5.

Quizan, Edwin T. "Duha ka Bangkay," November 5.

Tigulo, Tommy T. "Sa Pagtandog sang Kasing Kasing," July 23.

Villalobos, Rogelio. "Tinungkad nga Pagpasulabi," September 17.

1970

Bautista, Nenita S. "Sa Pagkatao Sang Lapsag," December 23.

Camacho, Pol A. "Tungod sa Kabikahan," March 25.

Defante, Raymundo G. "Gugma Ukon Katungdanan?" February 4.

Defante, Raymundo S. "Tingob nga Bayad," February 25.

______________. "Esfeamor," November 4.

Deferia, Desiderio T. "Ang Badigard," January 14.

______________. "Sa Pag-usoy Sang Banas," April 22.

Docdocil, Emilio Jr. "Ang Pagpili Sang Asawa," February 4.

Echevarria, Ariston Em. "Gaba," January 14.

______________. "Hitabu Sa Mambukal," November 4.

Educado, Sally J. "Ginliwas Ako ni Bulilaw," March 18.

Flora, Leopoldo. "Dayagnostik," February 11.

Garganera, Romeo G. "Panihol sa Kagab-ihon," February 11.

Gargantiel, Eugenio. "Dulot Sang Palahinandigan ni Kapitan Honorio," December 23.

Gibraltar, Luisa Defante. "Ang Gugma Sang Tindera," January 7.

Gonzalez, Ramon G. "Damang-Damang," March 18.

Joquiño, Antonio H. "May Iya Nga Datag," January 28.

Luza, Ismaelita Floro. "Ang Ilaga," January 14.

______________. "Kon si Kim si Blackie," March 18.

______________. "Ang Sugal sa Golgota," April 1, 1970.

Yap, Jose. "Kon Diin ang Kalipay," March 25.

1971

Aguilar, Narciso. "Rubas ang Binulig," March 10.

Gesulgon, Ray Gra. "Ang Dumuloaw," March 3.

Gonzalez, Ramon G. "Empleadong Inutil vs. Among Milyonaryo," March 17.

Joquiño, Antonio H. "Pangako," April 7.

Luza, Ismaelita Floro, "Duha Ka Iloy," December 22.

Magallanes, Nenita S. "Ati...Ati...Sa Bukid," February 24.

Palanog, Faustino T. "Patay nga Manggad," January 6, 1971.

Ramos, Faustino M. "Ang Hitabo sa Lulobngan," April 14, 1971.

Salasis, Josephus. "Ang Baganihan," January 27.

Siscar, Hernando. "Ang Utbong sa Dalan," February 10.

1972

Castaneres, Ariel B. "Si Victor Kag si Karina," November 29.

Frias, Rosalinda T. "Orasyon," April 5.

Jamolin, Mamerta J. "Ang Ila Amay," June 28.

Jedeliz, Nerio Jr. "Sadsaran sang Kalipay," March 1.

Joquiño, Antonio H. "Mga Kurit sa Kawayan," November 15.

Luza, Ismaelita Floro. "Mga Gabok," June 21.

________________. "Ang Duta Isa Ka Hiyas," November 22.

1973

Gonzaga, Leovigildo. "Pagpanumbalik," January 10.

Fajura, Jose M. "Gantangan," January 3.

References

Achebe, Chinua. "English and the African Writer." *Transition* 4(18): 27–30.

Abueg, Efren, ed. (1970). *Ang Manunulat.* Manila.

Adejare, Oluwole (1987). "Translation: A Distinctive Feature of African Literature in English." *Language and Style* vol. 20, no. 2, pp. 145-49.

Adisa, Opal Palmer (1990). "Duppy Get Her." *Caribbean New Wave*, ed. Stewart Brown. New Hampshire: Heinemann, p. 2.

Agpalo, Remigio (1973). *The Organic-Hierarchical Paradigm and Politics in The Philippines.* Quezon City: University of the Philippines Press.

Alejandro, Rufino (1980). *Ang Sining ng Pagsasalin.* Manila: Rex Bookstore.

Anderson, Benedict (1992). "Rereading Rizal." *The Manila Chronicle*, September 26–October 2, p. 11; "Noli Bowdlerized," *The Manila Chronicle*, October 3–9, p. 10.

Antonio, Lilia (1987). "Pagsasakatutubo sa Pagsasalin: Ang Nilalaman at Pamamaraan ng Pagsasalin ng Nobela sa Panahon ng Kolonyalismong Amerikano 1912–1940." Unpublished Doctoral Dissertation. Quezon City: University of the Philippines.

Aprieto, Pacifico (1987). *The Philippine Textbook Project: From the Textbook Board Secretariat to The Instructional Materials Corporation*. Quezon City: Instructional Materials Corporation, p. 25.

Aranas, Patricia Garcia (1990). "The Philippine Variety of English in Selected Universities in Metro Manila." *Philippine Studies* 38: 333–57.

Aronson, Ronald (1990). "The Post-Modern Condition: The End of Politics?" *The Post-Colonial Critic*, ed. Sarah Harasym. Routledge: New York and London, p. 22.

Asad, Talal (1986). "The Concept of Cultural Translation in British Social Anthropology." *Writing Culture: The Poetics and Politics of Anthropology*, ed. James Clifford and George E. Marcus. Berkeley: UCLA Press, p. 160.

Ashcroft, Bill, Gareth Griffiths, and Helen Tiffin (1989). *The Empire Writes Back: Theory and Practice in Post-Colonial Literatures*. London and New York: Routledge.

Bakhtin, M.M. (1940). "Epic and Novel." *The Dialogic Imagination: Four Essays*, ed. M. Holquist. Austin: University of Texas Press.

Barrantes, Vicente y Moreno (1889). *El Teatro Tagalo*. Madrid, pp. 20–21.

Batsleer, Jane (1985). *Rewriting English*. London: Methuen, Inc.

Bautista, Lourdes (1987). "Domains of English in the 21st Century." *The Role of English and its Maintenance in the Philippines*, ed. Andrew Gonzalez. Manila: Solidarity Publishing House, p. 75.

Benjamin, Walter (1955). "The Task of the Translator." *Illuminations*. New York: Harcourt and Brace.

Beyer, H. Otley, (1918-1920). *Ethnography of the Bisayan People.* Manila.

Bloom, Harold (1973). *The Anxiety of Influence*. New York: Oxford University Press, p. 70.

Bloomfield, Leonard (1933). *Language*. New York: Holt, Rhinehart, and Winston.

Bokamba, Eyamba G. (1982). "The Africanization of English." *The Other Tongue: English Across Cultures*, ed. Braj Kachru, New York: Pergamon Press.

Boxer, C.R. "Catalogue of Philippine Manuscripts." In the Lilly Library (Special Collections Library) of the Indiana University, Bloomington, Indiana.

Buhler, Karl (1985). "The Key Principle: The Sign Character of Language." *Semiotics*, ed. Robert Innis. Bloomington: Indiana University Press.

Capiz, Pascual (1960). "Politics and the English Language." *Diliman Review* vol. 8, no. 3.

Casper, Leonard (1980). "Introduction: Writing in the Vernacular." *Salimbibig*, ed. Joseph Galdon. Quezon City: Council for Living Traditions, pp. 4-6.

Catford, J.C. (1965). *A Linguistic Theory of Translation*. London: Oxford University Press.

Cheyfitz, Eric (1991). *The Poetics of Imperialism: Translation and Colonization from the Tempest to Tarzan*. New York: Oxford University Press.

Clifford, James and Marcus, George, eds. (1986). *Writing Culture: The Poetics and Politics of Anthropology*. Berkeley: University of California Press.

Colomb, Gregory (1990). "The Semiotic Study of Literary Works." *Tracing Literary Theory*, ed. Joseph Natoli. Urbana-Champaign, Illinois: University of Illinois Press.

Constantino, Ernesto (1974). "Editorial." *Literatura ng Pilipinas* vol. I, no. 1. Quezon City: Samahan Para sa mga Literatura ng Pilipinas.

__________ (1982). *Isinay Texts and Translations.* Tokyo: Institute for the Study of Languages and Cultures of Asia and Africa.

Constantino, Renato (1966). *The Miseducation of the Filipino.* Quezon City: Alemar-Phoenix.

Covar, Prospero (1988). *Tatlong Sanaysay.* Manila: Cultural Center of the Philippines.

Cruz, Isagani (1988). "The Future of Philippine Literature in English." *The Role of English and its Maintenance in the Philippines*, ed. Andrew B. Gonzalez, pp. 125–33.

Crystal, David (1985). "How Many Millions? The Statistics of English Today." *English Today* vol. 1, pp. 7–9.

Damaso, Consuelo, et al. (1987). *Philippine Drama in Six Philippine Languages.* Quezon City: Integrated Research Program 'A,' University of the Philippines.

Duque, Reynaldo, et al. (1988). *Kurditan: Mga Kuwentong Iluko.* Manila: Gumil Manila.

De Alva, Jorge Klor (1989). "Language, Politics and Translation: Colonial Discourse and Classical Nahuatl in New Spain." *The Art of Translation: Voices from the Field*, ed. Roseanna Warren. Boston: Northwestern University Press, pp. 143–62.

De Castro, Lourdes (1976). "Hiligaynon Literature." *Literature and Society: Cross-Cultural Perspectives*, ed. Roger Bresnahan. Makati: Jefferson Cultural Center.

Eagleton, Terry (1977). "Translation and Transformation." *Stand* vol. 29, no. 3, pp. 72–77.

__________ (1983). "The Rise of English." *Literary Theory.* Oxford: Basil Blackwell.

Eco, Umberto (1979). *A Theory of Semiotics.* Bloomington, Indiana: Indiana University Press.

____________ (1984). *Semiotics and the Philosophy of Language*. Bloomington: Indiana University Press.

____________ (1990). "Drift and Unlimited Semiosis." Distinguished Lecturer Series 1. Bloomington, Indiana: Institute of Advanced Study, Indiana University.

Edades, Jean and Hernandez, J. (1953). *English for Filipinos*. Quezon City: Hernandez and Edades.

Epistola, Nieves (1986). "English in the Twenty-First Century Philippines." Paper Read at the Annual Convention of the Linguistic Society of the Philippines. Manila: Philippine Normal College.

Eugenio, Damiana (1987). *Awit and Corrido: Philippine Metrical Romances*. Quezon City: University of the Philippines Press.

Evangelista, Sr. Socorro, S.Sp.S. (1977). "Magdalena Jalandoni, Hiligaynon Novelist." Unpublished Doctoral Dissertation. Quezon City: Ateneo de Manila University Press.

Even-Zohar (1990). "The Position of Translated Literature Within the Literary Polysystem." *Poetics Today* vol. 11, no. 1, pp. 45–51.

Fabian, Johannes (1986). *Language and Colonial Power: The Appropriation of Swahili in the Former Belgian Congo 1880-- 1938*. New York: Cambridge University Press.

Fansler, Dean S. (1916). "Metrical Romances in the Philippines." *Journal of American Folklore* vol. 29, pp. 203–81.

____________ (1937). "Philippine Folk Literature, a Synoptic Study on an Unpublished Manuscript Collection of Folktales." *Philippine Magazine*, vol. 34, pp. 208–09.

Fernandez, Doreen (1978). *The Iloilo Zarzuela*. Quezon City: Ateneo de Manila University Press.

Foucault, Michel (1970). *The Order of Things: An Archaeology of Knowledge*. Trans. Alan Sheridan-Smith. New York: Random House, Inc.).

______________(1977). *Power/Knowledge: Selected Interviews and Other Writings*, ed. Colin Gordon. New York: Random House, Inc.

Frawley, William (1984). "Prolegomenon to a Theory of Translation." *Translation: Literary, Linguistic, and Philosophical Perspectives*, ed. William Frawley. Newark: University of Delaware Press.

Goethe, Wolfgang von (1976). *Italienische Reise*, 2 vols. Frankfurt am Main: Insel Verlag. Cited in James Clifford and George Marcus (eds.), 1986.

Gonzaga, Encarnacion (1917). "Bisayan Literature: From Pre-Spanish Times to 1917." Unpublished Master's Thesis. Manila: University of the Philippines.

Gonzalez, Andrew and Alberca, Wilfredo (1978). *Philippine English of the Mass Media*. Manila: Linguistic Society of the Philippines.

Gonzalez, Andrew (1980). *Language and Nationalism*. Quezon City: Ateneo de Manila University Press.

______________ and Lourdes Bautista (1986). *Language Surveys in the Philippines 1966–1984*. Manila: De La Salle University Press.

______________ and ______________ (1988). "Domains of English in the 21st Century." *The Role of English and its Maintenance in the Philippines*, ed. Andrew Gonzalez. Manila: Solidaridad Publishing House.

Gonzalez, N.V.M. (1950) *A Season of Grace*. Manila: Bookmark, Inc.

Gorlee, Dinda (1989). "Wittgenstein, Translation and Semiotics." *Target*, The International Journal of Translation Studies vol. 1, no. 1, pp. 69–74.

Grimes, J.E. (1975). *The Thread of Discourse*. The Hague: Mouton.

Guillermo, Gelacio (1990). *Ang Panitikan ng Pambansang Demokrasya/The Literature of National Democracy*. Manila: Kalikasan Press.

Harrison, Regina (1989). *Signs, Songs, and Memory in the Andes: Translating Quechua Language and Culture*. Austin, Texas: University of Texas Press.

Hatim, Basil and Mason, Ian (1990). *Discourse and the Translator*. London and New York: Longman.

Hawkes, Terence (1977). *Structuralism and Semiotics*. Berkeley: University of California Press.

Hornby, Mary Snell (1988). *Translation Studies: An Integrated Approach*. Amsterdam/Philadelphia: John Benjamins Publishing Company.

Hosillos, Lucila V. (1976–1977). "Notes on Translation." *The Literary Apprentice* vol. 19, no. 1, pp. 130–31.

______________ (1984). "The Transmutation of the Western Short Story." *Originality as Vengeance in Philippine Literature*. Quezon City: New Day Publishers.

Ileto, Reynaldo C. (1979). *Pasyon and the Revolution, Popular Movements in the Philippines 1840–1910*. Ithaca, New York: Cornell University Press.

Iyer, Pico (1993, February 8). "The Empire Writes Back." *Time* vol. 141, no. 6, pp. 48–53.

Jacobson, Roman (1959). "On Linguistic Aspects of Translation." *On Translation*, ed. Ruben Brower. Cambridge: Harvard University Press.

Javier, Mariano (1990). "Joseph Montano's Travels in the Philippines and in the Malay Archipelago (1879–1881): A Translation and Critical Evaluation." Unpublished Doctoral Dissertation. Quezon City: University of the Philippines.

Jocano, F. Landa (1983). *The Hiligaynon: An Ethnography of Family and Community Life in the Western Bisayas Region*. Quezon City: University of the Philippines.

Jose, Vivencio (1987). "Identity and Liberation in Philippine Literature." *Kultura* vol. 2, no. 2, pp. 3–11.

Kachru, Braj (1982). *The Other Tongue*. London: Pergamon Press.

____________ (1986). *The Alchemy of English: The Spread, Functions and Models of Non-native Englishes*. Urbana, Illinois: University of Illinois Press.

____________ (1988 October). "The Sacred Cows of English." *English Today* vol. 16, pp. 3–8.

____________ (1990). "The Second Diaspora of English." *English in its Social Contexts: Essays in Historical Sociolinguistics*, ed. William Machan and Charles Scott. New York: Oxford University Press.

Kauffmann, Rev. J. (n.d.). *Visayan-English Dictionary*. Iloilo: La Editorial.

Lacaba, Jose F. (1991). *Sa Daigdig ng Kontradiksyon*. Manila: Anvil Publishing.

Llamzon, Teodoro (1969). *Standard Filipino English*. Manila: Ateneo de Manila University Press.

____________ (1983). "Essential Features of New Varieties in English." *Varieties of English in Southeast Asia*, ed. R.B. Noss (1983). Singapore: SEAMEO Regional Language Centre.

Lohafer, Susan and Carey, Jo Ellyn (1989). *Short Story Theory at the Crossroads*. Baton Rouge and London: Louisiana State University Press.

Longacre, Robert (1968). *Discourse, Paragraph, and Sentence Structure in Selected Philippine Languages.* Sta. Ana, California: Summer Institute of Philippine Linguistics, 1968.

Lucero, Rosario Cruz (1988). "Demonyo." *Ani* vol. 2, no. 4. Manila: Sentro ng Pangkultura ng Pilipinas, pp. 63–78.

______________ (1989). "Vernacular Literature: Philippine Literature's Other." *Kultura* vol. 2, no. 4, p. 13.

______________ (1990). "Komedya." *Ani* vol. 4, no. 3. Manila: Sentro ng Pangkultura ng Pilipinas, pp. 81–92.

______________ (1991). *Sugilanon*. Manila: De La Salle University Press.

Lumbera, Bienvenido (1967). "The Literary Relations of Tagalog Literature." In *Brown Heritage*, ed. Antonio Manuud. Quezon City: Ateneo de Manila University Press.

______________ (1986). *Tagalog Poetry 1570–1898: Tradition and Influences in its Development.* Quezon City: Ateneo de Manila University Press.

Maceda, Teresita G. (1986). *Mga Piling Kuwentong Sebuwano. Marcel M. Navarra.* Quezon City: University of the Philippines Press.

Marcella, Juanito (1970). "Ang Panitikang Hiligaynon." *Mga Piling Akdang Filipino*, ed. Efren Abueg. Manila: Kampi and Pioneer Printing House.

______________, ed. (1970). *Bahandi-i.* Manila: Lyceum Press, Inc.

"Magdalena G. Jalandoni: Writing at 85" (1977 December). *Pamana* 29, pp. 4–5.

Manuel, E. Arsenio (1958). "Tayabas Tagalog Awit Fragments from Quezon Province." *Folklore Studies* vol. 17, pp. 58–59.

Marcuse, Herbert (1976). *Counter-revolution and Revolt.* Boston: Beacon Press.

McCrum, Robert, et al. (1986). *The Story of English.* New York: Viking Press.

McGuire, Susan Bassett (1988). *Translation Studies.* London and New York: Routledge.

Mercado, Leonardo (1972). "Visayan Grammar." *Philippine Studies* vol. 20, p. 213.

Mojares, Resil (1983). *Origins and Rise of the Filipino Novel: A Generic Study of the Novel until 1940.* Quezon City: University of the Philippines Press.

Mulato, Santiago Alv (1986, May–April). "Maragsod: Hiligaynon Grammar." *Yuhum.*

_______________ (1989, June). "The Hiligaynon." *Ani* vol. III, no. 2, p. 3.

Naipul, V.S. (1969). *A House for Mr. Biswas.* Harmondsworth: Penguin.

Nava, Cecilia Locsin (1990). "Pagtan-aw sa Kalibutan: A Study of Ilonggo History and Society in the Novel of Ramon L. Muzones." Unpublished Doctoral Dissertation. Quezon City: University of the Philippines.

Newmark, Peter (1988). *A Textbook of Translation.* New York and London: Prentice Hall.

Ngugi wa' Thiong'o (1986). *Decolonizing the Mind: The Politics of Language in African Literature.* New Hampshire: Heinemann.

_______________ (1990). "English: Language of the World?" *The Yale Journal of Criticism* vol. 4, no. 1, pp. 269–93.

Nida, Eugene (1964). *Toward a Science of Translating.* Leiden: E.J. Brill.

Nida, Eugene and Taber, Charles (1974). *The Theory and Practice of Translation*. Leiden, Netherlands: E.J. Brill.

Ong, Walter J. (1982). *Orality and Literacy*. London: Routledge.

Pambansang Samahan sa Linggwistikang Pilipino, Ink. (1985). *Linggwistika at Panitikan*. Manila: Rex Bookstore.

Pascasio, Emy (1988). "The Present Role and Domains of English in the Philippines." *The Role of English and its Maintenance in the Philippines*, ed. Andrew B. Gonzalez. Manila: Solidaridad Publishing House, pp. 125–33.

Peirce, Charles (1897). "Logic as Semiotic: The Theory of Signs." *Semiotics*, ed. Robert Innis (1985). Bloomington, Indiana: Indiana University Press.

Philippine English Studies and Comparative Literature Association "Convention Proceedings" (1989). Quezon City: Department of English and Comparative Literature, University of the Philippines.

Quirk, Randolph (1990 January). "Language Varieties and Standard Language." *English Today* vol. 22, pp. 3–10.

Quirk, Randolph and H.G. Widdowson, eds. (1985). *English in the World: Teaching and Learning the Language and Literatures*. Cambridge: Cambridge University Press.

Rafael, Vicente (1988). *Contracting Colonialism*. Quezon City: Ateneo de Manila University Press.

Rao, Raja (1943). *Kanthapura*. London: Oxford University Press.

Regalado, Iñigo Ed. (1939). *Ang Pag-unlad ng Nobelang Tagalog*. Manila: Institute of National Language.

Reyes, Soledad (1984). "The Romance Mode in Philippine Literature." *Philippine Studies* vol. 32, pp. 163–80.

Ruiz, Macario (1968). "A Study of the Behavior of Hiligaynon Verb Roots with Particular Reference to the Actor and Goal Focus Affixes." A Report Presented to the National Science Development Board, Philippines. Iloilo City: University Research Center, Central Philippines University.

Said, Edward (1976). *Beginnings and Methods*. New York: Columbia University Press.

Santiago, Alfonso (1976). *Sining ng Pagsasaling-Wika*. Manila: Rex Bookstore.

Schultz, Emily A. (1990). *Dialogue at the Margins*. Wisconsin: University of Wisconsin at Madison Press.

Scott, William Henry (1982). "History of the Inarticulate." *Cracks in the Parchment Curtain and Other Essays on Philippine History*. Quezon City: New Day Publishers.

Sebeok, Thomas A. ed. (1975). *The Tell-tale Sign*. Netherlands: The Peter de Ridder Press.

_______________ (1986). "Semiotics in the United States." *American Signatures*. Norman: University of Oklahoma Press.

Seed, Patricia (1991). " 'Failing to Marvel': Atahualpa's Encounter with the Word." *Latin American Review* vol. 26, no. 1, pp. 7–32.

Sikat, Rogelio (1990). "Kasaysayan Bilang Panitikan: Pagsasalin at Ebalwasyon ng *The Forest* (*Ang Gubat*) ni William Pomeroy." Unpublished Master's Thesis. Quezon City: University of the Philippines.

_______________ (1991). "Tawagin Mang Tagalog o Filipino, Ang Pambansang Wika'y Narito Na." *Filipino III*. Quezon City: Instructional Materials Corporation.

Simpson, J.A. and Weiner, E.S.C., eds. (1989). *The Oxford English Dictionary*. Oxford: Clarendon Press.

Siskin, Jay (1987). "A Medieval Semiotics of Translation." *Semiotica* vol. 60, no. 1–2, pp. 103—28.

Smith, Larry E. (1987). *Discourse Across Cultures: Strategies in World Englishes*. London: Prentice-Hall.

Spivak, Gayatri Chakravorty (1990). In Harasym, S. ed. *The Post-Colonial Critic: Interviews, Strategies, Dialogues*. New York and London: Routledge.

Steiner, George (1975). *After Babel: Aspects of Language and Translation*. London: Oxford University Press.

_______________ (1975). *Why English?* Cited in Kachru, "The Sacred Cows of English," 1988.

Strevens, Peter (1982 June). "World English and the World's English—or, Whose Language Is It, Anyway?" *Journal of the Royal Society of Arts*, pp. 418–28.

Suleiman, Susan (1980). "Redundancy and the Readable Text." *Poetics Today* vol. 1, pp. 119–42.

Sobek, Maria Herrera (1990). *The Mexican Corrido: A Feminist Analysis*. Bloomington, Indiana: Indiana University Press.

Tacal, Sebastian A. (1989 June). "Nagre-entry si Takoy sa Abu-Dhabi." *Yuhum*.

Thumboo, Edwin (1991). "The Pragmatics of Meaning: Language as Identity in New English Literatures." *Pragmatics and Language Learning*. Monograph Series. Urbana-Champaign: Division of English as an International Language, University of Illinois.

Tinio, Rolando (1990). "An Approach to Translation." Paper Read at the Seminar on Translation. Manila: Presidential Committee on the Arts.

Todorov, Tzvetan (1982). *The Question of America: The Question of the Other*. Trans. Richard Howard. New York: Harper and Row Publishers.

Toury, Gideon (1986). "Translation: A Cultural-Semiotic Perspective." *Encyclopedic Dictionary of Semiotics*, ed. Thomas Sebeok. Berlin: Morton de Gruyter, pp. 1111–24.

Velasco, Yolanda (1952). "A Critical Study of Magdalena Jalandoni as a Novelist with Special Reference to *Ang Bantay Sa Patyo*." Unpublished Master's Thesis. Quezon City: University of the Philippines.

Villareal, Corazon D. (1990). "Ang Industriya ng Komiks: Noon at Ngayon." *Kultura* vol. 3, no. 3. Manila: Sentrong Pangkultura ng Pilipinas , pp. 47–55.

Volosinov, V.N. (1985). "Toward a Marxist Philosophy of Language." *Semiotics*, ed. Robert Innis. Bloomington, Indiana: Indiana University Press.

Weir, Anne Lowry (1982). "Style Range in New English Literature." *The Other Tongue: English Across Cultures*, ed. Braj Kachru, New York: Pergamon Press.

Watt, Ian (1957). *The Rise of the Novel: Studies in Defoe, Richardson and Fielding*. Berkeley: University of California Press.

Wolfenden, Elmer (1971). *Hiligaynon Reference Grammar*. Honolulu: University of Hawaii Press.

Worcester, Dean (1899). *The Philippine Islands*. New York: The Macmillan Co.

Interviews

Baterna, Quirino (sugilanon writer and editor-in-chief from 1992-1993 of the new *Hiligaynon*), Hotel Intercontinental, Makati, January 17, 1992.

Beltran, Herminio (coordinator, Division of Literature, Sentrong Pangkultura ng Pilipinas), CCP, February 21, 1992.

Burgos, Nestor (moderator for publications, Central Philippine University), Iloilo City, February 7, 1992.

Cabling, Mario (Tagalog novelist and former features editor of *Liwayway*), Liwayway Publishing Inc., January 23, 1992.

Campos, Felicisima (translator and head of the Filipino department, University of San Agustin, Iloilo), Iloilo City, February 3, 1992.

Duque, Reynaldo (Ilokano fictionist and translator), Liwayway Publishing Inc., January 28, 1992.

Deriada, Leoncio (Hiligaynon fictionist, essayist, and coordinator of the Sentro ng Wika, U.P. Visayas), Iloilo City, February 4, 1992.

Italia, Raymundo (Hiligaynon poet), Misola residence, Iloilo City, February 3, 1992.

Javellana, Ernesto (Hiligaynon sugilanon writer and translator), Liwayway Publishing Inc., January 23, 1992.

Joquiño, Antonio H. Jr. (sugilanon writer and editor-in-chief of *Yuhum*), Yuhum Publications, Iloilo City, February 3, 1992.

Manalo, Flaviano (sugilanon writer and moderator for publications, University of San Agustin, Iloilo), Iloilo City, February 4, 1992.

Misola, Agustin (Hiligaynon poet, essayist, fictionist, publisher), Misola residence, Iloilo City, February 3, 1992.

Mulato, Santiago Alv (Hiligaynon poet, essayist, and linguist), Sentro ng Wika Office, U.P. Visayas, Iloilo City, February 5, 1992.

Pineira, Cristina Gonzalez (Supervising Editor for Filipino, Instructional Materials Corporation), IMC Office, Quezon City, January 29, 1992.

Ravina, Clara, Ph.D. (Executive Director, Language Education Council of the Philippines—LEDCO), Faculty Center, U.P. Diliman, February 20, 1992.

Salandanan, Rodolfo S. (Editor-in-Chief, *Liwayway*), Liwayway Publishing Inc., January 28, 1992.

Serrano, Anthony (writer and translator), U.P. Creative Writing Center, February 24, 1992.

Sonza, Demy P. (Hiligaynon historian and member of the Provincial Board of Iloilo), Telephone interview, February 7, 1992.

Villa, Ligaya (Adviser of *Silayan*, Publication in Filipino of Iloilo National High School), Iloilo City, February 6, 1992.

Index

A

Abadilla, Alejandro, 102
Abadilla, Bayani, 105
Abeto, Quirico, 40
Abueg, Efren, 100, 110, 118
Academia Bisaya, 119
Achebe, Chinua, 62
The Adventures of the Rue Morgue, 87
Agpalo, Remigio E., 76
Aguilar, Faustino, 102
Aguinaldo, Rosalia, 100
Aklan, 8, 12
Alejandro, Rufino, 7
Alfonso, Oscar, 4
Allusion, process of, 68
Almanake, 14
Almario, Virgilio, 102
Altbach, Philip, 55
Alva, Jorge Klor de, 25
"The Ambitious Guest," 36
Anderson, Benedict, 13, 28, 87
Ani (Journal), 56, 130
Antique, 8, 12
Antonio, Teo, 102
Aprieto, Pacifico, 104
Arcellana, Francisco, 37
Arceo, Liwayway, 102
Arguilla, Manuel, 37
Arte del Idioma Bisaya-Hiligaino, 19, 42
Asad, Talal
on concept of cultural translation, 43
on languages, 55
Ashcroft, Bill, 58, 68
Awit, 38, 39, 40, 47, 49
Awit and Corrido, 56
Ayers, Edward, 14

B

Bahandi-i, 110
Bakhtin, M. M., 59, 89
Baltazar, Francisco (Balagtas), 101
Bannawag, 60, 99, 101
Barrantes, Vicente, Moreno, 41, 42, 46
Barthes, 54
Baterna, Quirino, 96, 126, 131
Batiduan, Elizabeth, 97
Beaugrande, Robert de, 7
Beltran, Herminio, 118, 132
Benjamin, 40
Bernardo Carpio, 38, 49, 50, 51
Bikolnon, 99
Bisaya, 36, 60, 99
Bloomfield, Leonard, 78, 79

Bokay nga Owak (The White Raven), 37
Bonifacio, Andres, 49, 50, 51
Borges, Jorge Luis, 54
Brillantes, Gregorio, 37
Buhler, Karl, 31
Bukaneg, Pedro, 102
Bulletin Publications, 99
"Bunyag-Takas" (A Refusal of Ritual), 65, 86, 110
  discussed, 113, 115
Butiña, Francisco, 18

C

Cabling, Mario, 99
Cagayan de Oro City, 104
Cahologan Sang Confesion General (Significance of the General Confession), 19
Calantahon nga tacus mapamalandongan sang mga casaquit sa purgatorio cag novena sa mga calag nga may matahum nga mga ejemplo sa tagsa ca adlao; decenario sa mga casaquit ni Jesus cag versos ni San Gregorio Papa nga may maramu nga indulgencias, 16-17
Campos, Felicisima Torres, 101
Cano, Zaragoza, 119
Capiz, 8, 12, 97
Caravana, Nemesio, 100
Catford, J. C., 26
Cebu, 103
Central Philippine University, 130
Cheyfitz, Eric, 26
China, 57
Clarey, Jo Ellyn, 36
Clavel, Leothiny, 88, 113
Coching, Gregorio C., 100
Comedia, 22, 47
Commonwealth Act No. 184, 126
Composo, 14
The Conquest of America: the Question of the Other, 25
Constantino, Ernesto, 57, 98
Constantino, Renato, 4
Constitution, Philippine
  1986, 6, 7, 101
  1987, 56, 98, 99, 103, 104
Contracting Colonialism: Tagalog Translation During the Early Years of Spanish Rule, 22, 30
Corpuz, Onofre D., 4
Corrido, 36-51 *passim*
  about, 14
  authorship, 44
  cited, 86, 87
  creative mis-reading, 44-51
  criticisms, 40
  described, 39-40
  genealogy, 46
  liberative potential, 49
  origins, 41-48
  translation as sub-version discussed, 36-51
  writer, 5, 64, 90
Corrido and the Sugilanon, discussed, 37-38, 54-55
Cotabato, 8
Covar, Prospero, 4, 76
Cruz, Andres Cristobal, 102
Cruz, Jose dela, 41
Cruz, Patricia, 102
Cuartero, Mariano (Fr.), 42, 43
Cultural Center of the Philippines, 56, 105
Cultural Research Association of the Philippines, 96

Culture
Eco's view, 28
Hiligaynon, 96, 97, 101
Culture and the word, discussed, 65-69
Culture-specific terms, 67, 73
Cursos de la Lengua Panayana, 42

D

Daigon sa Noche Buena (Carols on Christmas Eve), 14, 15
Davao, 8
De Guzman, Susana, 100
Del Mundo, Clodualdo, 100
"Demonyo," 111
Deriada, Leoncio, 97, 105, 130, 132
Diksyunaryo ng Wikang Filipino (Dictionary of the Filipino Language), 101
Discourse, 125, 126
Doce Pares de Francia, 38
Ang Doctor nga Nakahibalo sang Tanan (The Doctor Who Knew Everything), 14
Don Juan Gonzaga, 37
Don Juan Tiñoso, 38, 48
Duque, Reynaldo, 102, 118

E

Eagleton, Terry, 58
Eco, Umberto, 28, 63
Edades, Jean, 61
Edmundo, Son of Merced in the Kingdom of France, 47
Ejemplo ("for example"), 15, 16, 17, 18, 39, 41, 46, 54
El Filibusterismo, 3, 28
El Teatro Tagalog, 41
"english," syntax of
discussed, 69-80
English language, 54-90 *passim*
cited, 6, 7, 8, 9, 12
cultural imperialism, 58
elitism, 56, 57, 58
Filipino English, 63
liberative potential, 58, 59
Epics, 87
Eugenio, Damiana, 38, 40, 56, 57
Even-Zohar, 70
on the problem of translatability, 64
Executive Order No. 335, 104

F

Fabian, Johannes, 26
"Failing to Marvel: Atahualpa's Encounter with the Word," 29
Fansler, Dean, 40, 41-42, 47-48
Faulkner, William, 13
Fernandez, Doreen, 97
Fiction, Hiligaynon
discussed, 12-23, 32
Fil/english
rhetorical aspect discussed, 80-89
with the translator, 89-90
Fili see El Filibusterismo
Filipino, 3-132 *passim*
Filipino, use of
constitutional provision, 6, 56
The Financial Expert, 72
Floro-Luza, Ismaelita, 96, 113
Florante at Laura, 49
Flores, Julius, 36, 88, 97
Flores Por Maria, 15
"Frame," 5
France, 55
Francisco, Lazaro, 100

Frawley, William, 27
Fray Alonso de Mentrida, 42, 43
Fray Julian Martin, 42

G

"Ang Gaba sang Katubwan" (The Curse of the Sugarcane Fields), 36, 65, 82, 88, 89, 114
Galauran, Fausto J., 100
"Galilean consciousness," 59
Gawad Pambansang Alagad ni Balagtas, 126
General Monfredo, 37, 39
Gibraltar, Luisa Defante, 97
Goethe, 21
Gomez, Pablo S., 100
Gonzaga, Encarnacion, 40, 56
Gonzales, Abe S., 100
Gonzalez, N. V. M., 37, 61, 67, 68
Gorlee, Dinda, 27
Gramatica Hispania-Visaya, 19
Great Britain, 55, 65
Guevara, Jose J., 100
Guerrero, Leon Ma., 28
Guerrero, Milagros, 4
Gumban, Delfin, 96
Gumban, Eriberto, 119, 131

H

Hada Parubanu, 44
"Hara" (Queen), 100
Haring Villarba, 38
Harrison, Regina, 29, 30
Hatim, Basil, 27
Hawthorne, 36
Hemingway, Ernest, 13, 87
The Heritage of Ignorance, 40
Hernandez, Amado, 102
"hiligaynon" origin, 3
Hiligaynon
3-23, 54-90, 96-119, 123-32 *passim*
Hiligaynon (magazine), 8, 13, 36, 130, 131
Hiligaynon-Spanish dictionary, 42
Hiligaynon writer, 96
non-purist and purist, 118-19
Hinugpong nga mga Sugilanon 1936-1938 (Anthology of Short Prose), 12
Historia del Rey de Hungria, 41
Historia Famoso ni Bernardo Carpio, 50
Historia sang Dalaganan sa Guinharian sa España, 50
Hornedo, Florentino, 105
Hosillos, Lucila, 8, 37, 40, 49, 60, 61, 97, 110
A House for Mr. Biswas, 72
Ang Hunsoy Sungsongan Usab (The Empty Clay Pipe), 73
"Ang Hustisya sa Dagat" (Vengeance in the Sea), 65, 88, 89, 113, 116

I

Iloilo, 8, 12, 14, 40, 56, 96, 97, 101, 103, 114, 130
Ilonggo Language and Literature Foundation, Inc., 104
Inventive poetics of translation, 90
Ishiguro, Kazuo, 62
Italia, Raymundo, 131

J

Jakobson, Roman, 27
Jalandoni, Magdalena, 8, 12, 13, 36, 38, 86, 96, 100, 119, 126
  works cited, 37
Jalandoni, Marta, 37
Japan, 57
Jaro, Iloilo, 42
Javellana, Ernesto, 96
Joaquin, Nick, 37, 59
Jose, Vivencio, 4
Joquiño Sr., Antonio, 96

K

Kanthapura, 62
Kasingkasing sa Botelya (Lover in a Bottle), 37
Kinabuhi cag Pasion ni Jesucristo nga aton Guinoo, 38
Korea, 57
Kurditan, 97, 98

L

Lacaba, Emmanuel, 58
Lacaba, Jose, 117
Ladinos
  role in translation, 22, 30, 46, 47, 90
Lahi, 56
Landicho, Domingo, 102
Language policy, 57, 58
  of U.P., 98, 101
Libreria Panayana, 47
Linangan ng mga Wika sa Pilipinas, 101, 102
Literalness, 69, 70, 77, 78
"Literary Colonialism: Books in the Third World," 55
Liwayway (magazine), 60, 99, 100, 101, 126
Loan translations, 68
Locke, John, 124
Lohafer, Susan, 36
Lope de Vega, 50
Lopez, Salvador P.
Lozano, Raymundo Mejia, 42
Lucero, Rosario, 8, 59, 97, 110, 111, 112, 113, 115, 118
Lucibar, 37
Lumbera, Bienvenido, 4, 7, 22, 47, 60, 102
Luzon, 38

M

Magahum, Anghel, 12, 37, 40, 88, 96
Magic Ring Cycle, 47
Malay, Carolina, 58
Manalo, Flaviano, 131
Manila, 8, 12, 16, 22, 96, 97, 99, 126, 127, 130, 131, 132
Manuel, Arsenio E., 40-41
Ang Manunulat, 110, 111
Marcel Navarra: Mga Piling Kwentong Sebuwano, 98
Marcella, Jan, 96, 110, 111, 112, 118
Marcella, Juanito, 8, 36
Marxism, 9
Mass media and translation, 22
"Matapok ang Tambis" (The Branch Is Still Brittle), 65, 88
Matute, Genoveva, 102
Media monopolies and translations, 22

Mentrida, Alonso de (Fr.), 19
Menzi, Hans, 99
Metrical romances *see corridos*
Mga Ginto sa Iloilo (Golden Treasures from Iloilo), 101
Minguella, Toribio, 48
Misola, Agustin, 131, 132
Missionaries
  translation work, 42
Mo, Timothy, 62
Mocedades de Bernardo del Carpio, 50
Mojares, Resil, 7, 16, 37, 118
Moro-moro, 22, 47
Mulato, Santiago Alv., 97, 114, 131
Muzones, Ramon, 8, 13, 96, 100, 119, 126

N

Ang Nagsagad Caon Santol nga Tinubol (The One Who Ate Too Much Santol and So Became Constipated), 47
Nahuatl (Mexico), 25, 26
Naipul, V. S., 72
Narayan, R. K., 72
National language, 6, 7, 8, 58, 101-09 *passim*, 127, 130
  law, 126
National literature, 98, 99, 105, 130
Nava, Cecilia, 47, 97
Navarra, Marcel M., 36, 102
Negros Occidental, 8, 97
Nemenzo, Francisco, 4
Nida, Eugene, 63
Noli mé Tangere, 3, 4, 28
Norada, Conrado, 8, 13, 37, 96, 100, 126, 131
Novel, 37, 38
  studies made, 8
Novenas, 15, 16, 17, 39, 44, 87

O

Okri, Ben, 62
Ondaatje, Michael, 62
Oracion, 16, 17

P

Padre Juan kag Beata Maria (Father Juan and Blessed Mary), 37
"Ang Pagbalik" (The Apparition), 65, 88
Palanca Awards, 127
Pambansang Samahan sa Linggwistikang Filipino, Inc., 103
"Panaghoy sang Ginahandos nga Palpal" (Lamentation of a Stake), 110
Pananglet (for example), 14, 15, 16, 17
Panay, 97, 100
Panagmuyo, 16
"Pagpanumbalik" (Remembrances), 65, 70
Pardo de Tavera, Trinidad, 40
Pascasio, Emy, 57
Pasyon, 4, 5, 22, 30, 38
Pasyon and the Revolution: Popular Movements in the Philippines, 1840-1910, 4
Pasyong Pilapil, 38
Paz, Octavio, 54
Peirce, Charles S., 27, 28, 31, 124, 125
PEN Conference in Manila, 1977, 7
Perez, Pedro D., 19

Perfecto, Mariano (Bishop), 16, 17, 18, 21, 38
Philippine Drama: Twelve Plays in Six Philippine Languages, 57
Philippine Normal University, 102
Philippines, 4, 7, 8, 13, 14, 30, 37, 39, 56, 58, 62, 84
Pineda, Ponciano, 101, 102
"The Pit and the Pendulum," 36
Poe, Edgar Alan, 13, 36, 87
Pontivillar, 37
Power and translation, 64, 90
Principe Recarredo, 37
Presidential Committee on Culture and the Arts, 7
Prinsesa Florentina, 45
Print monopoly, 126
Printing press and translation, 126, 127
Provincial Council of Cebu, 103

Q

Quechua culture, 29, 30
Quezon City, 56

R

Radical left and translation, 22
Rafael, Vicente, 22, 30
Rao, Raja, 62
Ravelo, Mars, 100
Redundancy in translation, 84, 85, 86, 87
Re-frame
cited, 96, 123, 127, 129, 130, 132
meaning, 5, 6
Repetitiveness in translation, 86, 87
Regalado Inigo Ed., 37
Relacion de las Antiguedades deste reyno del Peru, 30
Representamen *see* sign
Representation
meaning, 28
Republic Cultural Heritage Award for Literature, 12, 126
Reyes, Edgardo, 102
Reyes, Soledad, 49
Rhetorical organization, 84
Rifattere, 54
Rizal, Jose P., 49
Roces Publications
policy, 99-100
Romblon, 8
Roullô, Romeo, 97
Rushdie, Salman, 62

S

"Sa Lawod sang Pangabuhi" (In the Sea of Life), 65, 113
Said, Edward, 45
Salandanan, Rodolfo, 101
SALIPI (Samahan para sa mga Literatura ng Pilipinas), 98
Santiago, Alfonso O., 7, 103
Santiago, Gervasio B., 100
Santos, Lope K., 102
Saussure, Ferdinand de, 124, 125
A Season of Grace, 67, 68, 72, 82
Sebeok, Thomas A., 28, 123
Secular works, 22
Seed, Patricia, 29, 30
Semiotic consciousness, 87
Semiotics, 124
Semiotics and the Philosophy of Language, 63
Sentrong Pangkultura ng Pilipinas, 130

Sermons, 39
Seth, Vikram, 62
Short story
  Filipino, 36, 37
  Western, 36
Short Story Theory at the Crossroads, 36
"Si Anabella," 12, 13, 17, 65, 88
Sign
  cited, 43, 63, 65, 123, 124, 125
  discussed, 25-33
Signs, Songs and Memory in the Andes: Translating Quechua Language and Culture, 29
Sikat, Rogelio, 55, 98, 102, 103
"Si Montor," 65
Sining ng Pagsasaling-Wika, 103
Sison, Jose Ma., 4, 58
SLATE Project, 102, 103
Soviet Union, 55
Spanish-Visayan dictionary, 42
Spivak, Gayatri, 90
Sterner, George, 63
Story of Edmundo, Son of Merced in the Kingdom of France, 44
Sugilanon
  cited, 8, 9, 12, 13, 36-51, 54-90, 96-119 *passim*, 124, 125
  genealogy, 32, 54
  sources discussed, 13-22
  ties with corrido, 54-55
  writer, 13, 96
Sugilanon, translation of
  analysis, 110-19
  from Hiligaynon to English, 57-90
  into Filipino, 96-119
Summer Institute of Linguistics, 7
Swahilis, 26

T

Tagalog
  and Ilocano, 107-08
  mentioned, 7, 9, 22, 30, 38, 39, 47, 50, 56, 60, 79, 99, 100, 102, 103, 104, 126, 127, 132
Tagalog or Filipino
  discussed, 105-10
"Taghoy" (Lamentation), 110
Tampad sa Kasanag, 36
Third World, 55, 62
Tibud nga Bulawan (The Golden Jar), 100
Tiempo, Edith L., 37
"Tig-alani" (Harvest Time), 65, 88
Tigbauan, Iloilo, 42
Tinio, Rolando, 7, 102
Todorov, Tzvetan, 25, 26
Torre, Serapion, 96, 119, 131
Torres, Cesar, 105
Toury, Gideon, 62
Translation, 3-132 *passim*
  as collective enterprise, 130
  aspects, 81
  audience, 62, 63
  categories, 39
  concepts of, 26, 27, 28
  counter-semiotic potentials, 29, 30
  cultural consideration, 31
  definition, 26, 27
  development affecting, 22
  equivalence in, 13, 64
  external, 103
  foreign works, 60
  Hiligaynon to English, 56-58
  internal, 103
  loss of meaning, 67
  post-colonial works, 25, 26, 27
  problem of language, 118

process of, 63, 64, 65, 68
rationale, 9
regional peculiarity, 118
semiotics of, 25-33
source and target texts, 63
spanish period, 16, 17, 18, 19, 20, 21
Translator and Fil/English discussed, 89-90
Translator and writer, 54, 67
Translator, Hiligaynon, 31, 32
Translator's role, 6, 7, 32, 33, 43, 59, 60, 61, 65, 68, 127

U

Ug Gianod Ako, (I Was Carried Away), 36
United States, 14, 55, 62, 65, 86, 96
University of the Philippines, 7
College of Arts and Letters, 6
Sentro ng Wikang Filipino, 6
Visayas Center (Iloilo), 56

V

Vadlit, Ulises M., 100
Values
colonial, 58
Western, 56
Velasquez, Tony, 100
Vernacular literature
mentioned, 9, 10, 40, 59, 60
weaknesses, 13
Vida nga Matahum ni Capinahan cag ni Bulanbulan sa Barrio nga Malapit sa Madiaas (The Beautiful Life of Capinahan and Bulanbulan in a Barrio near Madiaas), 47
Vida ni Bernardo Carpio cag ni Doña Jimena (The Life of Bernardo Carpio and Doña Jimena), 50
Vida ni Santa Zita, Criada O Hinuptan (Life of St. Zita the Servant), 18
Vidas, 18, 44
Villa, Jose Garcia, 58, 118
Villaluz, Prax S., 100
Visayas, 38, 39
Volosinov, V. N., 28

W

West Germany, 55
West Visayas, 3, 8
Wolfenden, Elmer, 74, 79, 81
Writing, 88
grants, 105, 106
inwardness, 89

X

Xavier University, 104

Y

Yamqui, Santa Cruz Pachacuti, 30
Yuhum (magazine), 13, 130

Z

Zaide, Gregorio, 4
Zarzuelas, 22